SLR TIPS & TECHNIQUES

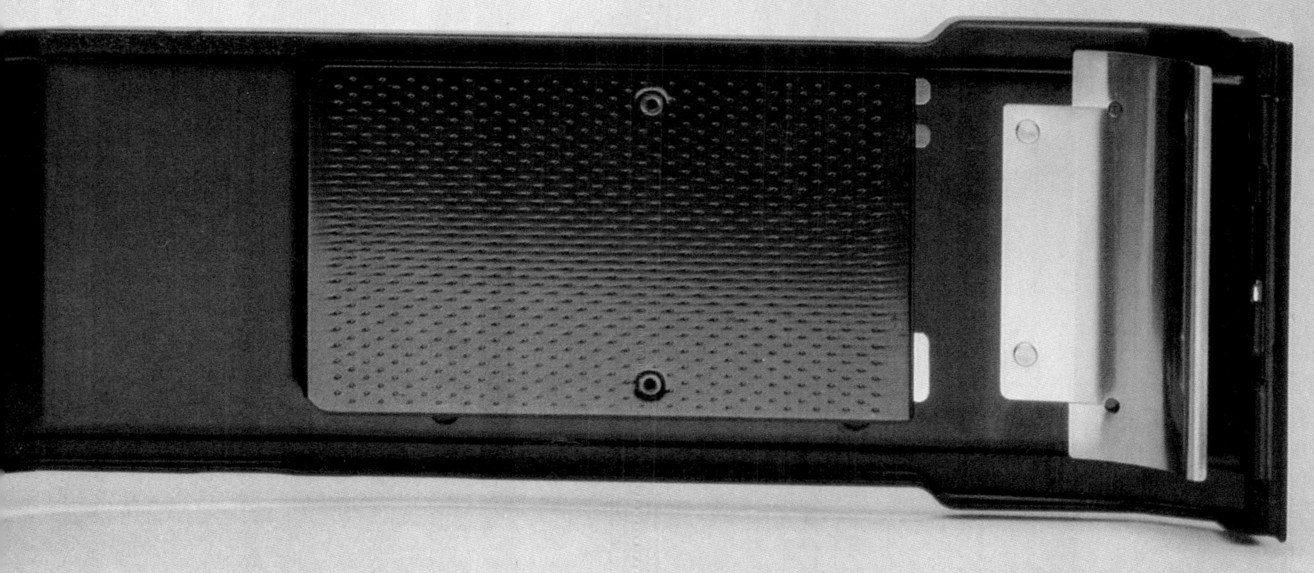

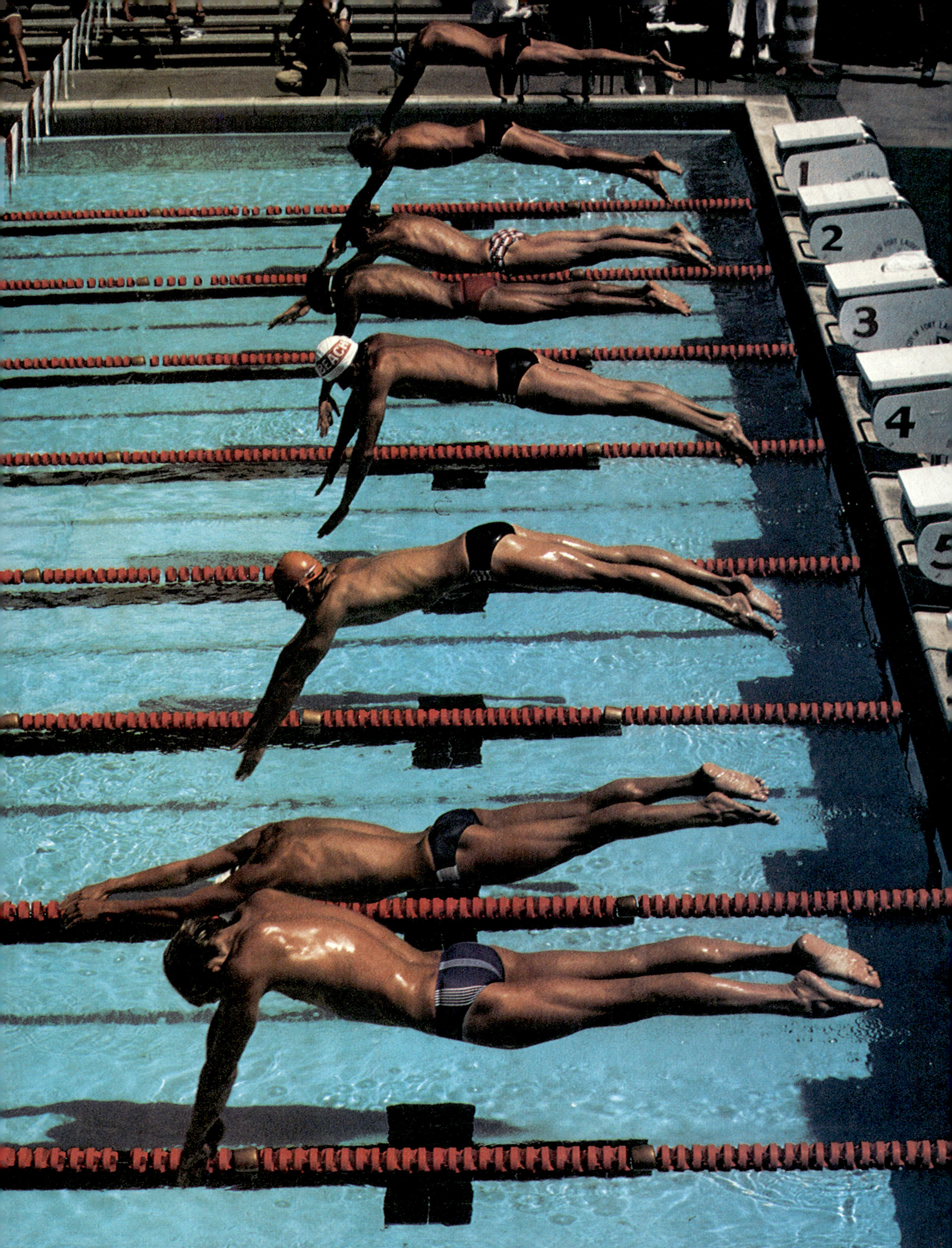
1
2
3
4
BEACH

SLR TIPS & TECHNIQUES

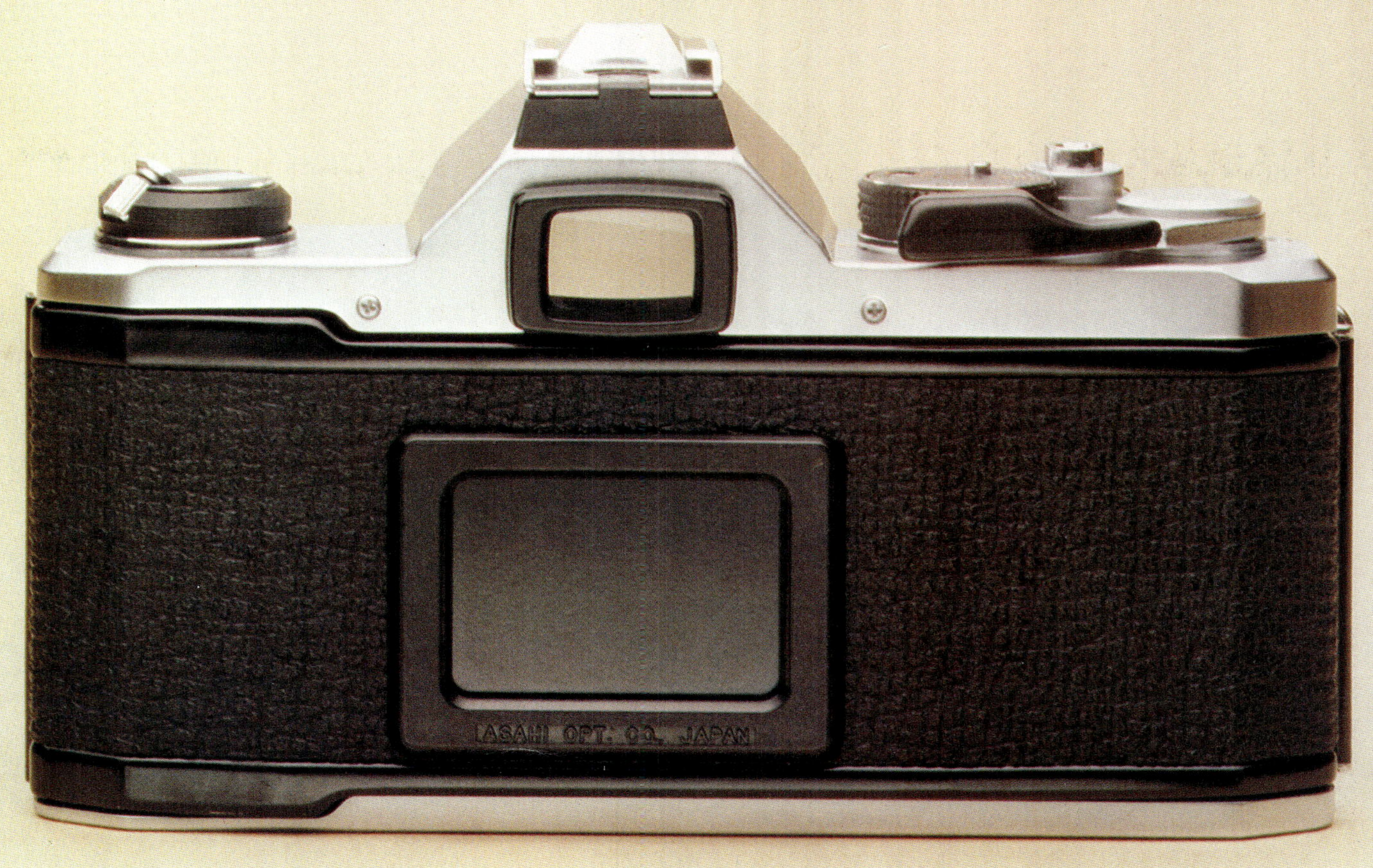

HPBooks®

Publisher: Rick Bailey
Editorial Director: Theodore DiSante
Editor: Vernon Gorter
Art Director: Don Burton
Book Manufacture: Anthony B. Narducci
Typography: Cindy Coatsworth, Michelle Claridge

Notice: This material was first created by David Kilpatrick for the magazine You and Your Camera, published in England by Eaglemoss Publications, Limited. It has been adapted and re-edited for North America by HPBooks. The information contained in this book is true and complete to the best of our knowledge. All recommendations are made without any guarantees on the part of Eaglemoss Publications Limited or HPBooks. The publishers disclaim all liability incurred in connection with the use of this information.

Published by HPBooks, Inc., P.O. Box 5367, Tucson, AZ 85703 602/888-2150
ISBN 0-89586-187-9 Library of Congress Catalog No. 82-82516

3rd Printing

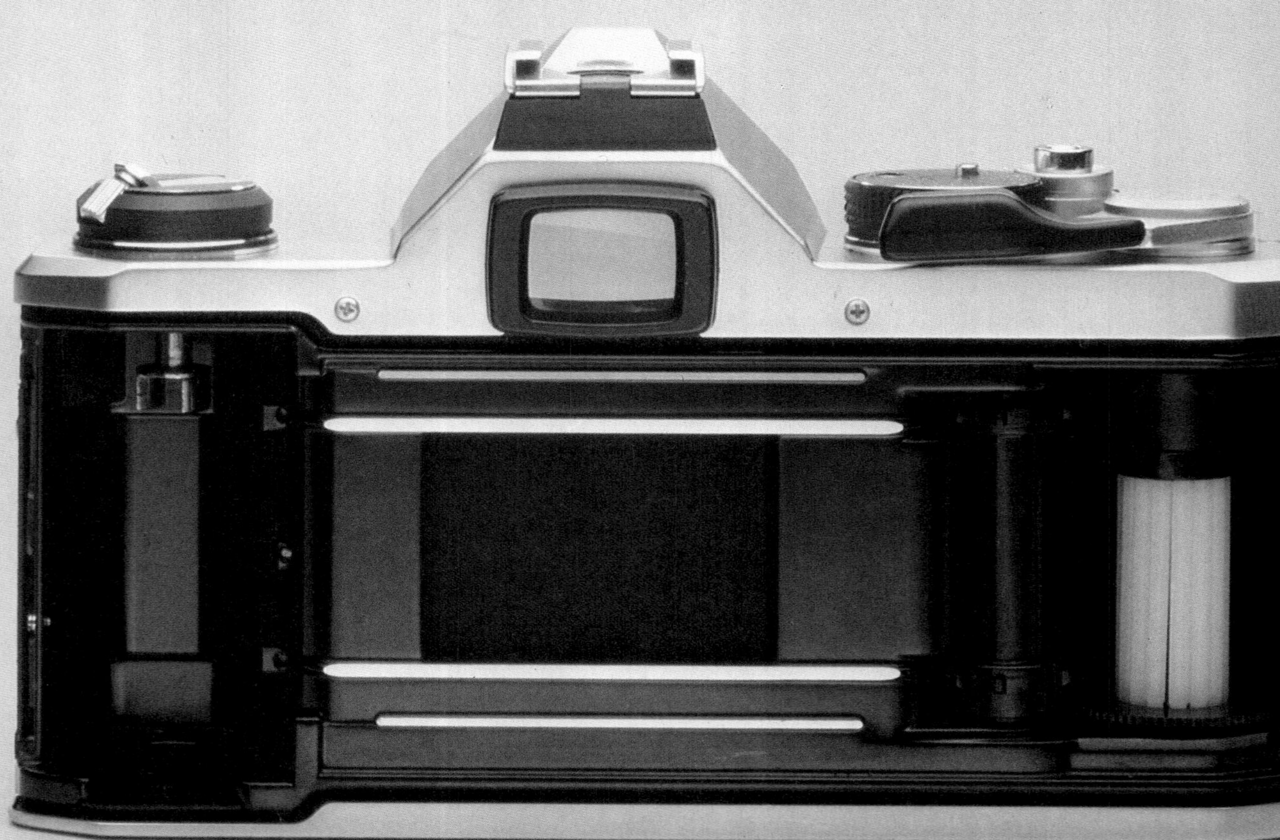

Contents

Front Cover Photos:
Portrait by Mike Buselle
Motorcyclist by David Kilpatrick
Flamingo by Tom Ives

Back Cover Photo:
Tom Ives

Quick Tips for Better Pictures

When you take a picture, you probably have a good idea of the results you want. A satisfying photo is one that reflects your mental image. A disappointing picture doesn't. In fact, it sometimes makes you wonder why you took the picture in the first place.

Photographic control lets you put images on film that meet your expectations. An understanding of photographic principles and camera operation can lead to better pictures. This book explains and illustrates the most important and practical methods you can use.

DO IT RIGHT

The pictures you see here show some of the most common photographic mistakes. You may recognize such faults in your own pictures. That's OK. All photographers have made such mistakes at one time or another. With this book, you'll learn how to avoid these problems. It takes a combination of technical and esthetic know-how.

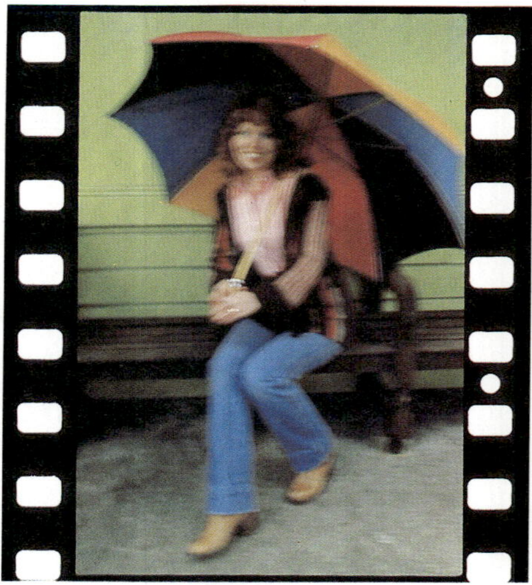

CAMERA SHAKE
Result—Whole image blurred.
Cause—Camera shake during exposure.
Possible Solutions—Rest the camera on something solid, such as a tree or wall. Lean against a solid support. Use a faster shutter speed. Use a tripod to hold the camera. Use a more sensitive film so you can use a faster shutter speed. Use flash. See pages 14 and 15 and 48 to 55.

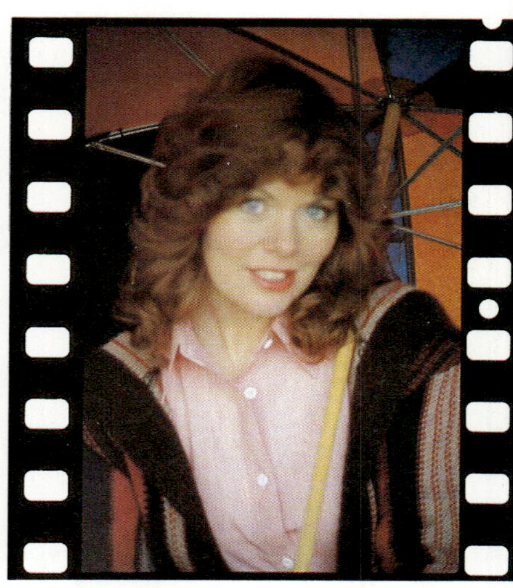

BAD FOCUS
Result—Part or all of the picture fuzzy.
Causes—Incorrect focusing. Too large an aperture. You may need a correction lens for the viewfinder eyepiece.
Possible Solutions—Learn how to carefully focus the viewfinder image. Use a smaller lens aperture for more depth of field. See your camera dealer or eye doctor to determine if you need a viewfinder correction lens. See pages 10 and 11.

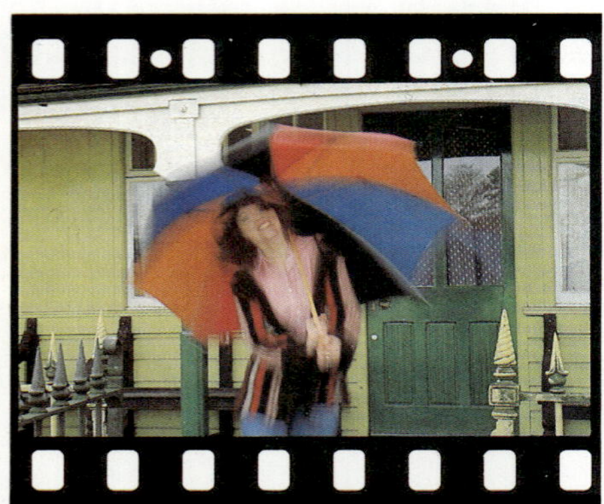

SUBJECT MOTION
Result—Main subject blurred. Background sharp.
Cause—Shutter speed too slow to stop subject motion on film.
Possible Solutions—Use a shutter speed that records the subject sharply. Pan the camera during exposure to record the main subject sharply and blur the background. Use flash to "freeze" the motion. Use a more sensitive film for a faster shutter speed or have subject stay still. See pages 14 to 17.

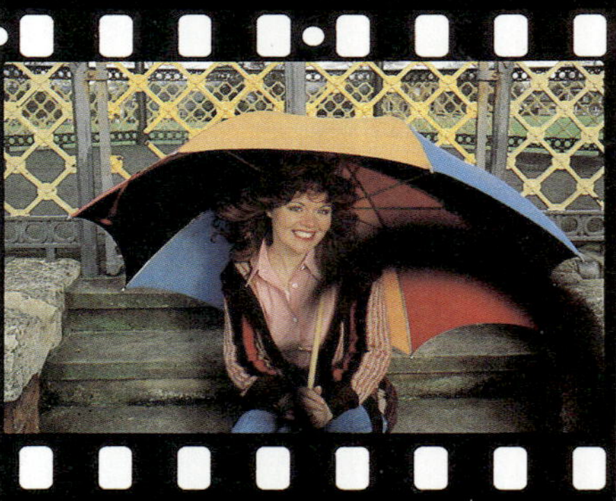

OBSTRUCTIONS
Result—Dark or bright indistinct images obstructing the main subject.
Causes—Foreground objects in view of the lens, such as leaves, twigs, fingertips, or cables.
Possible Solutions—View *all* parts of the scene that you can see in the viewfinder. Don't look at just the main subject. If your viewfinder doesn't show 100% of the image area, move the camera around to make sure no obstruction will be imaged at the edge of the frame. Preview depth of field before making the picture. See pages 8 to 9 and 62 to 69.

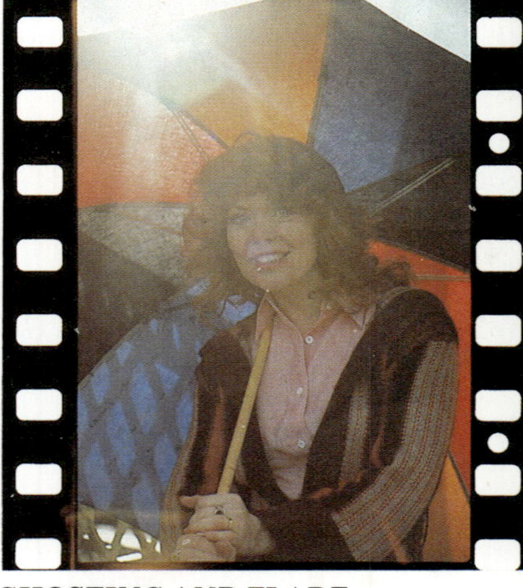

GHOSTING AND FLARE
Results—Image "washed out" and pale overall or in patches. Multiple reflections of lens aperture.
Cause—When light from a bright source enters the lens, unwanted multiple internal reflections occur.
Possible Solutions—Use a lens hood or your hand to shade the lens during exposure. Change composition to avoid the effect of flare. See page 44.

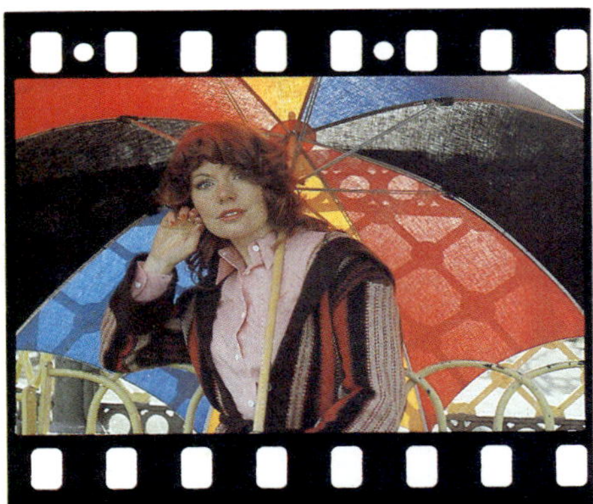

OVEREXPOSURE

Result—Picture too pale.

Causes—Too much exposure. The cause could be aperture, shutter speed or film-speed dial set incorrectly, camera meter in error or misinterpreted, non-average lighting conditions, flash used too close to subject.

Possible Solutions—Understand camera's exposure-control settings. Have meter tested. Bracket exposures in non-average lighting conditions. Use the recommended subject distance for your flash. See pages 18 to 25 and 50 to 55.

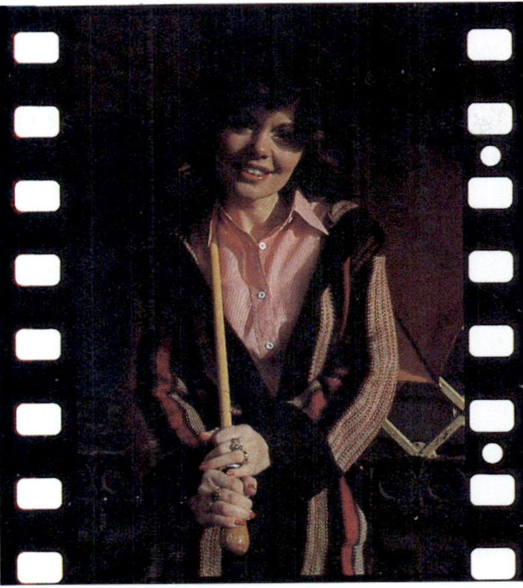

UNDEREXPOSURE

Result—Picture too dark.

Causes—Not enough exposure. Aperture, shutter speed or film-speed dial set incorrectly, camera meter in error or misinterpreted, non-average lighting, flash didn't fire or used too far from subject.

Possible Solutions—Understand camera's settings. Have meter tested. Bracket exposures. Use the recommended range of subject distances for flash or have it tested. See pages 18 to 25 and 48 to 49.

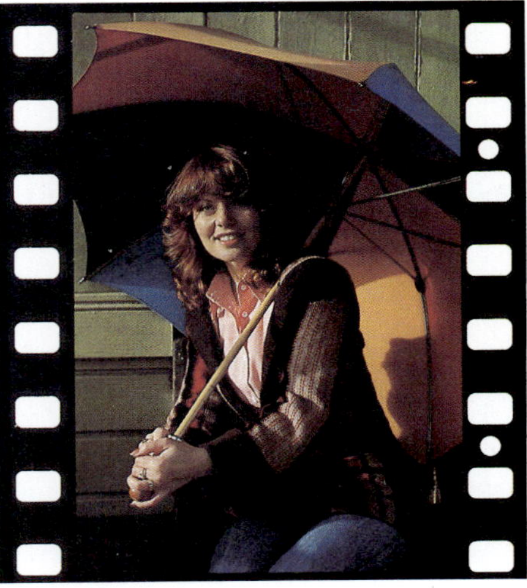

CONTRASTY LIGHTING

Results—Shadows very dark and lacking detail. Highlights too bright.

Cause—The scene's brightness range is too great for the film. When exposure is based on middle tones, bright areas reproduce too bright and dark areas too dark.

Possible Solutions—Brighten dark areas by using reflectors or fill lighting. Photograph subject in more even lighting. See pages 22 to 23 and 46 to 47.

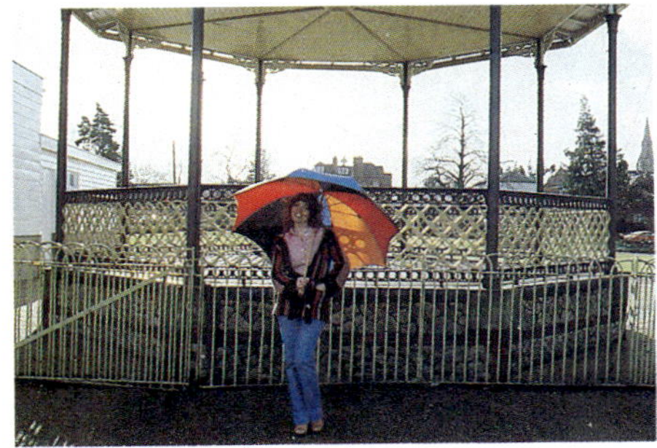

FILLING THE FRAME

Result—The main subject is too small and insignificant in the picture.

Causes—Poor composition. You are too far from the main subject.

Possible Solutions—Look at all of the image in the viewfinder. Don't concentrate on just the main subject. See what is in the corners or above and below the subject. Decide what you want on film, then compose accordingly or reposition the subject so you fill the frame with it. To do this, you may have to move in closer or use a longer-focal-length lens to exclude extraneous subject matter. See pages 8 to 9 and 64 to 65.

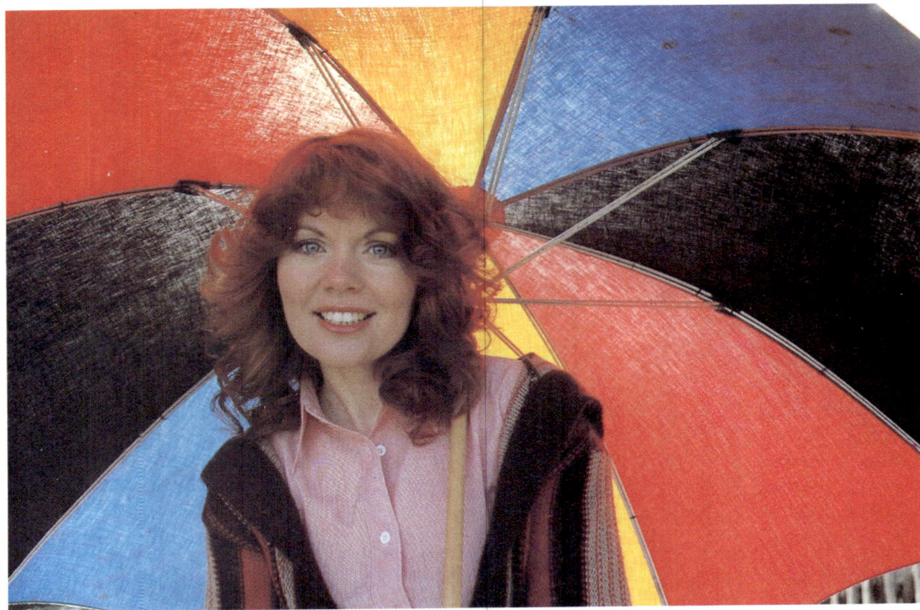

DOING IT RIGHT

This photo is the best of the bunch because it doesn't have any of the problems illustrated and described on these two pages. It is a simple and appealing picture made with both technical and artistic photographic controls. By understanding the principles and recommendations on the following pages, you can make pleasing pictures like this.

Using an SLR Viewfinder

The abbreviation *SLR* stands for *single-lens reflex.* A single lens makes an image that is upside down and laterally reversed by a mirror that reflects the image up to the camera's focusing screen. The right side of the scene appears to be on the left side of the image and vice-versa.

PENTAPRISM VIEWFINDER

Photographing with a reversed image can be confusing, especially with moving subjects. If the subject moves to the left, it looks as if it is moving to the right! For easier viewing, 35mm SLR camera manufacturers put a *pentaprism* viewfinder above the focusing screen. It is designed to present the image right side up and laterally correct. You see the image at eye level, by looking through an eyepiece at the back of the pentaprism finder.

In some cameras an exposure display is outside the image area, in others a display overlaps the image at the left or right side.

Most pentaprism viewfinders do not show 100% of the image made on film. Typically, you see between 90% and 98%. Your camera's instruction book will tell you how much you see. A cardboard slide mount masks a small part of the image area, so the image you see in the mount closely corresponds to the image you saw in the viewfinder.

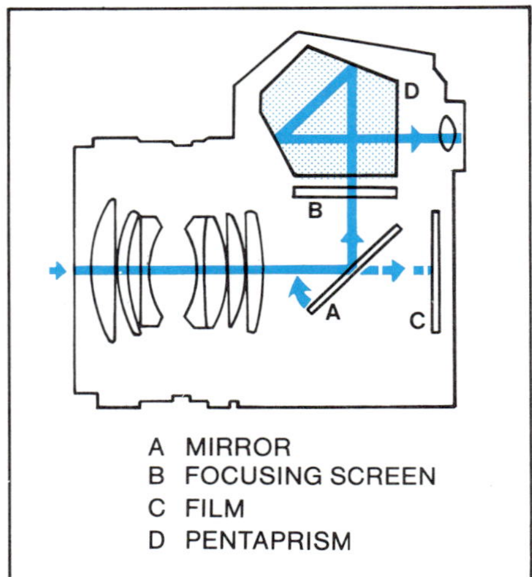

A MIRROR
B FOCUSING SCREEN
C FILM
D PENTAPRISM

WHEN YOU EXPOSE FILM

The drawing at above left shows how the camera forms the image you see and photograph. During viewing, the light from the lens reflects off the mirror and forms an image in the focusing screen.

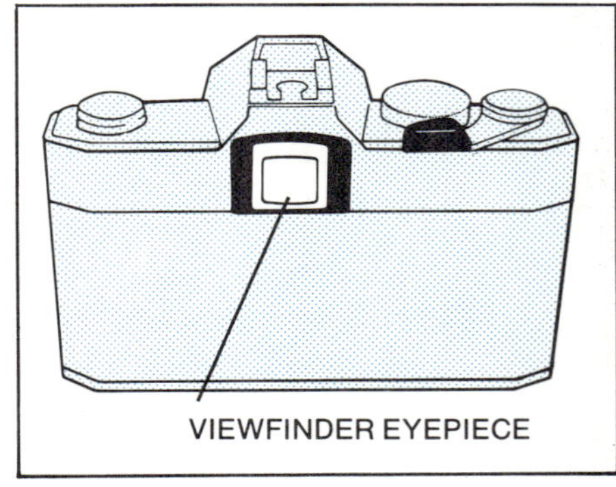

VIEWFINDER EYEPIECE

This image is reversed by the pentaprism finder and is visible through the eyepiece.

When you push the shutter button to expose film, the mirror swings up. This blacks out the viewing image. Then the camera shutter in front of the film plane opens and closes to expose film. After exposure, the mirror drops down so you can view the scene again.

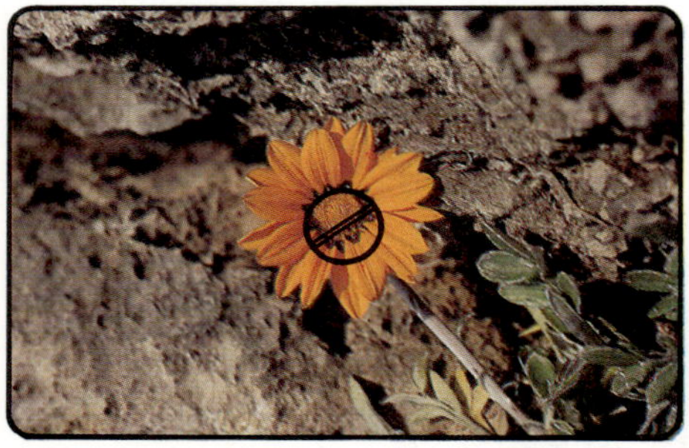

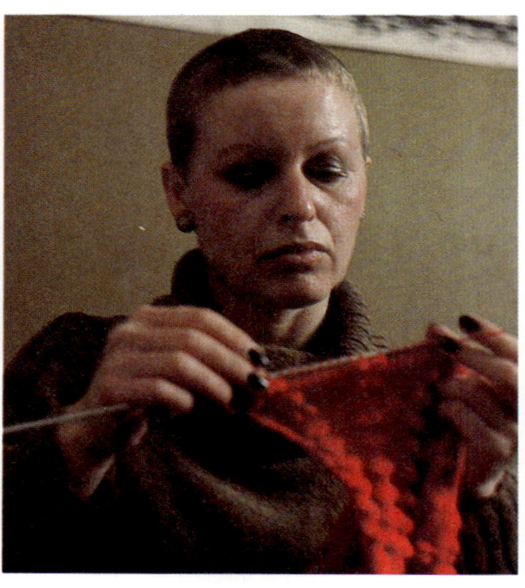

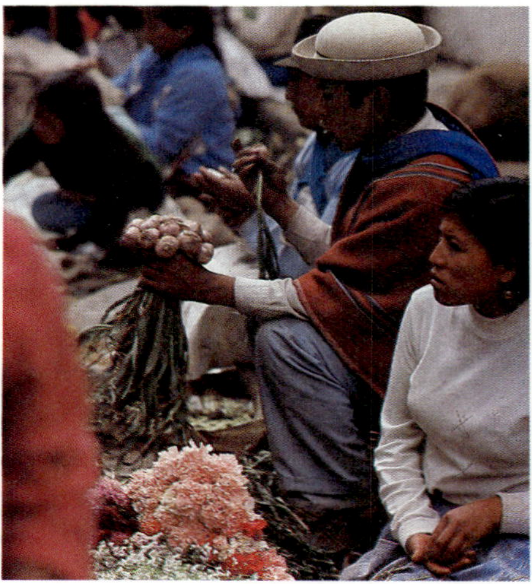

USING THE FOCUSING SCREEN

Modern focusing screens and lenses with large maximum apertures show a bright, clear image. Most scenes have a circular *focusing aid* at the center to help you find best focus.

The flower photo above is an example of a very common compositional error. The focusing aid was used as an aiming device, giving a "bulls-eye composition." The photographer focused on the main subject with the focusing aid, but didn't consider the best location for the flower in the picture.

The portrait, above right, suffers from "cut-off" composition. After focusing on the subject's face, the photographer didn't notice that one hand is "cut off" by the right side of the frame. In any portrait, be sure to inspect the entire viewfinder image to see if any important elements are accidentally excluded.

The third photo has an edge and corner problem sometimes called "intrusive composition." A brightly colored object on the left side draws your attention away from the main subjects.

Each of these problems is easy to solve. After composing and focusing, check composition again. Be sure to see *everything* the film will record. Train your eye to scan the image from corner to corner and edge to edge before taking the picture. This takes practice, but after a while you'll do it automatically. Then you'll compose better photos than before.

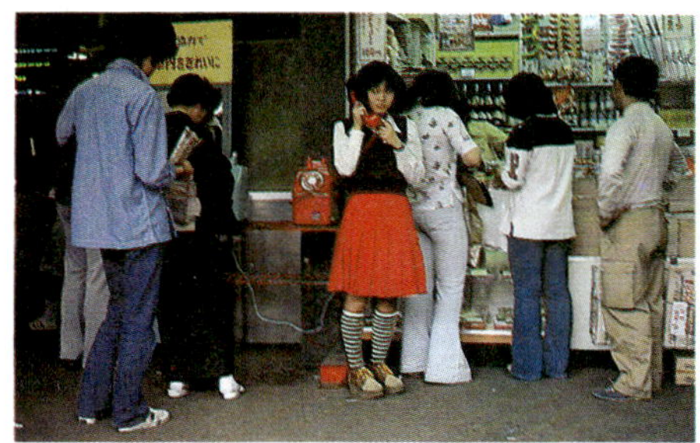

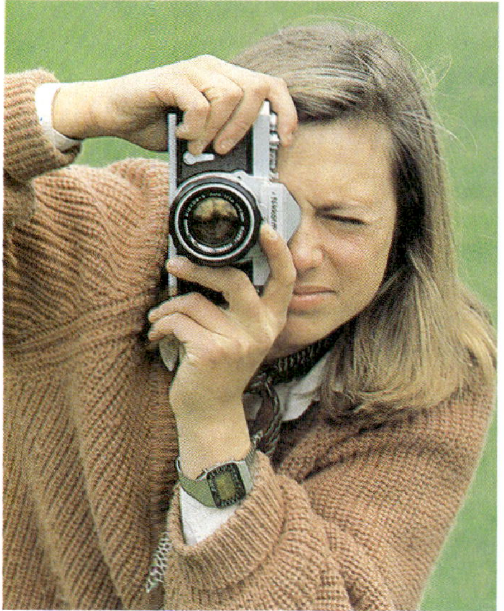

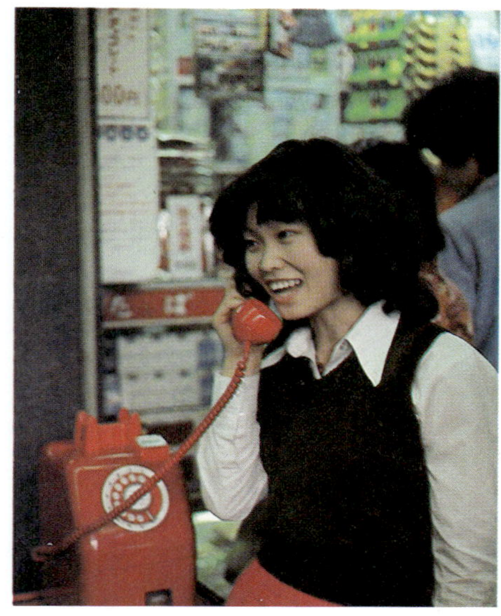

HORIZONTAL OR VERTICAL?

The natural tendency is to hold the camera horizontally. The long dimension of the rectangular image you see in the viewfinder is horizontal. This is called *horizontal format.*

Horizontal-format pictures are not appropriate for every scene. In the photo above, for example, the main subject is the woman at the center. However, the photographer was too far away and included too much distracting detail by using the camera horizontally.

For a vertical format, hold the camera as shown in the middle photo. Notice that the photographer is holding the camera with the shutter button on top. The left hand supports the camera and lens. Some people prefer to hold the camera with the shutter button on the bottom and use their right thumb to push the button. However you hold the camera for vertical-format photography, it should be easy and comfortable to switch from horizontal to vertical and back again.

The vertical-format photo, right, shows a better treatment of the subject. By moving in closer and using the camera vertically, the photographer excluded unnecessary detail. The main subject fills most of the frame. If you can't decide whether to shoot a scene with a horizontal or vertical format, try both. Later, you can decide which is best.

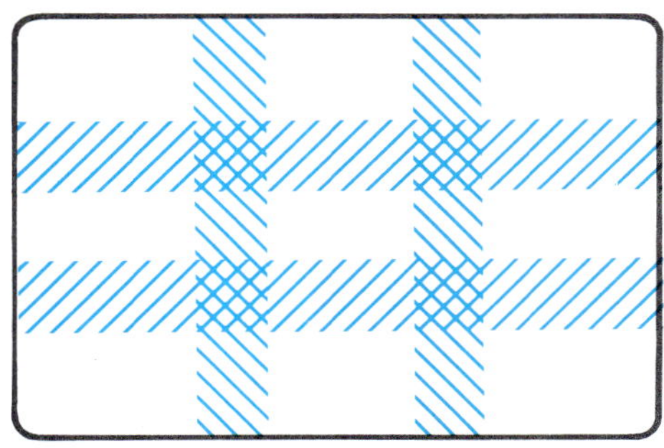

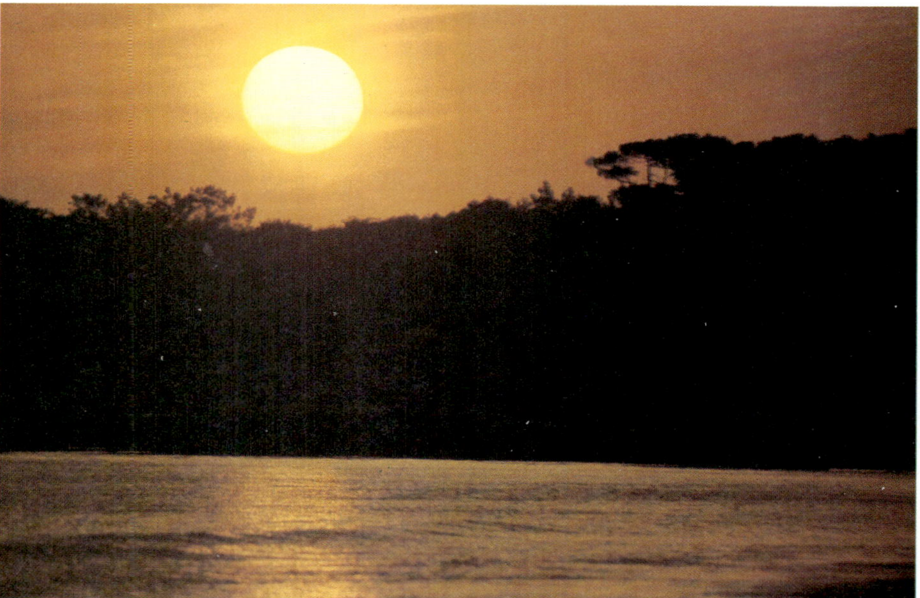

THE RULE OF THIRDS

Even an interesting subject can look dull in a symmetrical composition. Typically, the main subject looks best in a picture when it is off center, such as to one side and more toward the top or bottom. A compositional rule based on this idea states that zones about one-third in from the picture edges have visual attraction. And, areas where these zones intersect have the most eye-appeal.

The diagram above shows these zones and intersections. If you are photographing a scene with a horizon, consider placing the horizon in one of the horizontal zones. If a group portrait includes one tall person, place that person in one of the vertical zones rather than in the center. This will help direct the viewer's attention to that person. If the scene contains a small main element, try locating it at an intersection of zones.

The sunset photo uses some of these principles. The lines between trees and sky, and water and land, are in horizontal zones. The sun is near one of the intersections.

You needn't always use the "rule of thirds." Use it when it is the best way to record a scene. Using it too much can lead to repetitive pictures.

Focusing Techniques

Lack of sharpness is a common picture fault. Even though some negatives or slides may look sharp when you examine them, large images made from the originals aren't sharp.

For accurate focusing, you must use the lens focus control, the focusing screen, and the focusing aid correctly. In addition, you have to decide what part of the subject to focus on.

When you look through the camera viewfinder, an out-of-focus subject looks blurred and indistinct. As you turn the lens focus control, the image becomes more distinct. Eventually, the image is as sharp as it can be.

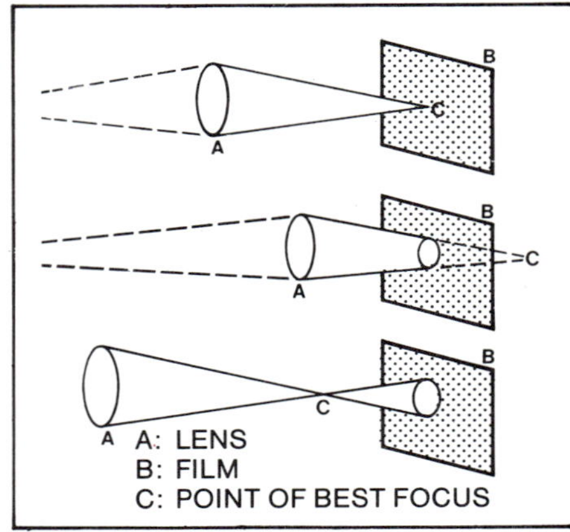

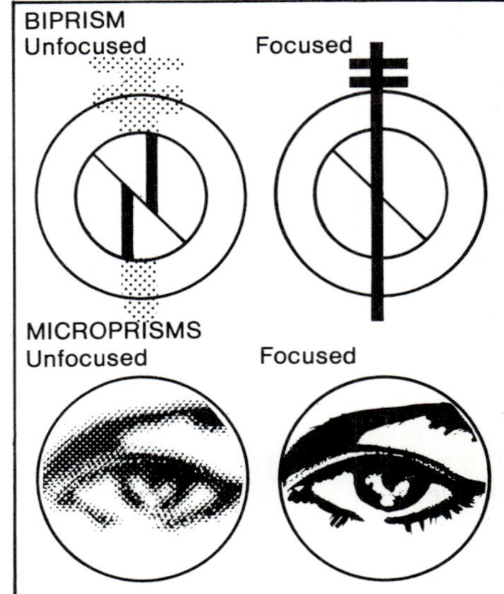

SHARP FOCUS

The drawing above shows how a lens (A) images a subject point on film (B). When the lens is adjusted for sharp focus, a cone of rays from the lens converges to a sharp point (C) on film.

If the lens is closer to the film, rays focus behind the film. However, the film intercepts the cone of rays, and a circular image results. If the lens is too far from the film, sharp focus occurs in front of the film. The film again intercepts a circular image, not a point.

A photographic image is a collection of points on film. If all of those points are relatively large circles, the image is hopelessly out of focus. When each point reproduces as a point, the image is sharp and distinct.

FOCUSING AIDS

The central part of a focusing screen can contain a focusing aid like a *biprism* or *microprism pattern*. Some screens use both.

A biprism makes an out-of-focus image appear split and an in-focus image look not split. This works well with scenes having straight lines and edges. A microprism pattern makes an out-of-focus image look textured or patterned. An in-focus image will look sharp and clear.

You can also use the ground glass (matte) focusing surface around the aid to help determine sharp focus.

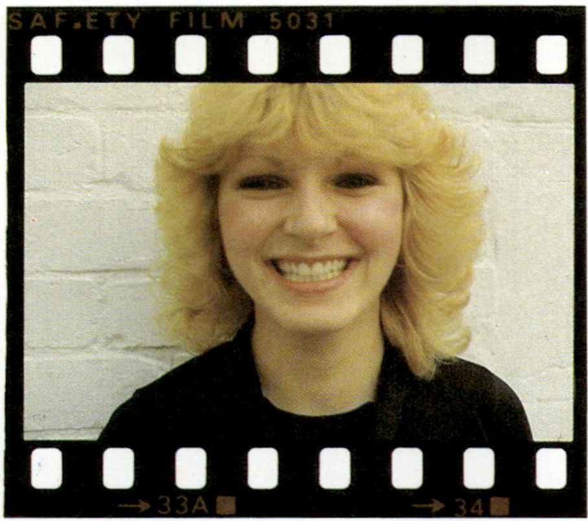

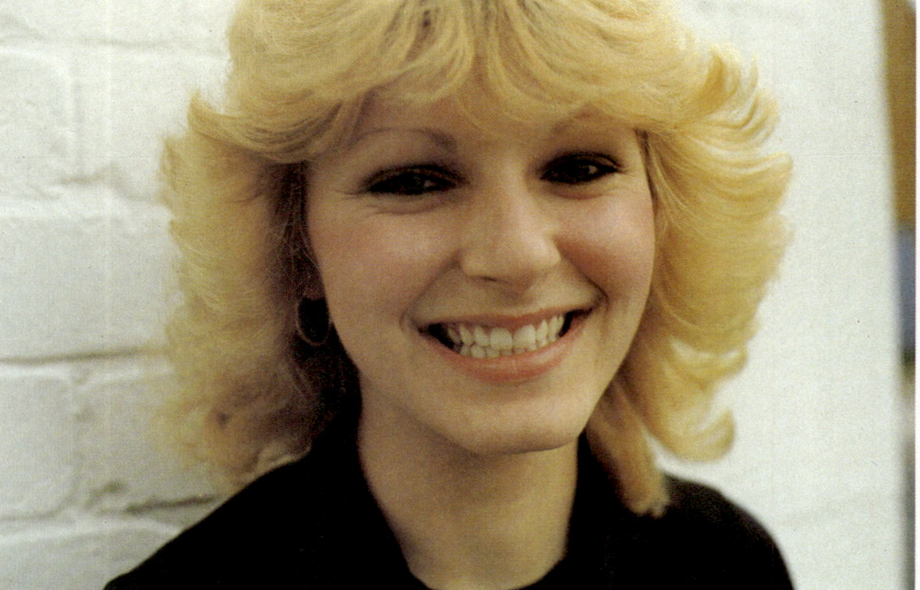

WHERE TO FOCUS

Choose carefully where you focus. Don't automatically focus on the clearest part of the subject. Instead, select the correct part, then try to find an easy-to-focus detail in it.

For example, in head-and-shoulder portraiture, the nose, teeth, ears or hair (as above) are often chosen as focus points because of their prominence or contrast with lighter or darker areas of the scene. If you are using a large lens aperture—with reduced depth of field—this may sacrifice sharp focus on the person's eyes. The subject's eyes must be in focus to capture the viewer's attention. Otherwise your picture will lack impact.

In portraiture, always use the subject's eyes or eyelashes as the focusing target. After finding sharp focus, adjust composition for the best overall result.

The eyes were used as the focusing target for the larger of the above pictures. Notice that even though part of the subject's shoulders and hair are blurred, the overall effect is a lively portrait.

HOW GOOD IS YOUR VISION?

It's possible that even though you make every effort to focus well, your pictures may be unsharp. If so, the fault may be a mismatch between your eyesight and the viewfinder.

When you view the focused image in an SLR viewfinder, the eyepiece should produce a sharp image for your relaxed eye. A standard viewfinder is designed for people with normal vision.

If you don't have normal vision or your glasses are not of the correct power, you may need an accessory eyepiece correction lens. Otherwise, a sharply focused image will look unsharp to your relaxed eye. The simplest way to select a correction lens is to go to your camera dealer and try different ones made by the manufacturer of your camera. Correction lenses mount on the viewing window at the back of the viewfinder.

Remove the camera lens and point the camera at a bright area while looking through the viewfinder. If the focusing-screen grain, corners and focusing aid look sharp to your relaxed eye, the eyepiece is OK. If they don't look sharp, try various correction lenses until the focusing screen looks sharp.

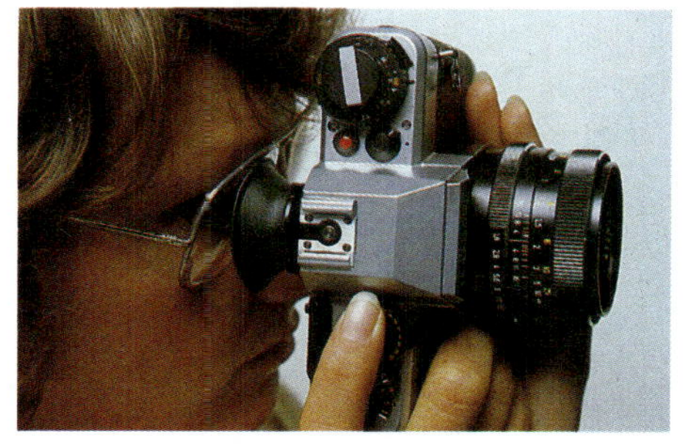

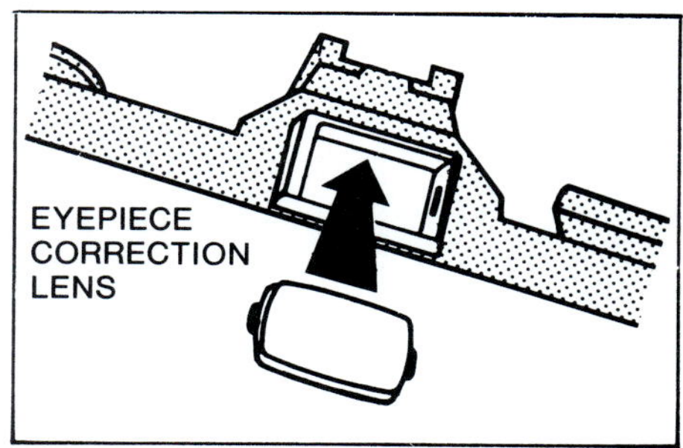

USING GLASSES

Even when wearing glasses and looking through a viewfinder, you should be able to see all of the focusing screen. Because your eye is farther from the eyepiece than usual, you may have to move your eye around to see the whole screen. To avoid scratching the eyeglass lens with the camera while it is to your eye, you can use a rubber eyecup. It will also help exclude stray light and therefore make the viewfinder image seem brighter for easier focusing. However, this can make eye-to-eyepiece separation even greater and reduce field of view more. The eyecup attaches to the camera's viewfinder eyepiece by screwing or clipping in.

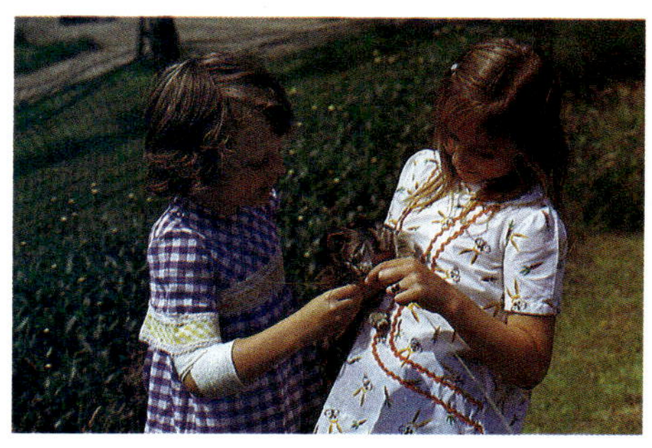

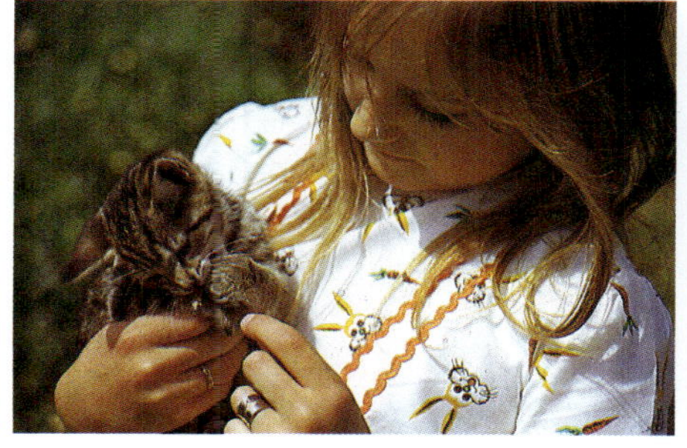

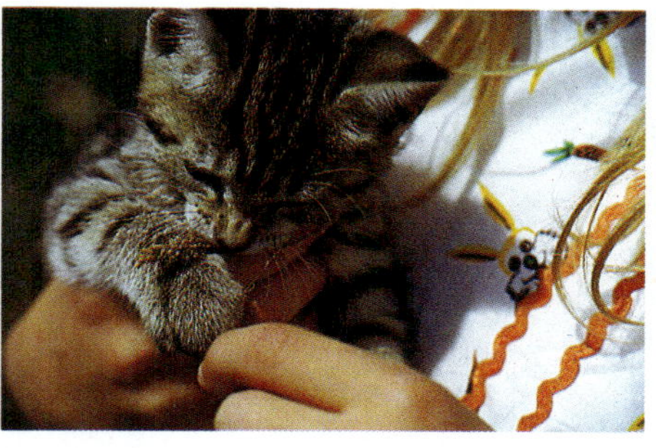

USING THE FOCUSING RANGE

The distance scale of your camera's 50mm lens shows the range of subject distances it can focus sharply, generally from about 18 inches (46cm) to infinity. If you set the infinity symbol (∞) at the lens focusing index, subjects farther away than about 30 feet (9m) are automatically in focus at any aperture. This makes focusing a faraway scene like a sunset easy.

Focusing errors are more noticeable as you focus on closer objects or use longer focal lengths. Even though much of your photography will be of subjects farther than about 3 feet (1m), you should be aware of the capability of a 50mm lens with closer subjects. It is sometimes necessary to move in close on a subject to exclude extraneous elements, thereby getting a more effective photo. This was done in the left photo to exclude background trees. For this image the girls, who were about 3 feet (1m) away from the photographer, are the main subjects.

Moving Closer—For the center photo, the photographer decided to show the girl holding the kitten. He moved in closer, about 2 feet (60cm) away, to exclude other elements. When close to the subject, you can set focus and keep the lens set. Then, if you or the subject moves slightly, you can move the camera back and forth until the image is in sharp focus again.

Closest Focus—The photo at right makes the kitten the main subject. Because the kitten is small, the photographer set the lens to its closest focus setting, about 18 inches (30cm). Then he moved closer to the kitten until its whiskers looked sharp in the viewfinder.

Depth Of Field—For any lens aperture, the zone of sharp focus—called *depth of field*—decreases as subject distance decreases. This is obvious in these three photos. In the photo at left, only the background looks blurred. In the middle picture, the girl's far shoulder also looks blurred. The photo at right shows that the back of the kitten is blurred.

Because of this effect, be sure to focus on the most important subject element when moving in close.

Aperture & Depth of Field

The lens aperture size controls the brightness of the image exposing film. The relationship between aperture and exposure is explained further on pages 18 and 19. Aperture also affects the zone of sharp focus, or *depth of field,* that you see in the image. Controlling depth of field is an important part of getting a satisfactory image.

APERTURE LOCATION

Inside the camera lens are overlapping metal blades arranged to form an adjustable opening. When you turn the lens aperture ring, these blades move, making the opening smaller or larger. The blade assembly is called the *diaphragm.* The opening is the *aperture.*

With most cameras, you can see the aperture change when you turn the aperture ring. To do this, remove the lens from the SLR. Look through the lens while turning the aperture ring. You'll notice that at large *f*-numbers, the opening is relatively small and at small *f*-numbers, the opening is relatively large.

ABOUT *f*-NUMBERS

Aperture settings are expressed as *f-numbers,* or *f-stops.* You can see the *f*-numbers, ranging from 3.5 to 22, on the lens aperture ring in the above photo. The *f*- is not engraved on the ring. The vertical yellow line above the ring is the focusing index. It also indicates the *f*-stop selected, in this case *f*-16.

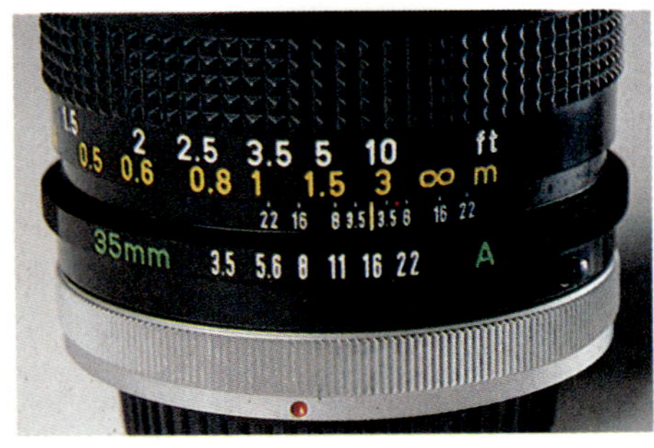

Standard aperture settings are *f*-1.4, *f*-2, *f*-2.8, *f*-4, *f*-5.6, *f*-8, *f*-11, *f*-16, *f*-22 and *f*-32. The smallest *f*-number is sometimes a non-standard value, such as *f*-1.8. As mentioned earlier, small numbers represent large openings and vice-versa.

Lensmakers calculate *f*-numbers by dividing lens focal length (F) by aperture size (d). The formula is:

$$f\text{-number} = F / d$$

Because lens focal length is fixed —except in the special case of a zoom lens—changing aperture size affects the calculated *f*-number. The calculation shows that as aperture size decreases, *f*-number increases.

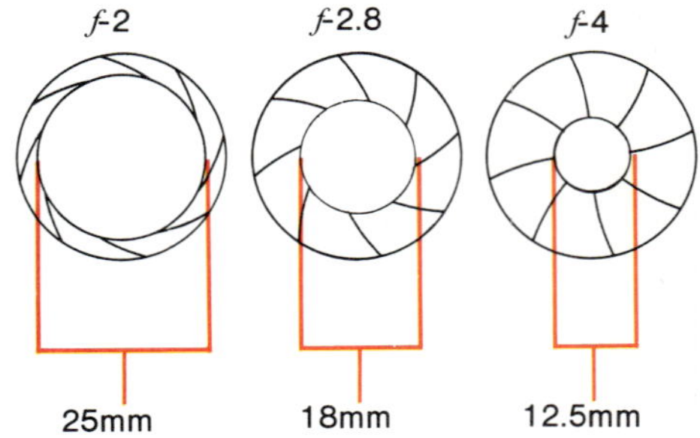

The drawing shows this with a 50mm lens. The bottom number is aperture diameter. Divide this number into lens focal length, 50mm, to get the *f*-number corresponding to that opening.

Exposure Steps—A standard *f*-number represents an image twice as bright as the next larger standard *f*-number, and vice-versa. For example, *f*-2.8 lets twice as much light reach the film as *f*-4 and half as much light as *f*-2. The exposure difference between adjacent *f*-numbers is called one *stop,* or *step.*

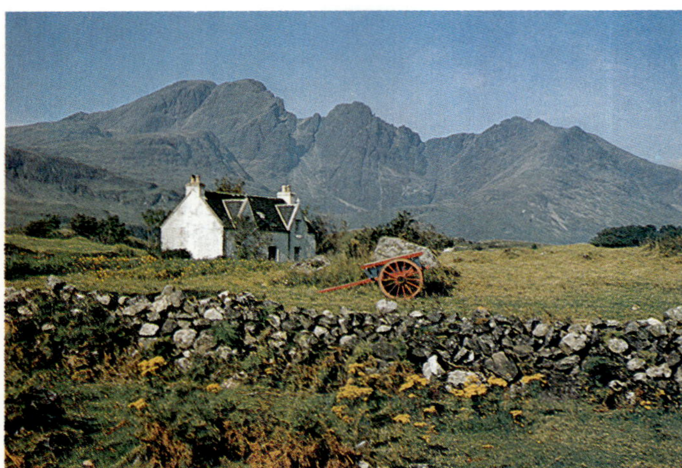

USING SMALL APERTURES

For maximum depth of field, use the largest *f*-number (smallest aperture). Typically, this is *f*-16, *f*-22 or *f*-32. Then set the infinity symbol (∞) on the distance scale to the far-limit depth of field index for that *f*-number. The subject distance indicated by the lens focusing index is called the *hyperfocal distance.* The near-limit distance is always half of the hyperfocal distance.

If you compose creatively and use extensive depth of field, sharp foreground elements can lead the viewer's eyes into the scene. Extensive depth of field also minimizes focusing errors.

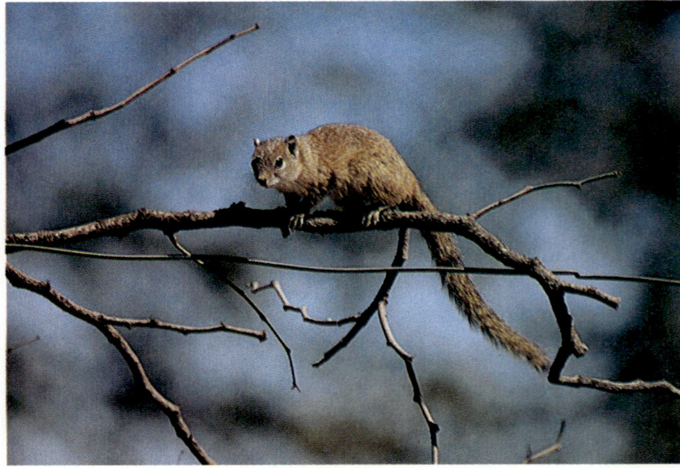

USING LARGE APERTURES

Not all photos benefit from a large zone of sharpness. Sometimes, it's best to have part of the composition blurred to emphasize the sharp elements. This is useful with portraits and some nature photography, as shown above. A sharp background or foreground would add confusion.

Use a small *f*-number (large aperture) to get shallow depth of field. Modern SLR lenses operate automatically—they show you the scene through the lens maximum aperture (smallest *f*-number) for the brightest image. Thus you see depth of field at the maximum lens aperture when looking at the focusing screen.

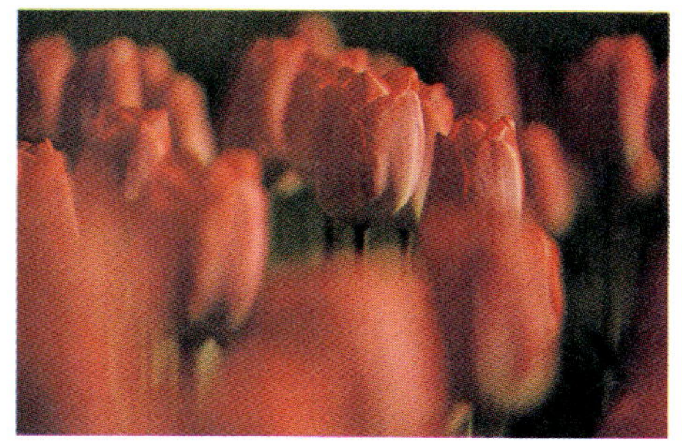

DEPTH OF FIELD

When we view a picture, it is natural to assume that the sharp parts of the image are most important and the blurred parts least important. When you control the sharp and blurred parts of the image, you can give the picture visual impact.

The zone of sharp focus in a picture is called *depth of field.* For a given image magnification, depth of field is affected only by aperture size. Large *f*-numbers, such as *f*-16, give more depth of field than small *f*-numbers, such as *f*-2.

You must decide if a zone of sharp focus is important to the picture. Choose lens aperture first to give the desired depth of field. Then adjust shutter speed for exposure. You can do this with manual or aperture-priority automatic cameras.

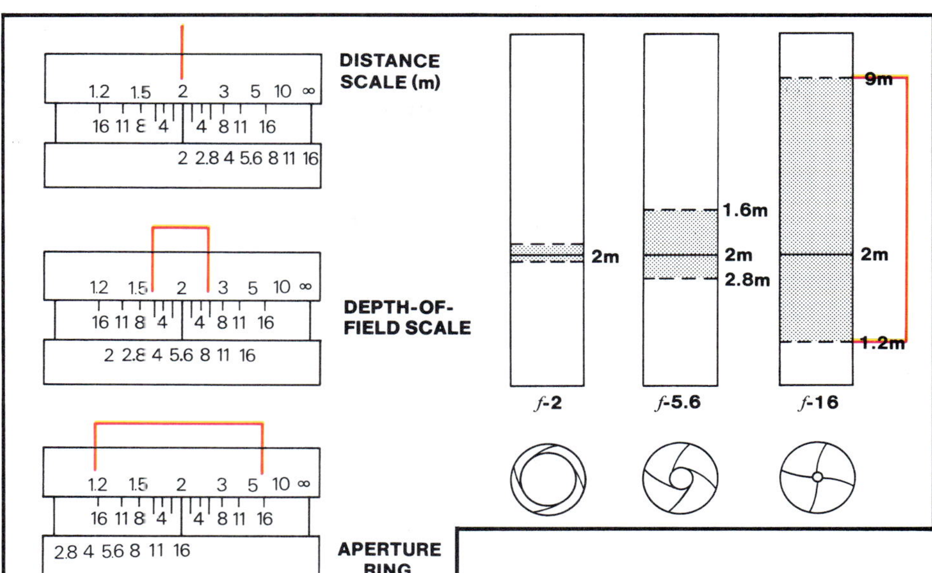

THE DEPTH-OF-FIELD SCALE

The diagram above shows how the lens depth-of-field scale indicates the zone of sharp focus. The scale shows pairs of index marks corresponding to *f*-numbers. These point to the distance scale.

At the maximum lens aperture of *f*-2, depth of field is minimal for a subject distance of 2m (6 feet), as indicated by the depth-of-field scale on the lens. At *f*-16, depth of field is from 1.2m to 9m (4.0 to 30 feet) with the lens still focused at 2m.

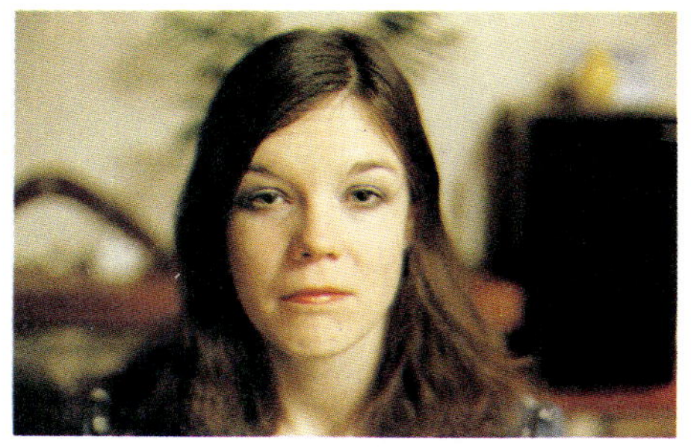

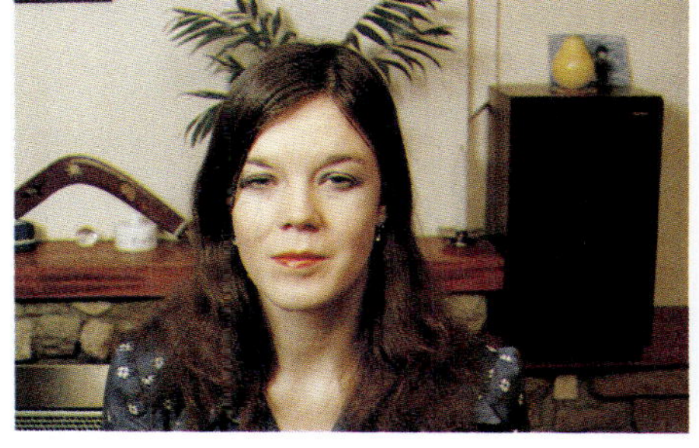

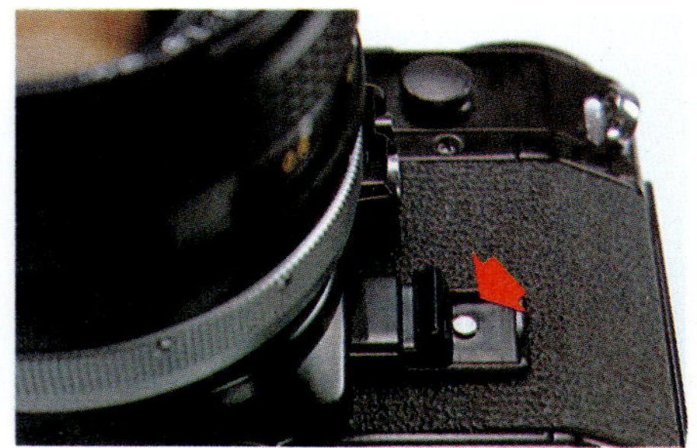

SEEING DEPTH OF FIELD

The photo above shows what you might see in the camera viewfinder when focusing. The main subject is sharp, but because you view the scene through the maximum lens aperture, depth of field appears shallow. The background and foreground, if any, are blurred and indistinct. This is how the picture will look if taken at maximum lens aperture.

If you use a larger *f*-number, the lens will *stop down* before exposure, while the focusing screen image is blacked out. The result is more depth of field, as shown in the center photo. Intrusive background elements may now be sharp in the picture—and in this case seemingly growing out of the subject's head!

Consider depth of field *every time* you take a picture. Often, using the depth-of-field scale on the lens is all you need to do. Sometimes, you will prefer to evaluate depth of field visually instead of measuring or estimating subject distances.

To do this, view the scene through the aperture that will be used to make the exposure. Push the depth-of-field preview button, if the camera has one. Most do. The photo at upper right shows one location for the button. See your camera's instruction manual.

When pushed, the button *stops down* the lens to the selected aperture. This darkens the viewing image if you've chosen an aperture smaller than the maximum opening. It also shows you what is in focus. You can keep the button depressed and adjust lens aperture and focusing ring for best effect.

Because the viewfinder image darkens, it is sometimes difficult to judge the zone of sharp focus exactly. Generally, you should use an aperture one step smaller than the one that *visually* gives the desired effect.

Shutter Speed & Image Sharpness

The *shutter-speed dial* is the other control you adjust for good exposure. The shutter speed you select also affects how sharp a moving subject is recorded on film, assuming focus is correct.

Standard exposure times are from about 1/1000 second to 1 or 2 seconds. Fractional settings are represented on the shutter-speed dial by the reciprocal of the fraction. For example, 1/60 second is represented by the number 60.

Each standard shutter-speed setting gives twice as much exposure as the next fastest setting. The exposure difference is one step. Doubling and halving exposure times have the same exposure effect as using adjacent standard *f*-stops. More on this later.

HOW THE SHUTTER WORKS

Modern 35mm SLR cameras use a *focal-plane shutter.* These have two opaque blinds or curtains. The first curtain is in front of the film when the shutter is cocked (1). The second is wound up on a roller.

When you push the shutter button, the first curtain begins uncovering the film (2). After a specific time, the second curtain is released and "chases" the first curtain (3). This covers the film again, ending exposure. When you cock the shutter, both curtains return, as shown in step 1.

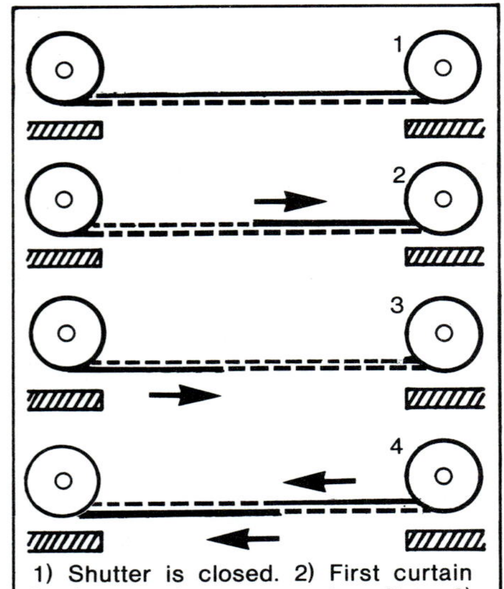

1) Shutter is closed. 2) First curtain begins moving, uncovering film. 3) Second curtain released, follows first curtain. 4) After exposure, shutter is recocked.

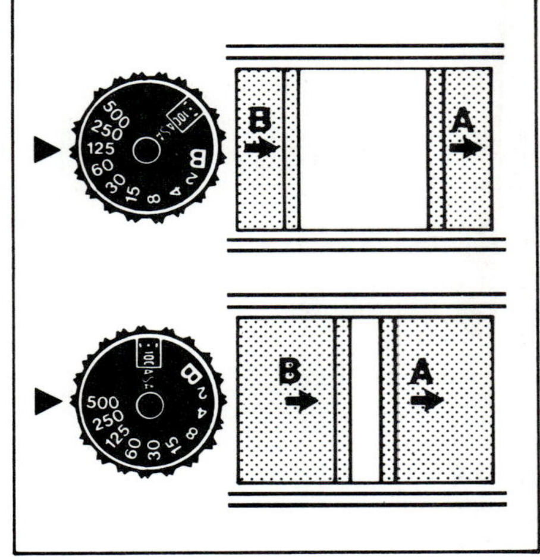

What Is Exposure Time?—Exposure time is the interval between the start of the first curtain and the start of the second curtain, as shown above. Essentially, a traveling slit moves across the film frame during exposure. A slow shutter speed uses a wide slit due to the long time interval between curtain releases. A faster shutter speed requires a narrower slit.

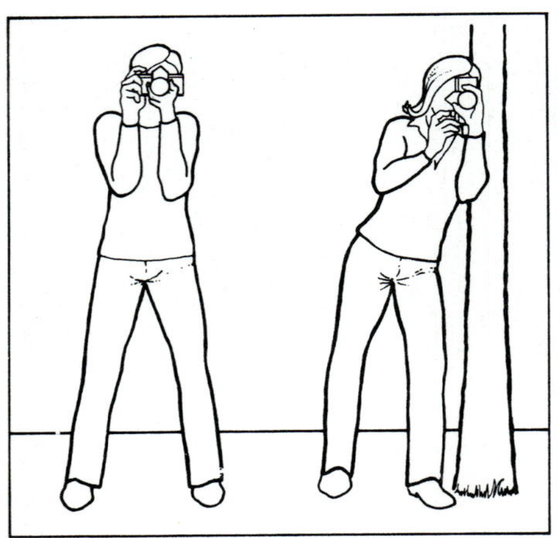

STANCE

When you stand while photographing, good balance is essential for sharp pictures. Not only will this help with slow shutter speeds, but it is also less fatiguing than an unbalanced stance.

Stand with your feet slightly farther apart than shoulder width. Bend your knees slightly. If you need extra support, or if you want to use a slow shutter speed, lean against a stable support, such as a tree or building.

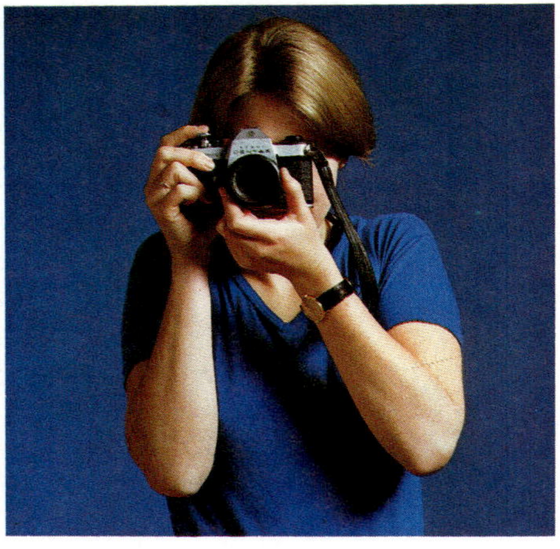

HOLDING THE CAMERA

While standing balanced, hold the camera steady. Here is a good way to hold a 35mm SLR camera. The right hand grips the side and the index finger depresses the shutter button. Left hand focuses the lens and the palm supports the base of the camera. The camera's pentaprism finder is against the photographer's forehead. Notice how the elbows are tucked in for stability and relaxed comfort.

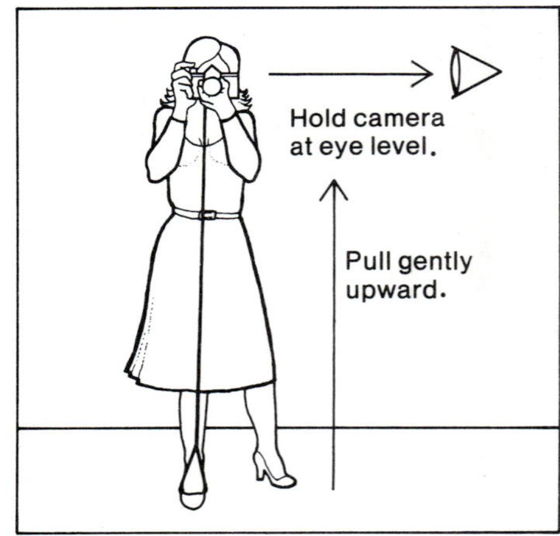

USE A CAMERA BRACE

Another way to stabilize the camera while handholding it is with steady upward tension. All you need is a piece of non-stretch cord with a loop at one end big enough for your foot to fit through. At the other end, attach a screw that fits the tripod mounting socket at the camera base.

The cord should be long enough that when your foot holds down one end, the camera can be comfortably held at eye level. Steady the camera by pulling up enough to tighten the cord.

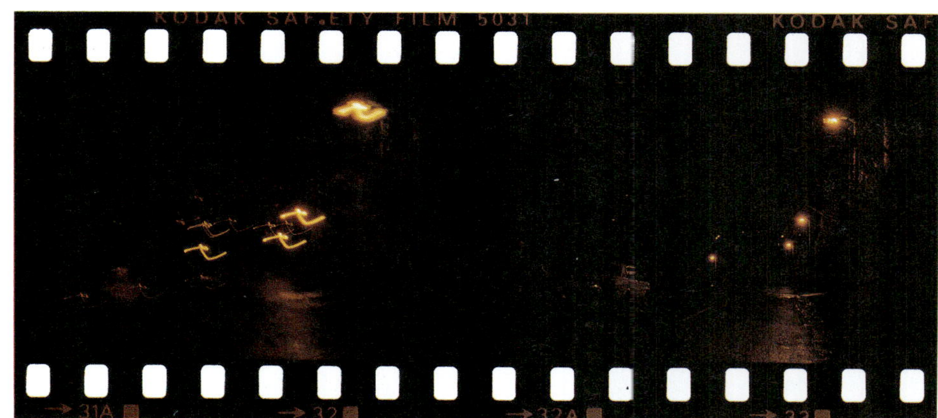

CAMERA SHAKE

Handholding the camera with slow shutter speeds can lead to overall image blur. As an approximate rule, the slowest shutter speed you should handhold is the reciprocal of lens focal length. For example, with a 50mm lens, you should be able to hold the camera still with a 1/60 second shutter speed. With a 200mm lens, the slowest shutter speed you should use is 1/250 second. With a 35mm lens, use no slower than 1/30 second.

Test Yourself—You can test yourself to find the slowest shutter speed you can handhold with a certain lens. Photograph one or more small bright lights in a dark area, as shown above. Take pictures at speeds faster than the slowest speed recommended by the rule. Also take pictures using slower speeds. Make notes of the exposure times.

Look at the processed film through a magnifying glass. Camera shake will show as streaks of light. The slowest speed that yielded a sharp image is your slow-speed limit for handholding with that lens. For example, the photo at left was exposed for 1/2 second. The other photo is sharp. It was exposed for 1/60 second.

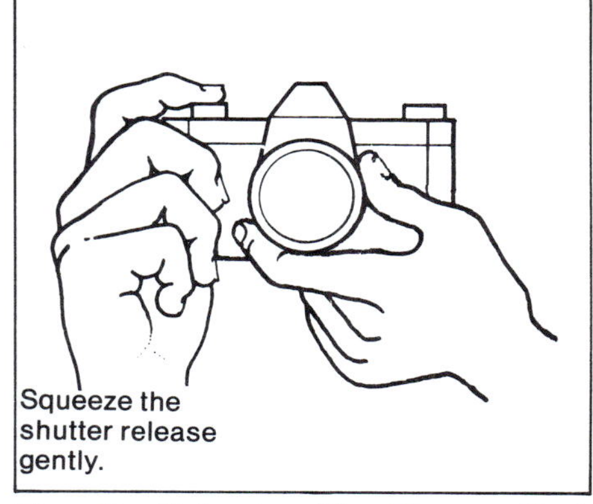

Squeeze the shutter release gently.

Tips On Releasing The Shutter—Push the shutter button gently to avoid camera shake. Take a breath and hold it, then push the button slowly. Hold it down until you can view the scene again, signifying that exposure is finished. The *wrong way* to release the shutter button is to jab it. This shakes the camera and causes blurred pictures.

The above drawing shows the best way to hold the camera. Use the palm of your left hand to support the camera base. Your hand absorbs any downward momentum that might be created by pushing the shutter button.

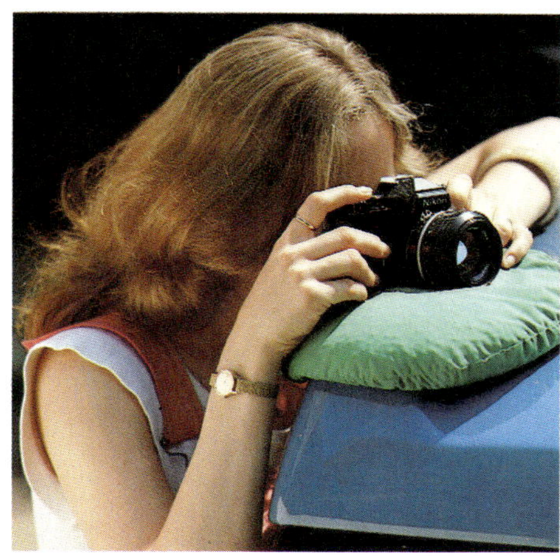

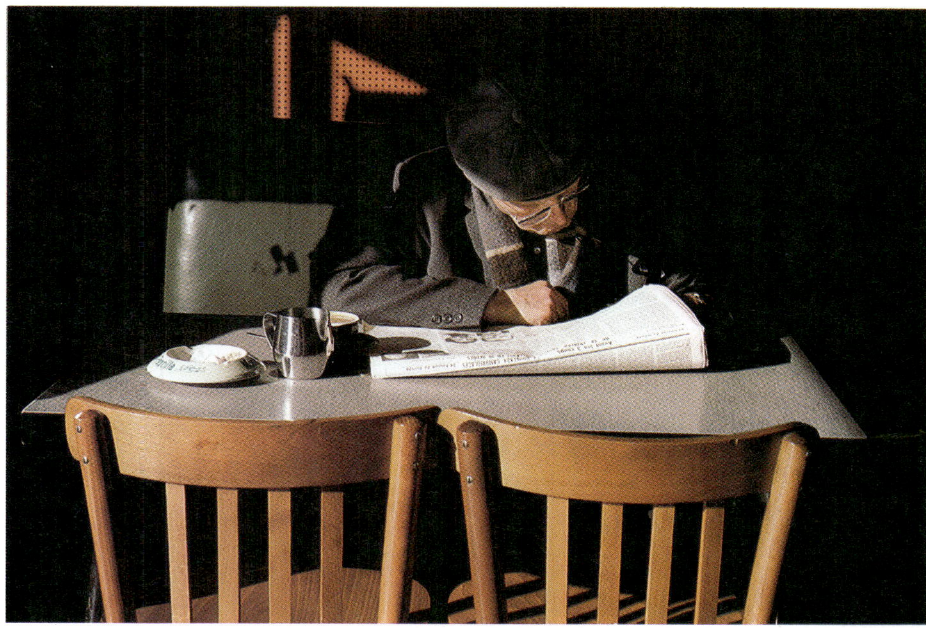

USING A BEAN BAG

If you want to use a shutter speed too slow to handhold and don't have a tripod, use a bean bag. Adjust its shape for correct aim and sturdy support of camera and lens. It's easy to make a bean bag. If you don't have one, use a rolled-up towel or piece of clothing as a substitute.

WHY BE SO CAREFUL?

The photo above is about the size of a standard color print. Its area is about 12 times larger than a 35mm negative or slide. Any blur in the original image would also have been 12 times as large in a print this size. Even if you can't see blur in the original, the enlargement may show it.

If you project a 35mm slide onto a 40-inch screen, faults are over 600 times as large! So, take sharp pictures. Using a tripod as much as possible minimizes image blur due to camera shake.

Shutter Speeds for Moving Subjects

Shutter-speed selection determines how sharp a moving subject will be recorded on film if there is good focus and no camera shake. If the subject is still, the image will not show any blur. If the subject is moving, the image may show blur. The amount of blur depends on both subject movement and shutter speed.

STOPPING MOVEMENT

The fast shutter speeds available on current SLRs—up to 1/4000 second on some models—will "freeze" most subject motions on film. When you use a fast speed, the subject doesn't move much during exposure, so the image is not blurred. The photo at far right was made with an exposure time of 1/1000 second.

Sometimes, you can use a very slow speed to *avoid* blur in your pictures. Be sure to use a tripod or other very firm camera support. In dim light, such as late dusk, you need a long exposure time to get enough light on film. If a moving subject is not very bright and does not stay in one place for very long, it may not be recorded on film. In the photo at left, shutter speed was 2 seconds. A pedestrian that walked by quickly was moving too fast to make an image on film.

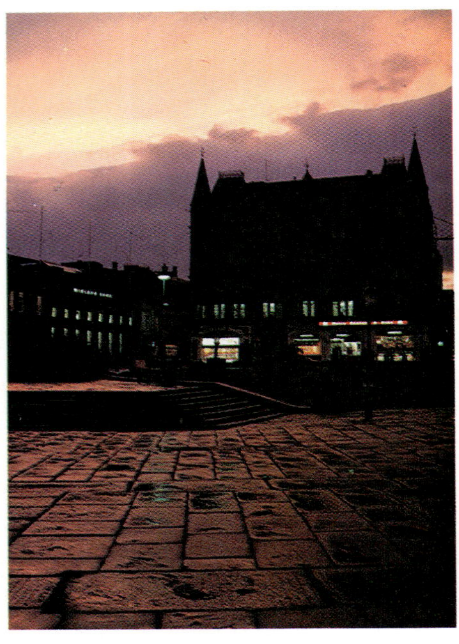

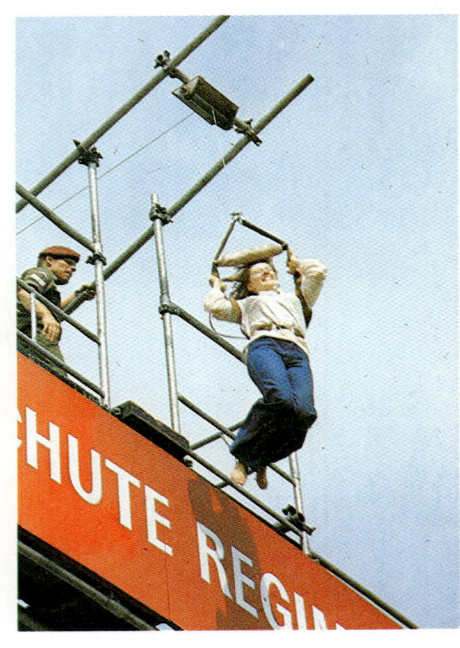

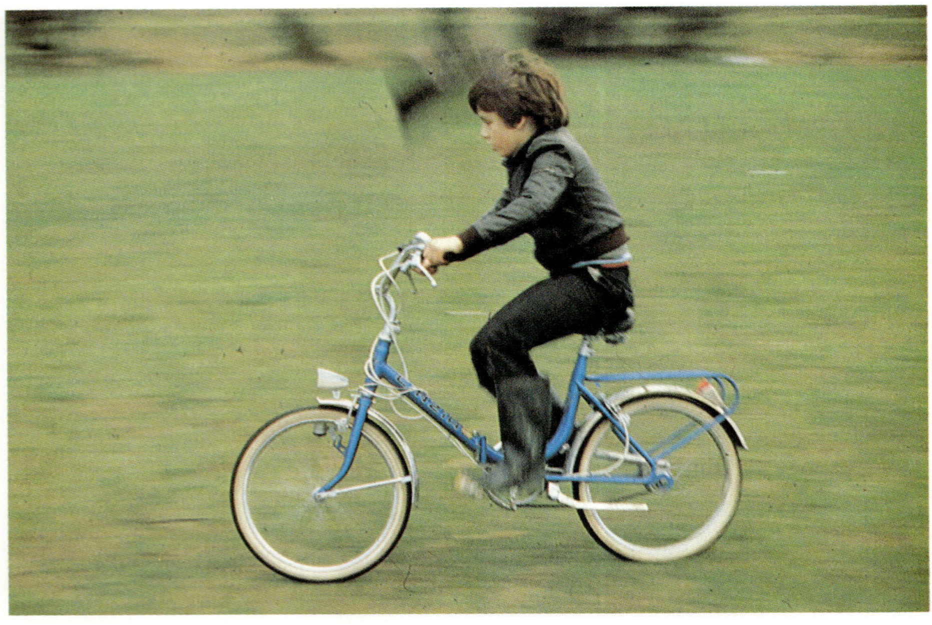

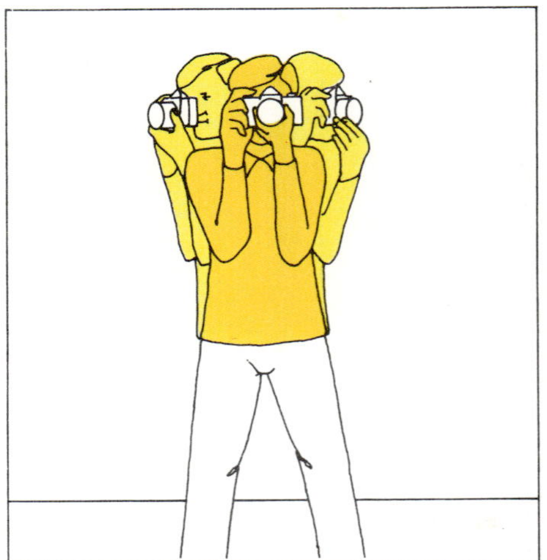

PANNING

A moving subject "frozen" on film sometimes lacks the impression of speed. If this detracts from the impact of the picture, consider following the subject by moving the camera during exposure. This is called *panning*. If you move the camera so the moving subject is relatively static on the film, the moving subject will look nearly sharp on film against a blurred background, as shown above. Because the rest of the scene is blurred, the photo gives the impression of motion.

Prefocus the lens to the approximate subject distance. Stand well balanced and begin moving the camera before exposure. While viewing the moving subject in the viewfinder, swing from the hips to follow subject motion. Expose film while panning and continue panning until exposure is finished.

Generally, you should use a shutter speed that would give a blurred image if you did not move the camera. Experiment and use the table on the opposite page as a guide.

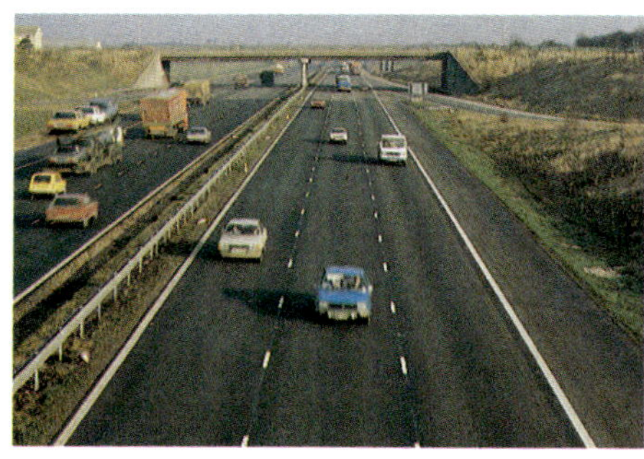

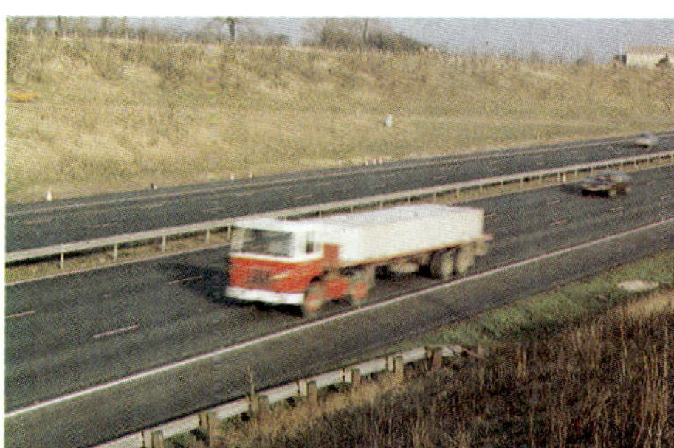

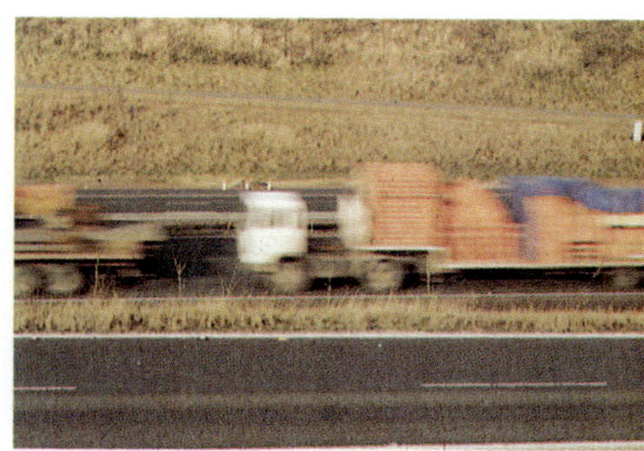

MOVING SUBJECTS

The exact effect a certain shutter speed and subject motion will have on the image is sometimes difficult to predict because of *other* variables involved. These include subject distance, image magnification, and the direction of travel.

All of the above photos were made with a shutter speed of 1/30 second. Image blur is minimal with distant cars moving directly toward or away from the camera, above left. Maximum image blur occurs with subjects moving directly across the field of view, above right. The center photo shows an intermediate blur. The truck was moving at 45° to the camera.

Use the table shown here to determine the slowest shutter speed that will freeze a certain subject traveling directly across your field of view. This information is based on using a 50mm lens. If you double lens focal length, use half the recommended time. If you halve focal length, you can double the recommended time.

If the subject moves at a 45° angle, you can use a shutter speed one step slower. If the subject moves directly toward or away from you, you can use a speed two steps slower.

Subject Distance	Subject Speed (mph) 1	2	4	8	15	30	60	125
5 ft.		1/250	1/500	1/1000	1/2000			
10 ft.	1/125	1/250	1/500	1/1000	1/2000			
25 ft.	1/60	1/125	1/250	1/500	1/1000	1/2000		
50 ft.	1/30	1/60	1/125	1/250	1/500	1/1000	1/2000	
100 ft.	1/15	1/30	1/60	1/125	1/250	1/500	1/1000	1/2000

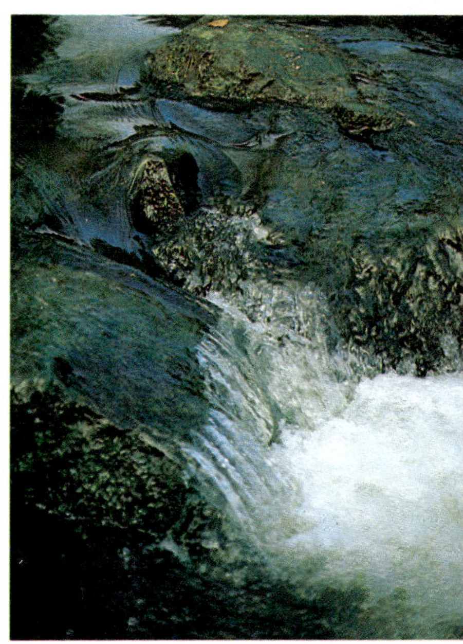

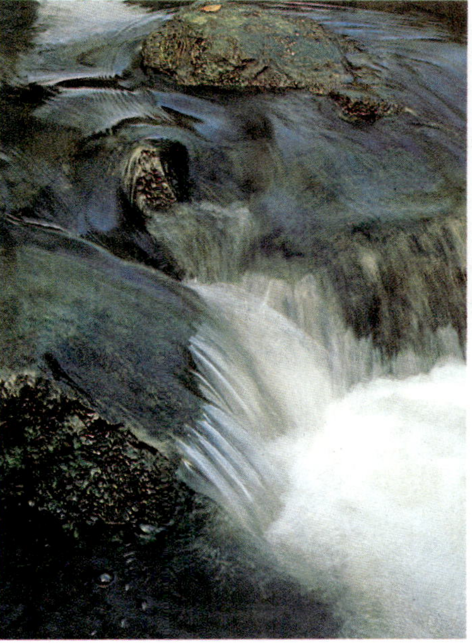

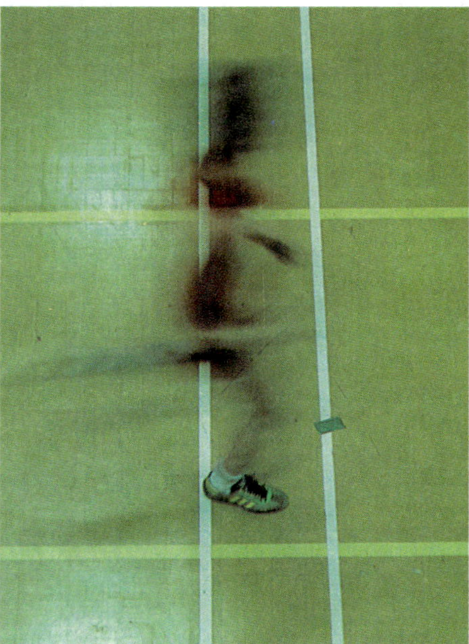

SHARP OR BLURRED?

The waterfall at left was photographed with a shutter speed of 1/1000 second. The resultant "frozen" motion looks artificial.

A shutter speed that gives image blur is sometimes a better choice. Moving water looks appealing when blurred. The center photo was made at 1/8 second. Because the camera was on a tripod, stationary details reproduce sharply.

In the photo at right, the only sharp part of the moving subject is the shoe. The viewer sees that the blur is a fast-moving runner. A slower speed would have also blurred the shoe, and a faster speed would have blurred less. Use shutter speed for creative image control.

Getting Good Exposures

A camera meter measures light reflected from the scene you see in the viewfinder. Then the camera recommends or makes appropriate exposure-control settings.

Shutter speed controls the time of exposure and lens aperture controls the relative brightness of the light striking the film. The combination results in exposure. As shown on the opposite page, you can use a variety of shutter-speed and aperture combinations to get the same exposure.

The bright parts of the scene expose film more than the darker parts. When exposed film is developed, this photographic effect is chemically transformed into image tone or color. In a negative, heavily exposed areas develop darker than less exposed areas. This *negative image* has the opposite tonality of the original scene. A print reverses the image again, so it looks correct.

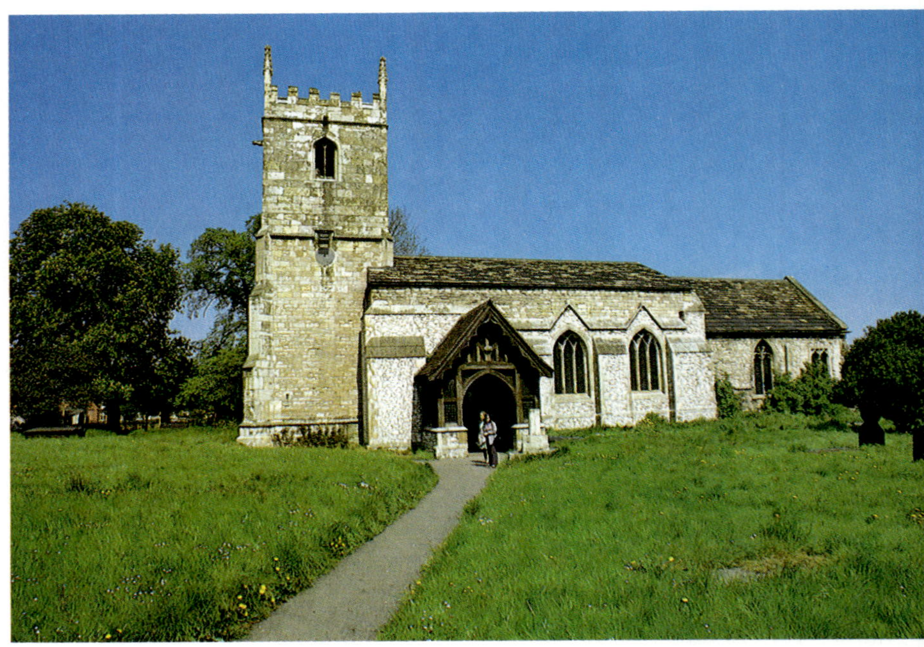

GOOD EXPOSURE

Camera meters are designed to recommend exposure-control settings that give good exposure of average scenes. The image above received good exposure. Dark areas reproduce black and there is much shadow detail. Bright areas also have detail. There is also a full range of tones and colors between these extremes.

CORRECT EXPOSURE

Exposure is the amount of light that strikes film. The amount of light is determined by intensity and exposure duration—controlled by lens aperture and shutter speed respectively. With the available ranges of apertures and shutter speeds, you can use many combinations of the two to get a certain exposure.

After you determine what exposure the film needs, you can choose aperture and shutter speed for a desired image effect, as shown on the next page.

You can get correct exposure in several ways. If you need great depth of field, use a small aperture and slow shutter speed. If you want to stop motion, use a fast shutter speed and a large lens aperture.

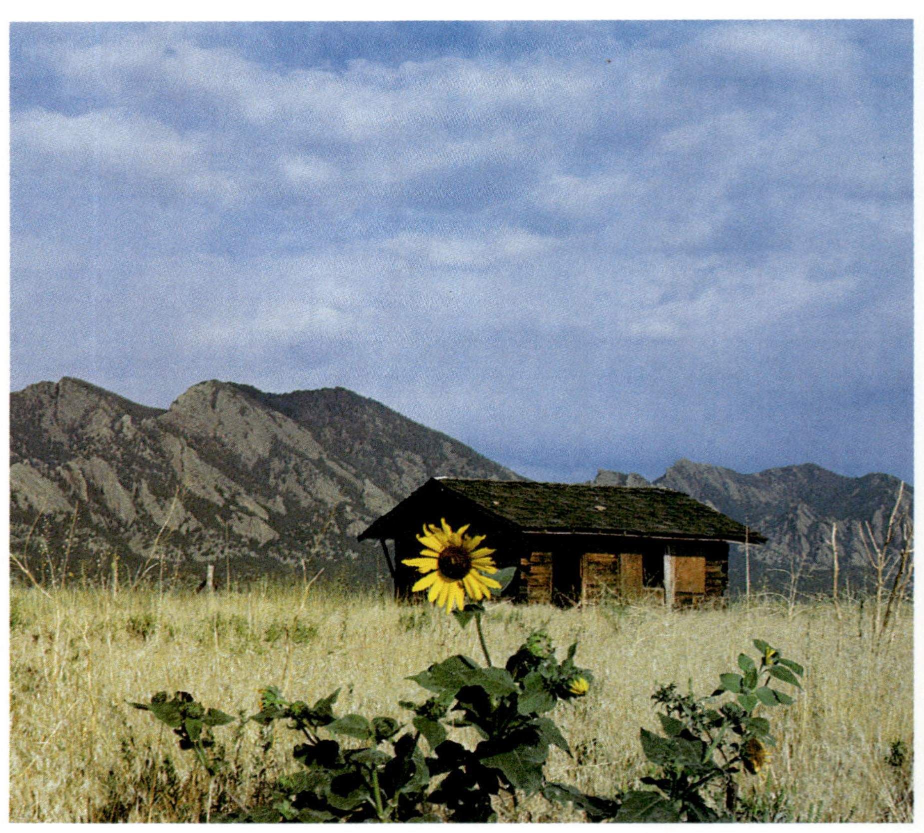

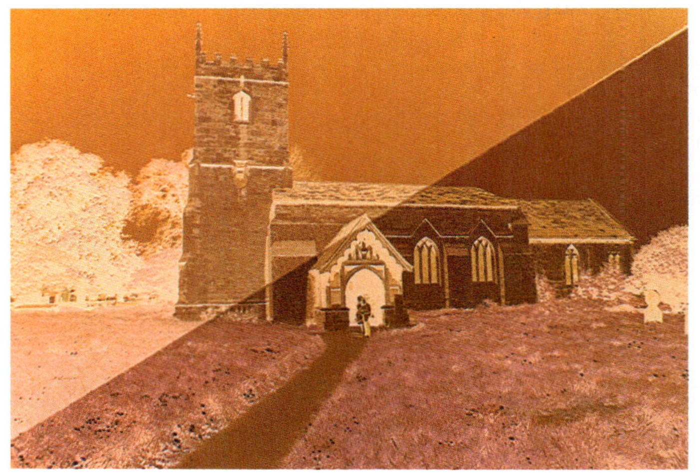

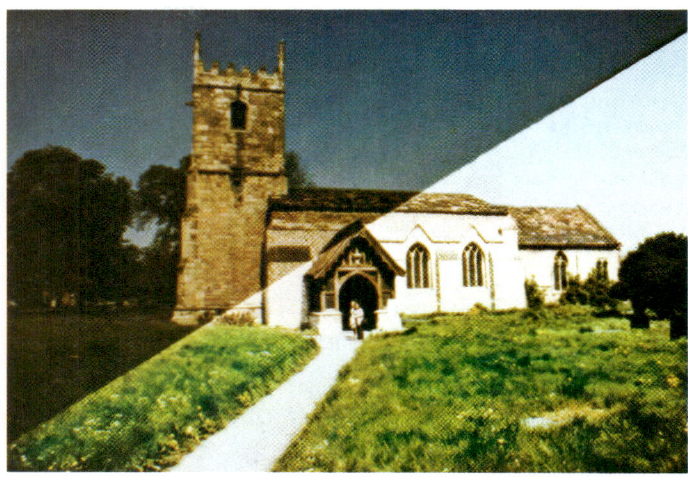

POORLY EXPOSED NEGATIVES

If a negative is exposed incorrectly, the film receives too much or too little light. The composite negative above shows the results of both.

The top part shows underexposure. The film did not receive enough exposure in the dark parts of the image, so those areas develop almost clear. Brighter areas do not develop as dark as they would in the case of good exposure. We say that the negative looks "thin." It is not as dark and contrasty as it should be.

The other part is an overexposed negative. Shadow areas have detail, but bright areas are too dark. They may be so dark that detail is lost.

PRINTS FROM BAD NEGATIVES

Due to negative underexposure, the top half appears dark and murky. There is little contrast or shadow detail. You can't put detail where none was recorded. The bottom half is too bright due to negative overexposure. Bright areas lack detail.

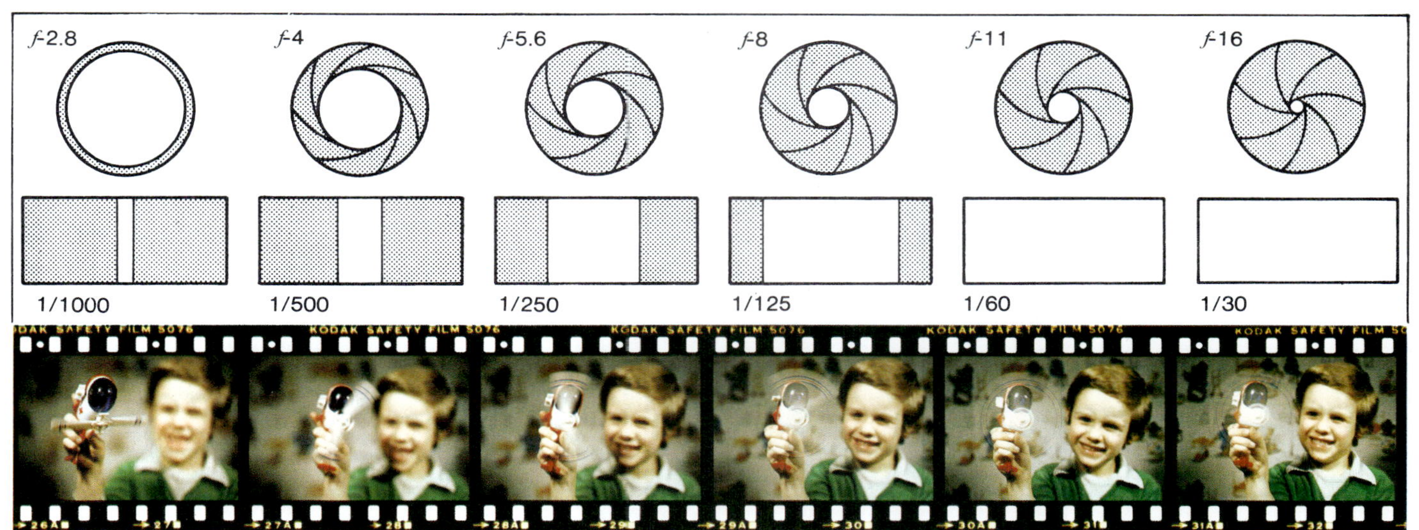

COMBINING APERTURE AND SHUTTER SPEED

The drawings above show the effect of changing aperture and shutter speed one exposure step at a time, maintaining the same effective exposure. When aperture is closed one step, from *f*-2.8 to *f*-4, the image is half as bright. To compensate, expose the film for twice as long.

The photos show the image effect of the settings. With fast shutter speeds and large apertures, movement of the toy helicopter blades is practically stopped and there is shallow depth of field. As *f*-number increases, so does depth of field. But because shutter speed must now be slower, the helicopter blades reproduce more blurred.

Choose aperture or shutter speed first for the desired image effect, then adjust the other to maintain good exposure.

Using Your Camera Meter

A built-in, through-the-lens (TTL) exposure meter measures the brightness of the image you see in the camera viewfinder. This helps you get good exposure most of the time.

A TTL meter is *coupled* to shutter-speed and lens aperture. As you adjust one of the exposure-control settings, the viewfinder exposure display indicates how to adjust the other for good exposure.

The meter operates while you view the scene through the maximum lens aperture, no matter where the lens aperture is set. This keeps the focusing screen image bright for easy focusing and composition. The lens aperture stops down after you push the shutter button and the mirror swings up. After exposure, the lens opens to maximum aperture again.

Some camera meters will also meter correctly while the lens is stopped down. This is useful if you use non-automatic lenses or want to visually judge depth of field and exposure-control settings at the same time. Check your camera manual to see if *stop-down metering* is possible with your model.

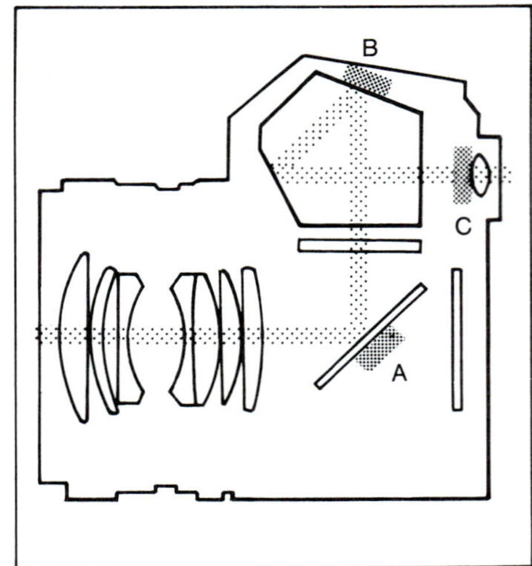

LIGHT-METERING CELLS

The diagram above shows three locations for light-metering cells. Some camera models use a cell behind or below the mirror (A), the cell reading light reflected from the film plane during exposure.

Other models use a cell at the top of the pentaprism (B) or behind it near the viewfinder eyepiece (C). The cell measures image brightness on the focusing screen.

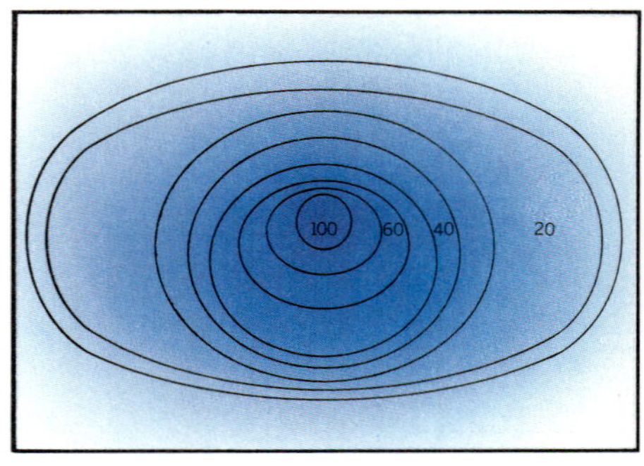

METERING PATTERNS

This is the way the meter measures light and dark parts of the scene within the viewing image. There are three basic types:

Full-frame averaging meters give equal emphasis to all parts of the frame. Light in the corners affects the meter the same way light in the center does. *Center-weighted* meters use a pattern that measures all of the frame, but has most sensitivity in the center, or bottom center, as shown above. The numbers and color tones represent relative sensitivity. You don't see this pattern on the focusing screen.

Semi-spot meters measure light in a well-defined area at the center of the frame and ignore other areas.

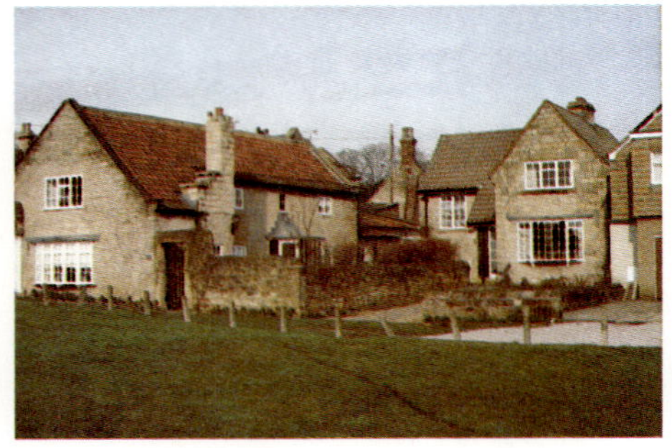

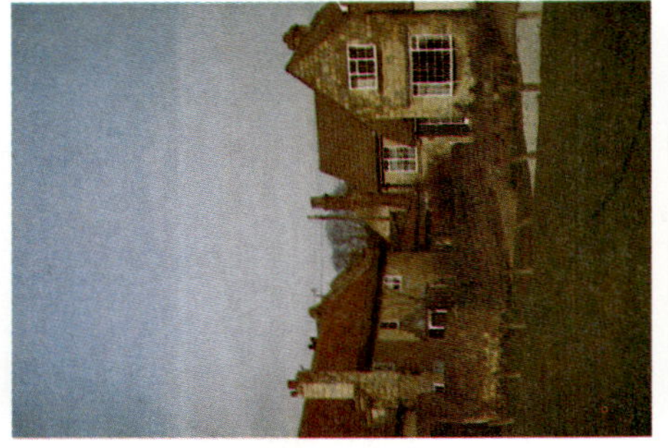

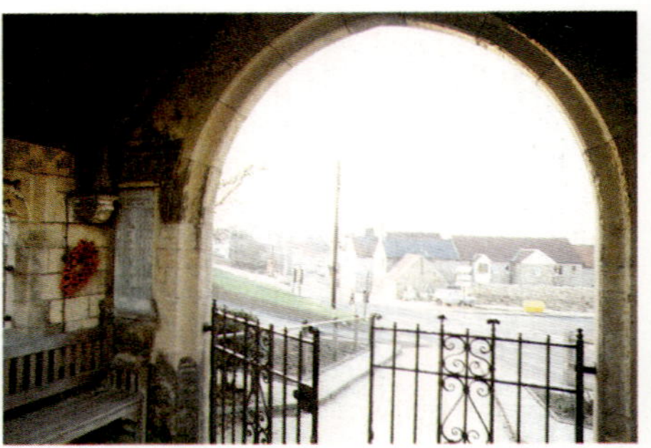

USING METERING PATTERNS

Most camera meters use a center-weighted or bottom-center-weighted pattern because most photographers put the main subject of interest at or near the center of the frame.

A bright sky can fool a full-frame averaging meter into thinking that the scene is brighter than it really is and therefore recommending underexposure. A center-weighted meter reduces this problem because the sky is usually above the center of the composition, where there is less metering sensitivity. The left photo above was made with center-weighted metering. The important parts of the scene—houses and grass—are in the most sensitive part of the metering pattern. The meter bases exposure mainly on these elements.

Fooled Meter—This design works well most of the time, but it can be fooled, for example when the camera is held for vertical-format pictures. Then maximum sensitivity is no longer bottom center-weighted. Even though you may photograph essentially the same scene, the meter may recommend different exposure settings.

This is what happened. The bright sky affected the meter too much. The meter recommended less exposure than with the horizontal-format photo.

SELECTIVE METERING

An *average* scene has relatively equal amounts of bright and dark areas. The brightness range from bright to dark is about seven exposure steps. The meter sees these areas as an average brightness and determines good exposure based on this average. Most of the scenes we photograph fit into this category.

However, if the scene has a longer brightness range than about seven steps, or is predominantly bright or dark, it is not average, and can give exposure problems. Usually the solution is to meter selectively the part of the scene you want reproduced normally and base exposure on it.

Inside/Outside Scene—Scenes showing inside and outside areas usually have a long brightness range. If you base exposure on inside details, such as on the arch-

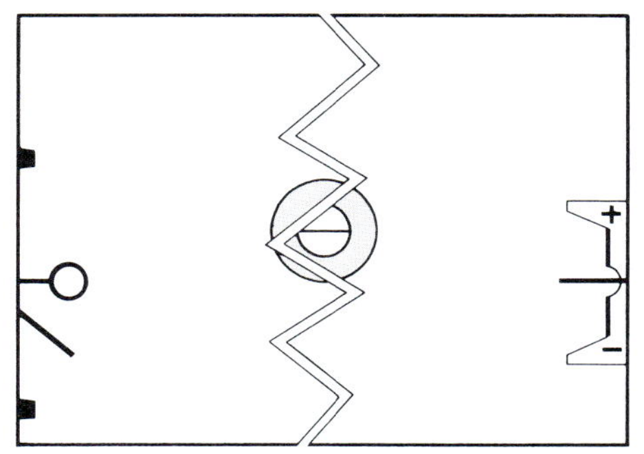

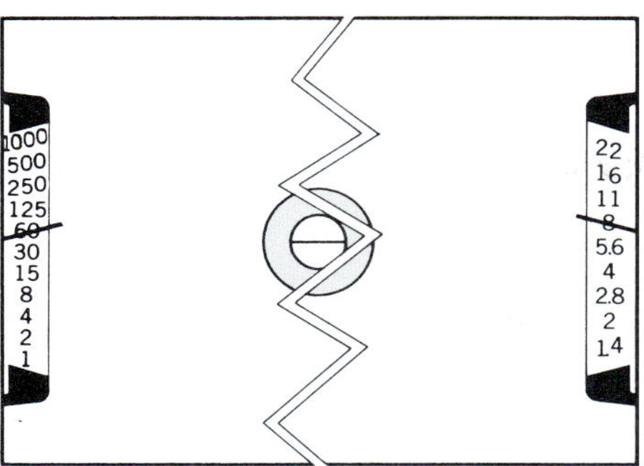

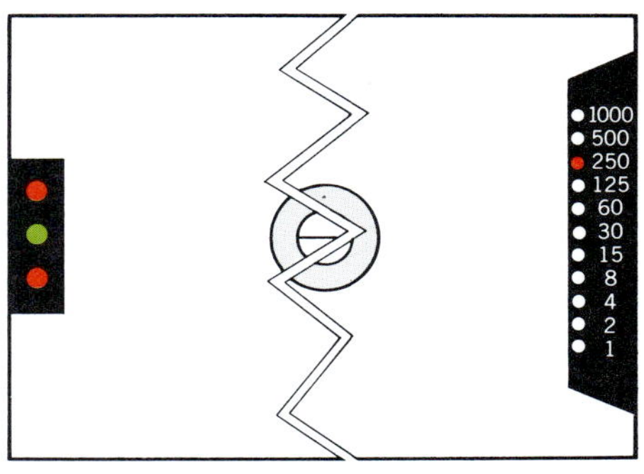

VIEWFINDER DISPLAYS

With a TTL meter you can judge good exposure while viewing the scene. You observe the viewfinder display and adjust exposure-control settings until the display indicates good exposure. Some common viewfinder displays are shown.

Match Needle—The left drawing above shows this manual-metering display. Typically, the shutter-speed dial is coupled to the straight needle and the aperture ring to the needle with the circle. Each moves as you adjust exposure controls. Exposure is correct when the two needles are aligned.

Needle Centering—The other display, above, indicates good exposure when the needle is centered. For more exposure, move the needle up toward +, for less exposure, down toward −

Scale Displays—Some cameras display the selected aperture or shutter speed in the viewfinder. This is very convenient. Two types are shown above.

Typically, you set aperture or shutter speed by looking at the camera exterior or a window in the viewfinder. A scale in the viewfinder display then shows what the *other* setting should be for best exposure. This is the way many automatic cameras work. With an aperture-priority camera, the needle indicates shutter speed, as at left. The display for a shutter-priority camera shows the automatically selected aperture. When you use the camera manually, set the indicated setting manually for good exposure.

Electronic Displays—Modern electronic alternatives for some of the displays shown are *light-emitting diodes* (LEDs) and *liquid crystal displays* (LCDs). An LED display is bright and easily visible in dark areas, but it uses more power.

The illustration above shows LEDs. At left is a centering display. Exposure is correct when the center green LED lights. The top red LED indicates overexposure, the bottom red LED underexposure. Only one LED lights at a time.

The right side shows a scale display. An LED indicates the shutter speed.

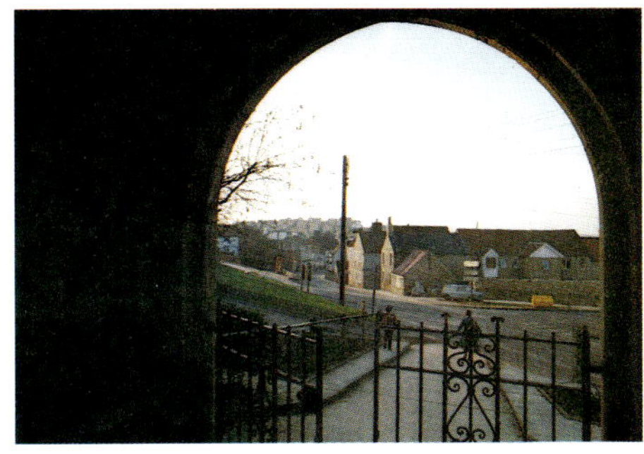

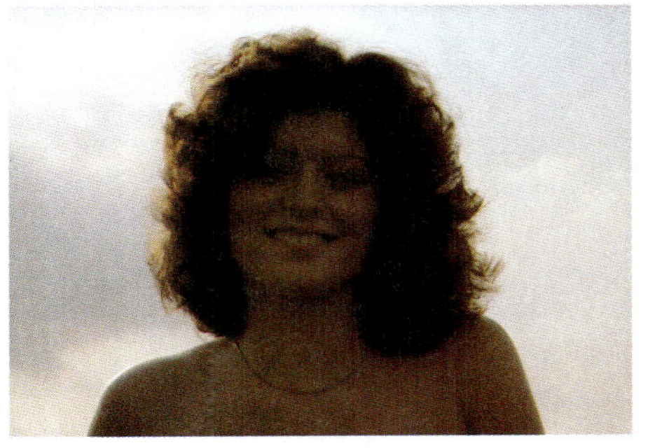

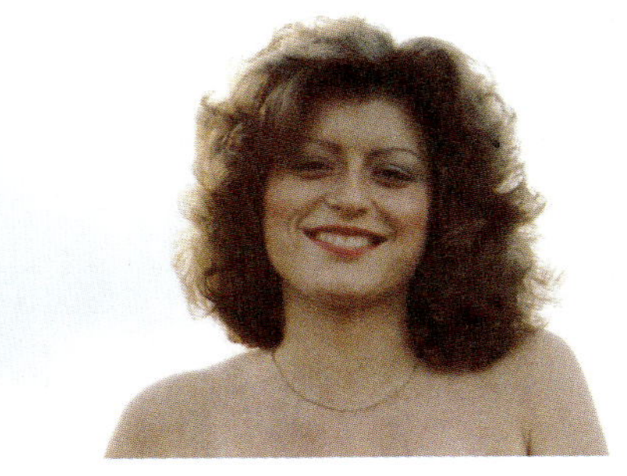

way in the first photo, these areas reproduce OK. However, outside elements—which are much brighter than inside elements—are relatively overexposed and reproduced "washed out."

For this composition, outside areas are of main interest. For best exposure of these areas, selectively meter them. Move camera position to exclude the effect of inside darkness while metering. Set exposure-control settings and move to your original location to take the picture. Doing this will give a better picture, as shown in the photo above.

Backlit Scene—A common photo situation is photographing a person in front of a bright sky or light source. This type of scene has a long brightness range because the light illuminating the front of the person is much more dim than the light from the background. If you meter normally, the bright background light makes the meter recommend settings that give good exposure for the background. This makes the person reproduce dark. If you want to silhouette the subject, selectively meter the background light.

To reproduce detail in the person, however, selectively meter the subject. Move up close to the person and fill the viewfinder with the image. Meter and manually set exposure-control settings. Move to your original position to take the picture. This gives more exposure than the first case. It'll overexpose the background.

If your camera is automatic, you can use the *Exposure-Compensation Dial* instead of metering selectively. In this case, you would set the dial to +1 or 2X for one step more exposure.

35mm SLR Metering Operations

Because there are many 35mm SLR cameras available, it can be confusing to choose one that is right for you. In addition to considering price, size, weight and location of camera controls, you also have to decide what kind of metering system you want in a camera.

Current 35mm SLR cameras have a built-in, *through-the-lens* (TTL) light meter that measures the light through the lens. The *metering pattern* was described on the previous two pages.

A TTL meter is convenient because it eliminates some of the problems of using a separate, handheld meter to determine exposure-control settings. The main problem with a handheld meter is that it often doesn't measure the same scene you see in the viewfinder. It can measure light reflected from more or less scene than you see, which may lead to incorrect exposure.

MANUAL AND AUTOMATIC METERS

A variety of TTL meters are used in today's 35mm SLRs. They can be divided

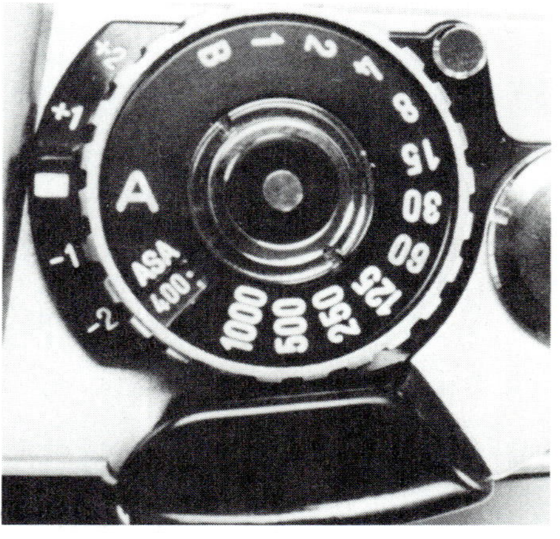

into two basic groups—manual and automatic exposure control. With manual operation, *you* adjust aperture and shutter speed until the meter display indicates that exposure is correct. The way the meter indicates correct exposure depends on the *exposure display* visible in the camera viewfinder. Some of these displays are described later.

An automatic camera sets aperture, shutter speed or *both* for you. Three types of automatic cameras are available—*shutter priority, aperture priority* and *programmed.* They are described on these two pages. For extra creative control, most automatic cameras let you interpret the scene and give more or less exposure than the camera would automatically. You do this with a control called the *Exposure-Compensation Dial.* One is pictured here. This gives more or less exposure. The dial has detents for 1/3 or 1/2 step intervals.

In addition, some automatic cameras give you the option of using automatic or manual exposure control. Some *multi-mode* cameras offer more than one automatic metering system.

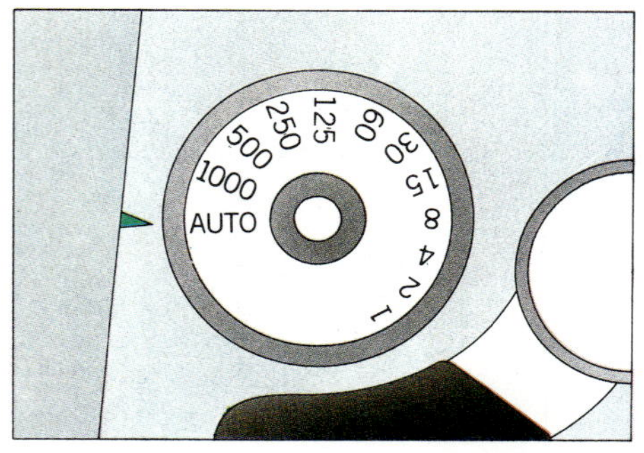

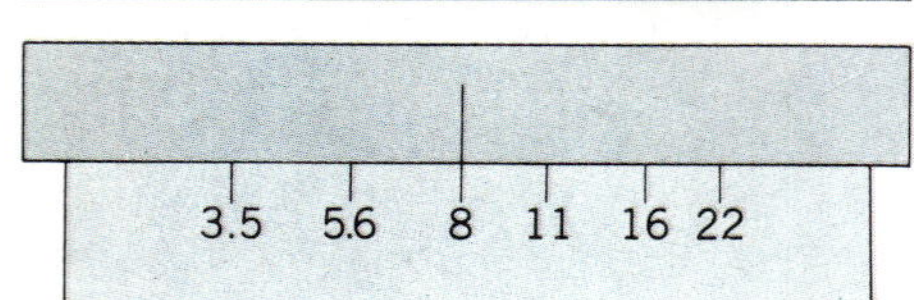

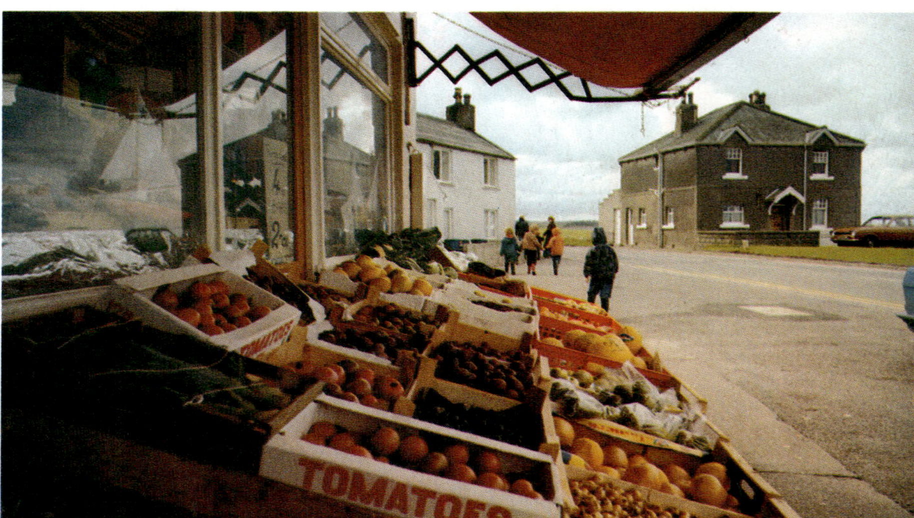

APERTURE-PRIORITY OPERATION

Aperture priority is the opposite of shutter priority. The shutter-speed dial is set for automatic operation, as shown above. You select aperture, using the lens aperture ring. In this drawing, *f*-8 was selected.

The camera automatically sets the appropriate shutter speed for good exposure. This speed can be non-standard, such as 1/325 second. Some exposure displays indicate the approximate shutter speed selected. If the camera meter cannot find a shutter speed that will give good exposure with the selected aperture, the viewfinder display will give you a warning. Select a larger or smaller aperture until the meter indicates good exposure.

USING APERTURE PRIORITY

This mode is most convenient when your main consideration is *depth of field*—the depth of sharp focus in the image from foreground to background.

If your camera has a depth-of-field preview button, you can see depth of field before taking the picture and set aperture for the effect you want. Let the camera select the appropriate shutter speed.

Aperture priority works with mirror lenses or with non-automatic accessories between lens and camera body.

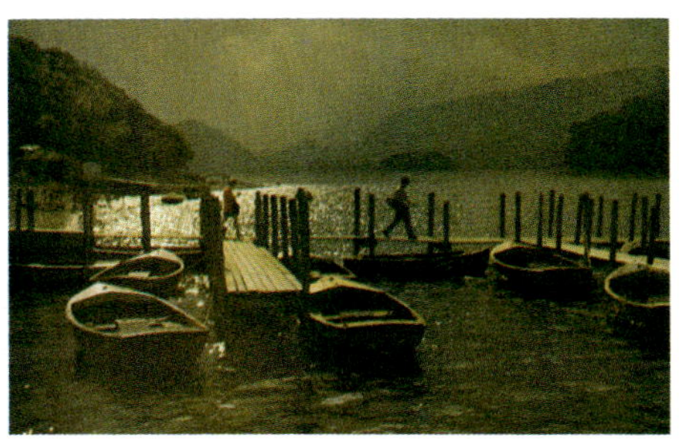

MANUAL OPERATION

You have to adjust both aperture and shutter speed before taking the picture. If the viewfinder exposure display doesn't show the settings, you may have to take the camera from your eye to adjust the controls. This can be time-consuming and inconvenient.

Usually, you'll already have set a certain shutter speed or aperture. Then you have only to adjust the other control to get good exposure. In addition, manual operation is useful to use exposure settings different than those recommended by the meter.

SHUTTER-PRIORITY OPERATION

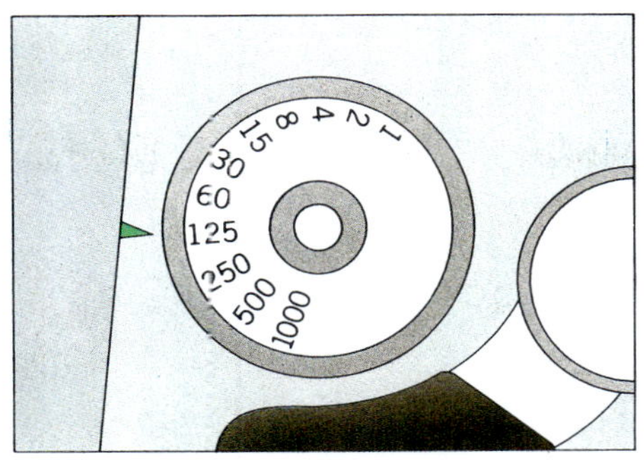

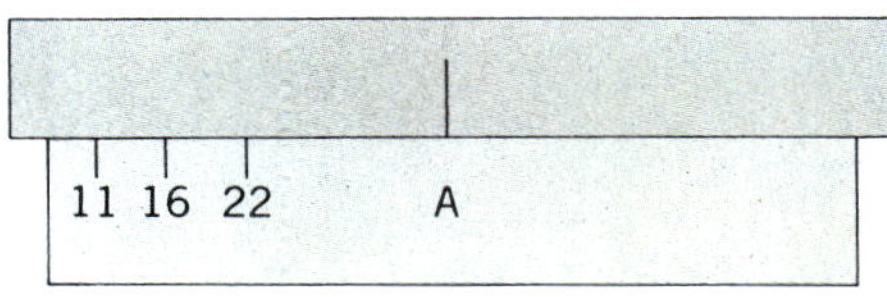

As shown in the drawing above, a shutter-priority camera has a shutter-speed control that you adjust manually. The camera automatically sets aperture to give best exposure. In this mode, the lens aperture ring is set to A for automatic operation.

If the camera cannot select an aperture that will give good exposure with the chosen shutter speed, the viewfinder display will warn you with a light or other indication.

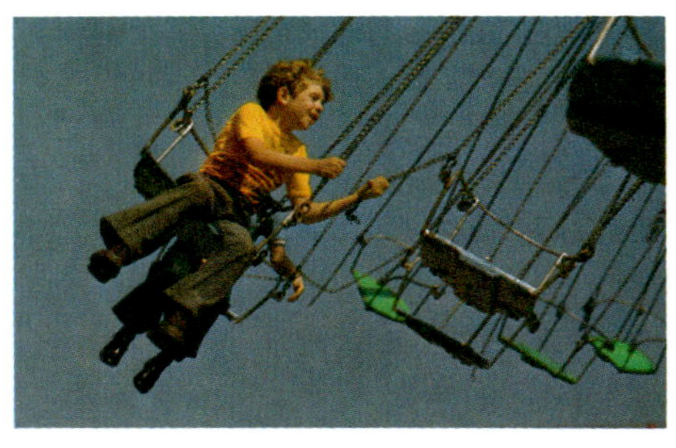

USING SHUTTER PRIORITY

This type of automatic operation is ideal if the major consideration is selecting the proper shutter speed. If you want to "freeze" subject motion on film, as shown above, select the fastest possible shutter speed and let the camera automatically set aperture. Or, if you want to hand-hold the camera in dim light, set shutter speed to a slow speed that you can hand-hold for a sharp image.

Shutter-priority automatic operation is not possible with a non-automatic accessory between the lens and camera body, such as an extension tube or bellows, or when you use a lens with a fixed aperture, such as a mirror lens.

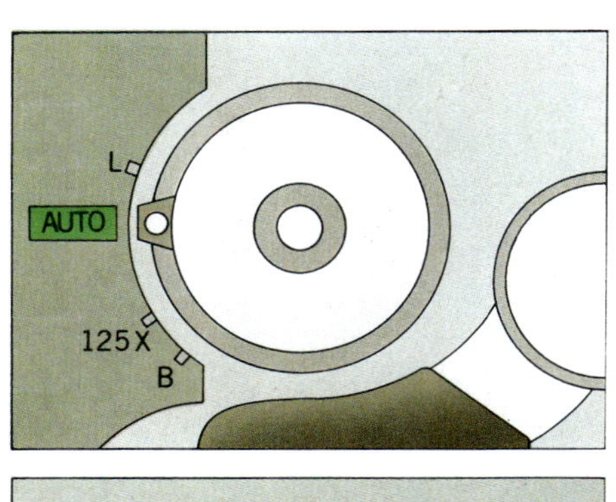

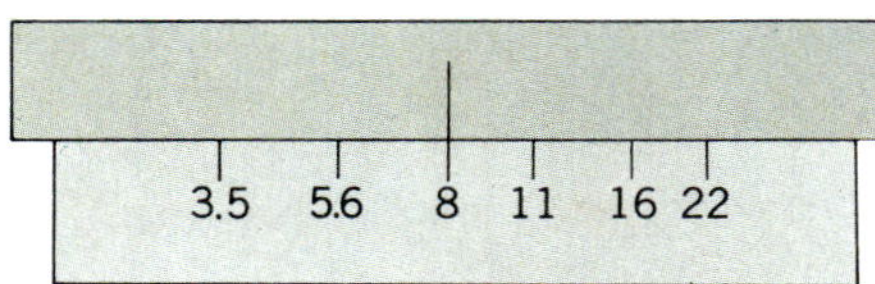

AUTOMATIC-ONLY CAMERAS

Typically, these are aperture-priority cameras. They do not have a control for manual use. The display may show the approximate shutter speed it selected, with an over- or underexposure indication if you have chosen an inappropriate aperture.

Because there is no manual mode, it is difficult to take pictures with exposure-control settings not recommended by the meter. You can use the Exposure-Compensation Dial if the camera has one.

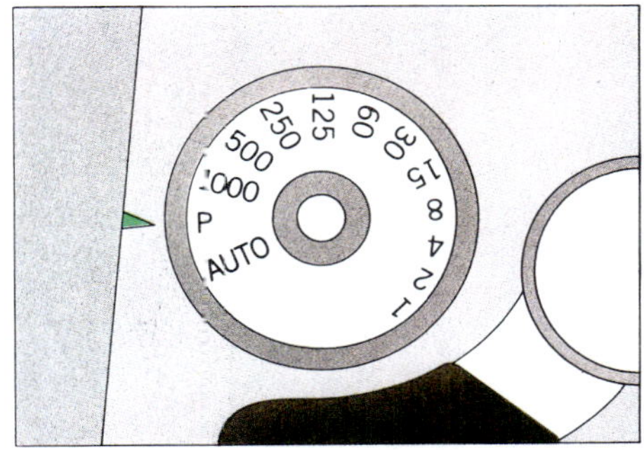

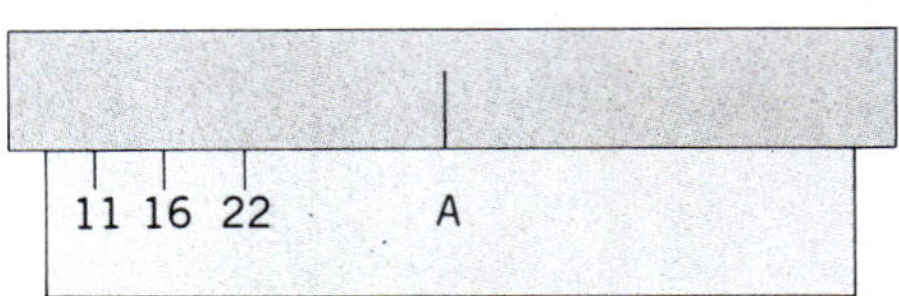

PROGRAMMED OPERATION

This type of camera sets *both* aperture and shutter speed automatically. In bright light, it uses a small aperture and fast shutter speed, in dim light a large aperture and slow speed. If the light is too dim, the exposure display shows a warning.

As you can see in the drawing above, with one brand you choose programmed operation by putting the lens on automatic and turning the shutter-speed dial to a setting that indicates *program,* such as P.

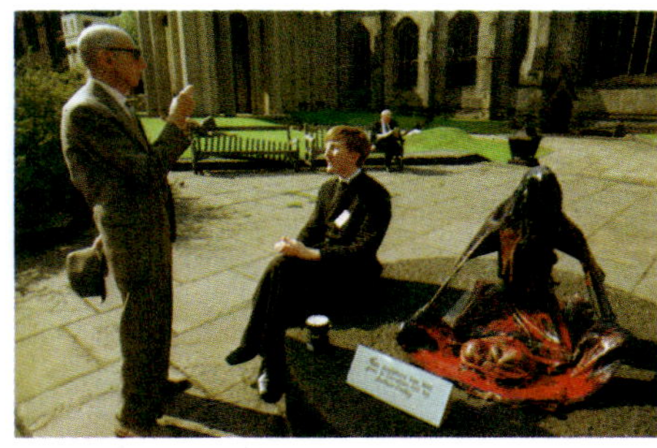

USING A PROGRAMMED CAMERA

You'll find this most convenient for general-purpose snapshot photography, when the most important considerations are good exposure. It's fine for candid shooting or unexpected "grab shots" when you want to think only about focusing.

Most cameras with programmed exposure capability are multi-mode. That is, they offer more than one kind of exposure control. You may never need to use the programmed mode. However, there may be times when you want to lend your camera to a photographic novice. Set the camera on programmed automatic and show the person how to load and advance film, focus and shoot.

More Tips for Better Exposures

Getting good exposures consistently requires understanding, observation and careful thought. Make exposure decisions after finding best composition. Good exposure of a boring scene will not make it an appealing picture! In fact, less-than-perfect exposure is sometimes OK if the composition and subject are interesting.

When determining best exposure for problem scenes, inspect all parts of the focusing-screen image. Consider your camera's metering pattern and how you want the image to look. Think about depth of field and subject motion. Select a preferred aperture or shutter speed, then determine the other setting. Preview depth of field if necessary. Make an exposure compensation if needed, or meter selectively.

CHECK YOUR METER

Meters are not foolproof. They may give erroneous recommendations. Therefore, it is sometimes helpful to check the meter recommendation against your experience or the film-maker's guidelines.

Sunny Day *f*-16 Rule—This rule is easy to remember. Outdoors on a bright sunny

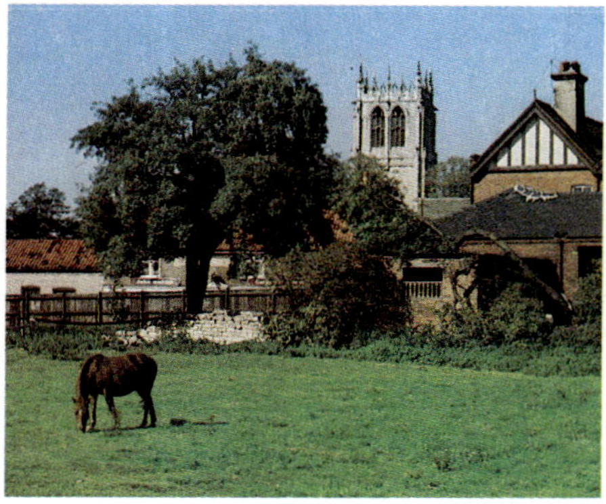

day, these settings give good exposure: *f*-16 and the reciprocal of film speed, in seconds. For example, if you use ASA 125 film, *f*-16 and 1/125 second give good exposure. Other combinations that give the same amount of light will work too, such as *f*-8 and 1/500 second.

If you were shooting a subject outdoors on a sunny day with ASA 125 film and the meter recommended a setting of *f*-2.8 and 1/15 second, you'd know something was wrong. This is the time to use the rule. Or, if you are photographing a non-average scene and want to base exposure on areas lit by the sun, use the rule as a guide.

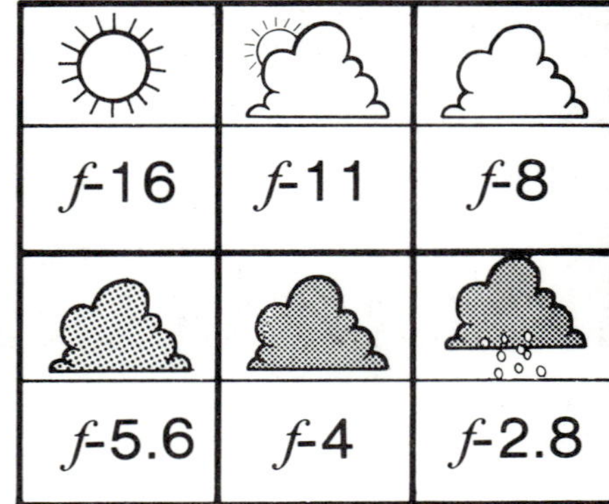

Using The Film Data Sheet—Film manufacturers supply a lot of useful information in the instruction sheet that comes with your film. Usually, one of the entries is an adaptation of the Sunny Day *f*-16 Rule for different kinds of outdoor light, as illustrated above. The recommended shutter speed for the *f*-numbers shown is the reciprocal of film speed in seconds. As the scene darkens—represented by more cloud cover—open the lens aperture.

Many data sheets also give recommendations for some indoor and nighttime scenes. Be sure to read data sheets to get best results with the film you use.

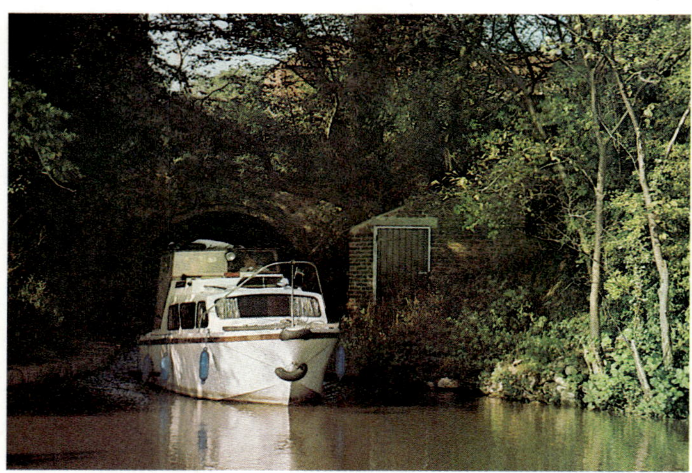

DARK BACKGROUNDS

Above is a good example of a predominantly dark scene. A camera meter "thinks" that it is an average scene in dim light. It recommends an exposure that reproduces the background in middle tones instead of dark ones. But the white boat would be overexposed and washed out.

To expose the boat correctly, you must adjust the recommendation. In this case, giving one step *less* exposure was correct and made the dark background reproduce darker than a middle tone. This reproduced the boat well.

Because the boat is directly lit by the sun, you could also use the Sunny Day *f*-16 rule.

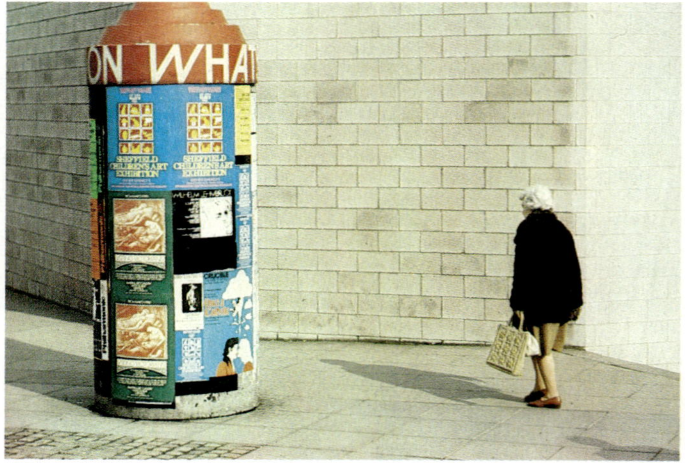

LIGHT BACKGROUNDS

The light wall is in direct sunlight, which makes the scene predominantly bright. Following the meter's recommendation would reproduce the wall in midtones, making other elements underexposed and too dark.

Solve this problem by giving the film *more* exposure than recommended. A correction between one and two steps is usually best. In this case, correction was 1-1/2 steps.

Other ways to solve the problem without using exposure compensation are to selectively meter the colorful column or use the Sunny Day *f*-16 Rule.

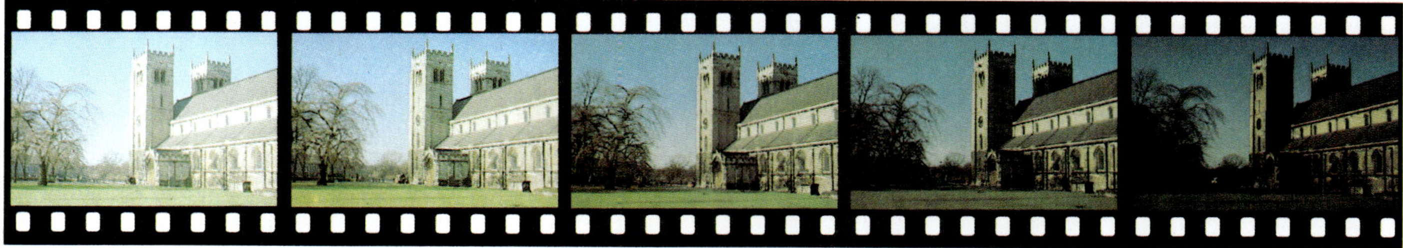

BRACKETING

There is a way to virtually guarantee a good exposure. Instead of making just one exposure and hoping it's correct, make several. Each frame is exposed with different exposure-control settings. This procedure is called *bracketing*.

Make what you think is the best exposure for the scene. Then expose more frames with more and less exposure. Some people bracket in full steps, some in half-steps. In the example above from left to right, bracketing was: two steps more exposure, one step more exposure, recommended exposure, one step less exposure and two steps less exposure. The photographer could choose the best slide after processing, and discard the rest.

How Much Bracketing?—How much you bracket depends on your uncertainty and how unusual or unrepeatable the scene is. If you will never see the scene again, bracket away! Five frames is not a lot of film in this case. Film is generally the least expensive part of photography when you compare it to the cost of your equipment, time and travel expenses.

As you become more experienced, you'll need to bracket less. Non-average scenes will become easier to handle, making your exposure judgement better and better. This is to your advantage when you have time for just one picture.

Follow these recommendations for slide film. When shooting negative film, do not bracket on the side of underexposure. It is impractical to make a good print from an underexposed negative.

Exposure Range—The film's *exposure range* is the range of brightnesses from light to dark that can be recorded. The brightest elements reproduce white and the darkest elements reproduce black. Film is designed to reproduce detail in scenes with a brightness range of about seven steps, 1:128, an average scene. Good exposure in most cases means reproducing all detail.

If the scene has a shorter brightness range, the film may record all detail even if you don't use the meter-recommended exposures. If the scene has a longer range, some scene detail will always be lost due to the limited film exposure range. Depending on how you set exposure, you can keep shadow or highlight detail or part of both, but not all of both.

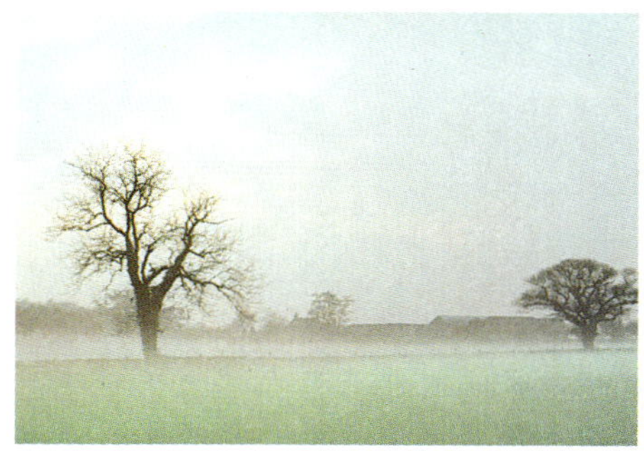

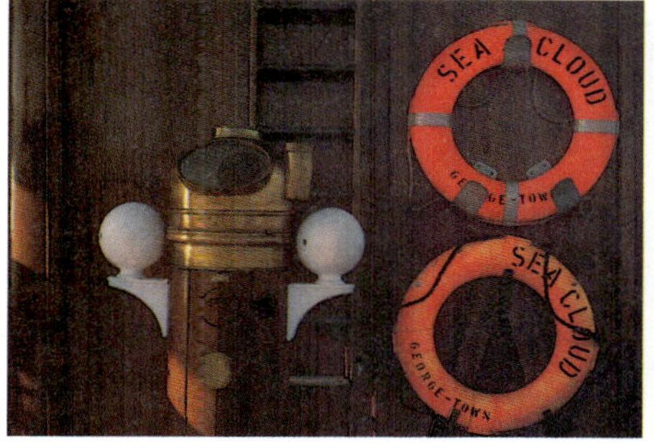

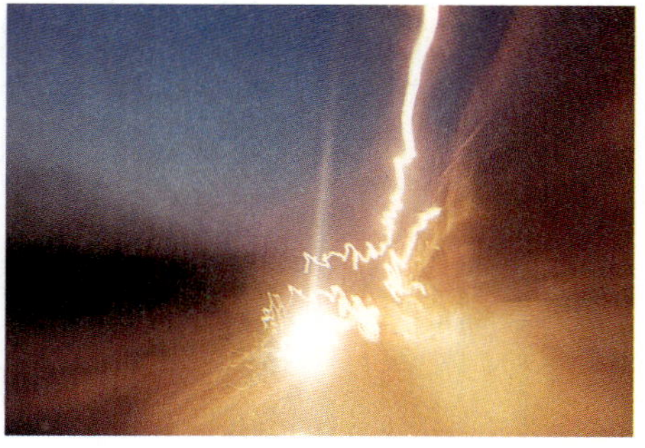

DELIBERATE OVEREXPOSURE

As shown, overexposure of color slide film lightens the image and can wash out color. Some scenes benefit from this treatment, making deliberate overexposure a useful creative control. Typically, the scene should have mostly light tones, such as the fog scene here.

When experimenting with this technique, be sure to expose a frame with normal recommended exposure. You can see if the special-effect image works better than the normally exposed one.

DELIBERATE UNDEREXPOSURE

Underexposure of color slide film darkens the image. It can give rich, "saturated" colors. This can increase the impact of some color pictures. Shadows reproduce as solid black, so if there is important detail in the shadows, don't use this technique. For best effect, detail should be in the light parts of the scene.

With slide film, creative underexposure from 1/2 to 1-1/2 steps is worth trying with strongly lit, textured subjects. The photo above was exposed with one step less exposure than the recommended reading. Also expose a frame normally when using this technique. Compare the two results.

LONG EXPOSURES

Some cameras have shutter speeds as long as 15 or 30 seconds. Others require using the B shutter setting for exposures longer than one second. When you depress the shutter button, the shutter stays open as long as the button is depressed.

Long exposures are fun when you want to record dark scenes, image blur or both. Above is a picture of a moving car taken from another car at *f*-5.6 for two seconds.

Because each low-light scene is different, it is difficult to give general recommendations other than these: Bracket extensively toward more exposure if your meter can read dim light levels. If it can't, bracket even more, starting with the recommended exposure on the film data sheet. For sharp pictures, use a tripod or other firm support. For creative blur, handholding is OK.

Choosing Film

A bewildering array of color and b&w films is available from your photo dealer. This section will help you choose the film you need.

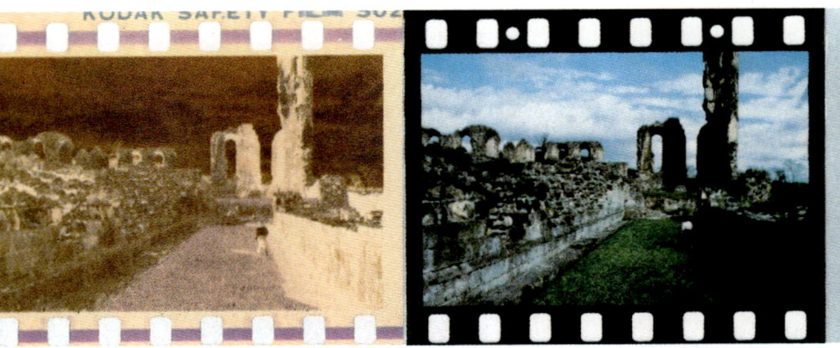

COLOR NEGATIVE FILM

The suffix *color* in a film name means color negative. People shoot this film (left picture) to get color prints. The overall orange color in the negative is there to compensate for two of the dyes in the film. The orange contributes to good color reproduction in the print.

Color negative film has a long exposure range, so it accommodates some overexposure without sacrificing too much image quality. This is one reason many photographers shoot with this film.

Another good reason is that it is easy to get additional copies from a good color negative. You can get small prints, big prints or color slides made from negatives. For more information, check with your photo dealer. If he doesn't offer the service, he can probably recommend a good lab.

Home-processing kits are available for color negative film. They can be convenient if you do your own color printing. However, even some professionals prefer to let automated labs process their negatives because they usually do a good job.

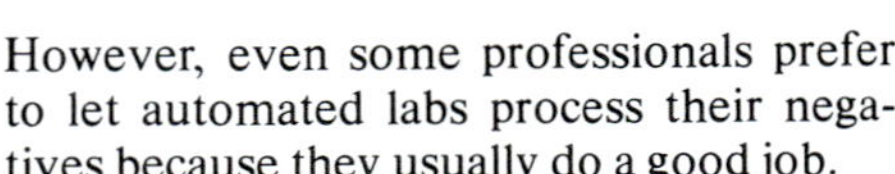

COLOR SLIDE FILM

The suffix *chrome* in a film name means it is color slide film. With slide film (center), the film you expose in the camera is made into a positive image by processing. Careful exposure is necessary to get the best possible slide. It is impractical to correct large exposure or color errors when printing or duplicating a slide.

Slides are used by photographers who like to project their images. You can always have prints made from your favorite slides, but generally the price is higher than for prints made from negatives. If you want to make many prints from a slide, have an *internegative* made first. This is a special color negative made from the slide. It ensures good reproduction from a good original image.

To duplicate your best slides onto slide film, use *slide-duplicating* film, available through your camera dealer. When you do it yourself, you can crop the image and change its color with filters. Most local labs will duplicate slides for a reasonable price.

Home-processing kits for slide films are easy to use. Total processing times are less than 30 minutes. You can shoot, process and have dry images for mounting in less than one hour.

You can use medium-speed films as general-purpose products for *most* picture situations. Select a slow or fast film when using one is the only way to get the specific photo you want.

If you aren't sure of what film speed to use, it makes sense to compromise with a medium-speed product. When you are likely to shoot a variety of subjects and scenes, use a medium-speed film.

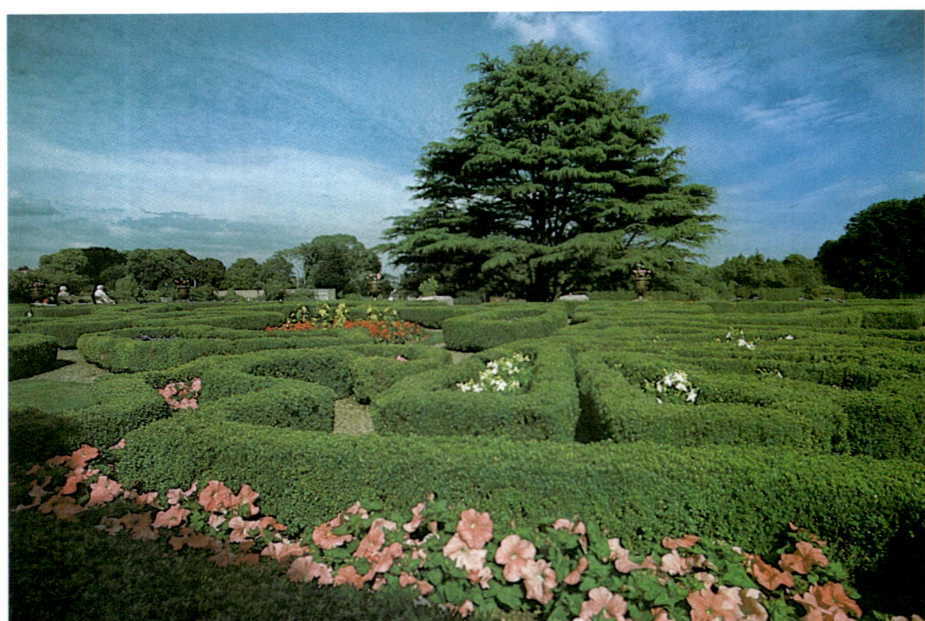

USING SLOW FILMS

Slow films have ASA speeds from 25 to 64. These include color slide and b&w films made by Kodak, Ilford and others. Kodachrome 25, Kodachrome 64 and Ektachrome 64 are popular slide films in this category. Ilford Pan F and Agfapan 25 are popular slow b&w films.

The main advantage of using a slow film is the ability to record detail clearly when you expose and focus carefully. Big enlargements are possible with 35mm images made on slow film. In fact, prints as large as 30x40 inches are possible from good negatives without noticeable graininess in the print. Slides made from slow-speed films show good image quality when projected onto large screens.

Use slow film when the light is bright. This lets you use fast shutter speeds so you can handhold the camera. Even so, using a tripod is always a good idea when you want to minimize camera shake for best sharpness in the picture.

If you want to use slow shutter speeds—for creative image blur for example—a slow film is fine. Use a slow film when large apertures are needed for shallow depth of field.

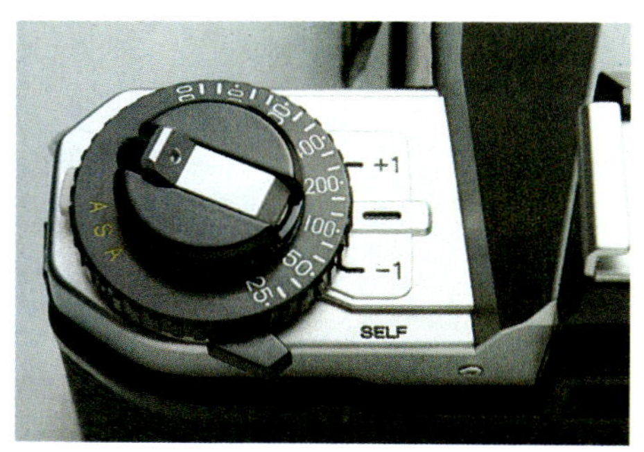

B&W NEGATIVE

The best reason to shoot b&w negative film is for total control of exposure, processing and printing. The steps are easy and fun. Several HPBooks give you information on b&w darkroom work. These books, chemicals, printing paper and darkroom accessories are available at most camera stores.

Today, few labs process and print b&w negatives. Rather, they pass on your exposed film to a local photographer who does it. Check with your lab to see how they handle b&w film. You may get a better price if you deal with the photographer directly.

FILM SPEED

This is a measure of a film's sensitivity to light. *Slow* films are less sensitive to light than *fast* films. *Medium-speed* films have intermediate sensitivity.

This does not necessarily mean that fast film is better than slow or medium-speed film. Films with different speeds are suitable for different applications. Each is appropriate for certain lighting conditions. The right film for you is one that does the job best for your needs.

Film speed is stated as ISO numbers, such as 125/22°. The first number is the ASA speed, which you set on the camera film-speed dial, above left. This tells the meter how sensitive the film is. The second number is the DIN film-speed specification, used in Europe. Forgetting to set the film-speed dial or doing it wrong leads to bad exposures.

USING MEDIUM-SPEED FILMS

This category includes ASA 100 to 200. Kodak Plus-X, Ilford FP4 and Agfapan 100 are b&w medium-speed films. Kodak, Fuji and others make many popular color negative and slide films. These include Ektachrome, Kodacolor, Fujichrome and Fujicolor films.

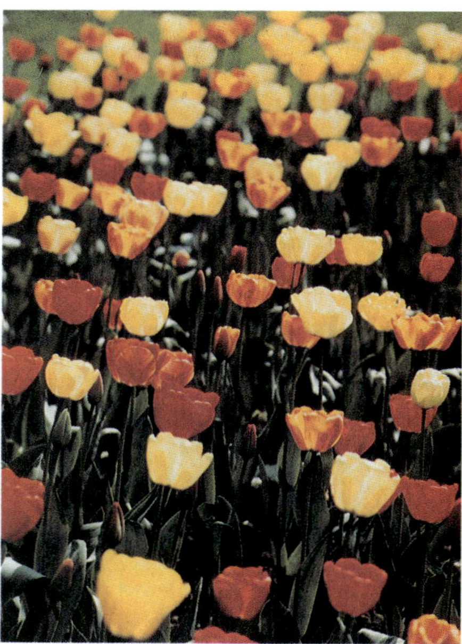

When carefully exposed and processed, medium-speed films give image quality almost as good as that of slow film. Because it is faster, you can use it in scenes with less light than normal and still handhold the camera.

USING FAST FILMS

This category includes films with ASA speeds greater than 200. Color slide, negative, and b&w films are available, made by Kodak, Fuji, Ilford, Agfa and others. The main advantage of a fast film is that you can shoot in dim light and still handhold the camera for sharp pictures.

Fast films use larger light-sensitive grains than slow and medium-speed films. Grain size limits the size of the enlargements you should make from 35mm negatives made on fast film. Generally, apparent graininess obscures image detail in an 11x14 inch print. With 3x5 or 5x7 inch prints, this shouldn't be a problem.

If recording fine detail is important, use a fast film only when you can't use a tripod in dim light. Fast films let you get depth of field with small apertures, action-freezing

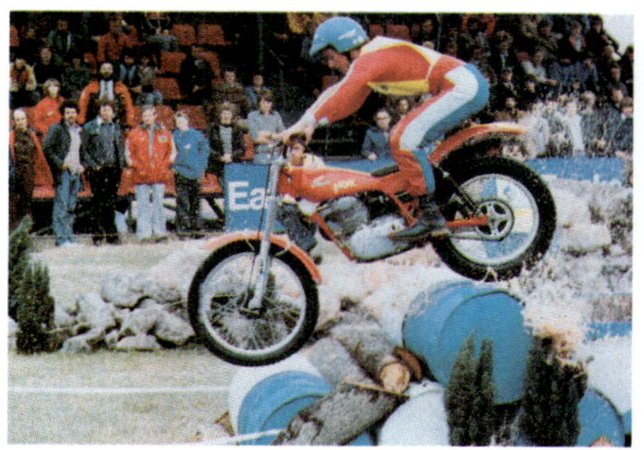

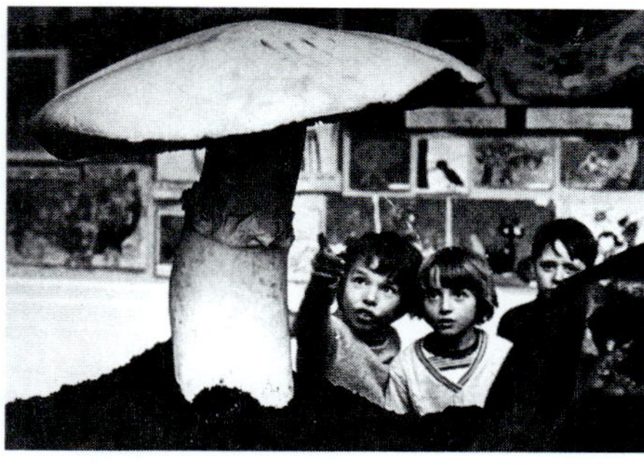

shutter speeds, or both when used in bright light. A pleasing picture does not have to be enlarged greatly to be effective. The two photos above prove this.

When taking pictures in bright daylight, your choice of exposure settings is limited due to film speed. According to the Sunny Day *f*-16 Rule, ASA 400 film requires *f*-16 at 1/500 second or *f*-11 at 1/1000 second. This limits your control of depth of field or prevents using a slow shutter speed for creative blur.

Loading & Unloading Film

Some photographers new to 35mm SLRs find film loading and unloading difficult when compared to the ease of an instant-loading camera. It is more time-consuming, but with practice and care, not difficult at all. Learning to do it right is crucial to getting good pictures. If the film doesn't advance because you loaded it wrong, you'll make 20, 24, or 36 exposures on one frame of film! You may even miss a once-in-a-lifetime picture. Don't let this happen to you. Take time to read and understand these tips.

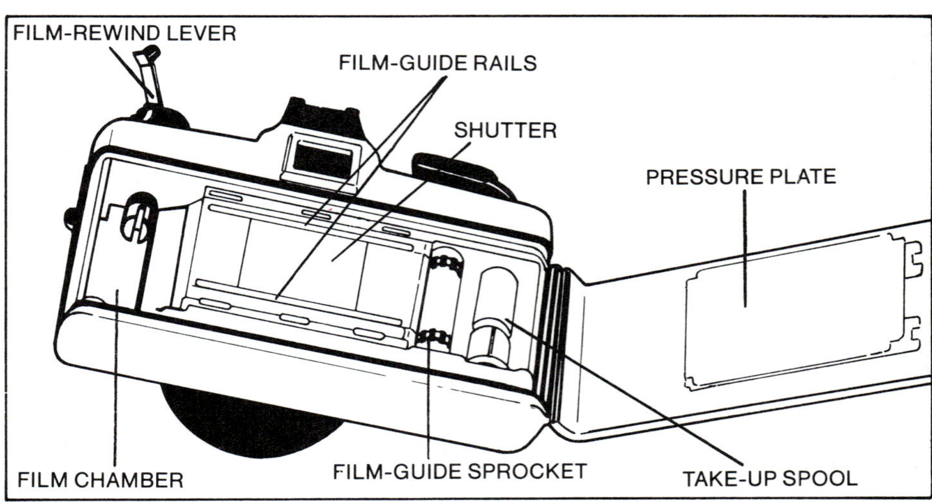

LOADING THE CAMERA

Load an empty camera in subdued, not direct, light. This minimizes the chance of light leaking into the cassette and exposing film. This kind of exposure is also called *fogging*. Lay the camera lens-side-down on a table or between your legs while you sit. Have the lens cap on to help protect the front lens element.

Open the camera back by pulling up the film-rewind knob on the top left side of the camera. The back will spring open, revealing the film chamber, shutter and take-up spool. Don't touch the shutter. It is fragile and costly to repair.

Put the cassette into the left chamber so the film leader points to the right. Push the rewind knob back down, and turn it if necessary so it returns fully. This engages the film cassette.

Pull the film leader across the shutter, film-guide rails and film-guide sprocket. Line up the film so it will fit on the film-guide sprockets. Tuck up to 1/2 inch of the film leader into a slot in the film take-up spool.

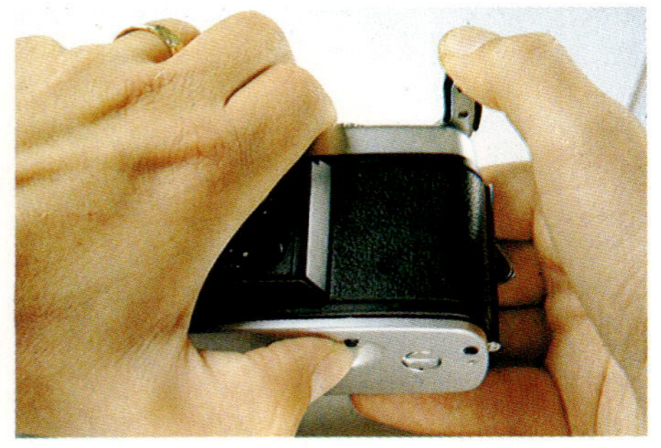

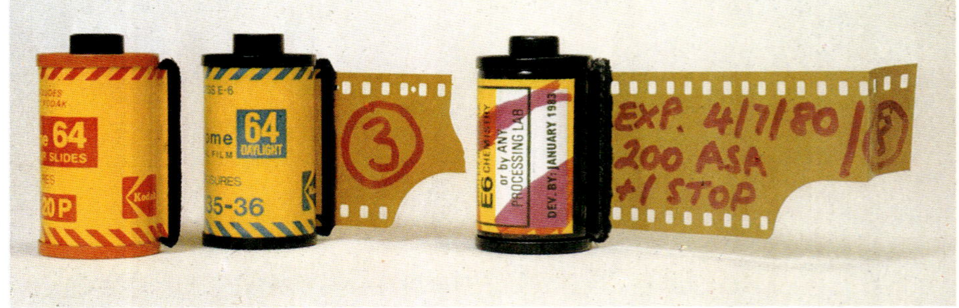

The counter advances every time you move the lever through its full travel, whether film is actually advancing or not. This is why it is good practice to check that the film-rewind knob rotates when you operate the film-advance lever.

Sometimes, even though the counter indicates that there are more frames to shoot, you won't be able to move the film-advance lever through a full stroke. Here are some possible reasons:

1) You loaded a shorter roll than you thought; 2) You advanced too much film before closing the camera back; 3) The film is jammed inside the camera; 4) The frame counter is broken.

To determine if all of the film is exposed, turn the film-rewind lever in both directions, see left photo. If it will move more than a half turn, film is still in the cassette. Rewind the film and have the camera checked.

REWINDING FILM

After the film is exposed, it is on the take-up spool. If you opened the camera at this stage, light would ruin the images. Wind the exposed film back into the cassette before opening the camera.

When the film-advance lever won't move any more, depress the film-rewind button. This button is on the bottom of most cameras, see left photo. Then rewind the film by turning the film-rewind crank clockwise, in the direction of the engraved arrow on or near the crank.

REWIND SLOWLY

Rewind the film slowly to avoid scratching the film or creating static electricity. As you wind the film back in the cassette, you feel a slight drag. This stops as soon as the film leader disengages from the take-up spool.

If you open the back of the camera at this time, you'll see the cassette with leader sticking out. Some people do it this way because the film acts as a seal for the felt light trap.

However, the exposed roll now resembles an unexposed roll! You might accidentally load it again later, double expose, and waste two sets of potentially good pictures. Avoid this by marking an exposed roll, as shown above. The center

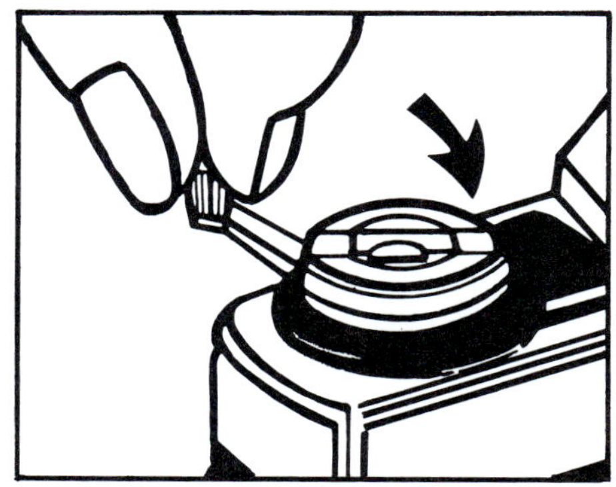

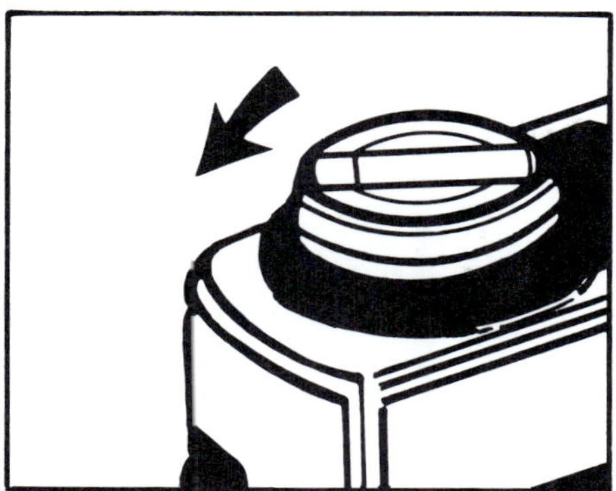

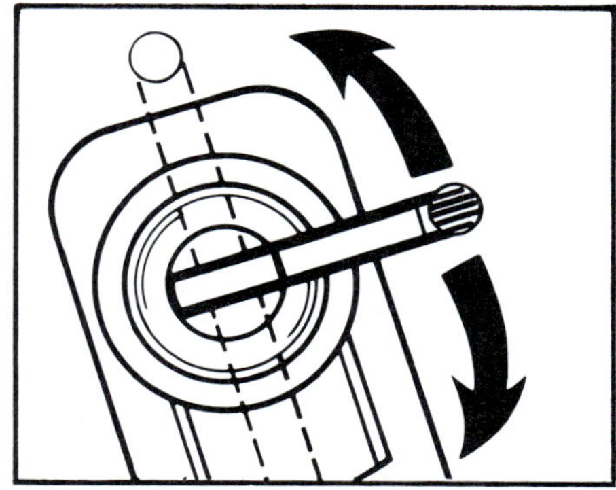

TAKE UP FILM SLACK

Advance film until holes on both sides of the film fit over teeth on the sprocket. Before closing the camera back, look at the cassette one last time to check the film speed printed on it. Check the film-speed dial to make sure it agrees with the speed printed on the film cassette.

Close the camera back. Take up the film slack by turning the film-rewind clockwise, in the direction of the arrow engraved on or near the unfolded lever. You'll feel more resistance as the film tightens. Stop when you feel resistance. You don't want to pull the film off the take-up pool or damage the wind mechanism.

ADVANCE FILM TO FRAME ONE

The next step is to advance the film to put an unexposed frame in front of the shutter. The film you pulled out of the cassette for loading—a length equal to about two frames—is now fogged and useless.

Advance film by pushing the shutter button and turning the film-advance lever. Do this twice. Because there is no more film slack in the cassette, the film-rewind knob will turn when film is advanced. This is an important check to be *sure* that film is actually advancing.

If the knob doesn't turn when you rotate the film-advance lever, the take-up spool isn't pulling film out of the cassette. Open the camera back again and start over.

FRAME COUNTER CHECK

As you advance film, watch the frame counter near the advance lever. When the camera back is open, the counter is automatically set to S. After you close the back and advance film twice to put an unexposed frame in place, the counter shows 0.

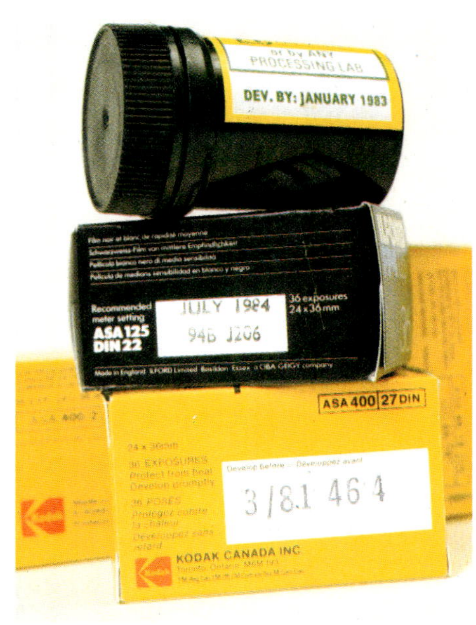

roll has most of the tongue torn off. The one at right is labeled with useful exposure information.

If you unload the camera in subdued light, you can rewind the film all the way into the cassette as shown at left. Wind until you feel no resistance. Open the camera back, remove the cassette and mark it with an indelible-ink pen if necessary. Keep it in subdued light until it is processed.

FILM EXPIRATION DATE

The carton holding the film indicates the film expiration date. This is the "deadline" for exposing and processing the film for best results. Because color film is more complex than b&w film, its expiration date is earlier than a b&w film made at the same time. With either type of film, proper storage can extend the useful life of unexposed film.

LONG-TERM STORAGE

If you store film at normal room temperature and humidity, use it by the expiration date. Film can deteriorate before this time if it gets too hot, or too damp due to high humidity. Film speed decreases and colors will change in color film.

The colder the film, the longer you can store it. If you use cold storage, keep the film boxed and in its plastic canister. Refrigerated storage slows film aging appreciably because most refrigerators are about 40F (4C). Freezing the film is even better. You can store frozen film indefinitely, and it will be OK years after the expiration date. Of course, this assumes that the film was never stored improperly before freezing.

When you are ready to use film that was stored in a refrigerator or freezer, let it warm up before using it. Refrigerated film needs at least two hours to warm. Let frozen film thaw overnight or for at least six hours. Avoid condensation on the film by keeping it sealed in its plastic canister until the warm-up time has elapsed.

AFTER EXPOSURE

To preserve the results of your good exposures, have exposed film processed as soon as possible. If you can't deliver the roll to the lab right away, store it in a refrigerator. Keep the exposed roll in its plastic canister to avoid light leakage and humidity changes.

Before giving the film to your lab, label the cassette with your name and address.

Building an SLR System

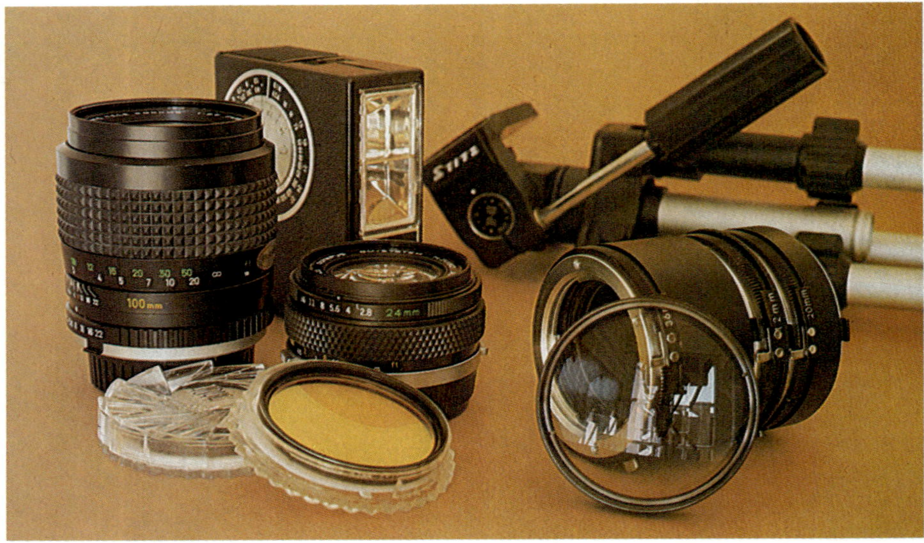

Most people buy a 35mm SLR with a standard 50mm lens. With this basic equipment you can make many satisfying pictures. Eventually you will miss some good pictures because of conditions that can't be handled with just a camera and 50mm lens.

If your camera is part of a *system,* you can add interchangeable accessories. These include lenses, viewfinders, focusing screens, autowinders and motor drives, special camera backs, filters, close-up equipment, electronic flash, tripods and more. Such accessories are made by both camera and independent manufacturers. With a system camera, you can be photographically versatile.

WHERE TO START

Use your basic camera and lens to become familiar with photographic technique. Don't buy an accessory first and then look for a way to use it. Consider purchasing a camera accessory *after* you've encountered a certain problem once or twice. This way, the accessories you acquire will be suited to your style of shooting.

The equipment shown here includes the most useful and popular accessories. With a choice of more than one lens you can bring distant subjects up close, or record wide-angle views and portray scenes in different ways. Filters let you control the way colors reproduce in b&w pictures. Or, use filters to control colors in color photography.

With a flash, you can take pictures in dim light or "freeze" a moving subject on film. A tripod holds the camera steady so you can use slow shutter speeds and get sharp results.

Close-up equipment, such as accessory close-up lenses or extension tubes, gives your 50mm lens the ability to focus closer than normal, for shooting small objects.

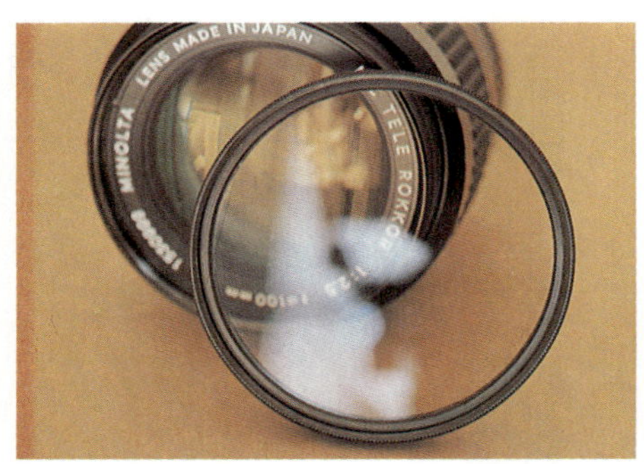

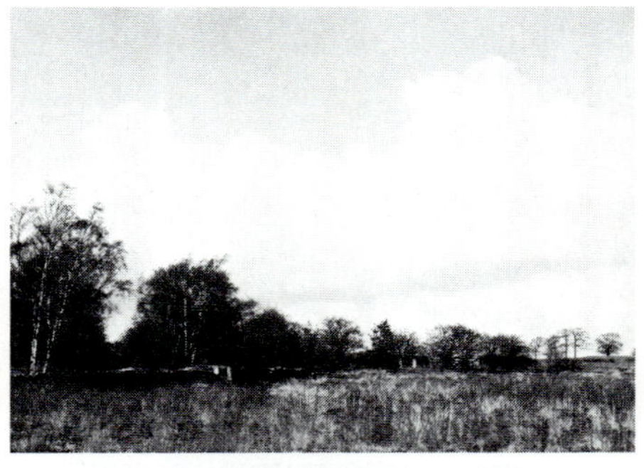

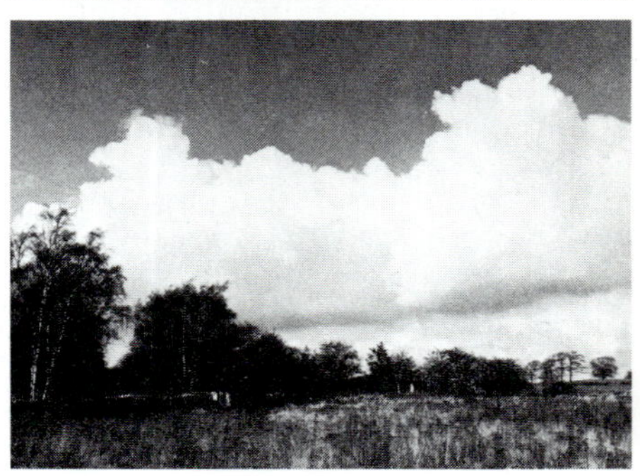

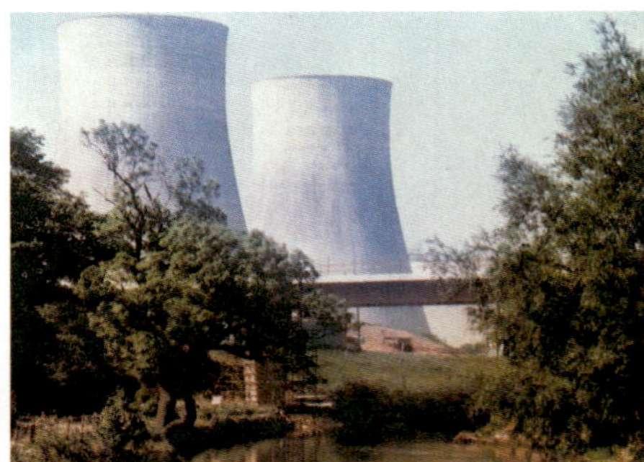

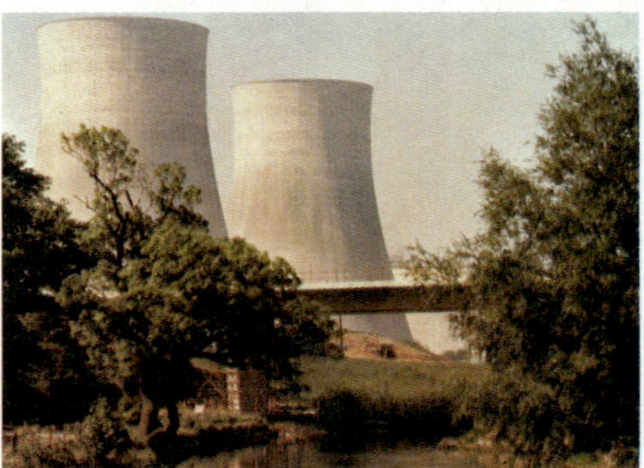

FILTERS

A filter is an accessory that fits over the lens and absorbs colors selectively so you can control the effect of light on film. Unlike a lens accessory that does optical tricks you see in the image, the effect of a filter is not always noticeable in the image. Two common examples are shown here. Filter techniques are also discussed on pages 58 and 59.

In b&w photography, you use filters to control the way colors reproduce as gray tones on film. A color filter makes its own color reproduce lighter but darkens all other colors. In the b&w examples shown here, no filter was used for the top photo. Both blue sky and clouds reproduce as the same tone. A yellow filter absorbs some blue light and makes the sky reproduce darker, as shown by the bottom photo.

To absorb the excess blue light in shadows or at high altitudes, use a skylight filter with color film. The top color photo was made without a filter. For the bottom photo, a pale pink skylight filter absorbed excess blue light to give a "warmer," more pleasing rendition on film.

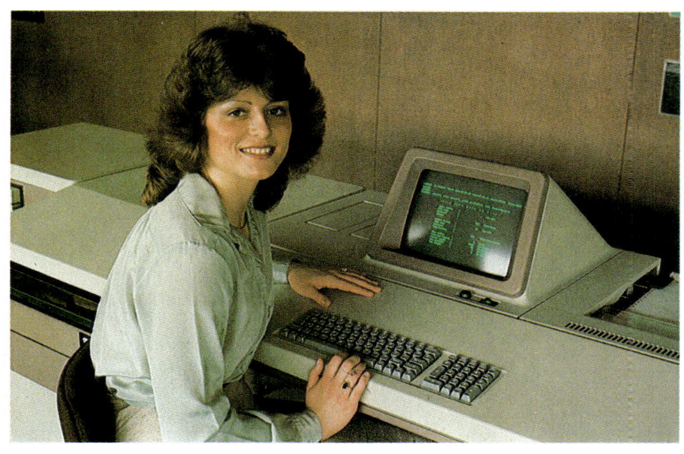

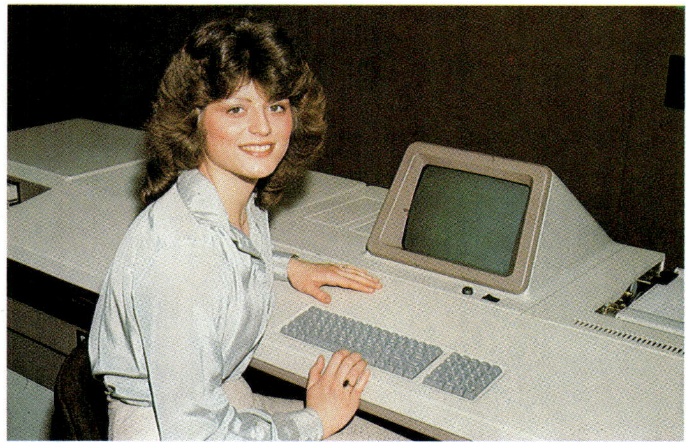

ACCESSORIES FOR LOW LIGHT

With a 50mm lens on your camera, it can be difficult to get sharp images while handholding the camera with shutter speeds slower than 1/60 second. If you use a faster shutter speed, the necessary aperture may be too large to give sufficient depth of field. Two accessories can help.

Use a tripod to hold the camera steady when you use shutter speeds slower than about 1/60 second with a 50mm lens. This eliminates camera shake. This is how the photo at left was made—1/15 second at *f*-8.

A tripod is usually unnecessary when you use a flash, as in the photo at right. With skill and experience, you can use flash to simulate natural lighting.

Flash duration is short enough to freeze most subject motion. Typically, the fastest camera shutter speed you can use with electronic flash is from 1/60 to 1/125 second. See pages 50 to 57.

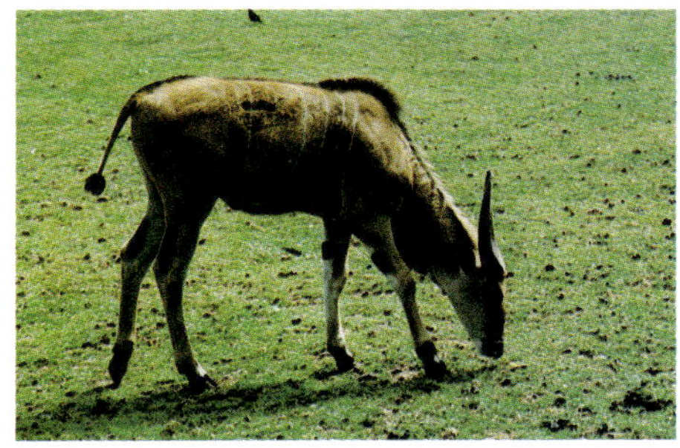

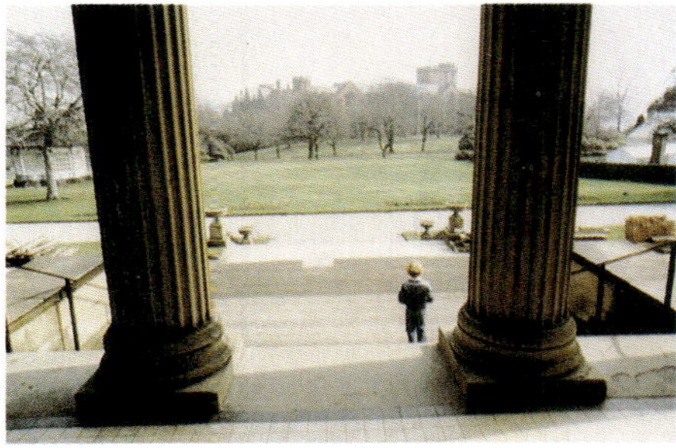

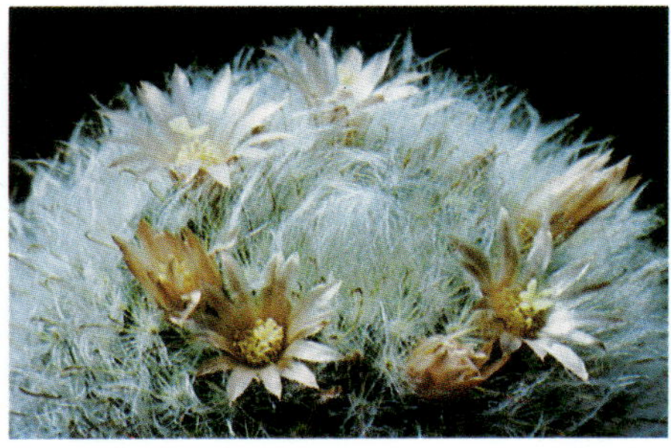

LONG-FOCAL-LENGTH LENS

For simplicity, a telephoto lens is defined here as a lens with a focal length longer than 50mm. The effect of such a lens is to make a faraway subject appear closer. It "sees" less of the scene than a 50mm lens.

Using a long-focal-length lens is convenient when you can't get close to a subject but you want to exclude background and foreground elements around it. This often applies to portraiture, sports and nature photography. You'll find more about long-focal-length lenses on pages 32 to 35.

WIDE-ANGLE LENS

This type of lens has a focal length shorter than 50mm. The effect is to show more of the scene than a 50mm lens. It has a wider *angle of view.* For example, a 24mm lens 10 feet (3m) from the main subject will see essentially the same view as a 50mm lens 18 feet (5.5m) away.

A wide-angle lens gives more depth of field than a 50mm lens at the same aperture and subject distance. Wide-angle lenses are, therefore, useful for scenes that benefit from having both foreground and background elements in sharp focus. See also pages 36 and 37.

CLOSE-UP ACCESSORIES

With a standard 50mm lens you can focus as close as about 18 inches (46cm). This will fill the frame horizontally with a subject about 13 inches (33cm) long. To fill the frame with smaller subjects, such as flowers or insects, use close-up accessories.

A *close-up lens* fits over the front of the lens. It acts as a magnifying glass, allowing you to focus closer to the subject to make a larger image. No exposure increase is required. A variety of close-up lenses is available. See pages 40 and 41.

Extension tubes fit between the camera lens and camera body to increase lens-to-film distance. More *extension* gives more magnification, but requires more exposure. If you use an *automatic* extension tube, the camera's TTL meter will recommend good exposure. See pages 42 and 43.

Telephoto Lenses

When using your SLR and its standard 50mm lens, you'll probably encounter some scenes that are frustrating to photograph. You'll want to get closer but can't, or you want to get a larger image of the subject on film than possible with the 50mm lens.

If this happens often, you need a *telephoto lens.* These are lenses with a focal length longer than 50mm. When you put one on your camera, it makes a larger image of the subject or lets you make an image of the same size from farther away. For example, a 100mm lens doubles the width and height of the image made by a 50mm lens.

The 100mm lens gives a larger the image, but sees a proportionately smaller *angle of view* than the 50mm lens. This is the angle between the two rays that determine the film frame. A 50mm lens sees an angle of about 46°. A 100mm lens sees about 24°. Longer focal lengths have even narrower angles of view.

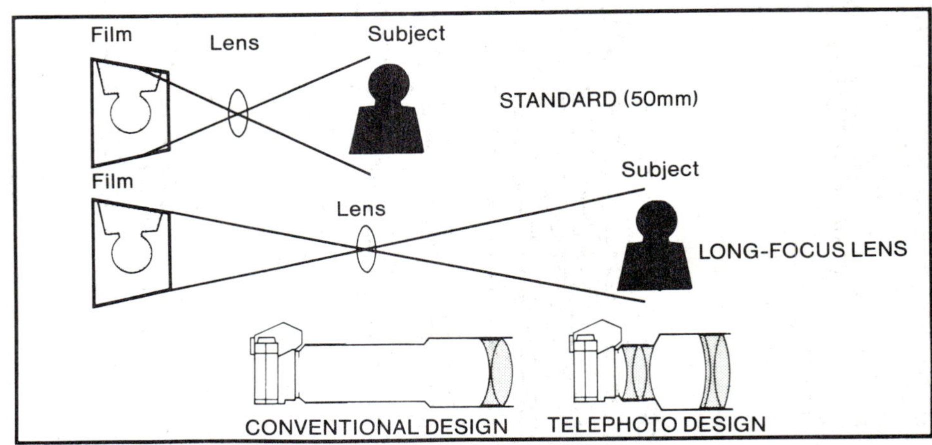

LENS DESIGN

The top sketch represents a 50mm lens imaging a subject. A lens that gives the same-size image at a farther subject distance has a longer focal length—measured from an optical point in the lens to the film. The same lens would give a bigger image at the subject distance shown for the 50mm lens.

A conventional long-focus lens is about as long as its focal length suggests. A *special* lens design—called *telephoto*—produces compact lenses with long focal length. The focal length is longer than the physical length of the lens. Lens designers achieve this by special means. Today the word *telephoto* is used to describe *any* lens with a focal length longer than 50mm. This book follows the same convention.

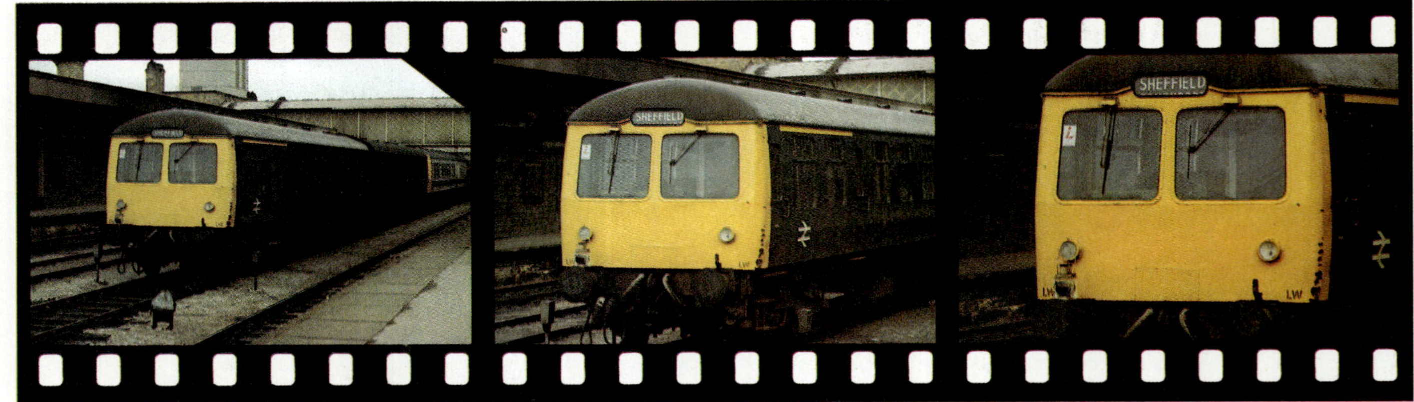

85mm LENS

This short a telephoto lens is sometimes called a *portrait lens* because it allows you to fill the frame with the subject's head and shoulders without getting too close and causing distortion of facial features.

Most 85mm lenses are compact and light. Some are very fast with a large maximum aperture such as *f*-2. These characteristics make them also useful as general-purpose lenses for scenes like that shown above.

135mm LENS

This photo was taken from the same position as the one at left. Notice that it "pulls in" the subject more than the 85mm lens.

Typically, this moderate telephoto is only slightly larger than the 85mm lens. Maximum aperture for most 135mm lenses is about *f*-3.5. It, too, is a useful portrait lens.

200mm LENS

The 200mm lens is in the range of lenses called *long telephotos.* It is the biggest of the three lenses discussed here, but modern designs are still amazingly light and compact. Maximum apertures are about *f*-4.

A 200mm lens is ideal for outdoor action scenes. Some will focus as close as five or six feet. If you can get near the action, you're almost guaranteed some exciting "close-ups."

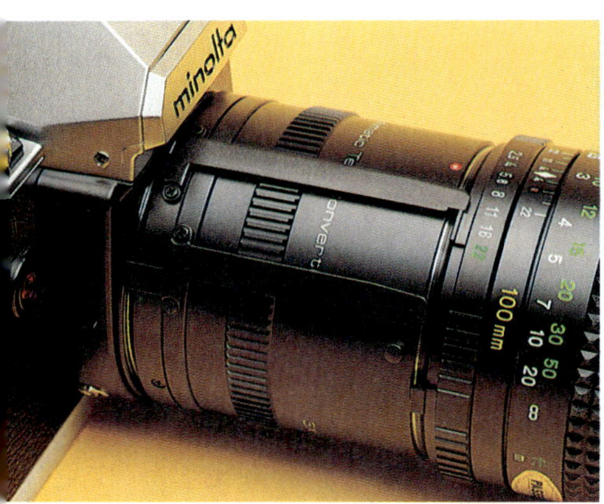

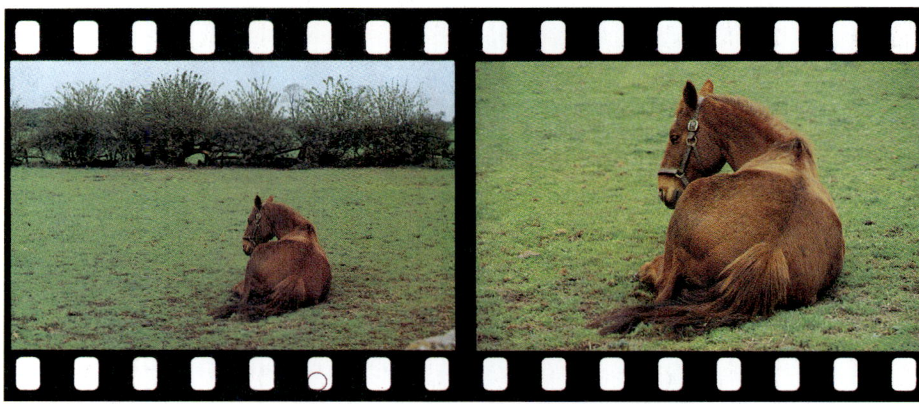

TELECONVERTERS

An easy way to have telephoto capability without buying another camera lens is to use a *teleconverter.* This optical accessory fits between lens and camera body—shown above—to effectively lengthen focal length. Teleconverters are labelled to indicate their magnifying ability.

A 2X teleconverter doubles the focal length of the lens used with it. If you use your 50mm lens with a 2X teleconverter, the assembly acts like a 100mm lens. See the two photos above right. A 3X teleconverter makes the assembly act like a 150mm lens. You can use a teleconverter with any lens, so if you later buy a 200mm lens, a 2X teleconverter can make it into a 400mm lens.

Exposure—The converter requires an exposure correction. A 2X converter necessitates a two-step compensation and a 3X teleconverter requires approximately three steps. With an *automatic* teleconverter, the camera meter automatically makes the needed correction.

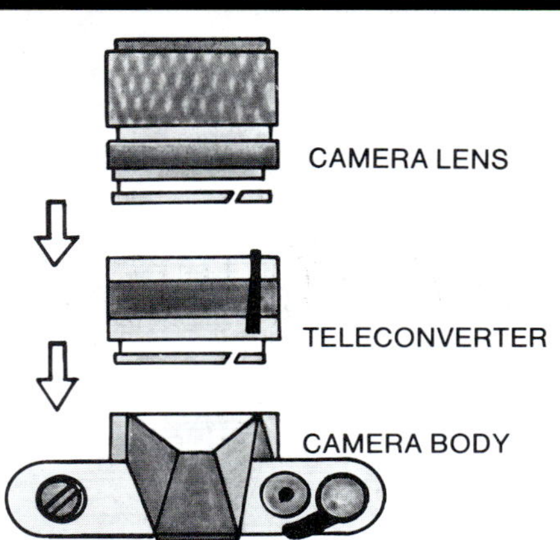

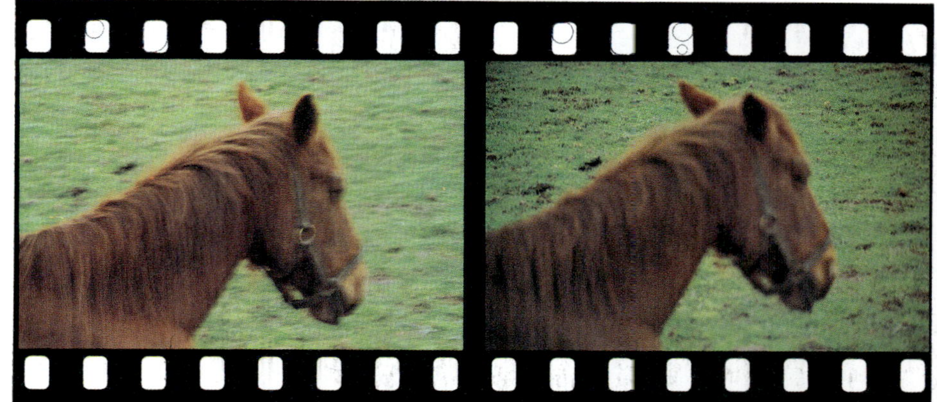

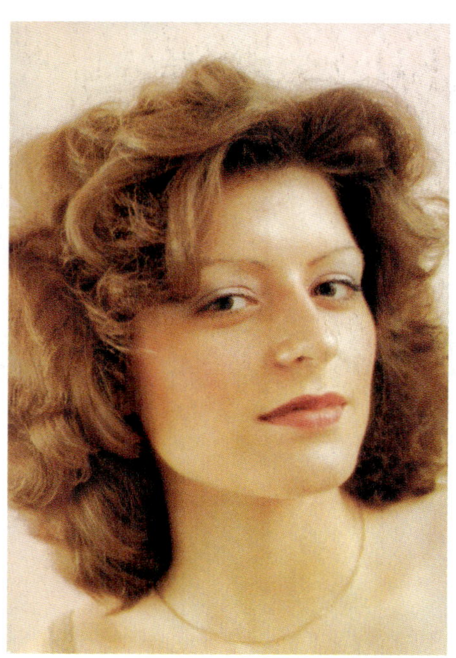

USING A TELEPHOTO

Weight and length of a telephoto lens make it more difficult to handhold the camera than when using a 50mm lens. As mentioned earlier, the slowest shutter speed you should handhold is approximately the reciprocal of lens focal length. Therefore, don't handhold the camera at shutter speeds slower than 1/250 second when using a 200mm lens. Otherwise, camera shake can contribute to image blur, above left.

In addition, the focusing screen image is usually not as bright as with a standard 50mm lens. This is because maximum apertures are usually smaller in telephotos. For any aperture, a telephoto lens also gives a shallower depth of field than a 50mm lens. Sometimes, this makes focusing more difficult, as shown above.

The portrait at right was made with a 100mm lens. Moderate telephotos are ideal for head-and-shoulder portraiture. Notice that the image fills the frame and facial features aren't distorted. The photographer was about four feet from the subject—not too far for easy communication, nor too close to intimidate.

Long Telephoto Lenses

Telephoto lenses with focal lengths longer than about 250mm can offer exciting views of distant scenes. Two kinds are available. Some use lenses only and are called *conventional* telephoto lenses. Others use lenses and mirrors. These are called *mirror,* or *catadioptric* lenses. One is shown at right.

CONVENTIONAL LENSES

The most popular of these are usually no longer than 18 inches (450mm). They have various features, some of which follow.

Internal focusing lenses are compact and don't change length as you focus. Elements inside the lens move with cam action, making focusing slower but more accurate.

Aspheric lenses use specially designed elements that help improve image quality. These lenses are expensive. *Fluorite* lenses use one or more elements made of crystal, not glass. The result is a light, compact, fast lens with a long focal length.

MIRROR LENSES

Mirror lenses are available in focal lengths from 250mm to 2000mm. These long-focal-length lenses have specially shaped optical-quality mirrors that reflect light rays back and forth in the lens. This "folds" the optical path, making the lens compact. Glass lens elements are also used.

This design results in a physically short and wide lens. A mirror lens is typically lighter than a conventional lens of the same focal length. For example, typical 500mm mirror lenses are about six inches long and weigh about 20 ounces. These features make it is easier to handhold than a conventional 500mm lens.

Design considerations limit the lens to a fixed aperture—*f*-8 with a typical 500mm mirror lens. You control exposure by changing shutter speed or using a *neutral-density* filter to absorb light. A ring that holds the filters is inside the lens. You install or dial in the light-absorbing filter you need for good exposure. Because a mirror lens is non-automatic, you can't use it on a shutter-priority camera operating automatically.

Image Effects—The viewfinder image created by a mirror lens is relatively dim and of low contrast. This can make focusing difficult. For accurate results, focus on

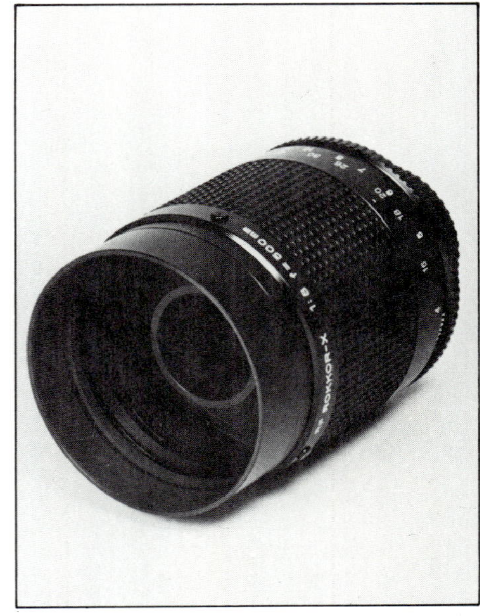

sharp, contrasty areas. Use the all-matte part of the focusing screen.

Out-of-focus points of small highlights reproduce as blurred bright circles—see below. Good subjects for this effect are highlights on water or light coming through trees.

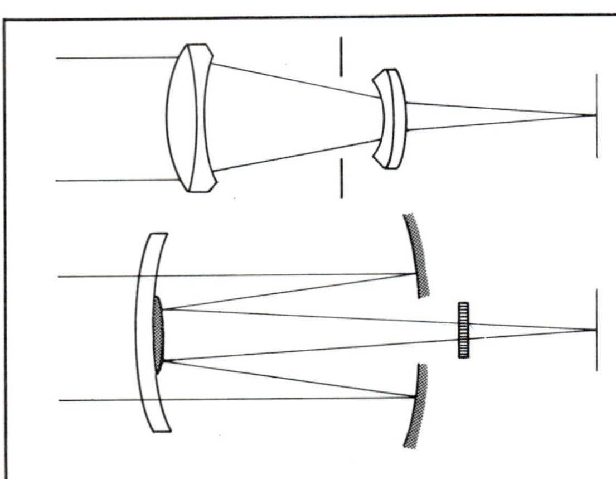

The telephoto lens has a special construction which allows it to be made much shorter than its actual focal length. This requires extra lens elements at the rear of the lens.

The mirror lens uses mirrors and lenses. The light path through the lens is shown here. The lens tends to be thick but much shorter than a telephoto.

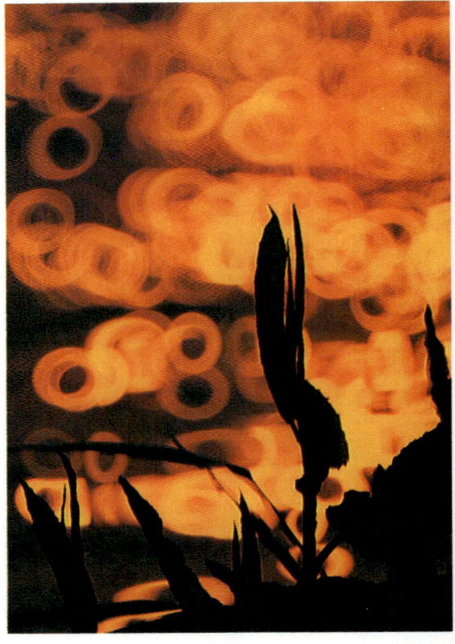

COMMON CHARACTERISTICS

Long-focal-length lenses produce similar results, whether they are of conventional or mirror design. They have narrow angles of view. The image may not look sharp because of dust and atmospheric or heat haze between you and the distant scene. You can minimize some of the effect by photographing contrasty subjects.

The long-focal-length lens does not give extensive depth of field. An unimportant car behind the subject may become a big unfocused yellow blur in the image.

Photographs have extreme spatial compression—background objects tend to look larger than you'd expect. For example, look at the sunset photo on the next page. Due to spatial compression, the sun seems too big relative to the size of the lighthouse. This is not necessarily a fault. You can make the effect work, as it does here.

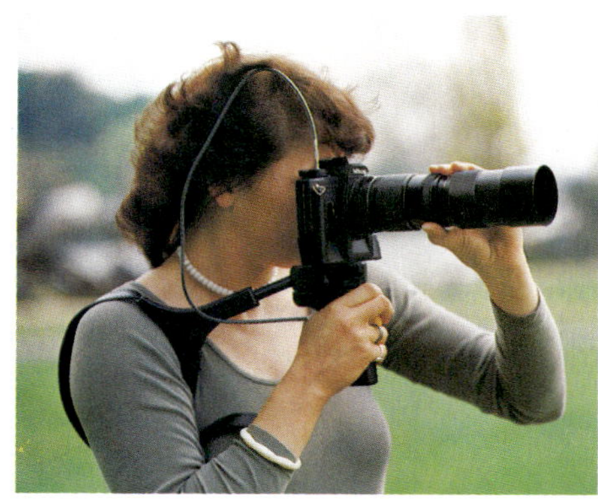

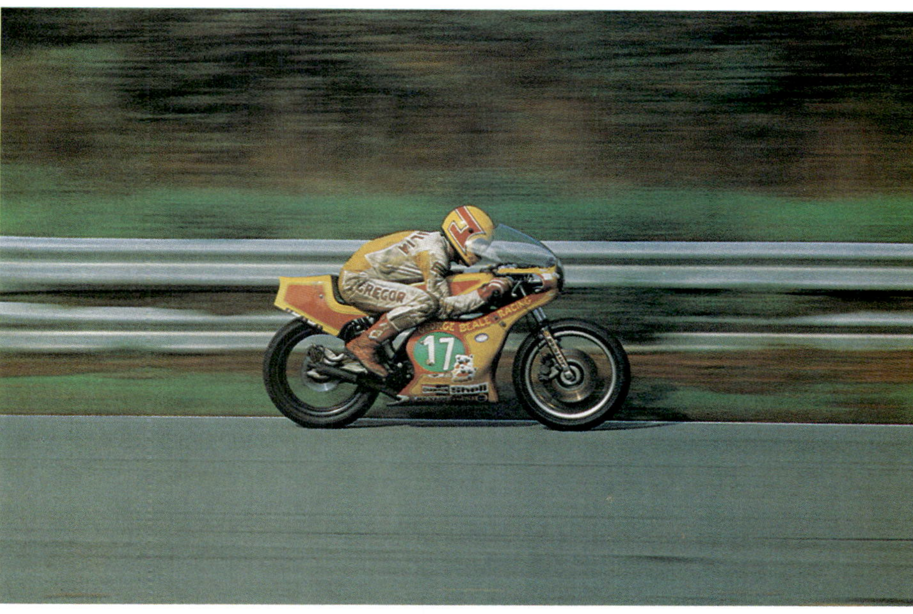

HOLDING A LONG LENS

With a long lens, rigid support is essential to prevent camera shake. It is impractical to handhold conventional lenses with focal lengths longer than 300mm with shutter speeds slower than 1/250 second. For best image quality, always use a tripod.

Some long lenses have a rotating tripod socket that helps balance the weight of the camera and lens. You can also use a pistol grip and shoulder stock, shown above, to help steady the assembly. Your shoulder and gripping hand steady the camera at two points. Your focusing hand supplies another point of support. Pushing the trigger on the pistol grip actuates the camera shutter button.

For some applications, like sports photography, you can use slower-than-recommended handheld shutter speeds when panning. This is how the photo of the motorcyclist was made. See page 16 for tips on panning.

MORE ABOUT LONG-FOCAL-LENGTH LENSES

Slowest Shutter Speed for Handholding

Lens	Speed
300mm	1/250
400mm	1/500
500mm	1/500
600mm	1/500
1000mm	1/1000
2000mm	1/2000

Angles of View for Long Lenses

Lens	Angle of View
300mm	8°
400mm	6°
500mm	5°
600mm	4°
1000mm	2.5°
2000mm	1.3°

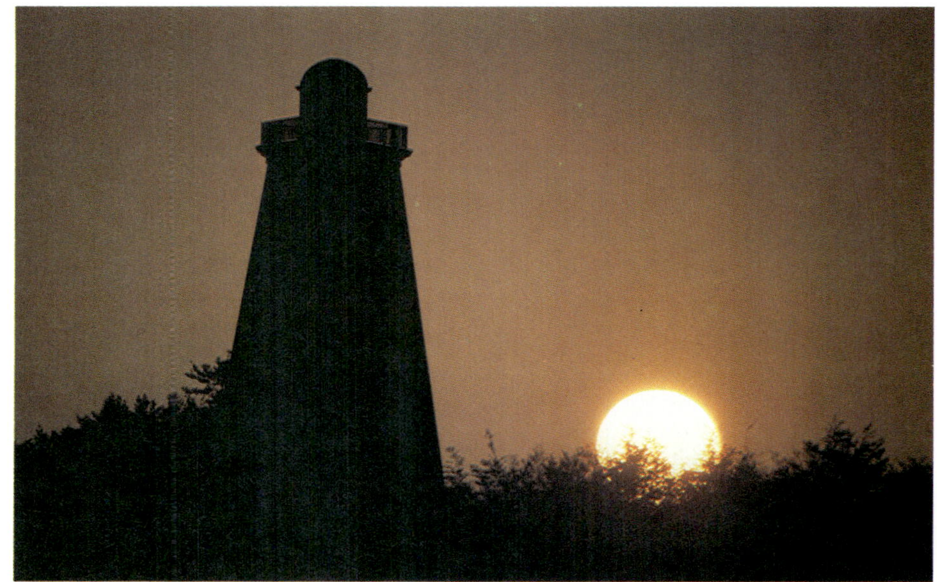

Wide-Angle Lenses

You'll eventually encounter a scene that is too close to photograph well with a 50mm lens. You'll want to back up but can't. Perhaps you are in a room and want to photograph three walls and part of the ceiling on one frame. If standing in one corner, as far away as possible, won't do it, then you need a *wide-angle* lens.

A wide-angle lens is one with a focal length shorter than 50mm. The effect of a wide-angle lens is to show a wider view of the subject than a 50mm lens shows. The illustrations below show how angle of view increases as focal length decreases.

Because a wide-angle lens includes more in the picture than a 50mm lens at the same location, each part of the scene is smaller than in the 50mm image. This characteristic gives wide-angle lenses another useful feature—they offer more extensive depth of field than the 50mm lens when used at the same aperture and location.

For example, if you use a 24mm lens at *f*-16 and set the lens to the hyperfocal distance (4.6 feet, 1.5m), everything from 2.3 feet (70cm) to infinity is in sharp focus. Using an aperture of *f*-22 extends the near-limit distance even closer!

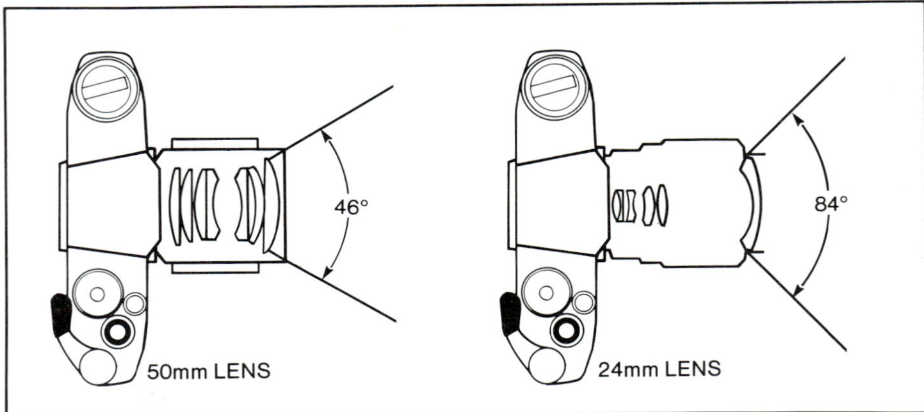

ANGLE OF VIEW FOR WIDE-ANGLE LENSES	
Lens	**Angle of View**
50mm	46°
35mm	63°
28mm	75°
24mm	84°
20mm	94°
17mm	104°

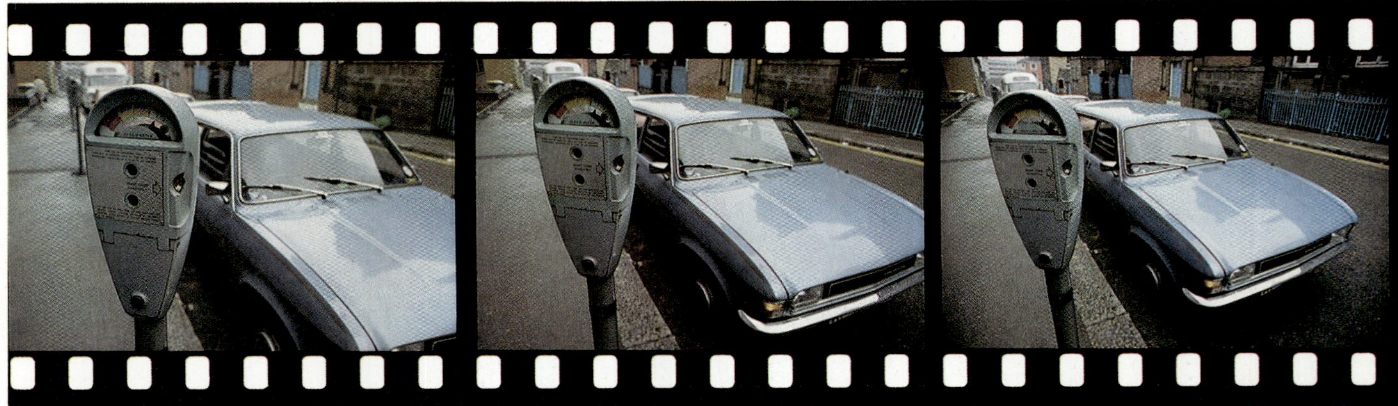

35mm LENS

This lens shows slightly more of the scene than a 50mm lens, but doesn't make the picture look obviously "wide-angle." Many photographers use a 35mm lens on their camera most of the time. It's ideal if you often photograph nearby subjects, such as groups of people indoors.

Most electronic flash covers the area seen by a 35mm lens, so that the picture will not have dark corners due to poor light coverage.

28mm LENS

The three pictures you see here were made from the same camera position. The 28mm lens shows the wide-angle effect by including much more area than the 35mm lens. Notice how the 28mm view makes each element proportionately smaller.

The 28mm lens is ideal for some architectural, landscape and interior photography. It shows a lot of the scene without your having to be far away.

24mm LENS

Use this lens for a more dramatic wide-angle effect. The increased angle of view causes increased image distortion. Straight lines near the edges of the scene appear curved. This is unflattering to many subjects, especially people, but can be used creatively with others, such as landscapes.

You may need a special attachment for your flash head with a 24mm or 28mm lens to spread out the beam to cover evenly the angle of view seen by the lens. This avoids dark corners.

WIDE-ANGLE CONVERTERS

You can turn a standard 50mm camera lens into a wide-angle lens by using a *wide-angle converter.* This accessory screws into the front filter threads of the lens, as shown in the drawing right. This is an inexpensive way to try wide-angle photography. Later, when you want better image quality, you can get a separate wide-angle lens for your camera.

A wide-angle converter does not change the effective aperture of the lens or alter the infinity setting of the focus scale. The converter provides a closer minimum focusing distance. The converter also makes the focusing scale inaccurate, so set focus visually.

Typically a wide-angle converter will turn a 50mm lens into the equivalent of a 30mm lens, or a 35mm lens to 21mm. The photos above show a scene imaged with a 50mm lens and with the same lens with a wide-angle converter.

A wide-angle converter that makes a standard 50mm lens into the equivalent of an 8mm lens is called *fisheye.* The assembly has an angle of view of about 180°! The effect is to curve straight lines in the image. Because of the image distortion, this converter isn't useful for general-purpose shooting. Use it for special effect or technical situations requiring shooting large areas at close distances.

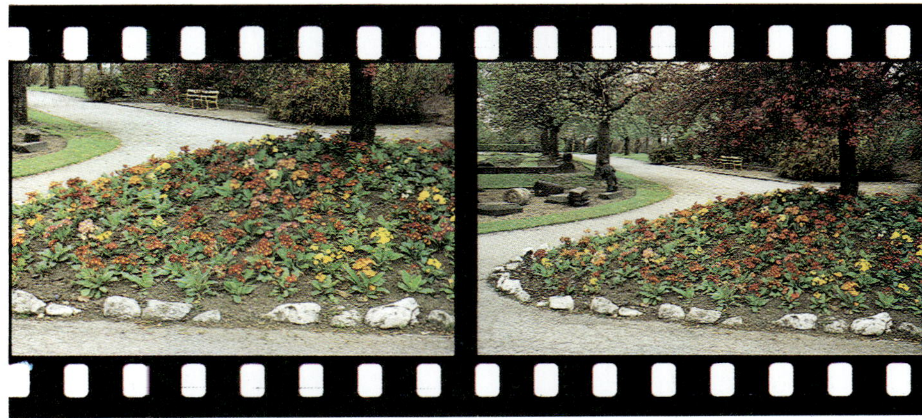

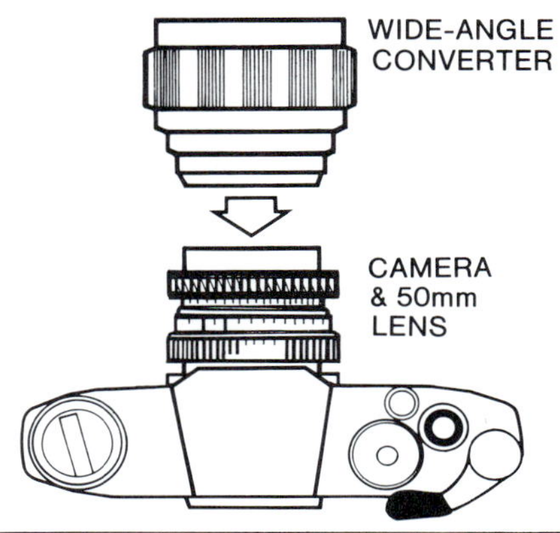

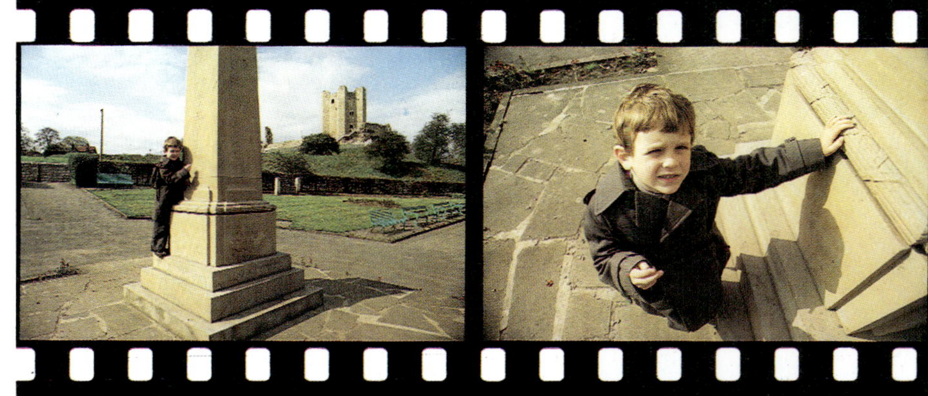

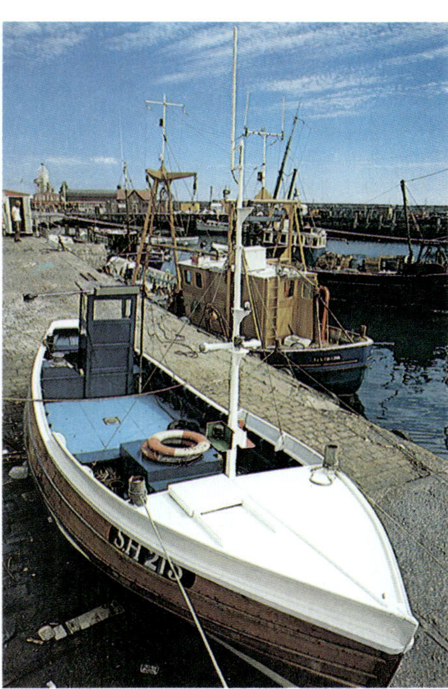

ADVANTAGES & DISADVANTAGES

With a wide-angle lens you can emphasize foreground objects against an expansive background. The extensive depth of field provided by a short focal length is beneficial.

When you first begin using a wide-angle lens, you'll be amazed at how much you can include in the picture, even when photographing close up. However, when you look at your processed pictures you may see that *too many* things are in view, diluting the impact of the main subject. For example, in the photo above left, the boy is too small and the photo lacks impact. If he were closer, the picture would be better.

In the photo at right the viewpoint is dramatic. Photographing a close subject can add interesting image distortion.

You can use these wide-angle characteristics by careful and thoughtful consideration of the scene you see in the viewfinder. Train yourself to see everything that will be recorded on film.

Zoom Lenses

Having a few lenses for your SLR camera lets you photograph a scene in many ways, or practically guarantees that you can find the right lens to make the picture you envision. Changing lenses on modern cameras is quick and easy, but not always practical in fast-moving situations. You may be changing lenses while a picture opportunity goes by. This is why some professionals use more than one camera while working. Instead of switching lenses, they switch cameras—each having a different focal-length lens.

Having and carrying a camera for each lens isn't practical for most photographers. The alternative is one camera with a zoom lens. The lens has a control that lets you change focal length and angle of view.

The zoom control is shown in the above illustration. Turning the zoom ring moves lens elements in the camera to change lens focal length and angle of view. With modern zooms, focus does not change with focal length.

Some zooms have a "one-touch" ring. This design combines the focus control with the zooming control. You turn the ring to focus and push or pull the ring to adjust focal length.

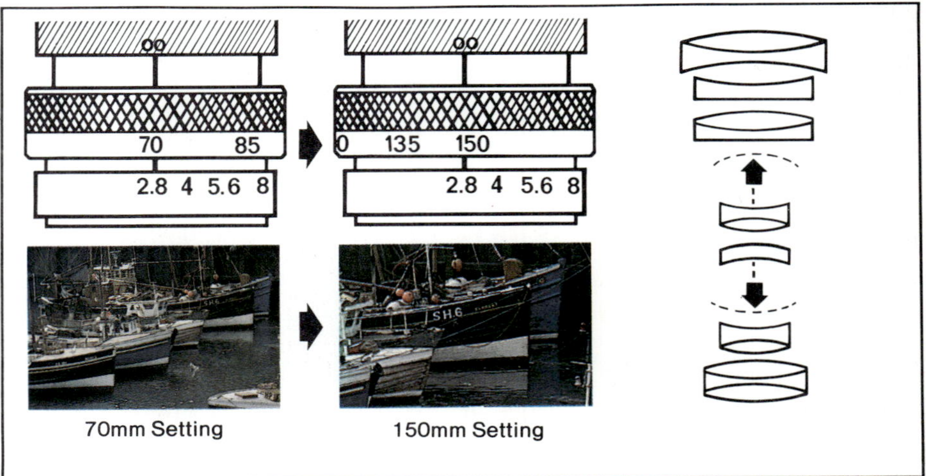

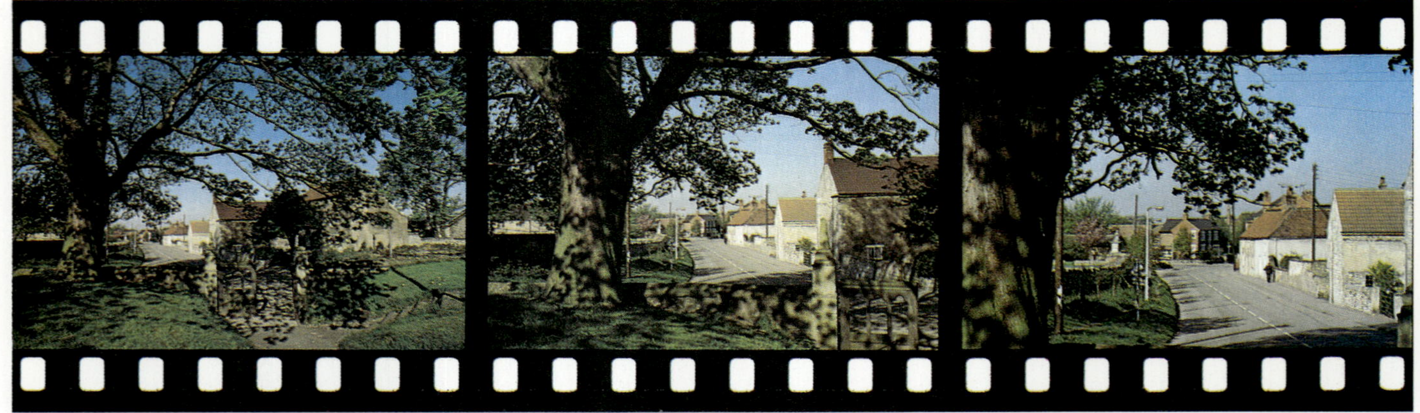

OTHER AVAILABLE ZOOMS

Good-quality zooms used to be impractical or expensive to make. This is no longer true. Many manufacturers are now creating a large variety of reasonably priced wide-angle, mid-range and moderate telephoto zooms. They can give image quality that is indistinguishable from that given by fixed-focal-length lenses.

If you consider the number of lenses that one zoom represents, you can see that even an expensive one is a bargain. Depending on your needs, you may need only two lenses—a wide-angle to standard zoom and a telephoto zoom. Generally, the only disadvantages compared to fixed-focal-length lenses are limited maximum aperture, size and weight.

Wide-Angle Zooms—There are two types. Some have just wide-angle focal lengths, such as 21-35mm or 24-40mm. This kind may have *two* maximum apertures. For example, when used at minimum focal length, one brand has an aperture of *f*-3.5. At maximum focal length, maximum aperture is *f*-4. Intermediate focal lengths have intermediate maximum aperture. The camera meter automatically compensates for this.

The other type of wide-angle zoom has mid-range focal lengths too—from wide-angle to standard or wide-angle to moderate focal lengths, such as 28-50mm, 35-70mm or 28-105mm. The latter was used for the above photos.

Moderate Telephoto Zooms—These are popular because they give telephoto effect but are small and light. Some useful zooms in this category are 43-86mm and 70-150mm. If you use a 2X teleconverter with the zoom, you can extend the focal-length range even more.

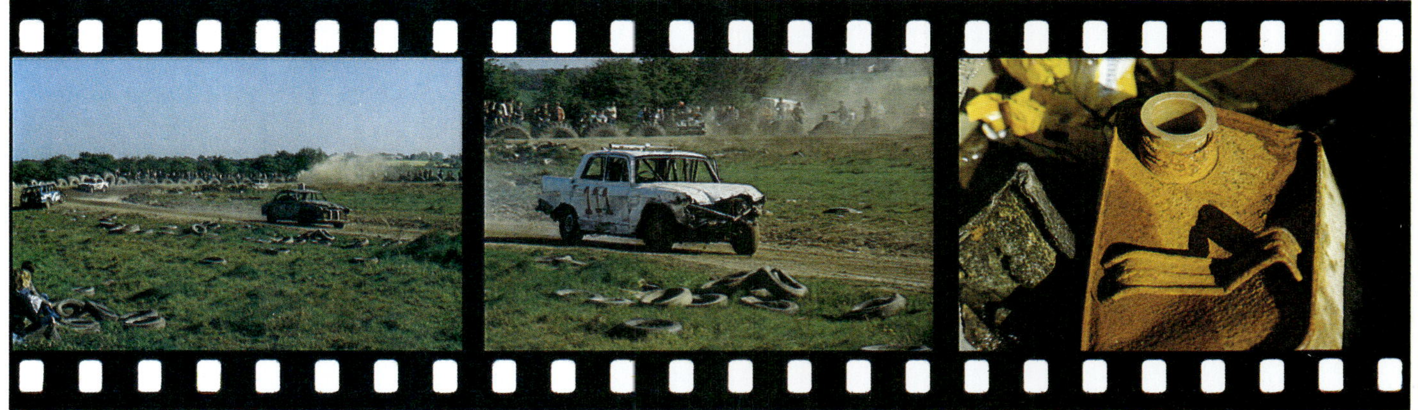

ZOOM RATIO

This indicates the zooming range of the lens. You find it by dividing the smallest focal length into the largest. For example, a 70-210mm zoom has a ratio of 3.

The left and center photos above show a scene photographed with a 70-210mm zoom. When using a lens with a large zoom ratio, you can get many different images without changing camera position. This is convenient with faraway subjects.

For this reason, zooms with the longest focal lengths, such as telephoto zooms (80-200mm, 50-300mm, 200-600mm), usually have the highest zoom ratios. Moderate-focal-length and wide-angle zooms usually have a ratio of 2 or smaller. This is because moving a small distance has a proportionately larger effect with these focal lengths than with telephoto focal lengths.

A greater zoom ratio also means a larger and heavier lens. For example, an 80-200mm zoom is about the same size as—or larger than—a 200mm fixed-focal-length lens. Select the slowest shutter speed you can handhold based on maximum focal length.

CLOSE-FOCUSING ZOOMS

A useful feature of some zooms is close-focus capability. By pushing a button and turning a ring or engaging some other mechanism you can focus closer than normal. Typically, maximum magnification with this kind of lens is about 0.3.

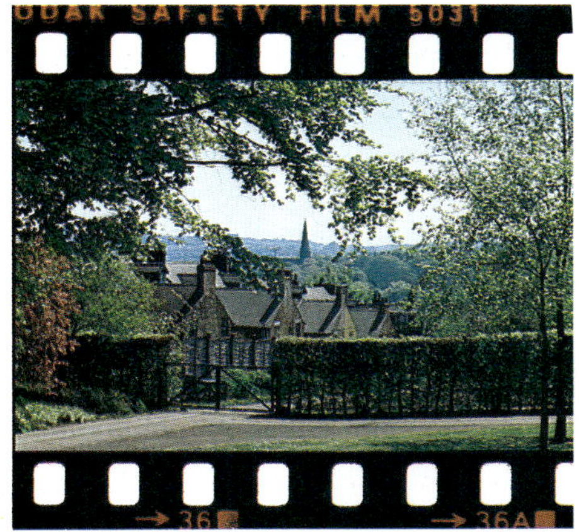

ZOOMING EFFECTS

The streaked effect in the photo above resulted from zooming during exposure. To do it, mount the camera on a tripod, keep the main subject in the center of the frame, and select a small lens aperture so shutter speed is slower than 1/8 second. Make the exposure *while operating* the zoom control, either decreasing or increasing focal length. Focal length was increased during exposure of this image. Camera settings were 1/4 second at *f*-22.

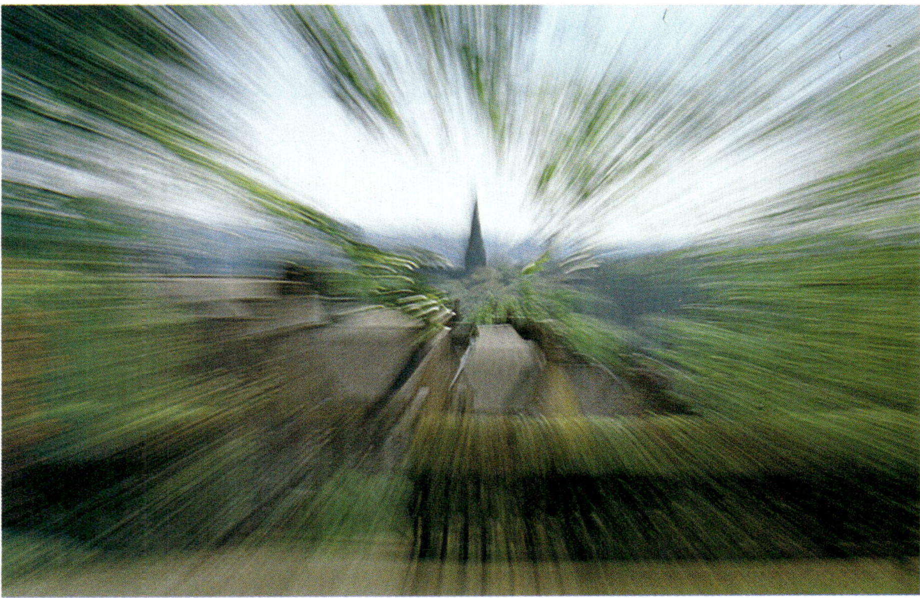

With slower speeds you can get a good effect by zooming during part of the exposure. This gives a partly streaked image.

Simple Accessories for Close-Ups

When you focus a lens on close subjects, you move the lens away from the film and toward the subject by turning the focusing ring. This increases *image distance* between lens and film.

As image distance increases, *image magnification* increases. This is the height of the subject on film divided by its actual height. This definition means that magnification can be smaller than life-size (1.0). For example, if the image is twice as tall as the actual subject, magnification is 2.0. If the image is half as tall as the subject, magnification is 1/2, or 0.5.

With a standard 50mm lens, you can't focus on subjects closer than about 18 inches (46cm). Maximum magnification is about 0.11. At closest focus, you can't fill the long dimension of the frame with a subject shorter than about 13 inches (33cm). If you want to photograph flowers or insects and exclude surrounding objects, you can't do it with only a standard 50mm lens.

Close-up photography is making pictures with image magnification from about 0.1 to 1.0.

MAGNIFICATION WITH ACCESSORY CLOSE-UP LENSES

Camera Lens	Close-Up Lens	Maximum Subject Distance mm	Maximum Subject Distance in.	Minimum Subject Distance mm	Minimum Subject Distance in.	Magnification min	Magnification max
50mm	1	1000	40	333	13	0.05	0.17
	2	500	20	250	10	0.10	0.22
	3	333	13	200	7.9	0.15	0.28
	3+1	250	10	167	6.2	0.20	0.33
	3+2	200	7.9	143	5.6	0.25	0.39
	3+2+1	167	6.2	125	4.9	0.30	0.45
	10	100	3.9	83	3.3	0.50	0.67

Note: Doubling camera lens focal length will also double minimum magnification.

This table shows magnification ranges with common close-up lenses and a 50mm camera lens. In each case, maximum magnification occurs at minimum subject distance.

WHAT YOU NEED

The accessories discussed here are screw-in close-up lenses and extension tubes. These are made by camera manufacturers and independent suppliers for 35mm SLR cameras. They make close-ups easy because you see the same image the film records and exposure metering is fast and accurate.

Extension tubes and close-up lenses work differently. An extension tube fits between camera and lens. It increases image distance, which also increases image magnification. A close-up lens screws into the front filter threads of the lens. It acts as a magnifier.

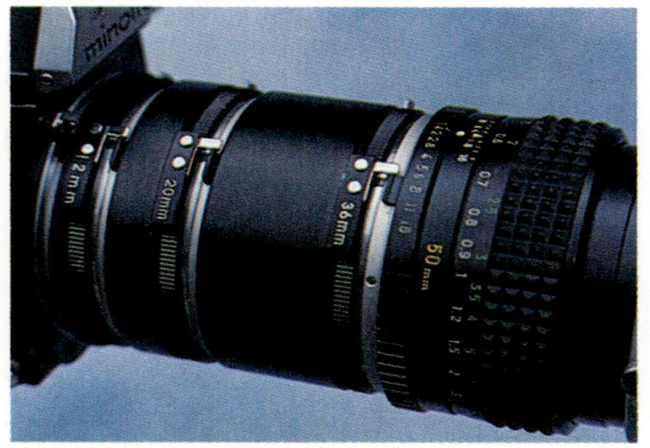

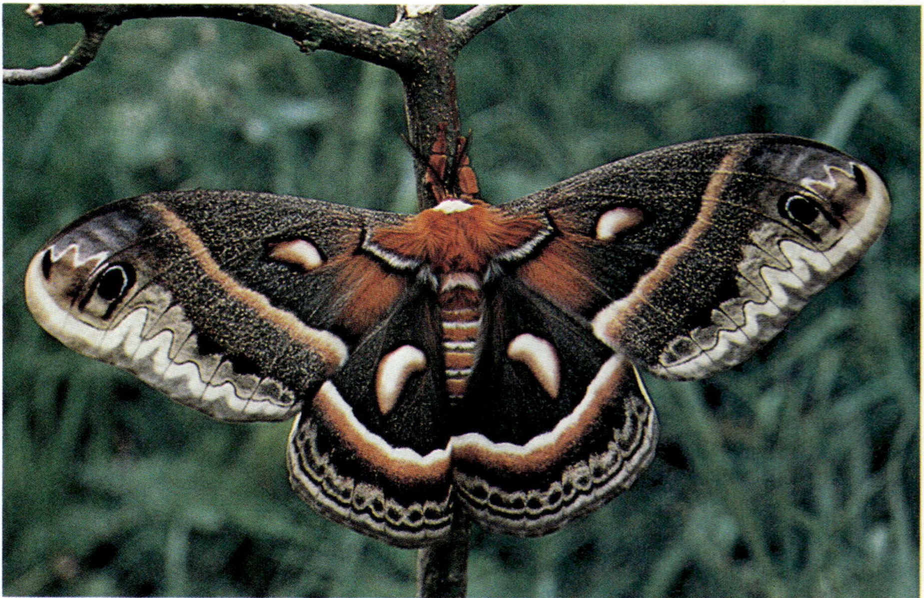

USING EXTENSION TUBES

Extension tubes give additional distance between camera lens and camera body. They are available in sets of various extensions. You mount the tube to the camera like mounting a lens. Mounting lens to tube is like mounting lens to camera. Modern, *automatic* tubes preserve the automatic features of the camera lens. This makes focusing and metering easy.

Extension tubes change the focusing range of the camera lens. Magnification with different extension tubes and a 50mm lens is shown in the table opposite.

Minimum magnification occurs when the lens is focused at infinity. Turning the lens focusing ring lets you focus on closer subjects. You can increase magnification by adding another extension tube.

Exposure—Increasing magnification makes the image dimmer. This requires an exposure correction. For example, with image magnification of 0.5, film needs an extra exposure step. See table opposite.

Use fast film when you want to hand-hold the camera and get sharp pictures. For best results, use a tripod to steady the camera during exposure. Focus carefully. Increasing magnification rapidly decreases depth of field, so you can't use depth of field to correct for slight focusing errors.

USING CLOSE-UP LENSES

The glass in a close-up lens is curved, giving it optical power to magnify. This changes the focusing range of the camera lens. Two of the major advantages of using a close-up lens are low price and the fact that no exposure correction is necessary.

Labeling Close-Up Lenses—Most are classified in *diopters.* This is the reciprocal of lens focal length expressed in meters. For example, a +1 diopter lens has a focal length of 1m, or 1000mm (40 inches); a +3 has a focal length of 333mm (13 inches). Buying a set of +1, +2 and +3 close-up lenses is a good idea because you can combine them for more magnification.

Knowing the focal length is useful for calculating minimum magnification and maximum shooting distance. With the camera lens set to infinity, the space between the close-up lens and subject is equal to the focal length of the close-up lens. For example, when you use a +2 lens, maximum shooting distance is about 50cm or 20 inches.

Turning the lens focusing ring away from infinity reduces shooting distance and increases magnification. Find focus by moving the lens closer to the subject until the viewfinder image is sharp. This is how the left photo was made with a +2 close-up lens and a 50mm camera lens.

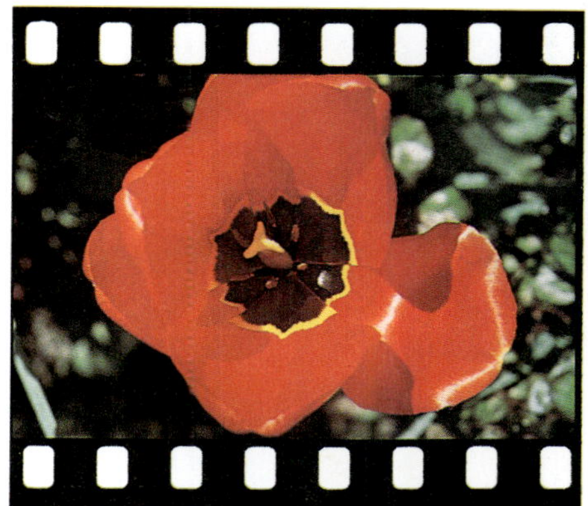

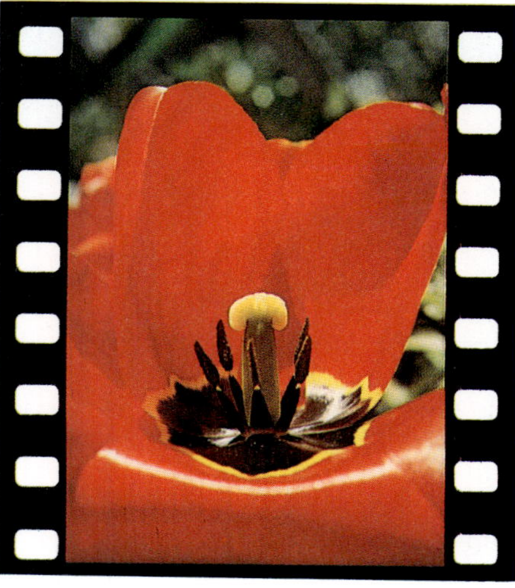

Minimum magnification occurs with the lens set to infinity. Camera lens focal length (mm) divided by close-up lens focal length (mm) equals minimum magnification. For example, with the +3 lens, minimum magnification is 50mm/333mm = 0.15. Focusing closer increases magnification.

You can combine close-up lenses for more magnification. The photo at right was made with +3 and +1 close-up lenses, for a magnification of about 0.20, or 1/5 life-size. For best image quality, put the one with the larger diopter rating closer to the camera lens.

Try to use small lens apertures, and put the most important subject elements in the central part of the frame, where sharpness is best.

50mm CAMERA LENS AND EXTENSION TUBES		
Tube Extension (mm)	Magnification Range	Approximate Exposure Correction (steps)
5	0.1 - 0.2	1/3
10	0.2 - 0.3	1/2
15	0.3 - 0.4	2/3
20	0.4 - 0.5	1
25	0.5 - 0.6	1
30	0.6 - 0.7	1-1/3
35	0.7 - 0.8	1-1/2
40	0.8 - 0.9	1-2/3
45	0.9 - 1.0	2

Accessories for Macro Photography

This category involves life-size images and larger. It requires some different equipment and shooting methods than close-up photography. The principles of magnification and extension that were described in the previous section apply here, too.

Calculating Values—Determine magnification by comparing the length of the film frame with the actual length of the subject. The 35mm frame is 24mm x 36mm—approximately 1 by 1-1/2 inches. Measure the subject length and divide it into frame length. Use a millimeter scale. For example, if the subject is 18mm long and you want it to fill the frame horizontally, then magnification is 36mm/18mm = 2.0.

You can determine the necessary extension (X) for a desired magnification (M) by using this formula:

$$X = M \times F$$

F is lens focal length. For example, if you use a 50mm lens and want a magnification of 1.0, use tubes that give 50mm of extension. Use the lens set at infinity.

REVERSING THE LENS

When using a standard 50mm lens for magnifications of 1.0 or bigger, you'll get best image quality if the lens is reverse-mounted, as above. To do this, you need an *adapter ring*. It screws into the filter threads at the front of the lens. The other side of the ring attaches to the camera body. You control aperture *manually*.

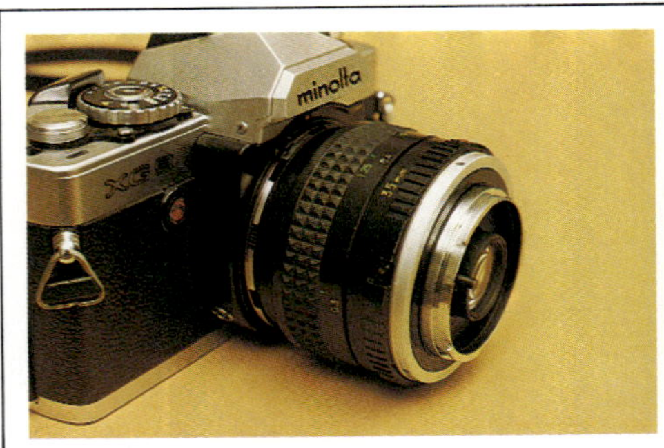

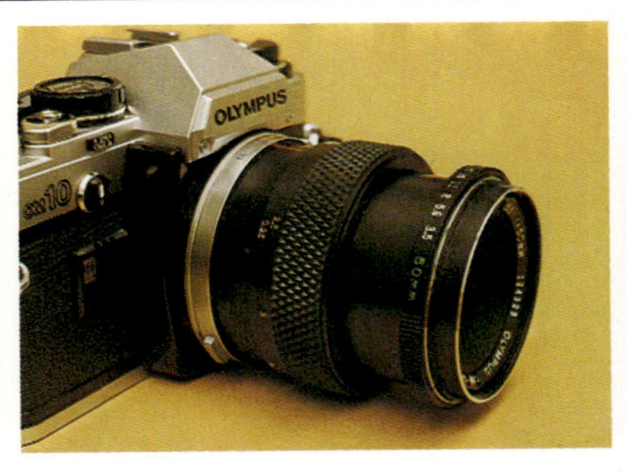

For magnifications of 1.0 and greater, calculate extension using the formula given. The result is approximate with a 50mm lens. The result is in error with a reversed wide-angle or telephoto lens. Reversed wide-angle lenses give very high magnifications with little or no extension. Reversed telephoto lenses give less magnification than you'd expect.

MACRO LENS

This lens has a larger-than-normal extension built into its focus travel. Common macro lenses have 50mm focal length, making them convenient for general-purpose photography, too. A macro lens is designed to give best image quality in the close-up and macro ranges.

Most 50mm macro lenses have 25mm of extension available. This gives a maximum magnification of 0.5 with the lens alone! If you get a 25mm extension tube for the lens, you can extend this up to life-size.

Some lens manufacturers make 100mm and 200mm macro lenses. The advantage of these is greater shooting distance.

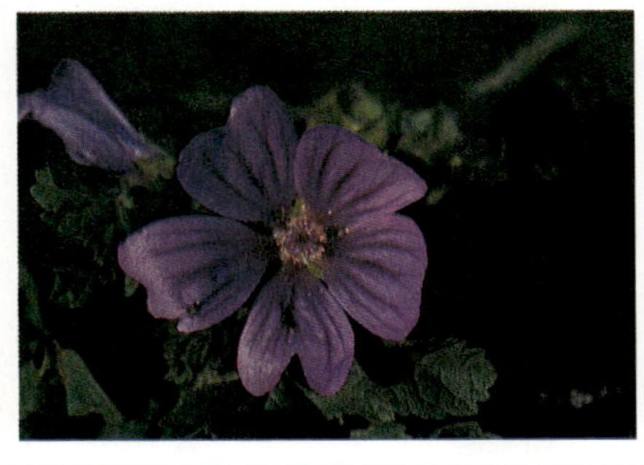

0.5 MAGNIFICATION

This flower was shot at a magnification of 0.5, or 1/2 life-size. There are a few ways to do this. You could use a 50mm macro lens fully extended 25mm. The lens has a scale that indicates image magnification. Sometimes the scale shows *reproduction ratio*. A magnification of 0.5 (1/2) is a reproduction ratio of 1:2.

You could use a bellows extended half the focal length of the lens in use, with the lens set at infinity. For example, if using a 35mm lens on bellows, an extension of 17.5mm gives a magnification of 0.5.

LIFE-SIZE

For this photo, the flower was photographed with a magnification of 1.0. Compare the length of a petal in this picture with the same petal in the picture at left. It is twice as long, meaning magnification is twice as great.

Get life-size magnification with any lens by using an extension *equal* to lens focal length. You can use extension tubes, a bellows or both in combination. Use the smallest practical aperture.

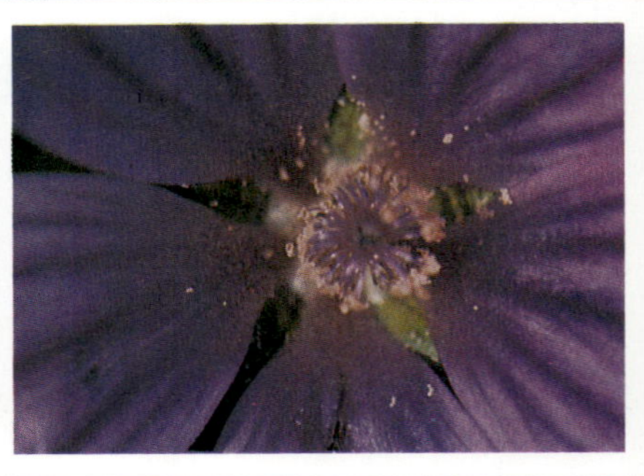

2.0 MAGNIFICATION

Here, magnification was doubled again. Notice that depth of field decreased radically. Sometimes, the smallest lens aperture won't give enough depth of field. This can limit the amount of image control you want. The best way to solve the problem is to photograph flat objects or compose so the out-of-focus elements look OK. It is usually advisable to put best focus near the front of the subject.

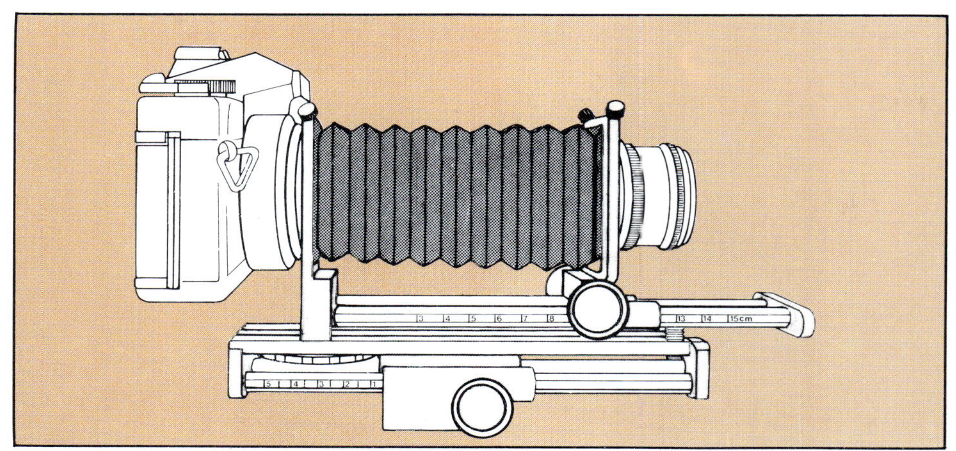

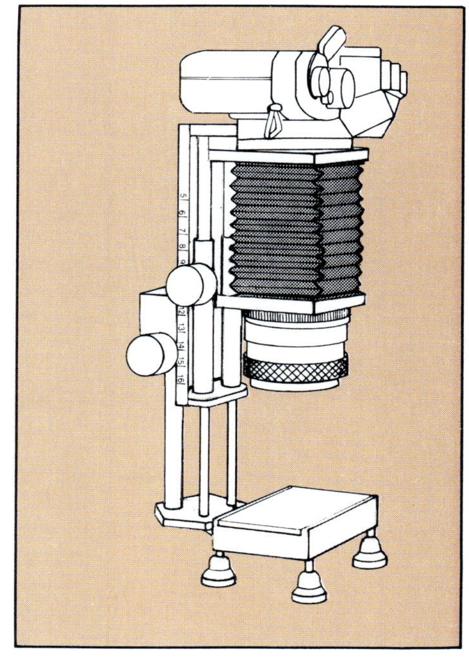

BELLOWS

A bellows fits between lens and camera. It allows changing magnification quickly. A bellows usually provides more magnification than a set of extension tubes because the bellows is larger. Some manufacturers also make extension tubes with adjustable extension.

First, decide on the necessary magnification (M) for a certain subject. Then use the formula X = M x F to find extension (X). Set the lens focus control to infinity to simplify the procedure. Set the bellows to the desired amount of extension by observing a scale on the bellows.

Tips With Bellows—Models designed for 35mm SLR cameras typically have extension from about 30mm to 150mm. With a 50mm lens set to infinity, this gives a magnification range of 0.6 to 3.0.

When using ordinary lenses, reverse the lens for magnifications greater than 1.0. There are some special lenses that do not require reversing at high magnifications.

For convenience and bright viewing, get a bellows that operates the lens automatically. Always mount the bellows on a tripod or other firm support.

When photographing flat objects, such as coins, use a focusing stand, shown at right.

EXPOSURE CORRECTION

Another problem with increasing magnification is the necessary exposure correction. Exposure increase depends on the *square* of magnification. Here is the formula to calculate the Exposure Correction Factor (ECF):

$$ECF = (1 + M)^2$$

M is magnification. At a magnification of 2, for example, ECF is 9. Set the camera to give 9 times as much exposure as an ordinary scene in the same light. Converting ECF values, which are multipliers, into exposure steps is done in the accompanying table.

EXPOSURE CORRECTION FACTORS TO EXPOSURE STEPS

ECF	Steps
1	0
1.5	1/2
2	1
2.5	1-1/3
3	1-2/3
4	2
5.7	2-1/2
8	3

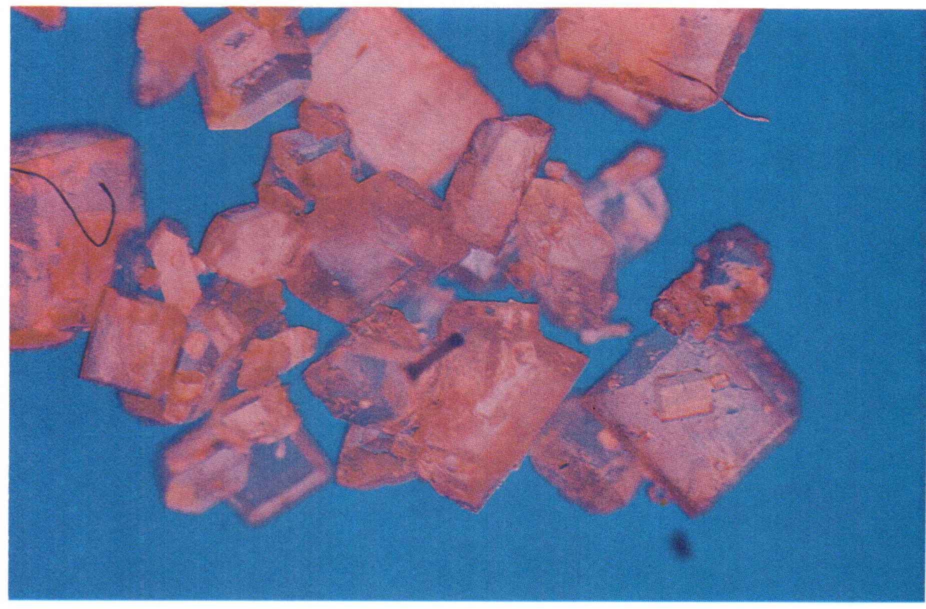

A TTL camera meter will automatically compensate for ECF, if the image brightness is within the meter's sensitivity range. If it isn't, use a handheld accessory meter to measure the light striking the subject, then correct based on the formula and table.

More SLR Accessories

As you acquire more lenses and accessories like flash, close-up equipment and filters, you have to consider how to carry and store them. It's frustrating when you need a piece of photographic equipment and realize that you left it at home!

The best solution is a carrying case. There are many styles and sizes. What you need depends on your current equipment, what you expect to own in the future, and your style of shooting. Always get a case bigger than one that just holds what you have. Thus, if you buy or borrow an extra lens or camera, the case has room for it.

Soft Or Hard Case?—When you carry a a soft case on a shoulder strap, the case conforms to your body. However, a hard case better protects your equipment in case of rough shocks.

Both types are available with removable and adjustable dividers, so you can customize the case to fit your equipment. This lets you use the case for a variety of tasks, depending on what you need to carry.

Hard cases are made of fiberboard or aluminum. The latter is most expensive, durable and attractive. Or, consider a hard case with a leather or plastic covering.

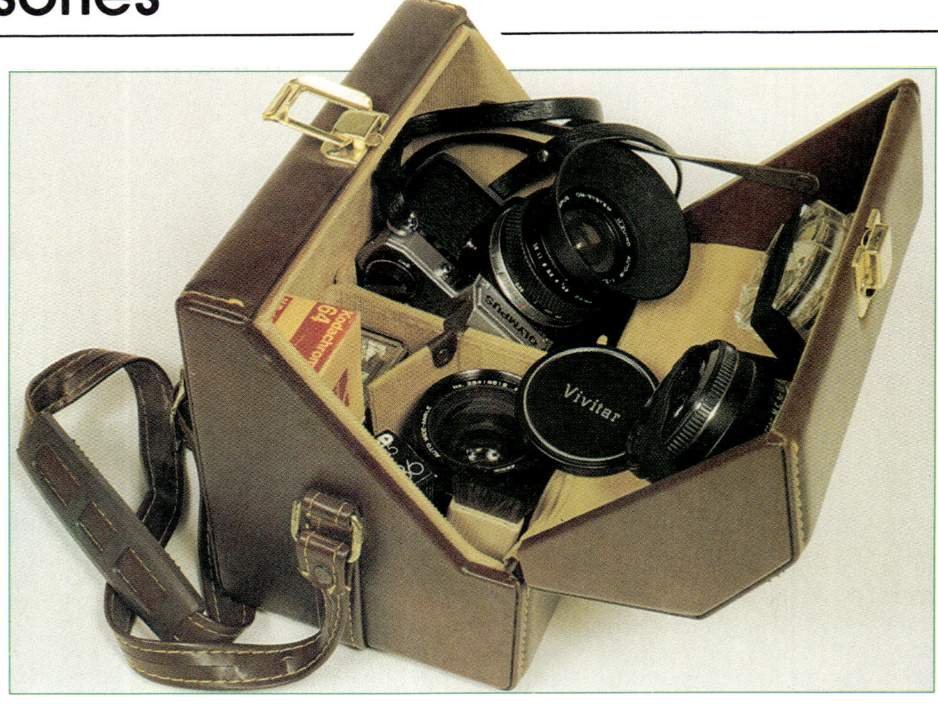

Soft cases are made of leather, imitation leather, or tough, waterproof nylon or canvas. Typically, this type of case is not as well padded on the inside as a hard case. It is usually lighter than a hard case holding the same amount of equipment.

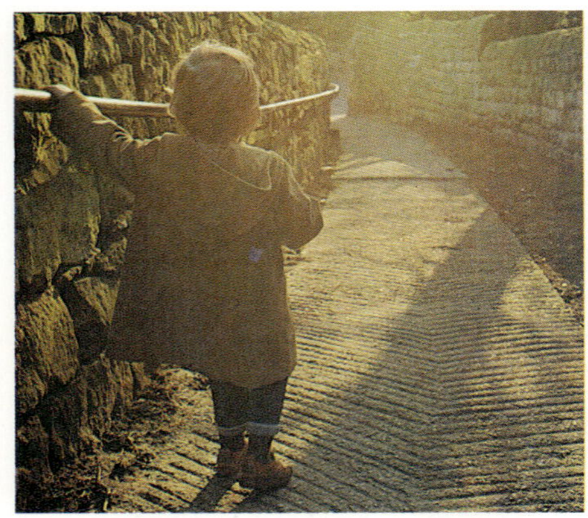

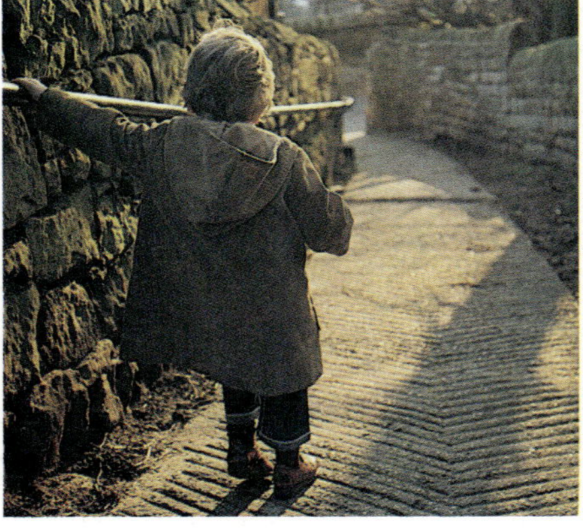

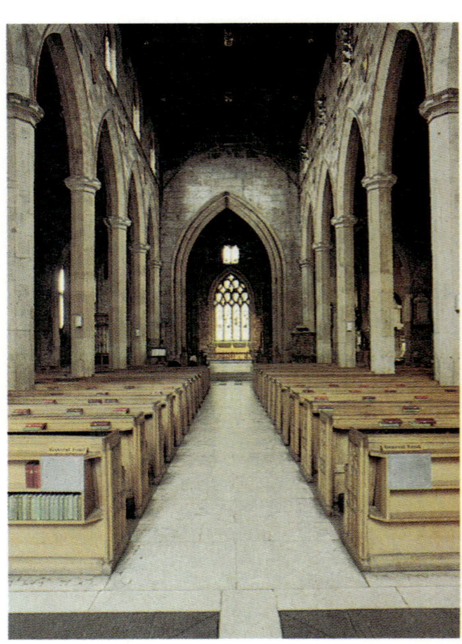

WHAT IS FLARE?

Flare is unfocused light that exposes film. It is bright light shining directly into the lens. This light is reflected and lightens bright and dark areas, decreasing image contrast. You may also see *ghost images* of the lens aperture. On film these look like geometric shapes.

In the above photo, the camera was pointed toward the setting sun. Direct light from the sun entered the lens and created a golden haze that obscures image detail.

Avoiding Flare—Minimize flare by blocking direct light from the lens. Change camera angle slightly and use a lens shade. Be sure to use one designed for your lens. If the shade is too big, it won't be effective. If it's too narrow, it intrudes into the picture area and darkens corners.

LONG EXPOSURES

Many interior scenes look best photographed with natural light, which is usually dim. Use a tripod or other device to hold the camera steady. A cable release also helps prevent camera vibrations when you trip the shutter.

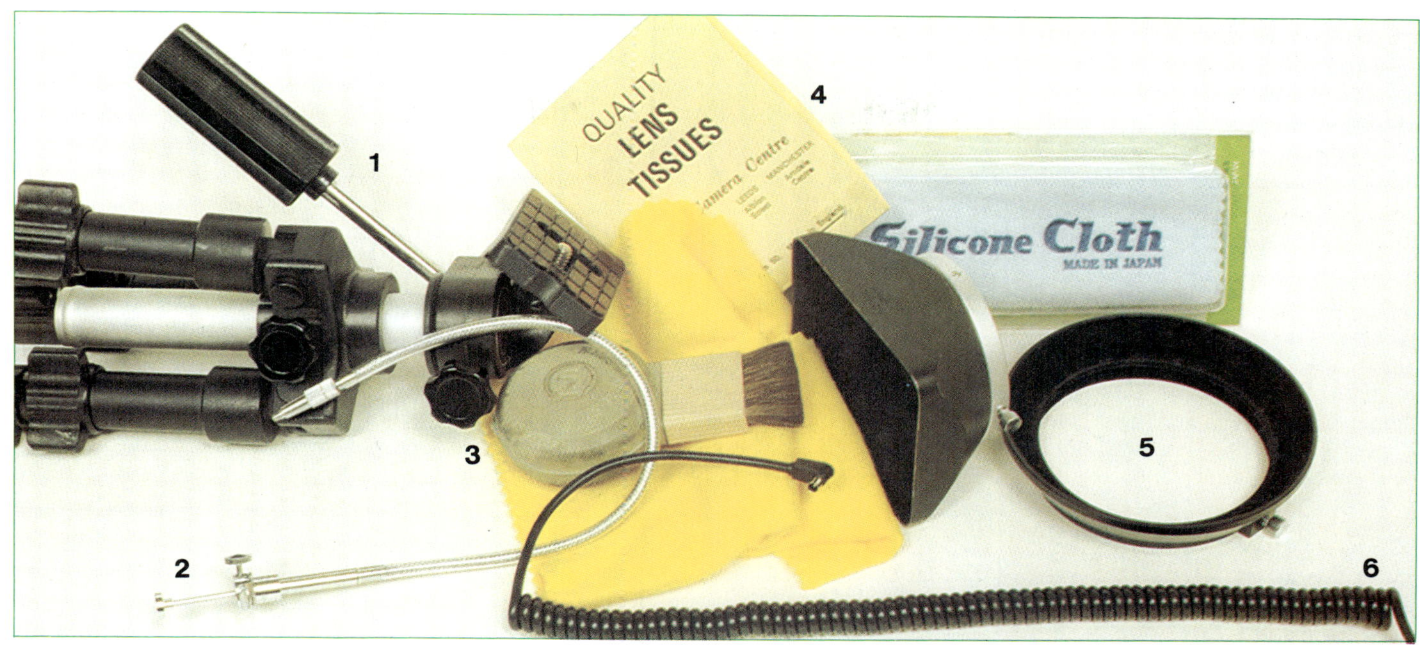

USEFUL ACCESSORIES

If you don't have a tripod (1) yet, consider getting one. It's a useful aid that can help you get a good picture when hand-holding the camera is impractical. When using a tripod to steady the camera for slow exposures, use a cable release (2). It trips the camera shutter with less vibration than your finger.

Carry a cleaning kit that includes a blower brush (3), lens tissue (4) and fluid, and a polishing cloth. Clean equipment works best.

Use a lens shade (5) to prevent flare from degrading image quality when shooting toward the light. A flash extension cord (6) lets you use the flash off-camera for some lighting effects.

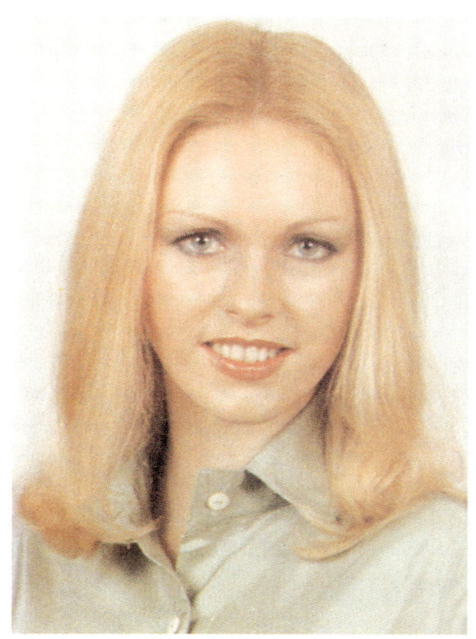

Formal portraits done indoors benefit from a tripod-mounted camera. You can set up a certain composition and maintain it. This lets you adjust lighting, subject pose and other elements in the scene without putting down the camera.

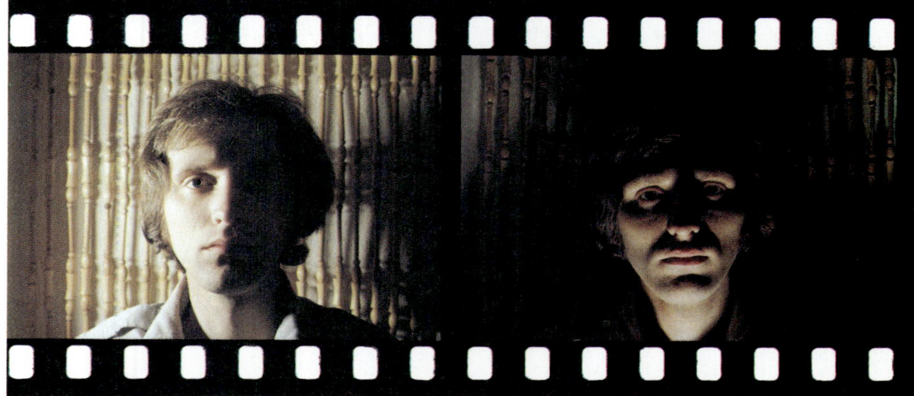

OFF-CAMERA FLASH

If you always use a flash attached to the top of a camera, the lighting effect in your pictures will be the same. The front of the subject is evenly lit and casts a dark shadow on a nearby background, if there is one. Even though this is fine for many of your pictures, you should strive for some visual variety when possible.

An easy way is to use the flash off camera. Using an automatic-exposure flash is simplest. If using a manual flash, use flash-to-subject distance in the guide-number (GN) formula.

Use a flash extension cord that is at least as long as your arm. You can then hold the flash in your left hand and the camera in your right. This way you can position the flash quickly and easily for best lighting effect. If you have a longer cord, use an assistant or lightstand to hold the flash.

For a large shadow area, hold the flash to one side of the subject. This is called *side lighting* and is shown in the photo above left. For more bright areas and less shadow, move the flash closer to the front of the subject. The other photo was made with the flash held below the subject.

How Light Affects Pictures

Photography is as simple—and complicated—as recording light. When you understand and control the light exposing film, you are on your way to getting pictures you like. This section discusses doing this with natural light, but the principles also apply to artificial light from lamps and electronic flash.

SOURCE SIZE

The size of the light source and its distance from the subject is important. A *large* source is big or close to the subject, so that light comes from many directions, filling potential shadow areas with light. This gives even illumination, such as happens outdoors on a cloudy day. The sky acts as a large light source.

A *small* source is very directional—you can tell where it comes from by observing dark shadows in the scene. Although a bright sun in a clear sky is large, it is so far away that it acts as a small source.

A *medium* source gives in-between effects. It is about as large as it is far from the subject. You'll see shadows in the scene, but they will have detail in them. The light seems directional, and looks even in lit areas.

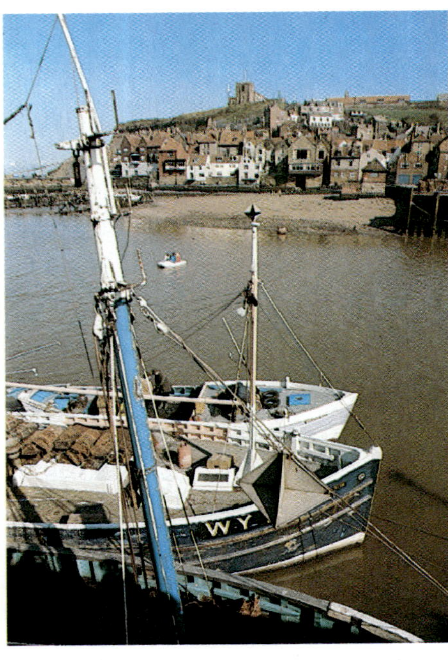

LIGHTING ANGLE

This is another important lighting characteristic. The angle between the light and the direction you point the lens determines what parts of the scene are lit and what parts are shaded.

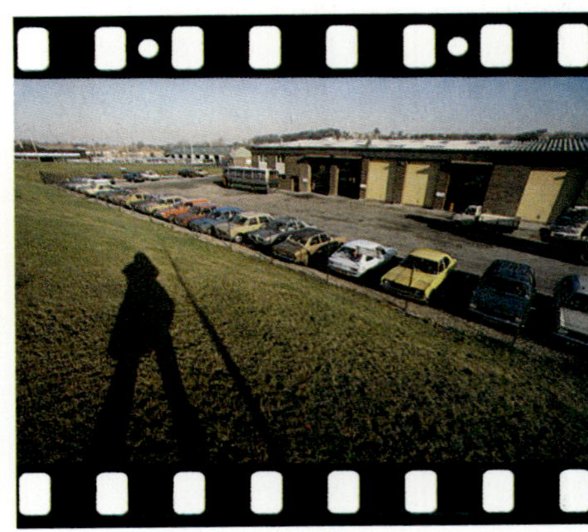

For example, common advice you've heard is to photograph a scene with the sun behind you. This guarantees that the sun illuminates everything in view. It gives a brightly lit scene (left) but doesn't necessarily give a picture with visual impact. Using the rule slavishly may also lead to pictures like the one above. When the sun is low, your shadow may intrude into the scene.

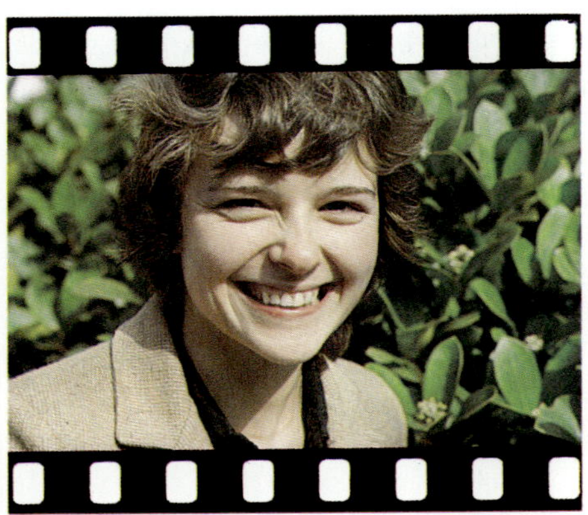

OUTDOOR PORTRAITS

Outdoors on a bright day, if the sun is behind you it can make your portrait subject squint. It can also cast unflattering shadows. This is shown above. The subject is smiling, but the result is less flattering than it could be.

Change Lighting Angle—For the second photo the photographer did not use the sun as a front light. Instead, he moved his subject so the sun lit her from behind. Notice the bright highlights on her hair. The light on her face was reflected light from nearby lit surfaces, such as a sidewalk. It was less bright than direct sunlight, but was from a much larger "source." The large-area reflector gave soft, even light. The subject didn't squint and was more relaxed.

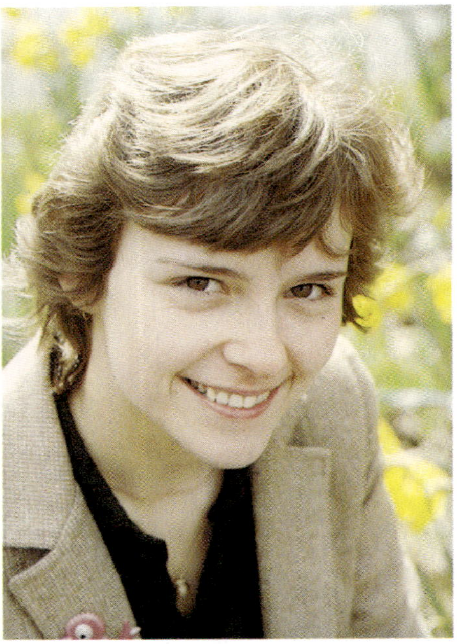

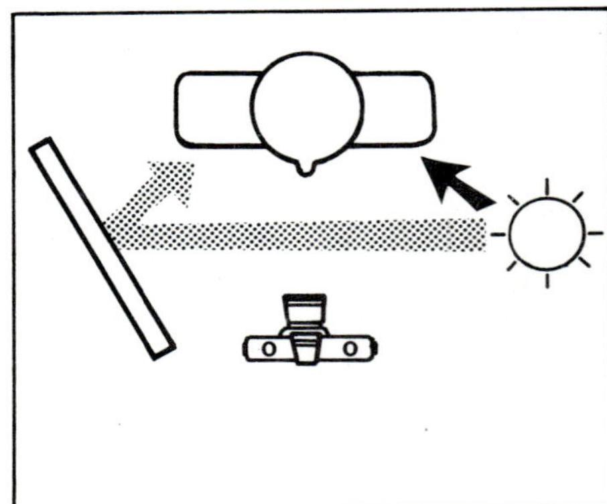

Use A Reflector—If you need more light on a subject lit from the back or side, use a reflector—see above. It adds *fill light* to brighten dark areas. You can see the effect as you move the reflector.

Use a large piece of white cardboard or a board covered with aluminum foil. With color film, don't use a colored board. It will tint the reflected light.

Have an assistant hold the shiny side of the board to reflect sunlight toward the subject. This will noticeably brighten dark areas, letting you use a faster shutter speed or smaller aperture.

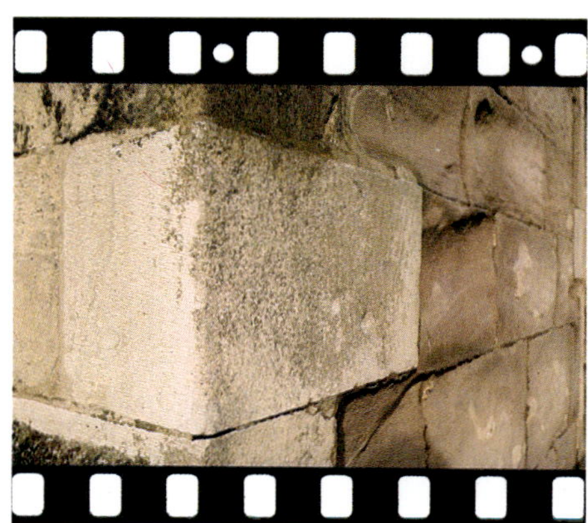

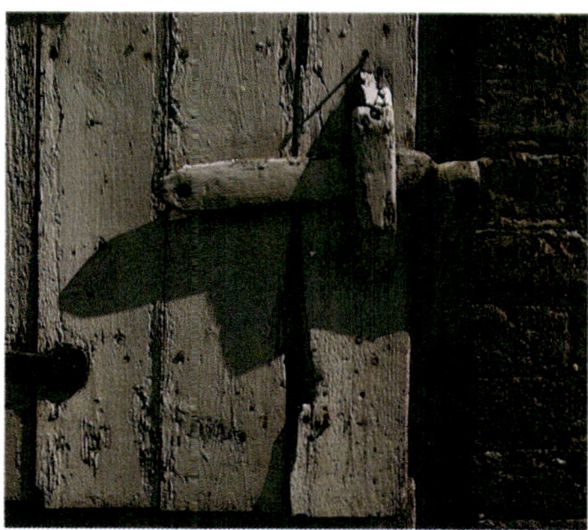

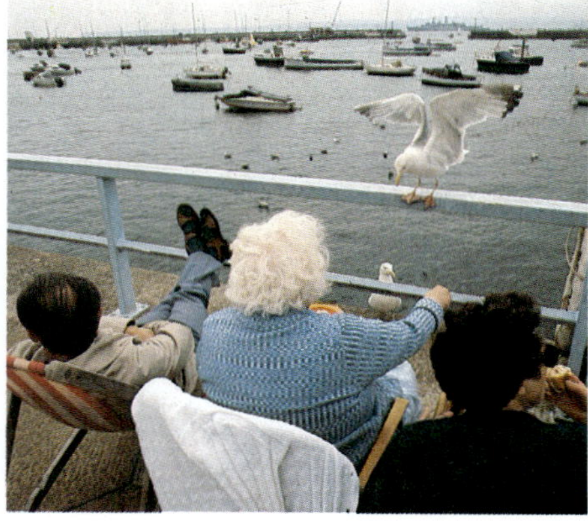

FRONT LIGHT

The above photo was shot with light from a large source behind the photographer. The lighting effect is even and shows minimal shadows, making the stone look flat and untextured.

Without shadows, a three-dimensional object can lack impact. Front light is best for flat objects without texture or when you *want* to minimize texture.

Sometimes, you want to emphasize subject form and shape, to make an image look three dimensional. This requires the right size and direction of light.

SIDE LIGHT

Light that comes from a source between 45° and 90° to the subject is called *side light.* The effect is that small bumps and depressions are lit on one side only, leaving the other in shadow. The relative sizes of the shadow and lit areas are visual clues to surface texture, as shown above. This gives an extra dimension to the photo, which usually makes it more interesting.

If you are photographing a textured surface, use a camera angle that exploits side lighting. Or, wait until the sun moves to give the effect.

LARGE-SOURCE LIGHTING

The above photo was made on an overcast day. A thick cloud layer spread out the light of the sun. This made the clouds act as a large light source.

Notice that everything is evenly lit. Because there is color in the scene, the picture doesn't lack impact. Details are easy to see.

Large-source lighting, also called *soft light,* is good for colorful scenes with much detail. Shadows won't obscure important elements.

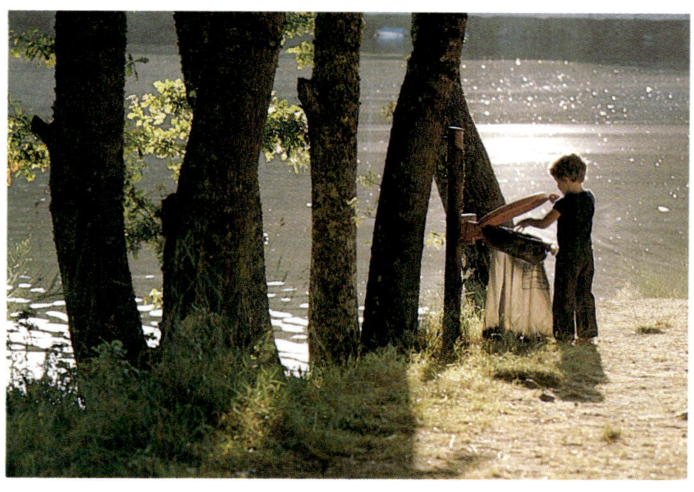

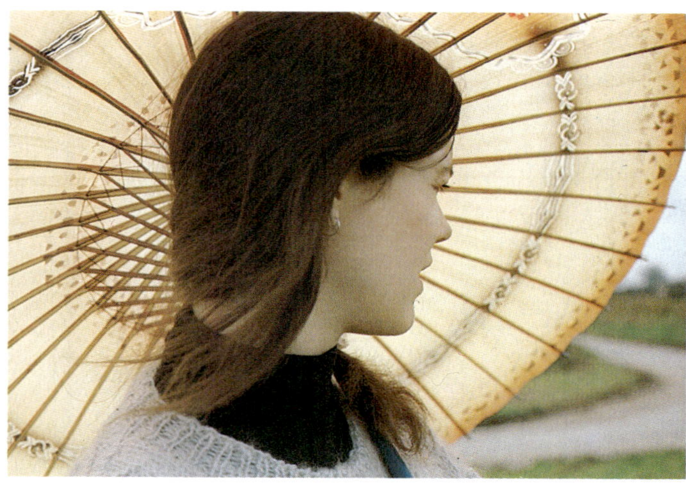

SHOOTING BACKLIT SUBJECTS

When you face the light illuminating the scene, the subject is lit from the back. This kind of lighting can give dramatic results. However, without a clear idea of what you want in the picture, you may not get an effective image.

As mentioned earlier, backlit scenes are non-average. This requires an understanding of how your camera meter works. Generally, you should base exposure on the areas you want to reproduce as midtones. Brighter elements reproduce lighter, and darker areas darker.

Dark Foreground—In the left photo, the photographer wanted to preserve the effect of the sunlight. He based exposure on the lit part of the foreground. What he did was move the camera until the lit foreground area was in the central part of the focusing screen. He metered and set the camera for the recommended exposure settings. Then he recomposed the scene as you see it here.

For the photo at right, the photographer took a close-up reading of the subject's face and hair. He used the recommended settings for the composition you see.

Shooting in Dim Light

Photographing in dim light can be more exciting and challenging than photographing by daylight or flash. During the day we see clearly, so we expect film to reproduce what we see. In dim light, things are different. We not only see less but also less brilliant color, detail and clarity. However, film can "add up" light and reproduce colors we can't see.

Modern lenses and film make dim-light photography easy. Typical maximum apertures of fast 50mm lenses are *f*-1.8, *f*-1.4 and *f*-1.2. The smaller the number, the greater the light-gathering ability. With a fast lens and fast film—ASA 400 or greater—you may be able to handhold the camera in dim light and get a sharp image.

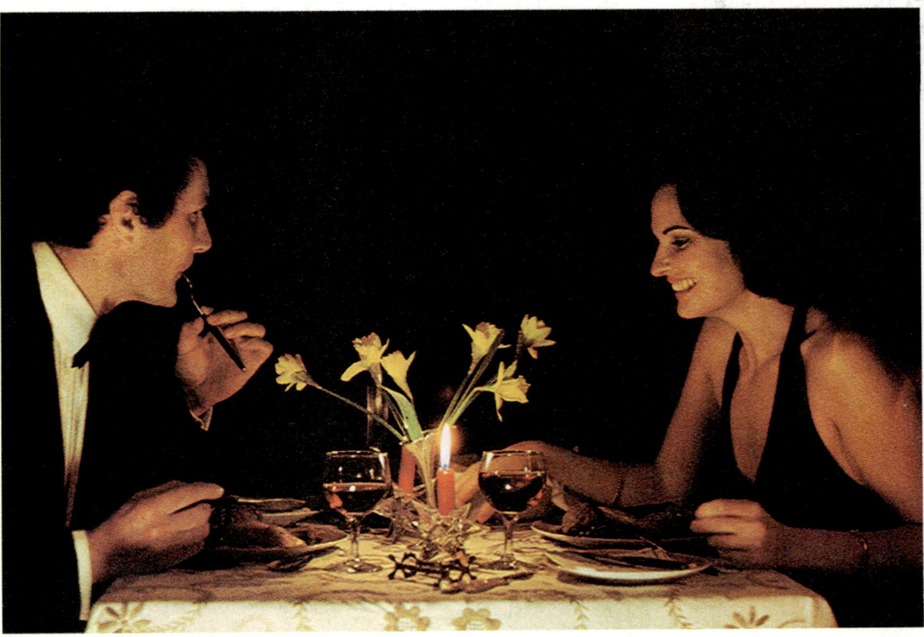

METERING

Most dim-light scenes are non-average. They may be too dim for the meter to measure accurately, and film needs more exposure than usual with exposures slower than 1/2 second, because of *reciprocity failure.* For these reasons bracketing in full steps toward more exposure is recommended if you want to be sure of getting the picture. The best general advice is to selectively meter the lit elements that you want to reproduce on film, and bracket extensively.

For the above photo, the photographer moved in close to view and meter the table, flowers, candle and wine. He set aperture and shutter speed, then recomposed the scene as you see it here. If he metered the scene you see, the lit areas would have been overexposed due to the dark background affecting the meter.

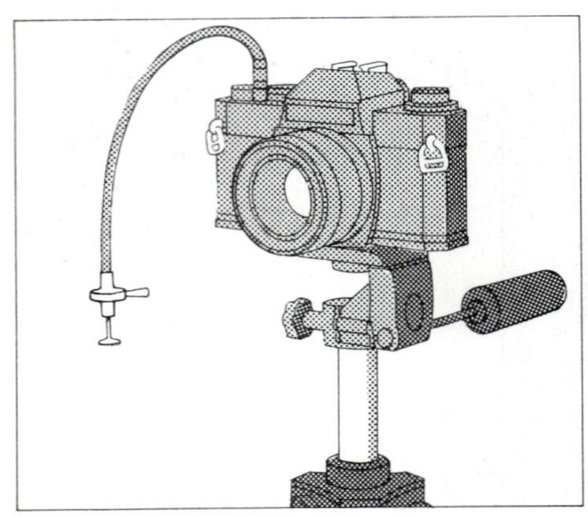

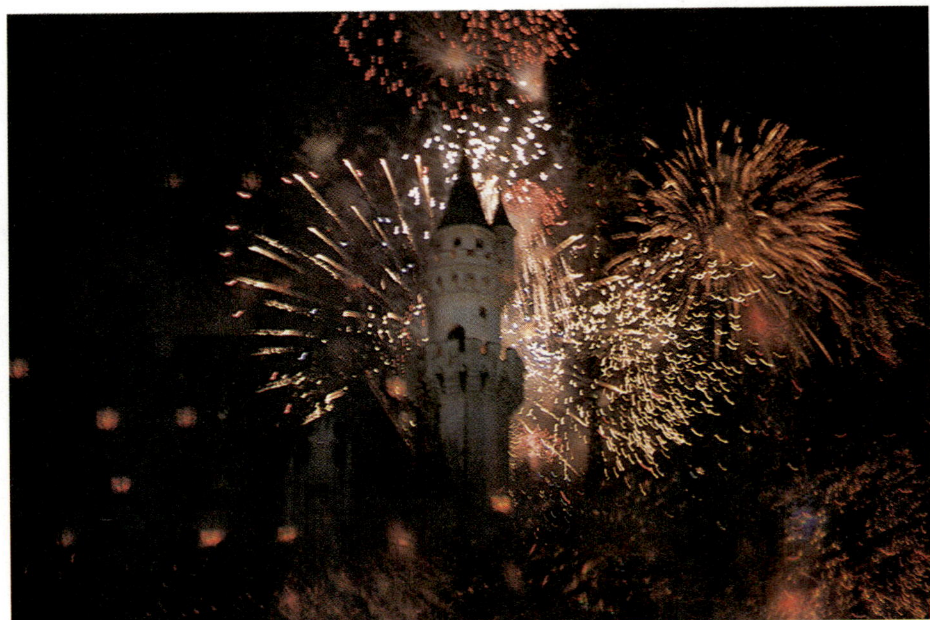

USING B

Sometimes, you'll want to expose film for a longer time than the camera's slowest shutter-speed setting. In these cases, mount the camera to a tripod, screw a cable-release into the shutter button, and set the shutter-speed dial to B.

At this setting, the shutter will stay open for as long as you depress the cable-release plunger. A locking plunger is convenient for exposures longer than a few seconds. Time the exposure, then close the shutter by releasing or unlocking the plunger.

Appropriate Subjects—Operating the camera this way is good for scenes with very low light, such as a landscape on a full-moon night. With ASA 400 slide film a good starting point is *f*-2.8 for 30 seconds. Bracket toward more exposure.

Using B is also useful when photographing moving lights like evening traffic or fireworks. The tripod holds the camera steady so buildings and other stationary elements reproduce sharply. Moving lights show as trails of color and light. With ASA 400 film, bracket exposures, beginning with settings of *f*-4 and 1 second.

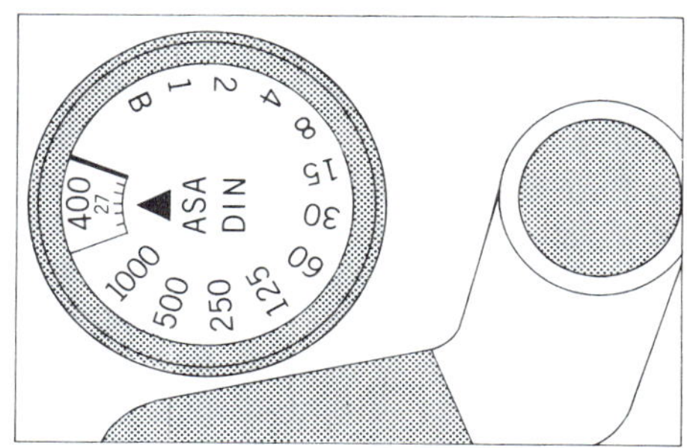

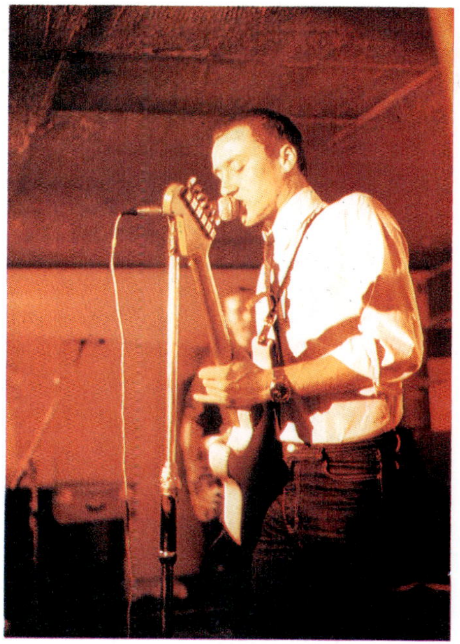

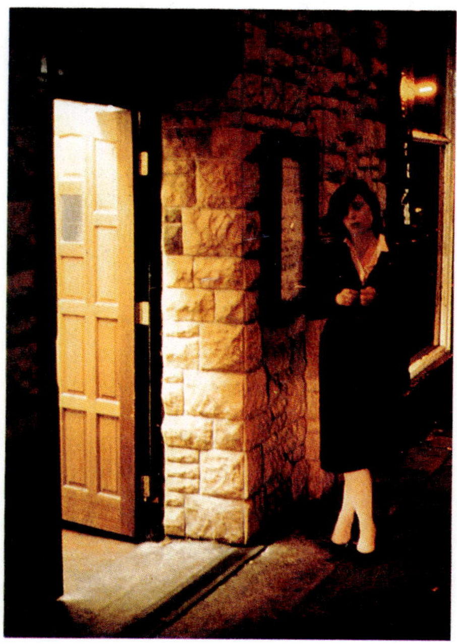

FAST FILMS

The fastest color and b&w negative films are ASA 400. The fastest color slide film is ASA 640. It gives best color reproduction with tungsten lamps. ASA 400 color slide and negative films give best color reproduction with daylight and flash.

Color Balance—Color film is designed to give best color with light that has a certain mix of red, blue and green. When film sensitivity matches the color content in the light, the film and light are *balanced.* And subject colors reproduce lifelike.

If color film and light aren't balanced, the image has a *color cast.* This can happen in dim-light shooting, as you can see in the photos here. Both are orange-yellow. Daylight-balanced film was used under low-level tungsten lights, which have relatively more red than daylight.

Some people do not mind this effect, others do. Whether the color cast is acceptable or not depends on the mood of the scene. For example, the candlelight scene is OK because the mood is "warm." If the photographer used a tungsten-balanced film, the color cast would have been less orange.

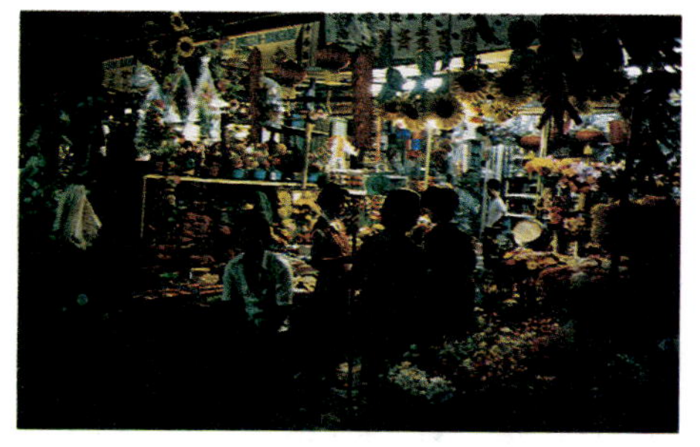

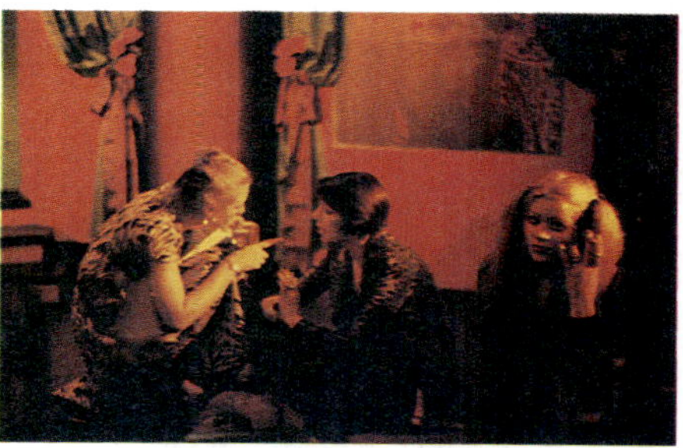

PUSH-PROCESSING FILM

You can "underexpose" some color-slide films by one step and still get good pictures. This is the same as using a film-speed setting of 800 on the camera when using ASA 400 color slide film. Doing it may help you handhold the camera in dim light.

The film lab can compensate for underexposure by developing the slide film for a longer time. This is called *push-processing.* Because the whole roll is processed at once, you have to expose the whole roll at the same speed, not just a few frames. Eastman Kodak offers one-step push-processing for E-6 Ektachrome slide films. Be sure to tell your photo dealer that you want push-processing for your film. Processing cost is slightly higher.

Some custom labs offer one-, two- or three-step push-processing for E-6-type films. Check with your photo dealer to see if he can recommend such a lab in your area. For a two-step speed increase, set the film-speed dial to 1600 when using ASA 400 film. For three steps, set 3200.

Do It Yourself—If you process E-6 type films yourself with an E-6 home-processing kit, you can do your own push-processing. It's easy. Extend first development time from the normal 7 minutes to 9 minutes for a one-step increase, or to 12-1/2 minutes for a two-step increase. Some photographers extend first development to 20 or 26 minutes for a three- and four-step increase respectively. All other processing steps are standard.

Image Quality—Push-processing fast film affects some image characteristics. Generally, the image looks grainier and has higher contrast than a regularly processed slide. Sometimes, a color cast occurs. The higher the speed increase, the more pronounced these effects.

Depending on the image, these changes may not be detrimental. Graininess in an image can add an appealing visual effect, as can higher contrast. And as described earlier, many low-light scenes reproduce with an unnatural color cast anyway. A slight color shift due to processing may be unnoticeable.

For these reasons, pushing fast film for a speed increase is a creative and experimental process. When doing it for the first time, shoot a variety of subjects to see which look best on film.

Using Electronic Flash

Knowing how and when to use electronic flash will expand your photographic horizons. With flash you can take pictures in dark places without having to use slow shutter speeds and large apertures. Because flash duration is very short—about 1/1000 second or less—you can "freeze" motion on film. Because *you* control the light, you can produce natural and unnatural lighting effects. Flash light also matches the color sensitivity of color daylight film, for good color reproduction.

MANUAL FLASH

This is the most basic type of flash. It creates a burst of light of the same intensity and duration every time. The flash connects to the camera by an electric cord or through an electronic connection in the mounting shoe. When you push the shutter button, the camera triggers the flash.

You base aperture setting on subject distance and film speed. Use the calculator dial (above left) on the flash unit. Set film speed on the dial. After focusing on the subject, check the lens distance scale for camera-to-subject distance. Look at the calculator scale to find the aperture corresponding to this distance. Set that aperture and shoot.

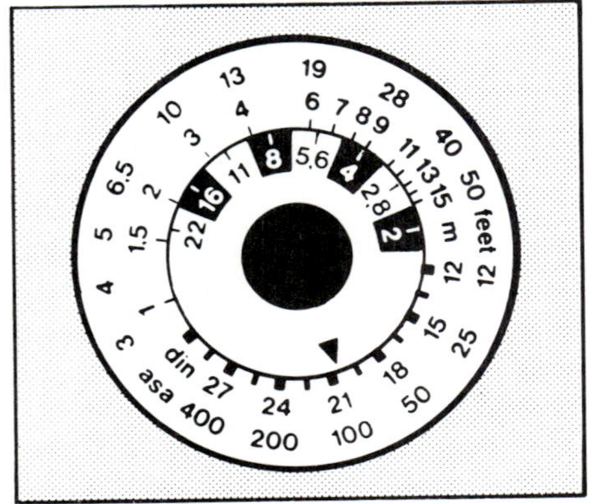

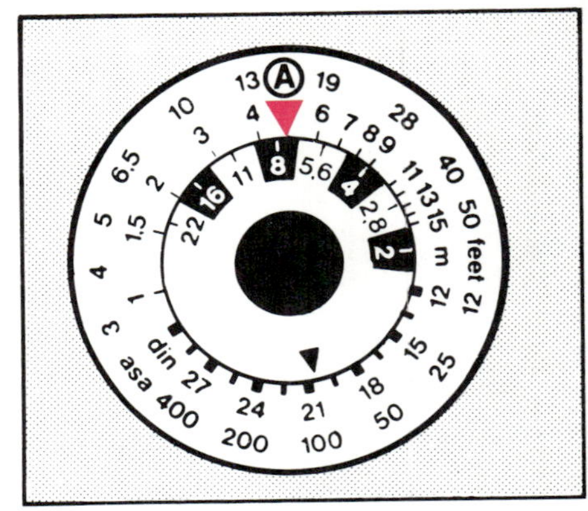

AUTOMATIC FLASH

Using flash manually can be time consuming. A quicker way is to use an automatic-exposure flash. It has a sensor that detects light reflected from the subject. When the detector decides that the subject has received enough light for good exposure, it turns the flash off. This feature can save battery power, giving more flashes than in manual operation.

An automatic flash has a different calculator dial than a manual flash. After setting film speed on the dial, find camera-to-subject distance from the lens distance scale and check the calculator dial. If the subject is closer than the distance indicated by the A on the scale, use the indicated aperture—in this example *f*-8—for automatic exposure. If the subject is farther, you must use the flash manually, as described. A switch on the flash puts it in auto or manual mode.

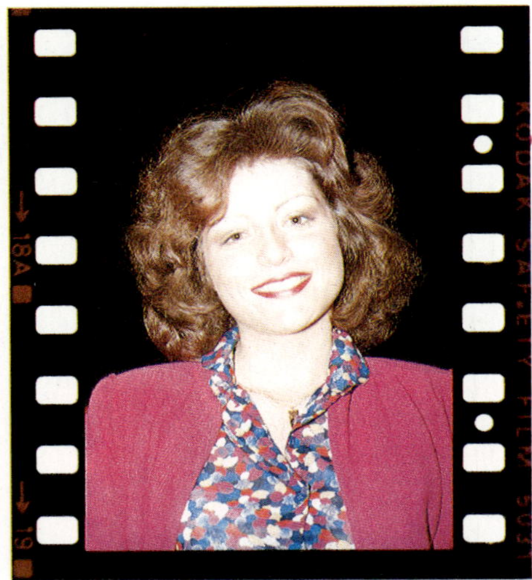

OVEREXPOSURE

Too much flash exposure gives an overexposed "washed-out" image. This can result from one or more of the following mistakes: setting a too-slow film speed on the calculator dial; reading the dial incorrectly; forgetting to set lens aperture; or being too close to the subject. These mistakes can happen when you change camera-to-subject distance and forget to check flash exposure.

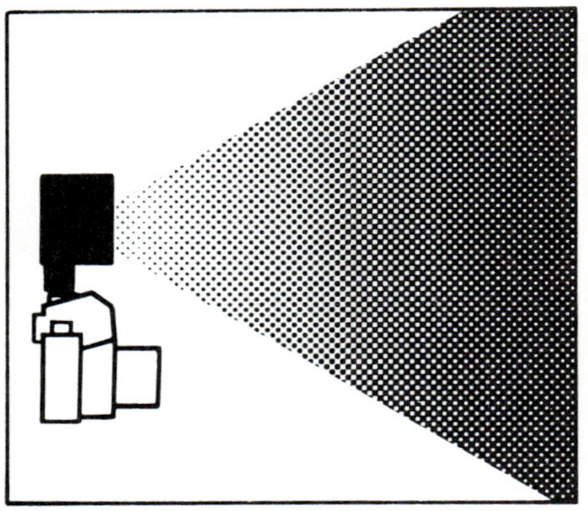

FLASH FALL-OFF

The above drawing shows how the light from a flash spreads out and covers a larger area as flash-to-subject distance increases. This is also indicated by the calculator dials shown at top. With manual flash for farther subjects, you need a bigger aperture for good exposure.

When you calculate good exposure, only subjects in a narrow range of distances are well exposed. Closer subjects receive too much light and are overexposed. Subjects farther away look dark on film. This effect is called *flash fall-off* and is shown in the photo of soccer players.

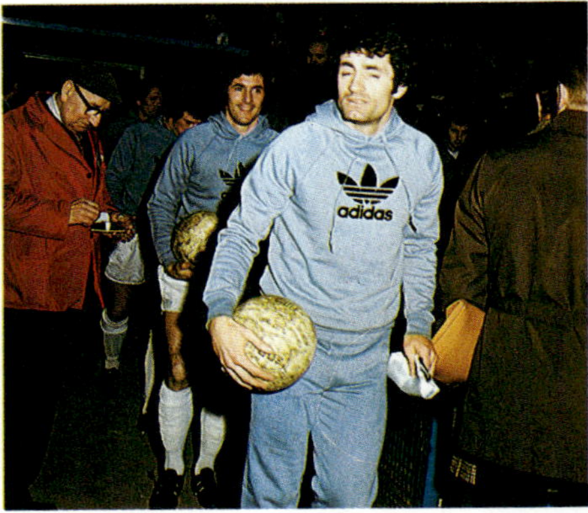

Avoiding Fall-Off—Minimize the problem by photographing subjects that are about the same distance from the flash. You may have to rearrange the scene or move farther away.

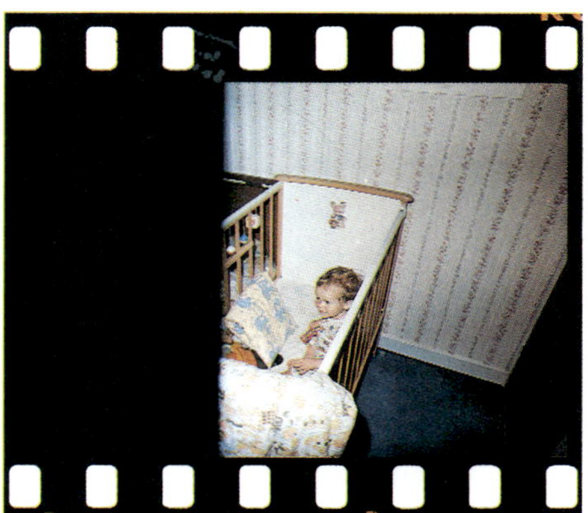

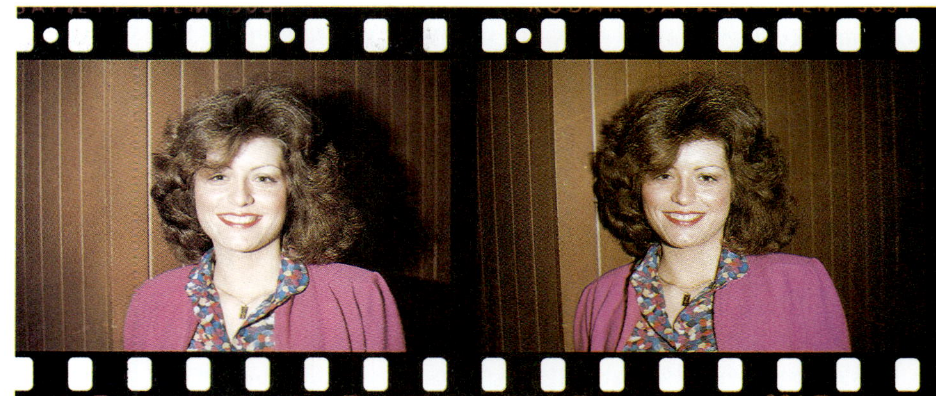

FLASH SYNCHRONIZATION

A focal-plane shutter uses a traveling slit to expose film. If you use too fast a shutter speed, only part of the frame would be exposed, as shown above.

You must expose film when the slit is as wide as the film frame. With horizontally-operating shutters, this happens at 1/60 second and slower. After uncovering the whole film frame, the first curtain triggers the flash, all of the film is exposed, then the second curtain moves to cover the film.

With vertically-operating shutters, the fastest flash sync speed is 1/90, 1/125 or 1/200 second. The camera shutter-speed dial usually indicates the fastest flash-sync speed.

DARK SHADOW

A camera-mounted flash gives almost front lighting. It clearly illuminates all front features of the subject, as shown above. Due to nearly front lighting, the subject casts a dark shadow on a nearby background. This happens because the flash is slightly beside and above the *lens axis*—the center line of the lens.

The shadow can add a confusing and unnecessary element into the photo. There are a few easy ways to eliminate it:

1) Move the subject away from the background, so the shadow falls out of the picture area.

2) Use a flash extension cord and hold the flash higher than the camera and pointing down. This way the subject casts a shadow behind and below the scene in view, as shown above.

3) Bounce the light from the ceiling or a nearby wall to create softer light. This kind of reflector spreads the light.

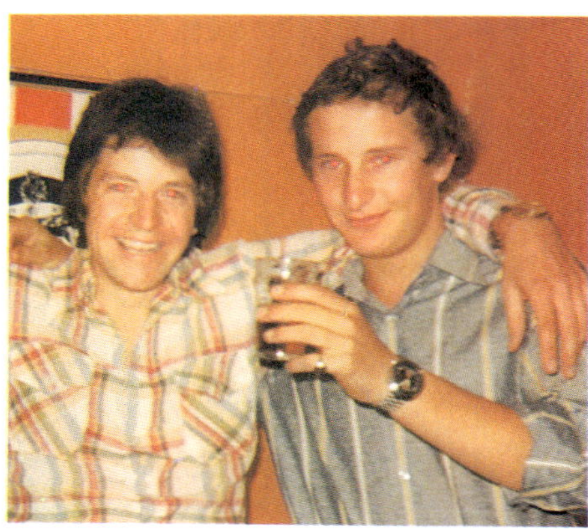

RED EYE

The above photo shows the effect called *red eye*. It happens when the flash is very close to the lens axis and the subject is looking directly into the lens. Light from the flash reflects from blood vessels in the person's retinas, recording on color film as red. The top drawing shows this. Usually, red eye occurs when you photograph in very dark conditions, when eye pupils are dilated.

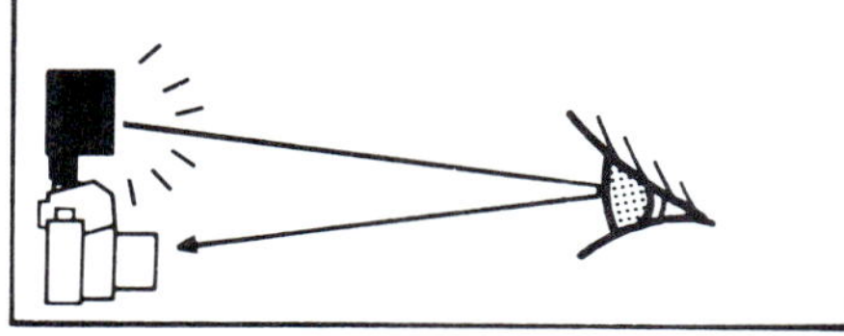

Avoiding Red Eye—If the flash window is not close to the lens axis, the reflection is out of the lens field of view, as shown in the bottom illustration. This happens naturally with some flashes mounted on-camera. Or, you can use a flash extension bracket and cord to move the flash up. The simplest solution is to ask the subject to look away slightly. Then you don't have to move the flash.

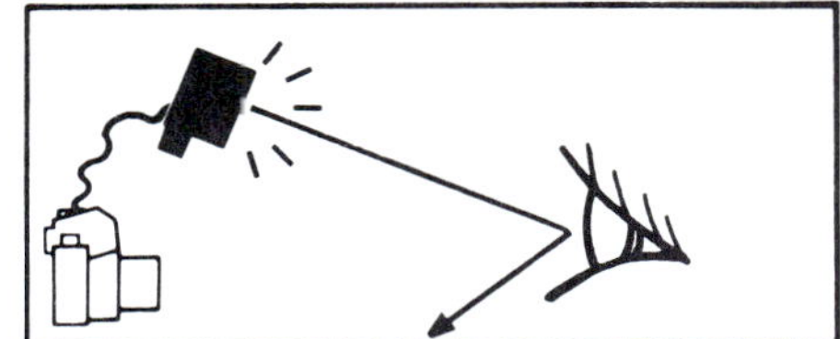

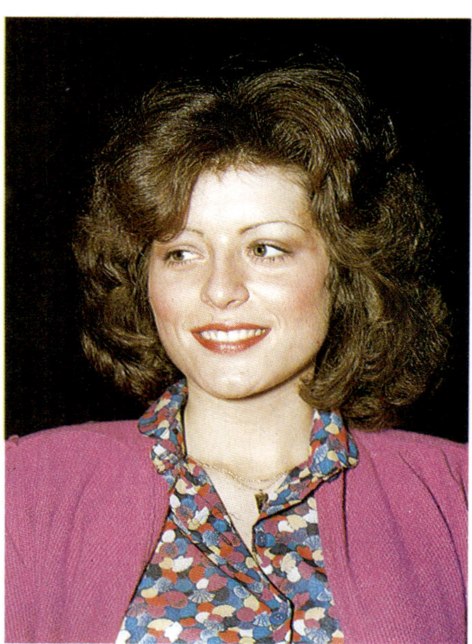

Controlling Electronic Flash

The previous section discussed basic operation of a manual or simple automatic flash. With either type of unit you can make good pictures. Flash and camera manufacturers also make units with many useful controls. Knowing how to use these lets you control flash lighting effects even more. This is essential due to the short flash duration, which prevents you from judging the lighting effect until you see a developed picture.

USING GUIDE NUMBERS

An easy way to calculate good exposure with manual flash is to use the flash guide number (GN). This number is the product of flash-to-subject distance (d)—in feet or meters—and the lens aperture (*f*-number) that gives good exposure with a certain film speed:

GN = *f*-number x d

Suppose GN is 56 for an ASA 100 film. If flash-to-subject distance is 10 feet, divide 56 by 10 to get lens aperture of *f*-5.6. This setting gives good exposure at 10 feet.

Or, if you want to use an aperture of *f*-4 for more shallow depth of field, divide 56 by 4 to get flash-to-subject distance of 14 feet. You can put the flash on the camera and stand 14 feet away, or put the flash on a light stand 14 feet from the subject. Remember, guide number is based on flash-to-subject distance, not camera-to-subject distance. The flash calculator dial would give the same recommendations as using GN calculations.

Flash manufacturers report a flash GN as an indicator of flash power. The higher the number, the more powerful the flash. Obviously, the GN also depends on the film speed. A GN for an ASA 25 film will be smaller than the GN for an ASA 100 film, assuming that actual flash power is the same. When you compare flashes by comparing guide numbers, be sure to consider the film speed.

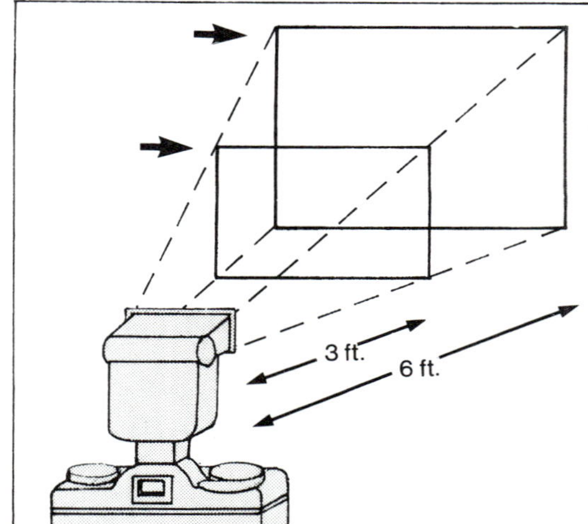

MORE ON FLASH FALL-OFF

Light spreads out as it travels farther. For example, as flash to subject distance doubles from 3 feet to 6 feet, the light covers an area four times as large. For good exposure at six feet, exposure must be four times as much. Opening lens aperture *two* steps is the way to do it. GN calculations show how this works. Suppose the GN is 48:

At 3 ft. *f*-number = 48/3 = *f*-16
At 6 ft. *f*-number = 48/6 = *f*-8

An *f*-8 aperture lets four times as much light (two steps) through the lens than an aperture of *f*-16.

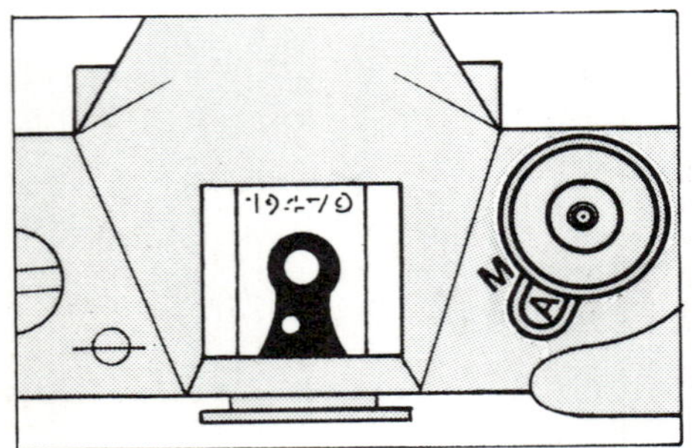

DEDICATED FLASH

Many current SLR cameras have one or more special flash units designed for them. These *dedicated flashes* connect to the camera hot shoe, shown above, and make an electronic connection to exposure controls.

What It Does—Typically, a dedicated flash automatically sets lens aperture and the fastest flash-sync speed for the camera. When you choose a distance range for automatic flash operation, the flash tells the camera what the appropriate aperture is. The camera sets it and shows it in the viewfinder display. In addition, some viewfinder displays indicate when the flash is charged and ready to use, and if you got good exposure in the automatic mode.

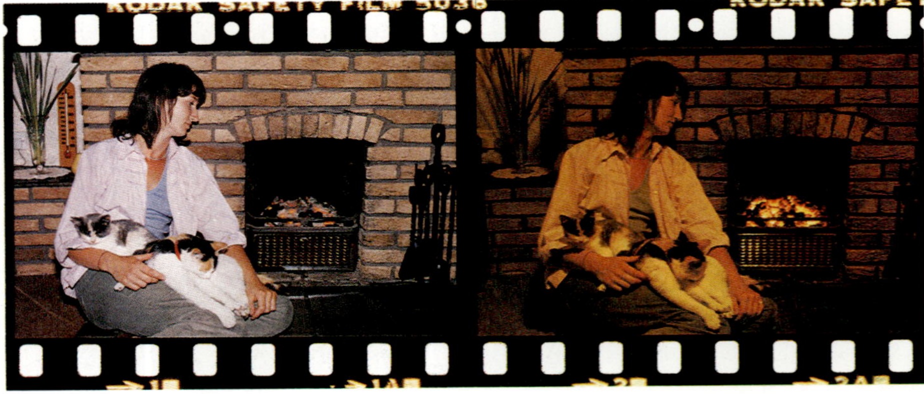

These convenient features help you avoid bad pictures. For example, after making a picture with natural light, you may forget to set the camera shutter-speed dial to a flash-sync speed for a flash picture. A dedicated flash does this automatically when you attach it to the camera and turn the flash on.

Or, you may forget to set lens aperture after setting the distance range of the flash calculator dial. Some dedicated flashes do this for you automatically.

The above two photos illustrate a mistake that can happen even with an automatic flash. The left-hand picture was well exposed by an auto flash. But the next frame was exposed before the flash had recycled, causing the camera to give an "available-light exposure." The orange cast is due to the warm roomlight that exposed the film.

If your dedicated flash-and-camera combination makes a flash-ready light glow in the viewfinder display, this won't happen to you.

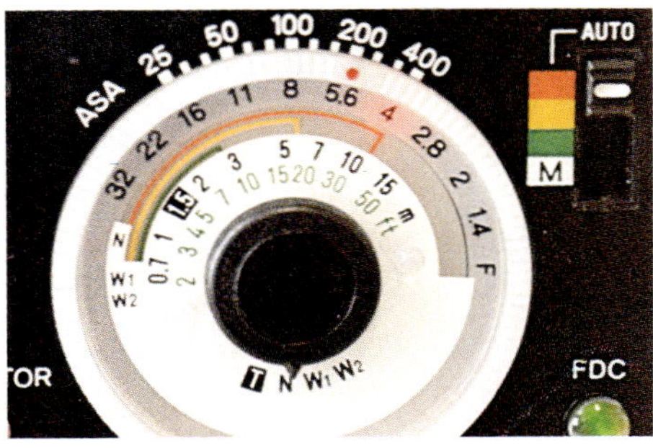

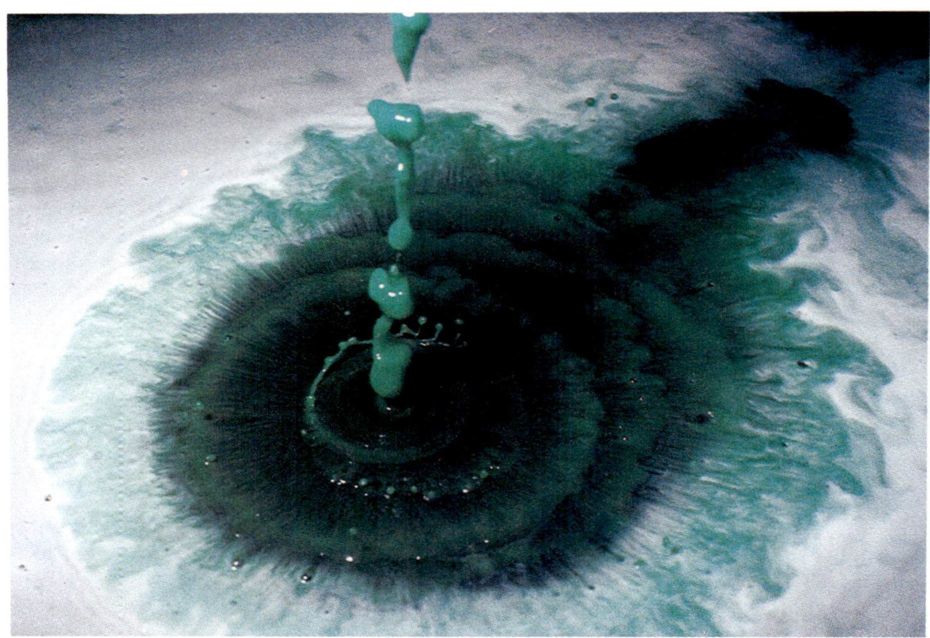

AUTO FLASH DISTANCE RANGES

Many current auto flashes have more than one distance range for automatic operation. A typical calculator dial for this kind of flash is shown above. If your subjects will be in a long distance range, up to 40 feet, you set the lens to *f*-4. This sets the flash for the farthest subject distance. If you photograph a subject that is much closer, the flash sensor automatically turns off the flash when it detects enough reflected light to indicate good exposure.

If the farthest distance in the range is closer, for example at 20 feet, then you can set the smaller lens aperture of *f*-8 for more depth of field.

Flash duration for close subjects is much shorter than with far subjects—sometimes as short as 1/20,000 second! This is how motion was stopped in the above photo. Less battery power per flash is used too. Manufacturers take advantage of this by using a flash circuit, called *thyristor,* that saves unused power for the next flash. This results in very quick recycling time.

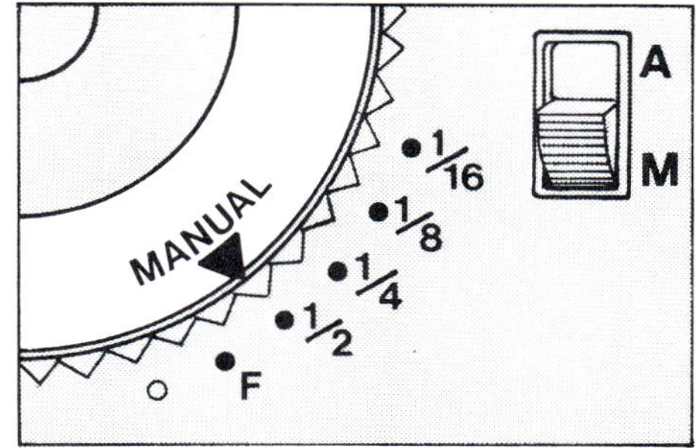

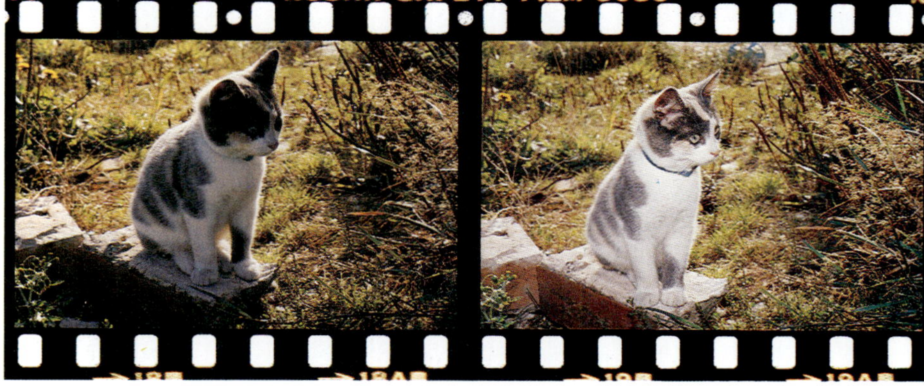

VARIABLE-POWER CONTROL

Some portable flash units have a control that lets you use less-than-maximum power in the auto or manual mode. As shown in the drawing, you can choose settings that decrease flash brightness in steps. This is sometimes helpful if you want to use a bigger lens aperture for shallow depth of field.

Or, you may want a fast recycling time. If each flash is of low power, then saved charging energy gets the flash ready almost right away for another burst of light. Use the 1/16 setting when using an autowinder to rapidly expose and advance film.

Turning the variable-power control also adjusts the calculator dial when used in the auto or manual mode. This helps guarantee that you won't underexpose film because you use less than full flash power.

Fill Flash—This is a useful technique for outdoor backlit scenes, such as the left-hand photo of the cat. You may want to clearly reproduce both background and foreground, instead of one being bright and the other dark. The solution is to brighten the dark foreground with fill light from a flash.

Set the camera's fastest flash sync speed. Meter the background light based on this speed. Determine aperture and set the lens. Set the flash to give one step less exposure than necessary for this aperture. Using a variable-power control lets you do this without changing viewpoint. This setting would "underexpose" the foreground subject with flash alone, but should give a good overall exposure, like the one at right. Bracket for best results.

Bounce-Flash Techniques

As described earlier, the size of the light source relative to subject distance determines certain lighting effects. A flash used on-camera is a small source because the flash window is small when compared to most subject distances. Typically, the subject casts dark shadows with hard edges. Flash used for side lighting emphasizes texture. These effects are not flattering with subjects like people. Look at the top left photo on the next page.

Increasing Source Size—Make a bigger source out of the flash. The easiest way is to bounce the light from a large pale surface, such as a wall or ceiling. Many portable flashes are designed for this application. They have tilting heads that can point directly at the subject, straight up, or at in-between angles. If your flash doesn't have a tilting head, use it off-camera and point it at the bounce surface.

As shown in the illustration, you tilt the flash window so the beam strikes the ceiling and reflects toward the subject. The bounce surface effectively becomes the light source. Because it is much bigger than the subject, softer more flattering light results. The light picks up color from the bounce surface. This can cause an unwanted color imbalance, as shown in the top right photo on the next page.

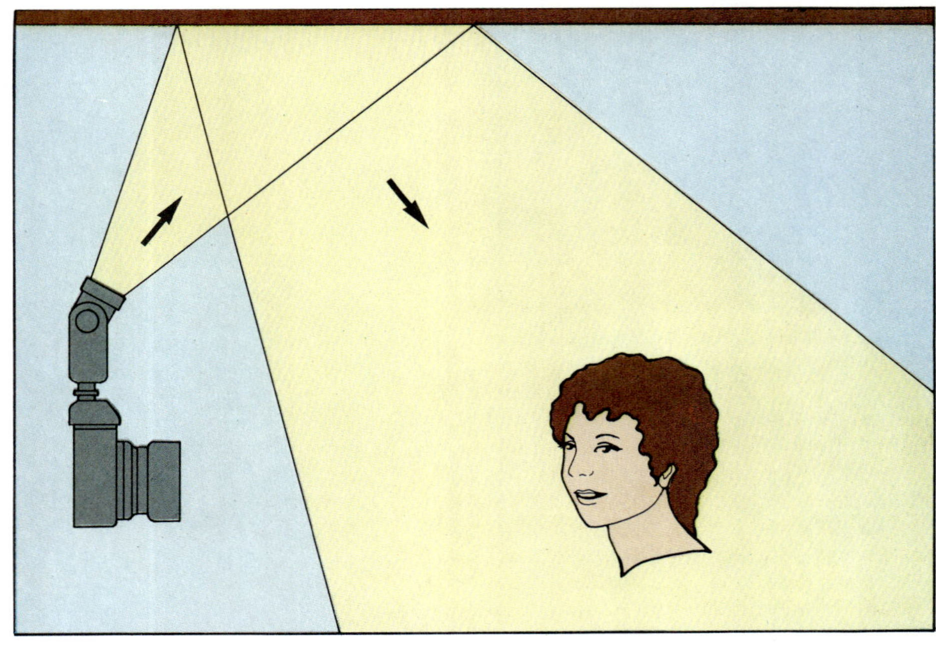

Flash-to-subject distance and angle of tilt are important. You don't want the reflected beam to miss the subject. Generally, you'll get the best lighting effect with a 45° tilt and a flash-to-subject distance about 1.4 times as far as flash-to-ceiling distance. Use bigger angles with closer subjects and smaller angles with farther subject.

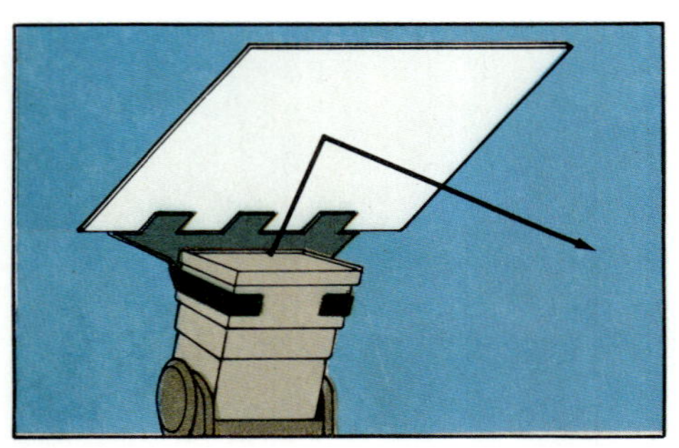

BOUNCE CARDS

Some tilting flashes have an accessory bounce card, shown above. This gadget or any portable white reflector is handy when the ceiling or wall is dark or far away.

Point the flash straight up and angle the bounce card. The angle of the card determines the direction of the reflected beam. Because the card is smaller than a wall or ceiling, the resulting light is not as soft.

The lighting direction is more frontal than from above. As shown in the photo at right, the effect can still be pleasing. An 8x12 inch white card was used as a portable reflector. Facial shadows are present, but they have soft edges and good detail.

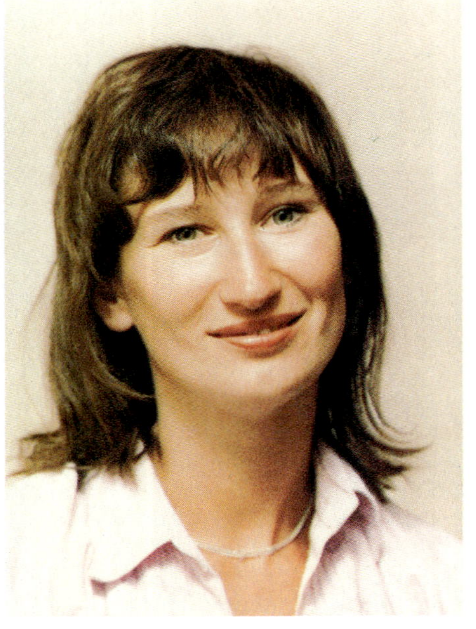

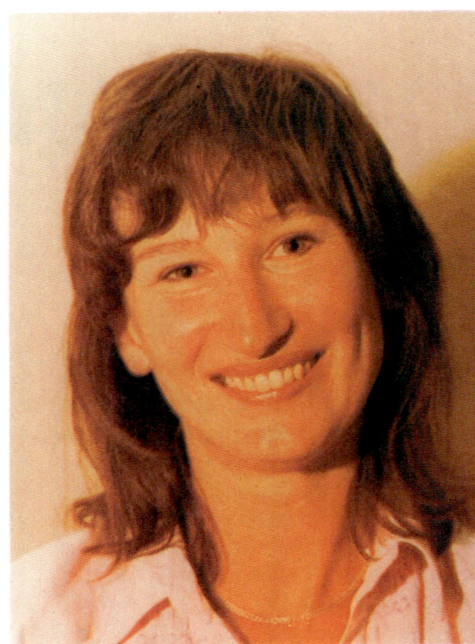

Don't use a brightly colored bounce surface or card when shooting color film. The reflected light picks up the color of the surface. This reproduces on film, as at right. Generally, a *slight* warm cast is acceptable in the image.

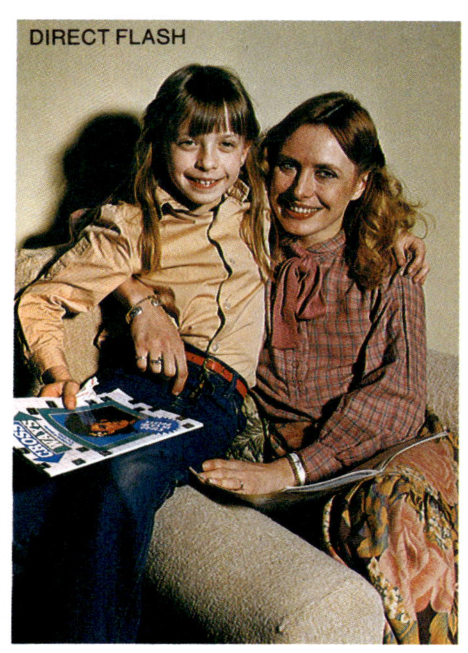

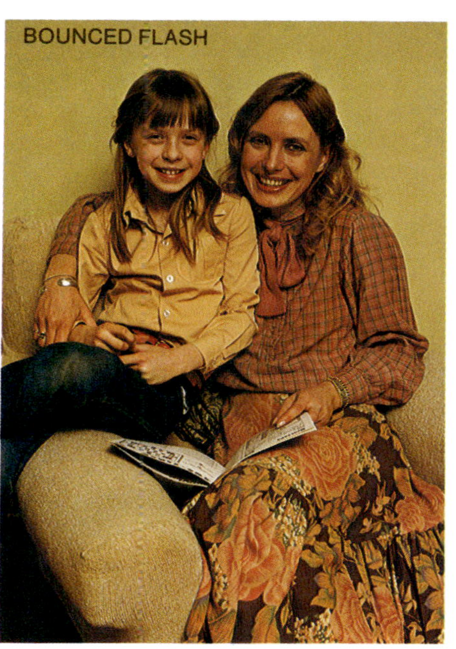

EXPOSURE CALCULATIONS

If the flash is mounted on the camera, using bounce flash makes flash-to-subject distance longer than camera-to-subject distance. Base exposure on the total distance the light travels—flash-to-bounce surface plus bounce surface-to-subject distance.

In addition, the bounce surface scatters and absorbs some of the light. Avoid underexposure by making an exposure correction.

How Much Correction?—Determine flash-to-subject distance by measuring or approximating flash-to-surface and surface-to-subject distances. Add them together. With a manual or automatic flash, use the flash GN or calculator dial to determine the initial aperture. Then correct for light scattering and absorption by opening the lens aperture *another* 1-1/2 to 2 steps.

The exact amount of correction depends on the nature of the bounce surface. The whiter and smoother the surface, the less correction necessary. Use one-step correction for smooth, bright white surfaces. With textured white ceilings and walls, use about 1-1/2 steps correction. Dirty or tinted surfaces require two-step adjustment.

If you use an automatic flash with a sensor pointed at the object, push the flash-test button before exposing film. A light will glow if the flash had enough power to make good exposure. If it didn't, adjust the flash for a longer distance range. Reset lens aperture based on this range.

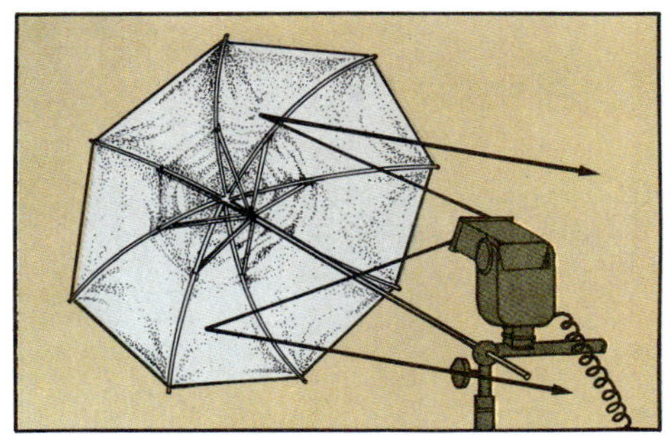

UMBRELLA REFLECTORS

For professional-quality pictures with a portable flash, consider using an umbrella reflector, shown above. These are available at camera stores. The flash points at the shiny inside surface of the reflector, which spreads out the beam to give soft, but directional lighting. Umbrellas designed for portable flash units create medium-source lighting effects, as shown in the portrait at right.

Use the flash off camera. Connect it to the camera with a flash extension cable. Unless your automatic flash has a detachable sensor that you can point at the subject, use the flash manually. Calculate flash-to-subject distance as described earlier.

Exposure correction depends on umbrella size, flash size and flash-to-umbrella distance. Shoot a test roll of slide film first to determine the proper exposure correction. Bracket with 1/2, 1, 1-1/2 and 2 *f*-stops of compensation for a variety of flash-to-umbrella distances. Take careful notes so you can repeat your best results.

Modeling Lamp—When using a flash and umbrella reflector, it's hard to judge the resultant lighting angle and shadow location. It's impossible to see these during the short flash duration.

Professional-quality flashes for umbrellas solve this problem by using a modeling lamp next to the flash tube. This tungsten lamp gives light constantly so you can see the lighting effect and adjust umbrella location for best effect.

Make your own modeling lamp for your umbrella by using a household light bulb in a standard bulb reflector. Hold it next to the flash and point it at the subject. You can then see how the lighting angle will look on film. Shadow darkness and edges will probably be different, however, because the two sources aren't the same size.

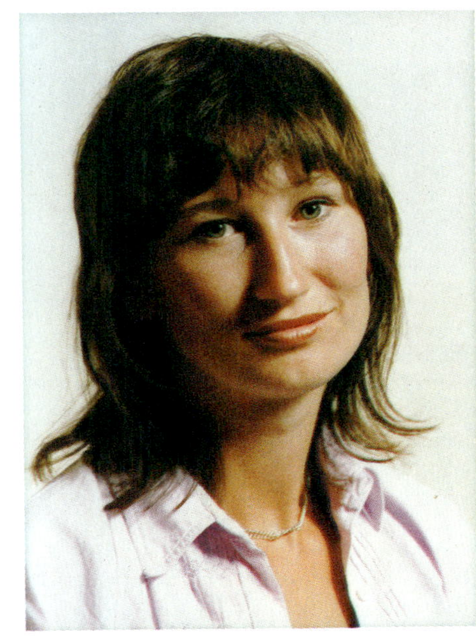

Special Flash Effects

When you're able to control flash lighting for good, natural-looking results, you'll probably want to try making some special-effect flash pictures. This is possible with many portable flashes and some special flash units and accessories. Some are pictured here.

STUDIO FLASH

At top left is a powerful, professional-quality studio flash that attaches to a stand, not your camera. The flash has a modeling lamp next to the flash tube. This model can be operated by batteries or with an AC cord you plug into your wall socket. The parabolic reflector on the flash body detaches, so you can attach light-shaping accessories that narrow the beam or spread it out for different lighting effects.

This kind of flash does not have an exposure-calculator dial. You determine exposure by using a handheld *flash meter* or metering the modeling lamp and making an exposure correction.

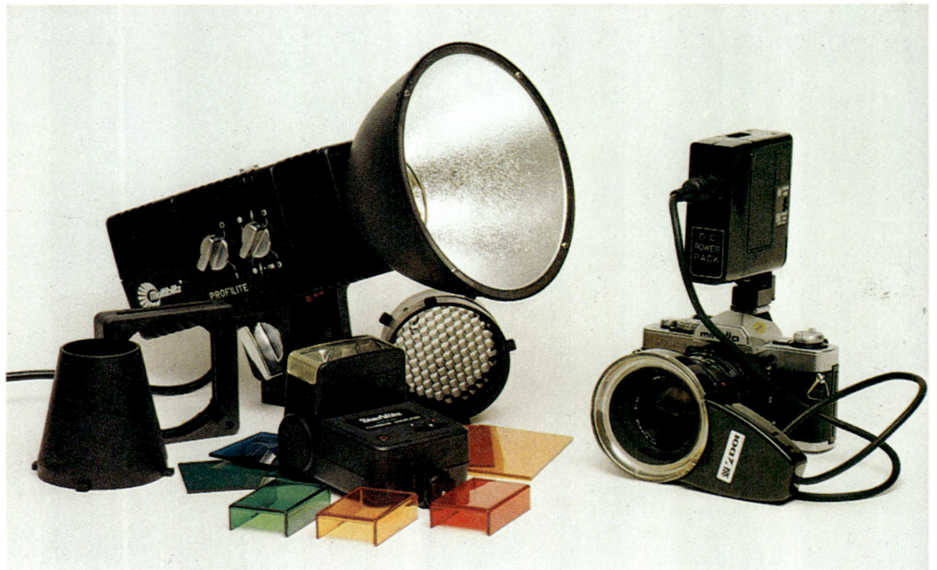

PORTABLE-FLASH ACCESSORIES

Many portable flashes can be used with accessories such as plastic filters, diffusers and lenses. Filters change the color of the light. Diffusers spread out the light for use with wide-angle camera lenses. Plastic lenses focus the light in a narrower beam to match the angle of view of a telephoto lens. This is useful for lighting a faraway subject photographed with a telephoto lens.

RING LIGHT

This special portable flash has a flash tube that surrounds the lens. Light from the flash is essentially on-axis, giving a lighting effect that is described on the next page.

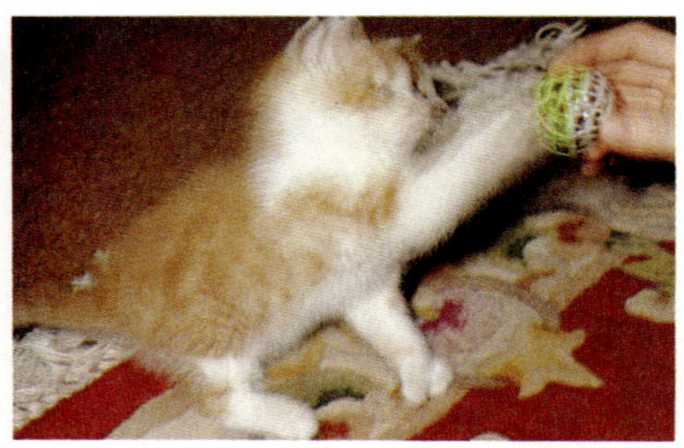

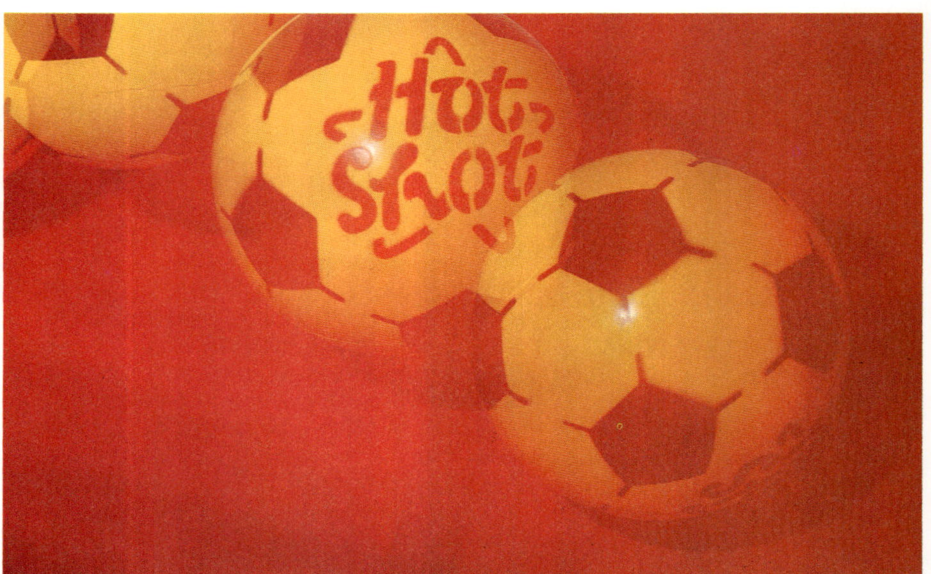

MULTIPLE-FLASH EFFECTS

If your auto flash has an energy-saving circuit, you can use it for exciting multiple-flash pictures of a moving subject. Each flash freezes part of subject motion, giving a *stroboscopic* effect.

Manually trigger the flash more than once while the shutter is wide open. Mount the camera on a tripod and set the shutter-speed dial to B or a shutter speed slower than one second. Darken room lights so ambient light doesn't affect exposure. Use a dark background.

For the fastest recycle time, use the largest aperture allowed by the flash and photograph a nearby subject. Open the shutter and *manually* trigger the flash two, four or eight times with the flash-test button. Close the shutter.

Exposure—The easiest way to get good exposure automatically with overlapping images, as in the cat photo, is to "trick" the flash in the following way: If making two exposures, set the flash film-speed dial to a speed that is twice actual film speed—set ASA 100 instead of ASA 50 for example. For four exposures double the setting again—to ASA 200 in this case. And for eight exposures, double it again—ASA 400. All exposures add to give a near-normal exposure.

When there is a dark background and little image overlap, as with the other photo, give full exposure to each image.

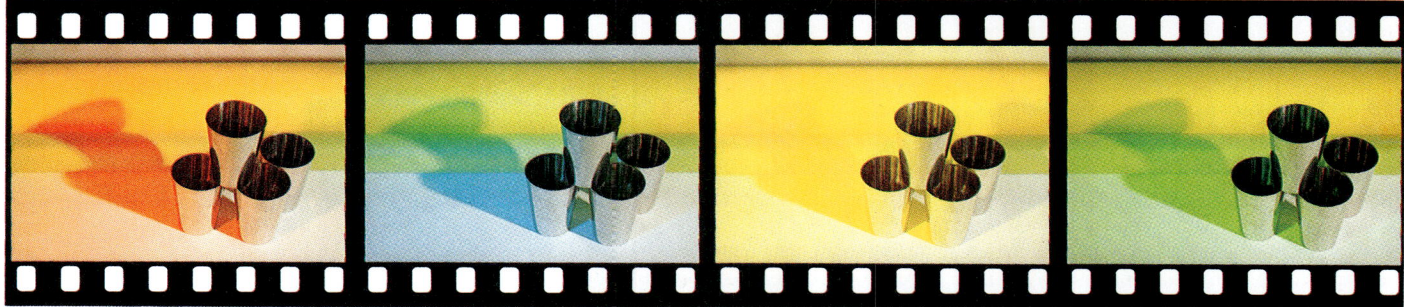

FILTERING FLASH

There are two ways to add creative color to scenes lit by flash. You can use a color filter over the camera lens or a color filter over the flash. This section describes the second case.

When you filter the flash, you can use practically any transparent colored material. It needn't have the optical quality of a lens filter. Colored acetate sheets work well. They are available from art-supply stores and come in a variety of colors. Cut one to size and tape it over the flash window. You can use more than one color over the window, but don't overlap colors unless you want to block a lot of light.

Some flash manufacturers make accessory filters for their flash models. Three filters are pictured at far right. The plastic filters clip over the flash window, coloring light produced by the flash.

Exposure Considerations—A colored filter absorbs light, coloring the light and making it less bright. Therefore, for good exposure you should correct for the light loss by opening lens aperture. Exactly how much more exposure is necessary depends on how dark the filter is.

If you use a pale filter, exposure correction may not be necessary. Colored light tints the scene. With dark filters, correction will be between one and two steps. Bracket for best results.

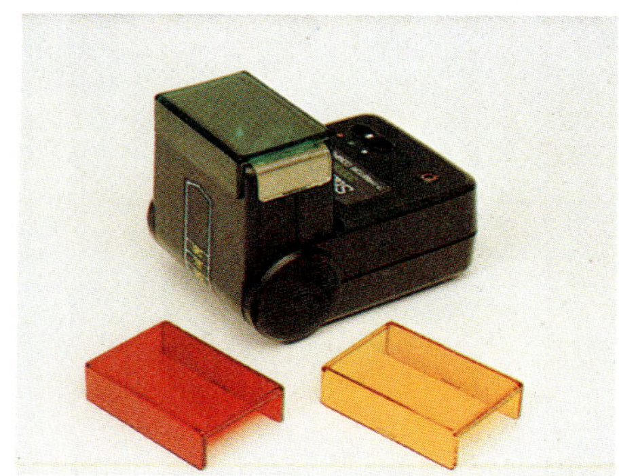

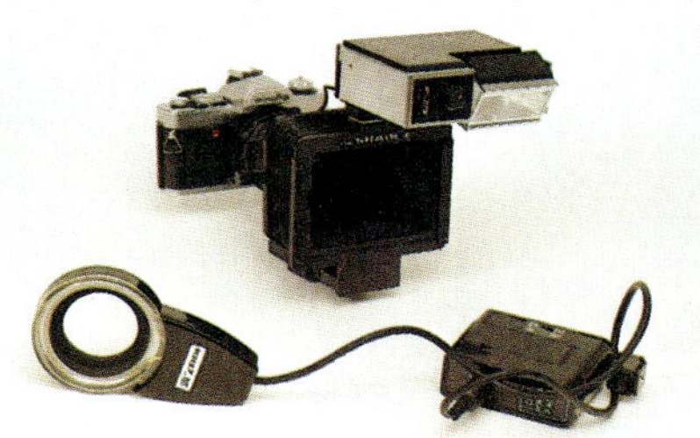

CLOSE-UP FLASH

If you light a close-up subject with a flash mounted on the camera hot shoe, the flash head may not be pointed accurately at the nearby subject. Much of the beam may miss it, and the image will be underexposed.

There are two ways to avoid the problem. One way is to tilt the flash at the subject. Use a flash with a tilting head and attach it to an adjustable lens shade, as shown in the above photo. This puts the flash close to the subject. The left photo of the cat was exposed with this setup. Exposure is good. But, because the flash pointed down, there are distinct shadows and the background is dark.

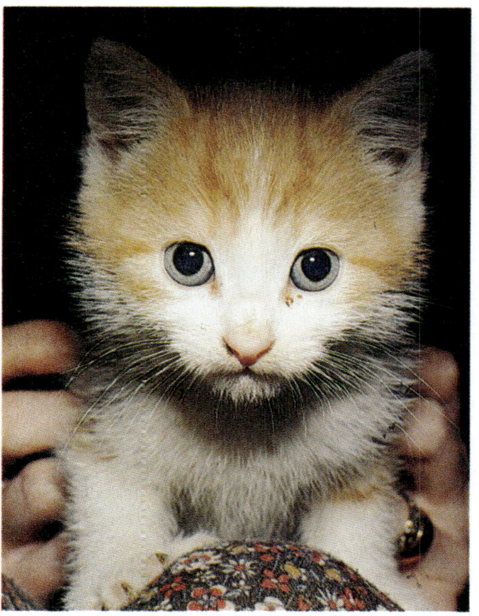

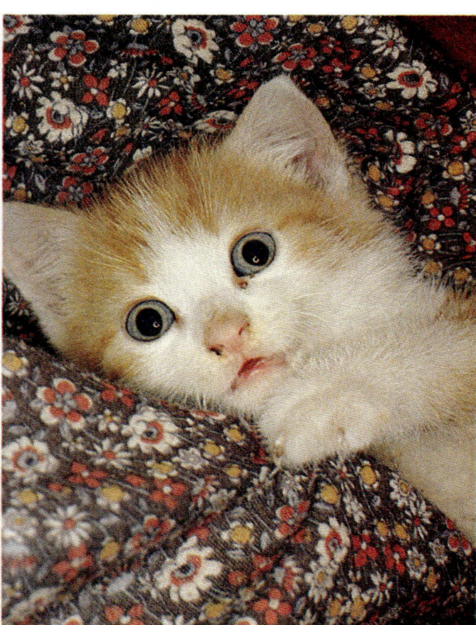

You can get better results with a ring flash, also shown in the photo above left. Because the flash tube surrounds the lens, it is practically on-axis. Front lighting is even and the subject hides its shadow. See the second cat photo. Notice that texture is less obvious, too.

Color Control with Filters

Color temperature is a way of expressing the mix of red, blue and green in a light source. The lower the color temperature, the redder the light. The higher the color temperature, the bluer the light. Daylight-balanced films are balanced for 5500K light—the approximate color of midday daylight and electronic flash. 3200K and 3400K are the color temperatures of photographic tungsten lamps. Tungsten-balanced color films are balanced for one or the other.

If color film is used with a light of a lower color temperature than it was designed for, a reddish color cast results. If used with a higher color temperature light, a bluish cast is reproduced on film.

FILTERS FOR COLOR FILM

Avoid these color casts when using imbalanced film and lights by using a *color-conversion* or *light-balancing filter* over the camera lens. Exposure correction is necessary for good exposure. A TTL meter does this automatically.

A bluish (80-series) filter absorbs reddish light so you can use daylight-balanced film with a tungsten lamp and still get good color balance. Conversely, use a yellowish (85-series) filter when shooting tungsten-balanced film in daylight or with flash.

COLOR CONVERSION AND LIGHT BALANCING FILTERS															
← Filters increasingly bluish (to raise color temperature of light)								Filters increasingly red-yellowish (to lower color temperature of light) →							
Color conversion filters				Light balancing filters				Light balancing filters						Color conversion filters		
80A	80B	80C	80D	82C	82B	82A	82	81	81A	81B	81C	81D	81EF	85C	85	85B
2	1-2/3	1	1/3	2/3	2/3	1/3	1/3	1/3	1/3	1/3	1/3	2/3	2/3	1/3	2/3	2/3
Exposure Correction Factors																

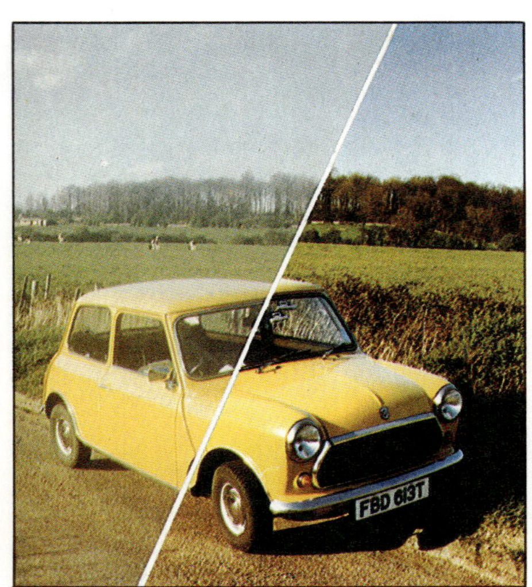

CUTTING HAZE

With a *skylight filter,* which is slightly pink, you can cut through haze and absorb some excess ultraviolet (UV) radiation and blue light. These reproduce on color film as shown in the left half of the photo. The right half shows a filtered result. A skylight filter is helpful with b&w film too.

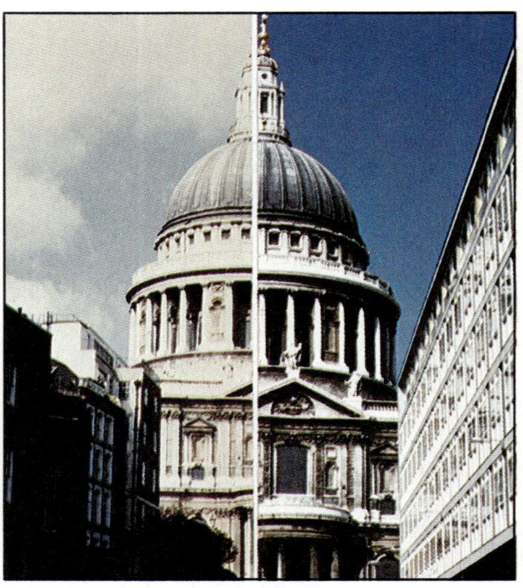

STRONGER COLORS

A *polarizing filter* can help you get stronger colors. See right half of photo. The filter has maximum effect on sky areas that are 90° to the sun.

After attaching the filter to the lens, rotate it and view the effect in the viewfinder. Take the picture when you like the effect. Check your camera instruction manual to see if your camera can meter through the filter. Not all can.

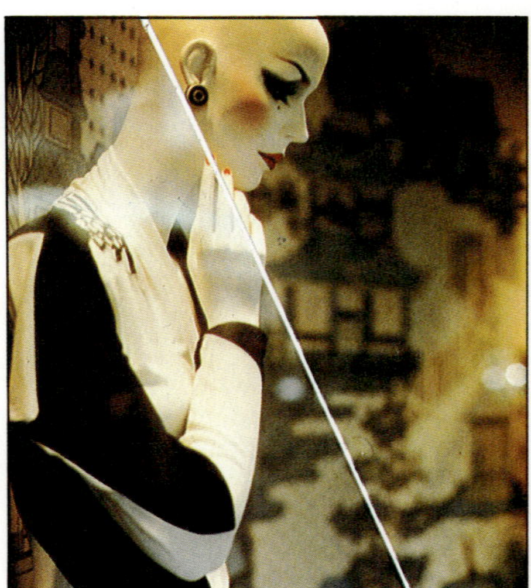

CUTTING REFLECTIONS

You can also use a polarizing filter to eliminate unwanted reflections. The left half shows an unfiltered picture. The right half was filtered. The effect is strongest when you are about 35° to the surface. Rotate the filter for best results.

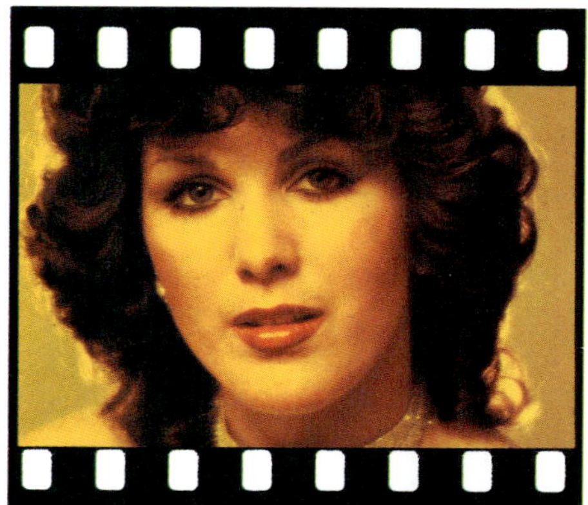

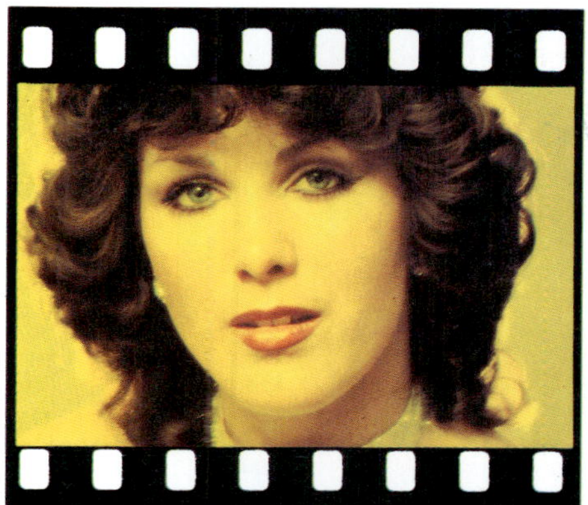

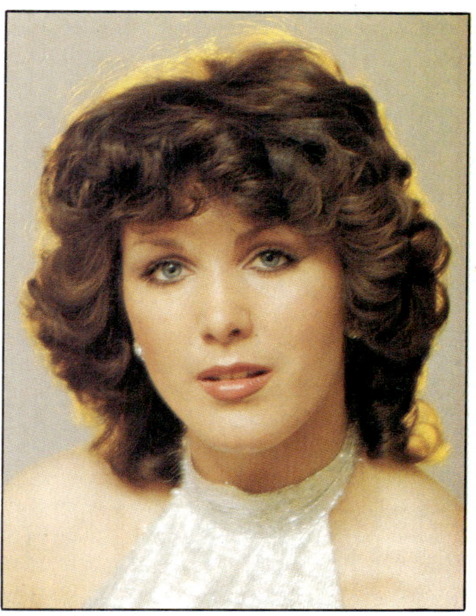

AVOIDING AN ORANGE CAST

The photo above was made using daylight film with tungsten light. The excess red in the light creates an objectionable color cast in the image.

If you shoot daylight film under 3200K tungsten light, use a blue 80A filter. It absorbs two steps of light. When using 3400K light, use a blue 80B filter.

Household tungsten lamps have a color temperature of about 2800K. There is no standard light-balancing filter to use with daylight film. If you use the 80A, most but not all of the excess red is absorbed. The leftover creates a slight orange cast. This may create an appealing warm mood in the picture.

FLUORESCENT LIGHT

Because of the way they make light, fluorescent tubes can't be assigned a color-temperature value. They create some "spikes" of light in certain colors. We don't notice them, but color film does. Typically, the result is a bluish-green cast on daylight color film, as in the center photo.

Avoid this color cast by using an amber-colored light-balancing filter. It gives life-like color balance when you shoot daylight film under general-purpose fluorescent bulbs, as shown above. This kind of filter has different names, such as FLD, FL-D or FL-DAY.

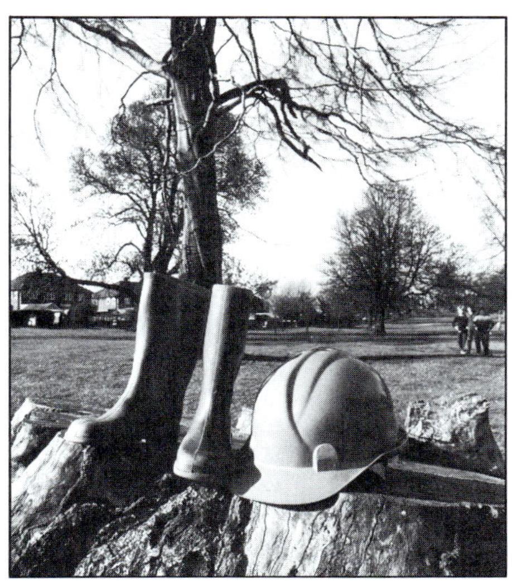

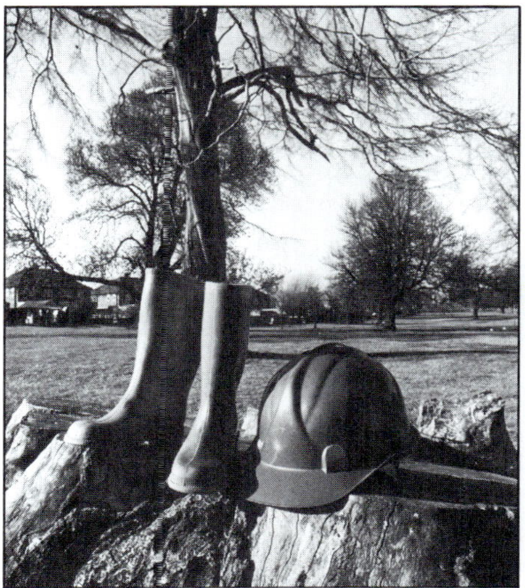

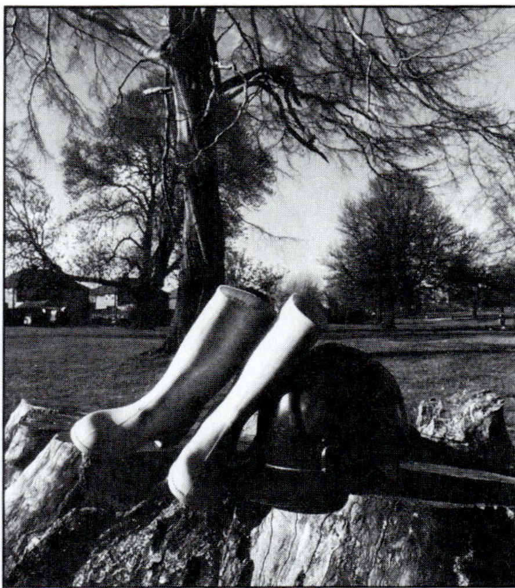

FILTERS FOR B&W FILM

Polarizing, skylight and some other filters can also be used with b&w film. You can also use color filters with b&w film. These filters change tone reproduction, letting you adjust the way tones contrast in the picture.

A color filter lightens objects of its color and darkens all others. For example, a yellow filter makes a lemon reproduce lighter than usual in the print, and makes a blue sky darker so it contrasts well with white clouds.

The photo at left was unfiltered. The boots are red, the hardhat blue, and the grass green. The center photo was shot through a yellow filter. Notice that the hardhat is darker. Other things changed slightly because the filter was pale yellow. A darker yellow filter would have changed them more.

The photo at right was shot through a 25A dark red filter. This lightened the boots dramatically and darkened the sky, hardhat and green grass.

Filters & Lens Accessories for Special Effects

Usually, you'll use a filter to correct some problem and make the best possible image. In this case, filter technique is not obvious to the viewer of the picture, who may like the picture, but not have any idea of what you did to make it good.

When you use a filter for a special effect, however, filter technique is usually apparent. The viewer knows something is different and can assume that you used a special accessory for the effect. When using filters and accessories for a special result, your challenge is to make the effect appropriate to the picture content.

FILTER OR LENS ACCESSORY?

A filter absorbs light. This usually necessitates exposure correction. A *lens accessory* performs some kind of optical trick, like making star patterns or diffusing the image. Exposure correction is usually unnecessary. A small selection of filters and lens accessories is shown here.

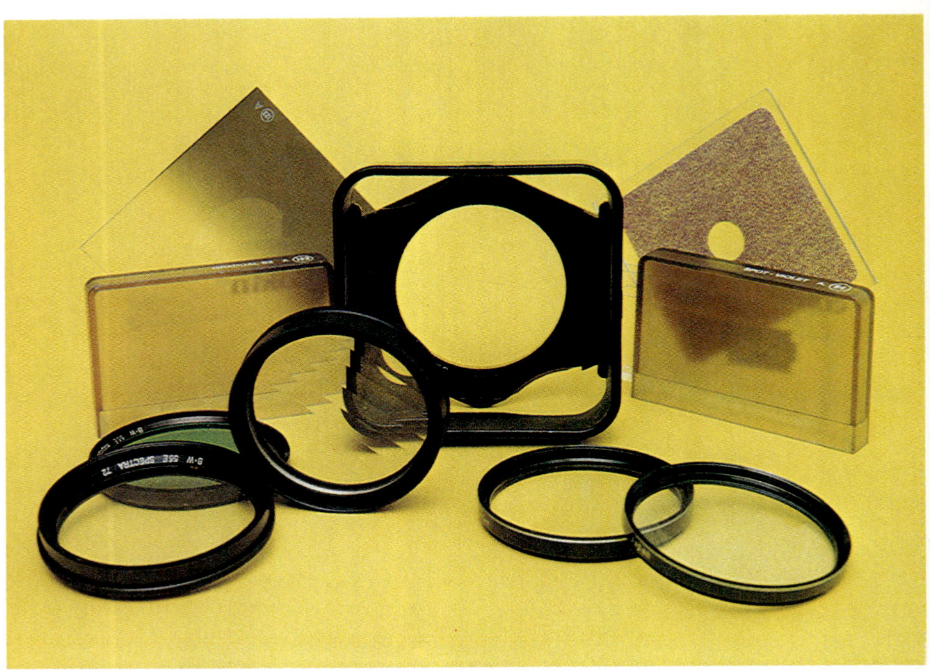

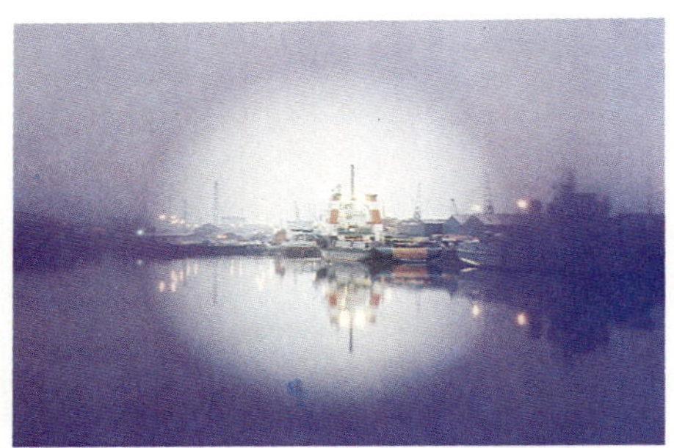

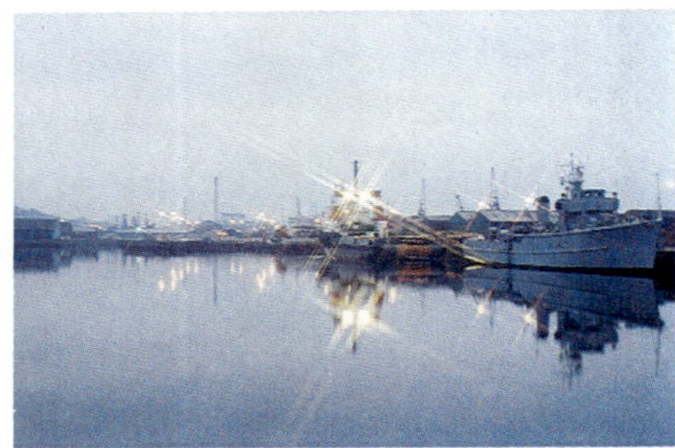

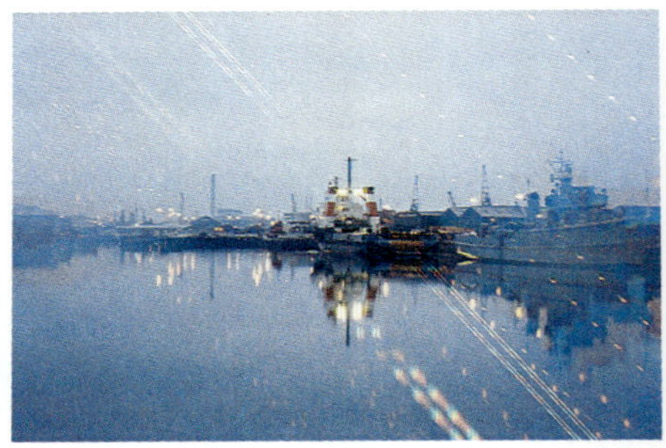

SPOT FILTERS

This is the common name for a colored filter with a clear central area. The effect is to emphasize the center of the image and subdue the rest with color.

The sharpness of the central circle's outline depends on lens aperture. The smaller the aperture, the sharper the circle, and vice-versa. This picture was made at *f*-8. Check the effect before you shoot by previewing depth of field. Spot filters are available in glass or plastic.

STAR MAKERS

Some people also call these lens accessories *cross screens* because a finely etched cross-screen pattern turns small bright highlights into star-like images, as shown above. This also causes slight image diffusion, but generally, it's not a bad effect.

Many kinds are available in glass and plastic. You can get star makers to make four-, six- or eight-pointed stars. Some rotate so you can orient the direction of the star lines any way you want. Generally, you'll get the best star effect with scenes having a medium-toned background.

COLOR-BURST

This accessory makes a small rainbow-like pattern out of a small bright highlight. The above photo was made with a color-burst accessory that creates a line pattern. You can also get color-burst lens accessories that give circular patterns.

The effect works best with small highlights in a predominantly dark field. It separates the light into its component colors. White light becomes a red, blue and green pattern. Yellow light is separated into its components red and green.

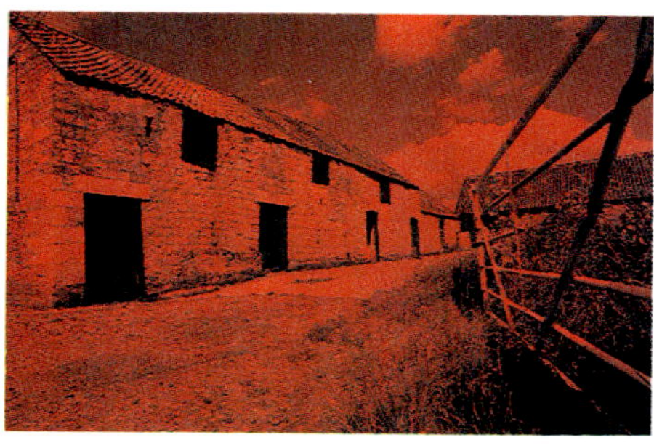

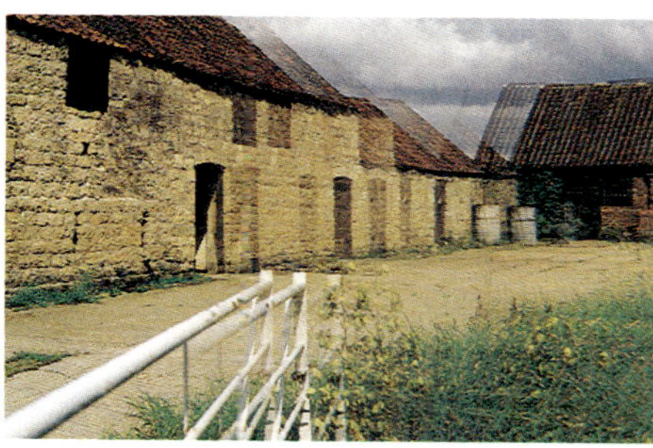

WHAT'S AVAILABLE

A huge variety of filters and lens accessories is available from your camera dealer. This section mentions only a few popular ones. Each filter and accessory manufacturer may have a different name for each type.

Glass—You can buy glass screw-in filters of different colors and sizes. Screw-in lens accessories are available too. The red photo above shows one creative way to use a red 25A filter with color film. The filter adds red to the whole picture.

In addition, you'll find glass diffusers, multiple-image makers and more. The other photo on this page shows how a *linear* multiple-image maker affects the picture. In this case three overlapping images are produced. You can also get a circular multiple-image maker. It gives three, five or six repetitive images around the central subject.

Filter System—A recent photographic innovation is a *filter system.* These are made by Cokin, Ambico, Hoya and others. You attach a plastic holder to the threads at the front of the lens. A holder is shown on the previous page with some other elements of the system.

The holder secures one or more plastic filters or lens accessories in front of the lens. You can move the filter or accessory up or down to get just the right effect.

Each filter system contains colored filters, diffusers, multiple-image makers, star-pattern makers, graduated filters and many more individual pieces that can improve your special-effect pictures.

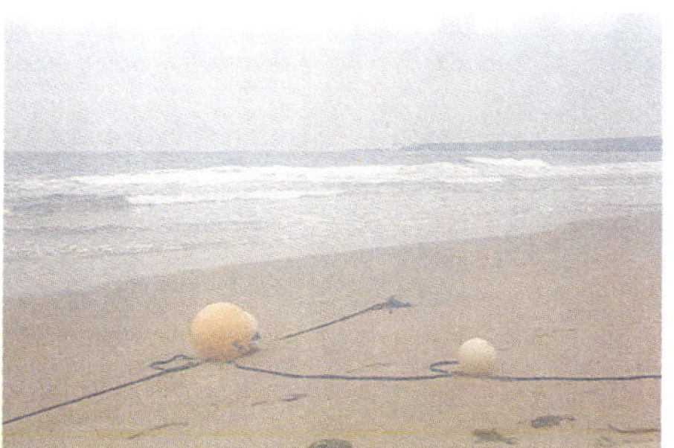

FOG ACCESSORY

Use this accessory if you want to add haze or fog effects to an otherwise clear scene. It makes the scene look misty and softens colors and tones, making it suitable for "moody" landscapes.

For best results, bracket exposures when using the fog filter. Slight overexposure may contribute an exagerrated misty effect. Fog accessories are available in glass and plastic and are also called *pastel filters.*

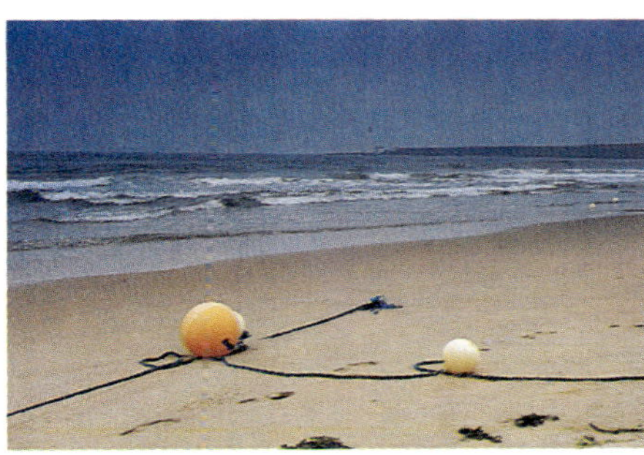

GRADUATED FILTERS

There is a gradual density or color transition between the two halves of the filter. This lets you selectively darken or color part of the picture area. A blue graduated filter was used for the above photo to make the sky dark blue.

Meter the scene without the filter in place. Use the recommended exposure settings or your best interpretation of the settings for exposing through the filter. Then put the filter in the holder and adjust it to give the effect you want.

If you use an aperture of *f*-8 or bigger, the transition between clear and colored areas is unnoticeable. Smaller apertures give a more abrupt transition. Check this effect by previewing depth of field.

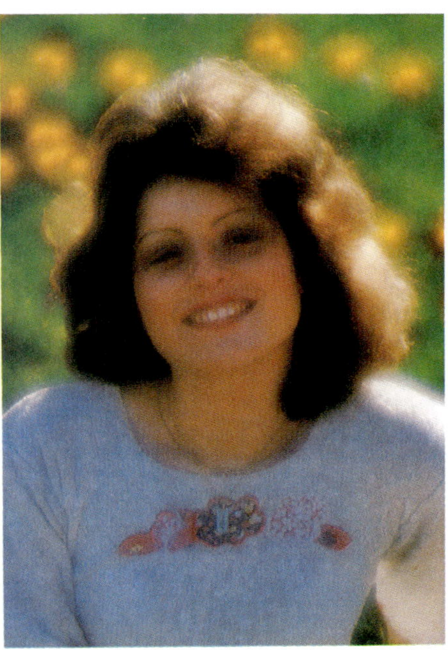

SOFT FOCUS

A soft-focus accessory spreads highlights into darker areas. Use one to make romantic-looking portraits.

Composing Better Photos

Making good pictures requires sound technical and artistic decisions. Most of the ideas presented in this book up to now help you make correct technical decisions—exposure, focusing, lens selection and so on. A good composition is useless if the picture is technically bad.

The rest of this book discusses creative considerations for making better photos. Some photographers say that this is more difficult than the technical part. Whether you agree or not, it should be obvious by now that good pictures don't happen accidentally. They happen when you control camera and subject to record what you want to see in the image.

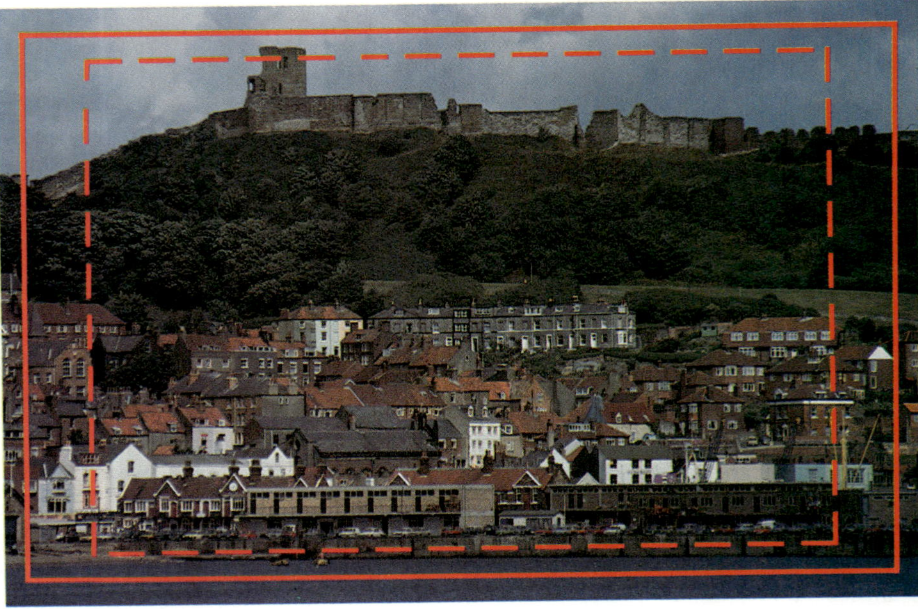

CAREFUL FRAMING

When you view a scene through the camera viewfinder, you automatically exclude part of the overall scene. Knowing what to exclude is just as important as knowing what to include. This is why you should carefully scan all of the image in the camera viewfinder before exposing film.

Most camera viewfinders show between 90% and 98% of the total picture area—indicated by the area inside the solid red line above. What you don't see approximates what the cardboard slide mount masks in a processed slide.

If you have prints made commercially from negatives, the crop is usually even farther in—as indicated by the dashed red line. Some labs offer full-frame prints, but most don't do it without special request. Either way, you should be aware of what will be *cropped* as compared to what you see in the viewfinder.

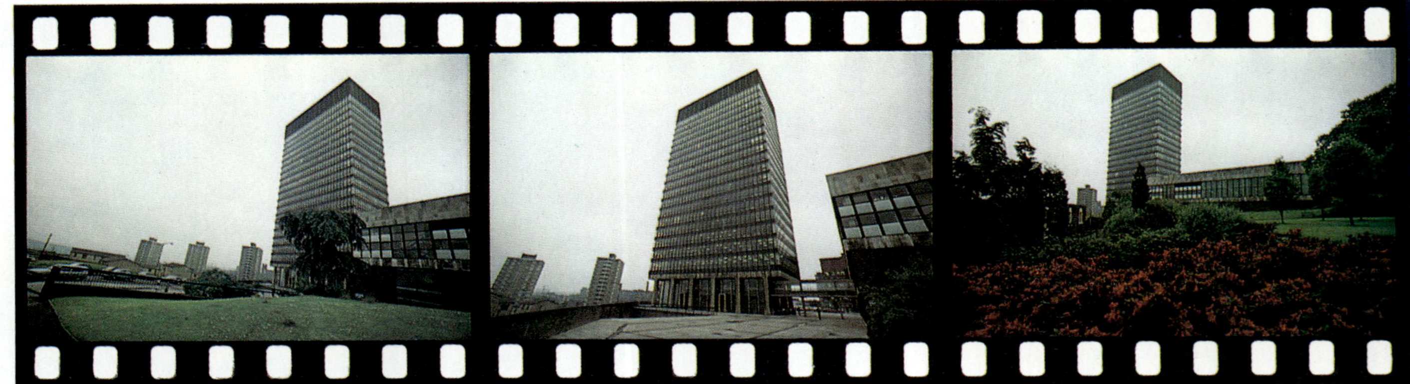

BALANCE

Most elements in a picture should be balanced, level, or oriented as we usually see them. For example, for the above right photo, the photographer tried to keep one edge of the building parallel to the side of the frame. This made the distant horizon no longer horizontal. This disadvantage outweighs any advantage gained in the way the foreground building looks.

In the middle photo, the horizon is level. Notice that vertical lines converge and buildings seem to lean. This is a characteristic of photographing tall things by tilting the camera. Even so, the effect is more pleasing than in the first photo.

Avoiding Converging Verticals—Back up to keep the camera back parallel to the building and still get all of it in view. This is sometimes easier said than done. And even if you can do it, there may be big empty spaces between you and your main subject.

Balancing Masses—For the above right photo, the photographer moved far away for a flattering view of the building. He used foliage to fill the foreground part of the frame. He balanced masses and filled the frame. You may have to use a different lens, shoot from ground level or use the camera for a vertical-format picture.

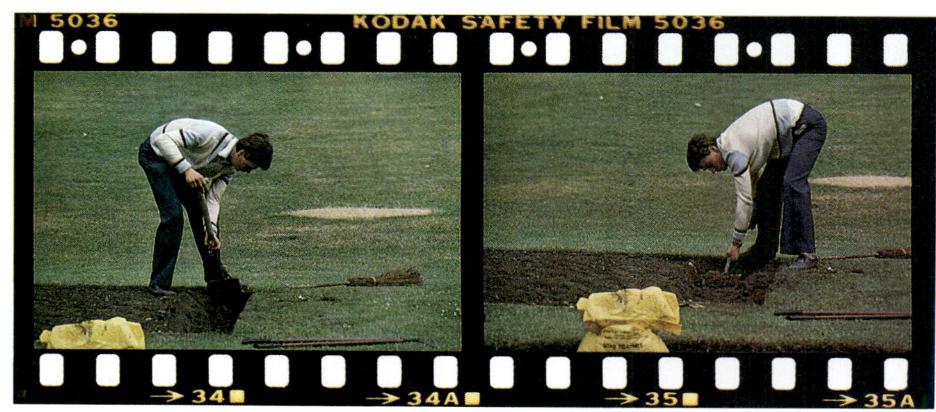

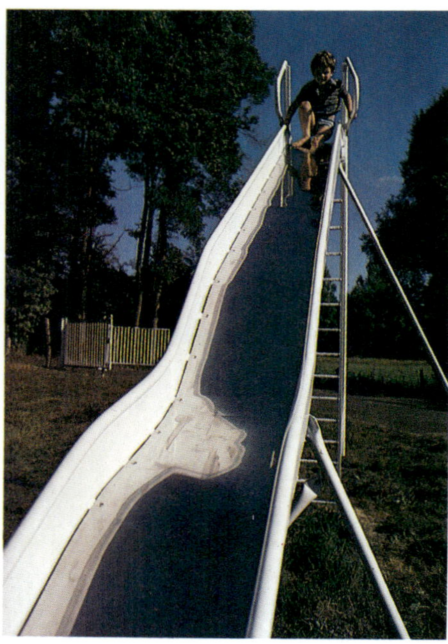

POSITIONING THE MAIN SUBJECT

The location and size of the main subject are important. If it is too small or in the wrong place, the viewer may not realize that it is your main subject. If it is too big, it may not relate well to other less important elements. Generally, other factors in the scene should support the main subject, completing the story conveyed by the subject.

You should also consider in which direction the subject faces. We usually scan things from left to right because this is the way we read. If the subject faces right our eyes are directed out of the picture away from the main subject. If the subject faces left, our eyes are stopped. They then concentrate on the main subject.

Check this effect with the photos of the gardener. Don't look at them at the same time, however. Cover one, then the other.

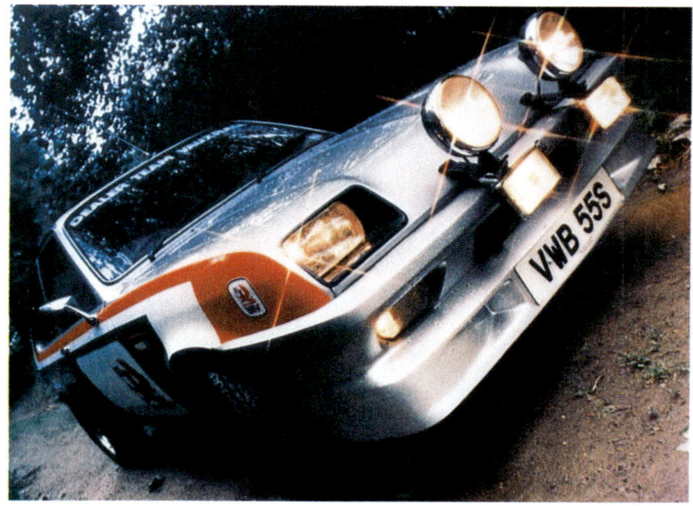

BREAKING THE RULES

Rules of composition are not absolute laws. Creative photographers sometimes break them to make an effective picture. The image of the sports car is a good example. The photographer deliberately made the subject unbalanced by using a low viewpoint and turning the camera, giving an impression of movement to an otherwise static subject.

Notice that the effect is exaggerated. A slight imbalance might be seen as a compositional fault, not as creative control.

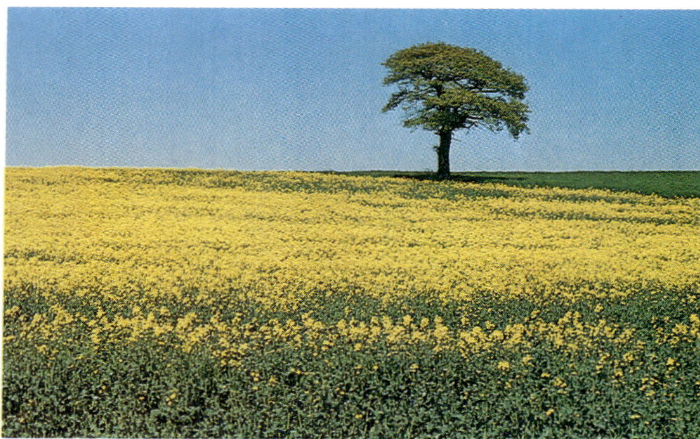

THE CLASSIC APPROACH

Painters traditionally have used the *rule of thirds* as a compositional tool to present a scene attractively. They divide the scene into thirds horizontally and vertically and locate main subject features near these divisions. The tree in the above photo is located where these vertical lines intersect.

This rule is useful with just about any scene. But break the rule when necessary, to get the best image.

Seeing in Color

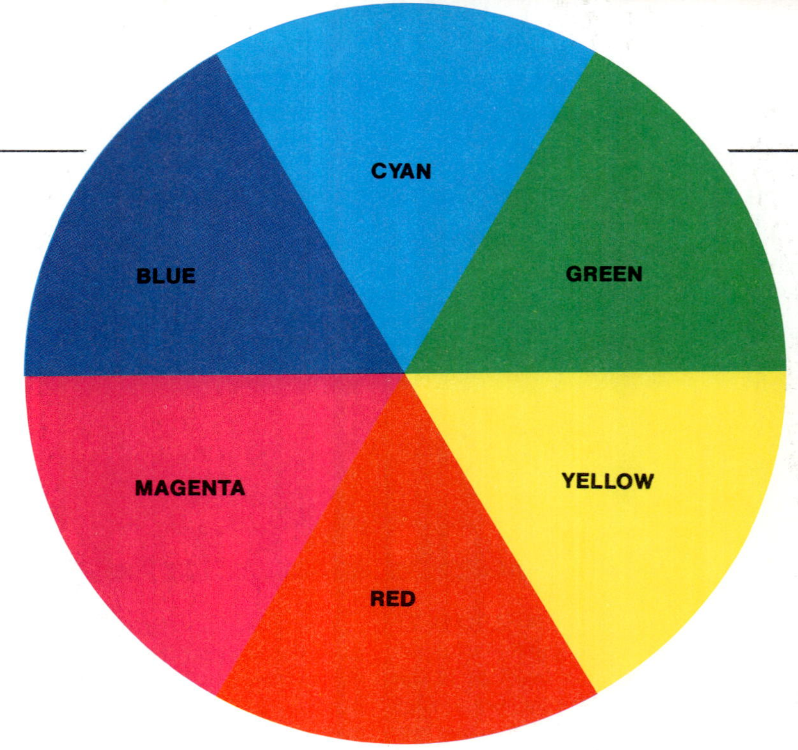

You can improve the impact of your color photos if you know the three basic ways that colors interact. They *contrast, harmonize* or *clash*. Generally, these reactions depend on where the colors are in the *color wheel,* shown at right. This is the range of colors that make white light, like sunlight.

Colors can be divided into two categories—*primary* and *complementary*. The primary colors of light are red, blue and green. Complementary colors are cyan, magenta and yellow. Artists working with pigments define primary colors differently.

The color wheel shows harmonizing colors next to each other. For example, yellow and green harmonize. Contrasting colors are separated by another color. Magenta and yellow contrast. Clashing colors are opposite each other, such as red and cyan. With this color wheel, clashing colors are *complements* of each other. Red and cyan, blue and yellow, and green and magenta are complements.

COLOR QUALITIES

These rules for contrast, harmony and clashing are generally true, but not always. Sometimes, such as on a hazy day, colors that normally contrast—such as blue and green—will harmonize. This happens because the strength of the colors are reduced. The strength or impact of color depends on these three factors—*hue, saturation* and *brightness*.

Hue is what distinguishes one color from another—green from yellow, for example. *Saturation* is the purity of the hue. A saturated red, for example, is composed only of pure red. No other colors are noticeable. *Brightness* is what we talk about when we say something is light or dark. A bright color seems to reflect more light than a dark one.

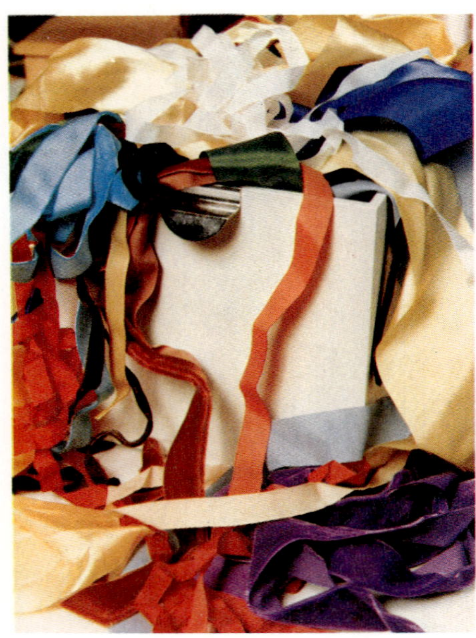

COLOR AS SUBJECT

This is an example of a composition that is interesting because of its varied colors. The subjects are ordinary—ribbons and a box—but it doesn't matter. Bright colors make the image good.

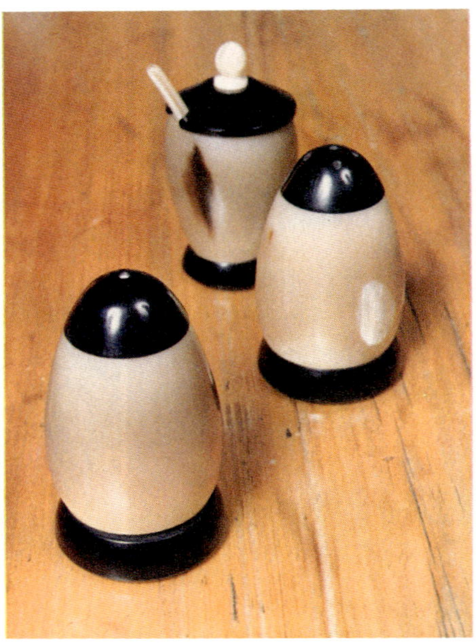

COLOR HARMONY

The warm brown tones of these elements harmonize and give a quiet, subdued feeling to the image.

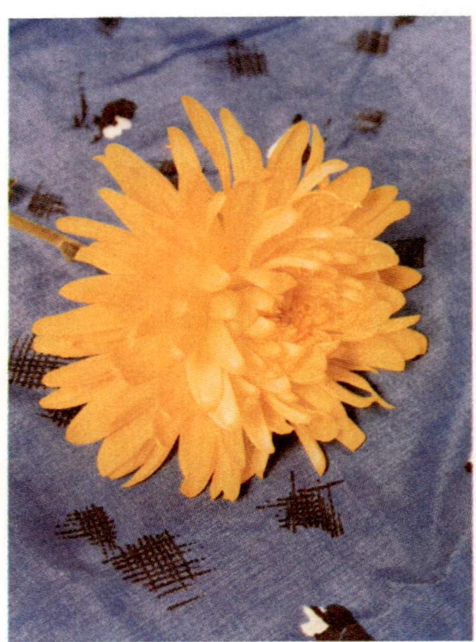

COLOR CONTRAST

Contrasting colors add depth to a picture. The redder of the two colors will seem closer than the other. Therefore, the redder color should be in the foreground.

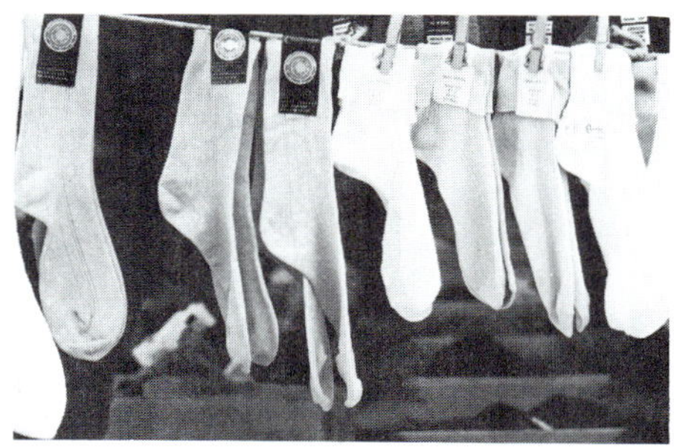

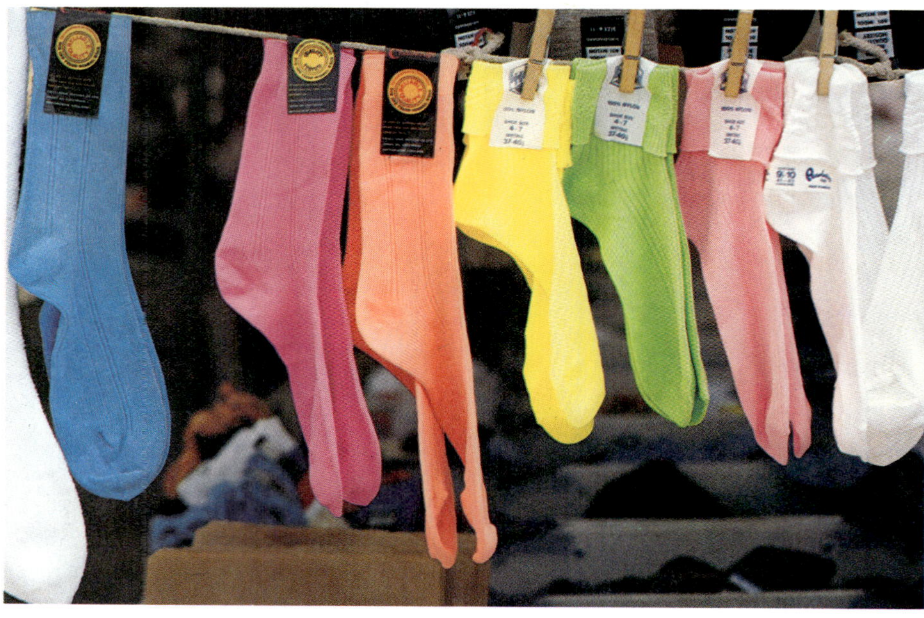

Hues shown in the color wheel are fully saturated, pure colors. They would be desaturated by the addition of white. Adding white (light) makes them pale, producing a pastel *tint.* Adding black by shading a color gives a *shade.*

A hazy day desaturates colors because of white haze between your eyes and a distant color. Color harmony is more likely with desaturated colors.

B&W OR COLOR?

The two photos above show that some scenes look great in color and boring in b&w. If you are attracted to a scene because of its colors, use color film. Save b&w film for scenes that have interesting tonal effects.

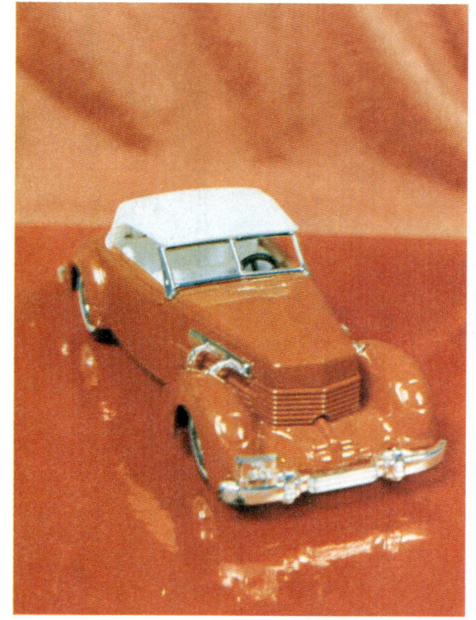

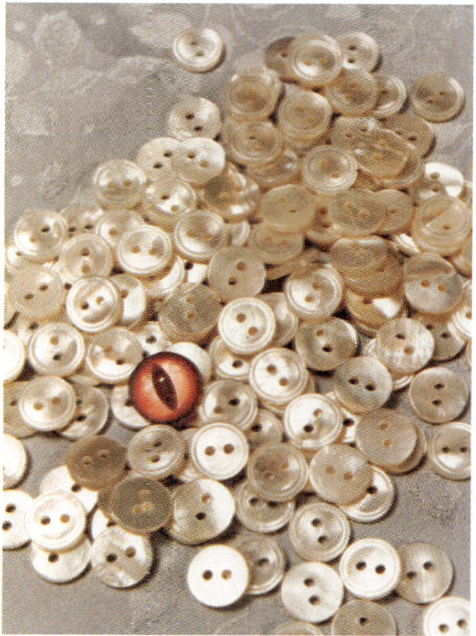

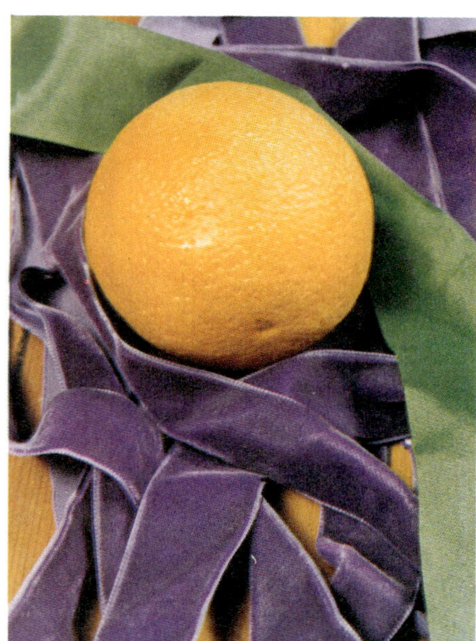

MONOCHROMATIC

This is a picture with predominantly one *(mono)* color *(chrome).* The effect is pleasing, but looks best if there is also a small area of neutral tone, such as white, gray or black.

ACCENT COLOR

This effect occurs when there is a small area of dominant color in a larger area of neutral or harmonizing colors. The accent color, such as the red button, becomes a focal point for the viewer's eyes.

POLYCHROMATIC COLORS

Many *(poly)* colors may work in a picture, as shown at far left, or not work, above. Contrasting colors may give a confusing composition.

Composing for Depth

One of the challenges of photography is to capture a three-dimensional scene in two dimensions. Making the picture look three dimensional requires careful composition, viewpoint and lens selection, foreground and background choice, and other elements. Some of the most important ones are described in this section.

ONE EXAMPLE

At right are four different pictures of the same scene. Each has its merits, but not all are good if depth is important to the picture's meaning.

Viewpoint—The two pictures at left illustrate how viewpoint affects depth. The lower photo is an overhead view. This flattens the scene, emphasizing only two dimensions. The top left photo was made from a lower angle—almost ground level. You see more into the distance. The viewer still knows what kind of plant is growing because the foreground is clear. In addition, he has a good idea of the size of the field and the contour of the land. And, the converging lines convey perspective.

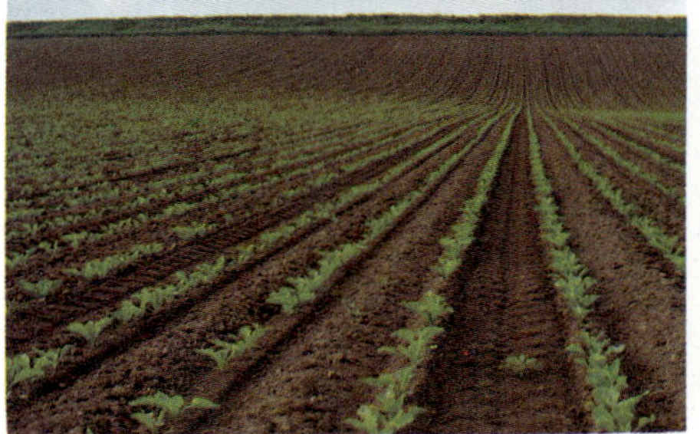

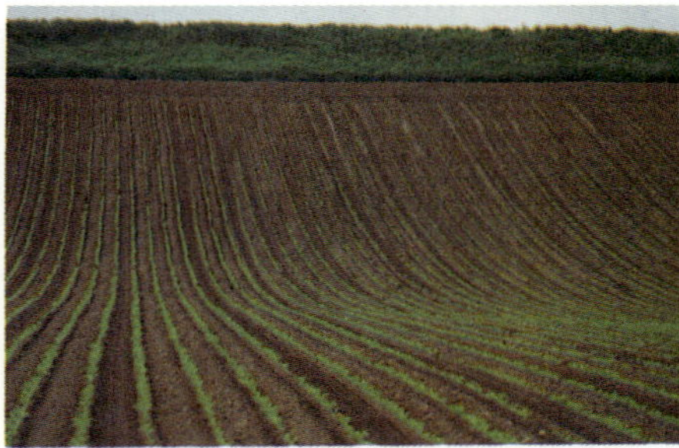

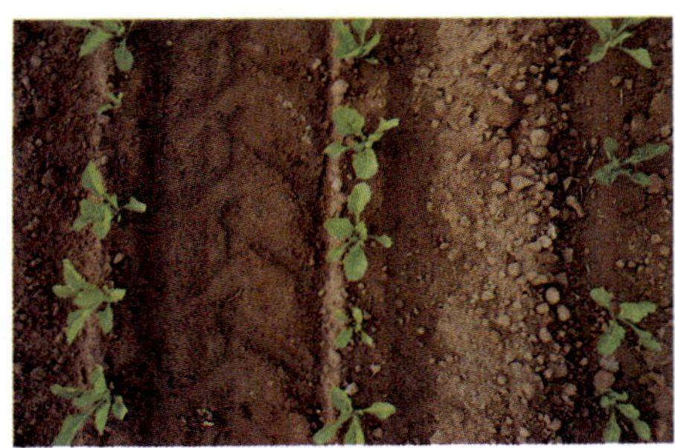

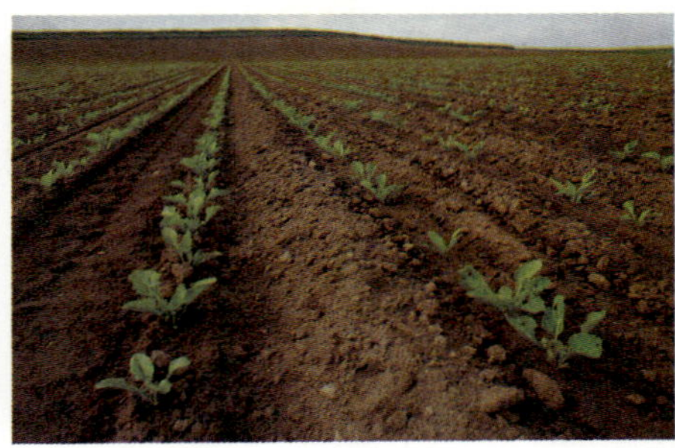

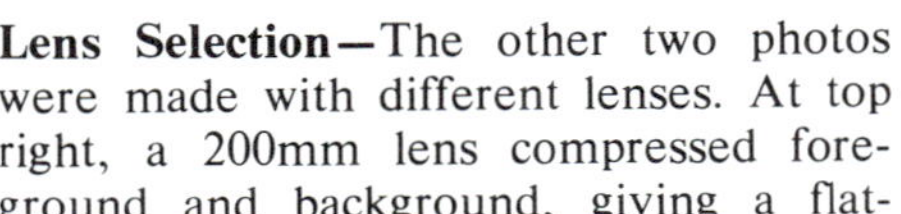

Lens Selection—The other two photos were made with different lenses. At top right, a 200mm lens compressed foreground and background, giving a flat-looking photo. The lower picture, made with a 24mm lens used low, shows foreground detail clearly contrasted against a vast expanse of background.

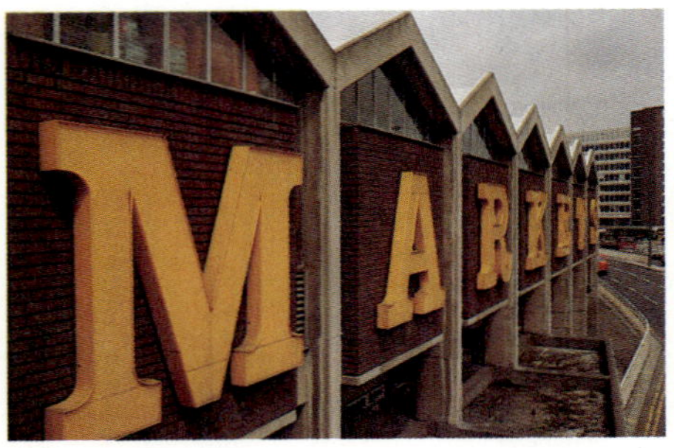

USING SCALE

We know from experience that receding objects look smaller as they get farther away. You can use changing scale to create depth in the scene, as was done above. The effect works best with similarly sized objects in a line.

Use a wide-angle lens and choose a shooting angle that puts one end of the line up close. This viewpoint makes the nearest element look very big and the farthest one very small, while in-between elements show the changing scale. If you use a small lens aperture for maximum depth of field, you may be able to get the whole line in sharp focus.

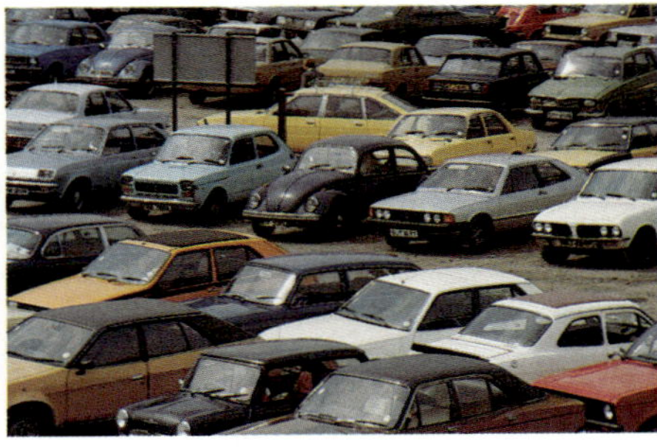

OVERLAPPING ELEMENTS

Suppose you use a telephoto lens, yet still want the impression of depth in the picture. The problem is that a telephoto lens seems to compress foreground and background. An effective solution is to select a viewpoint that makes things in the scene overlap. This gives the viewer a good indication of what is in front and what is farther away.

For the above photo, the photographer used a telephoto lens at a high viewpoint. This made the cars overlap, indicating the size of the distant parking lot.

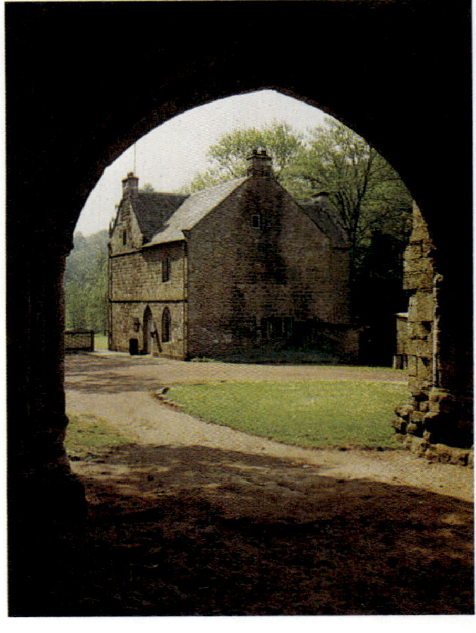

FRAME THE SUBJECT

When you surround a distant object with a foreground frame, the impression of depth is accentuated. The foreground-framing arch of this photo was obviously closer to the photographer than was the house.

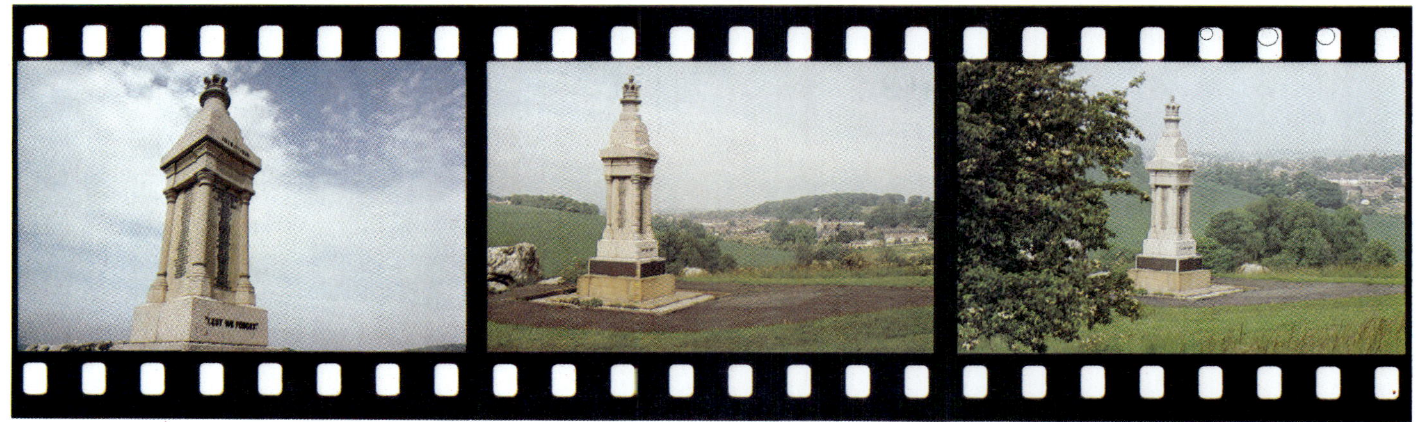

ESTABLISHING DEPTH

Pictures that have a three-dimensional look tell us a lot about the scene. We can see the relative sizes of elements and judge distances between them.

When you photograph a subject, consider telling the viewer as much as you can by establishing depth. For example, the above left photo of the monument doesn't indicate mass, height, or other dimensions. It could be big or small—you have no sure way of knowing by just looking at the picture.

Including Background—It helps to include a background, as was done above. Now you see a distant town and some trees. The monument's size is easier to judge relative to other elements. In addition, the viewer can assume that the monument is related to the town. In this case, background establishes scale and context too.

Including Foreground—By including a foreground subject, you can emphasize depth even more. This was done for this picture. A nearby element makes a distant element look even farther away. A foreground can also block or fill unsightly space that doesn't help the composition. Be careful, however, that foreground detail isn't so colorful or large that it distracts the viewer from the main subject.

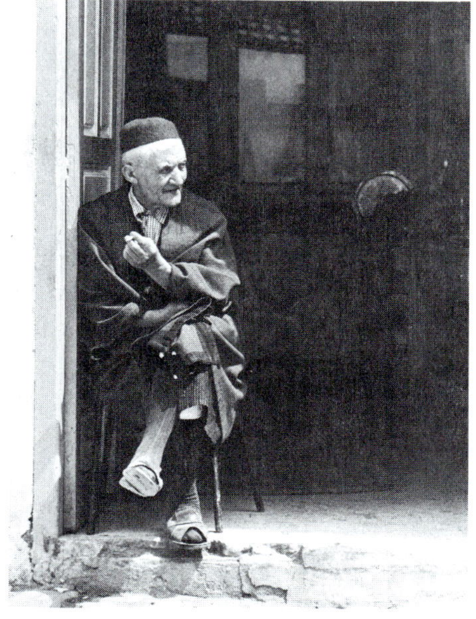

CONTRASTING TONES

With b&w film, you can emphasize depth with light and shade, translating them into contrasting bright and dark tones. Compose so distant and foreground subjects have contrasting brightnesses.

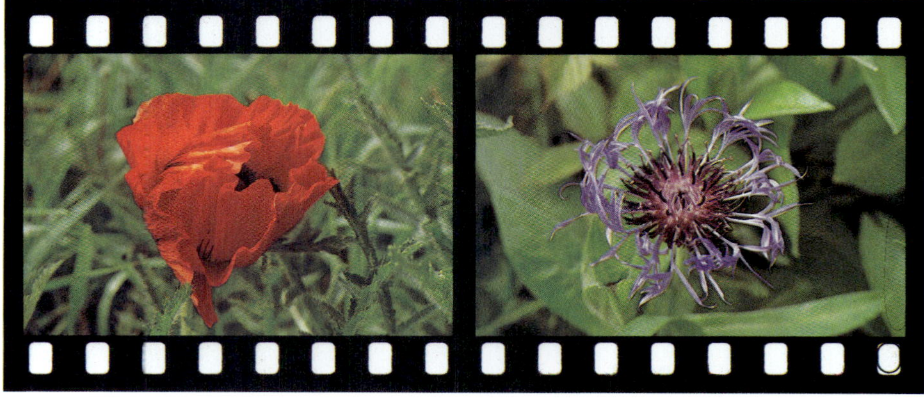

DOMINANT COLORS

Colors also play a role in depth effects. Generally, bright warm colors—red, yellow and orange—look close and relatively larger than other colors or tones.

Exploit this effect by using warm-colored foreground subjects and darker or cooler colors for the background. In the above picture of the poppy, the red flower gets your attention and makes the green foliage seem more distant. The photographer accentuated this effect by using a large aperture for shallow depth of field.

RECEDING COLORS

Cool colors, such as blues and greens, do not stand out well unless they are very bright. Therefore, they seem to recede, creating a flat-looking picture. Compare the above two photos and see how red/green contrast gives more depth than blue/green contrast.

Selective Focus

Controlling depth of field means selecting what you want in and out of focus. For creative composition you emphasize particular parts of the scene in view. Emphasize the main subject most. You can usually do this by putting it in sharp focus. Less important parts of the scene can blur. This is why selective focus—based on depth-of-field controls already described—is a valuable compositional tool.

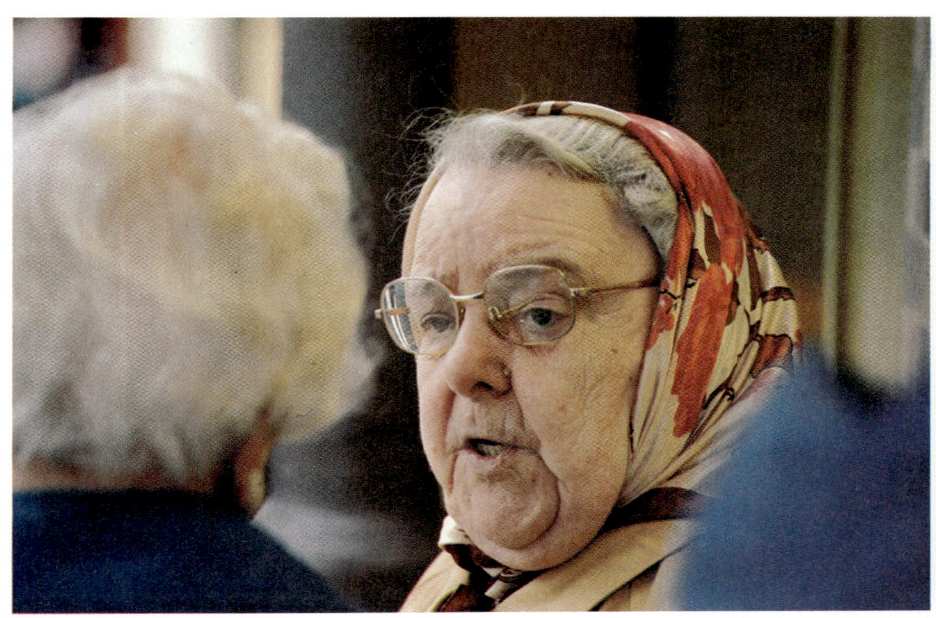

ISOLATING WITH BLUR

If most of the picture is out of focus, our eyes will naturally seek out and stop to view the focused part. It automatically becomes the main part of the subject because it is the only part that gives clear information.

For example, in the portrait here, the woman is the main subject because she is sharp. There is little detail in the out-of-focus person at left. The blue in the right corner is relatively unobtrusive because it is blurred.

This picture works by isolating the main subject in a field of blur. If all elements were sharp, you would give the woman's face less attention.

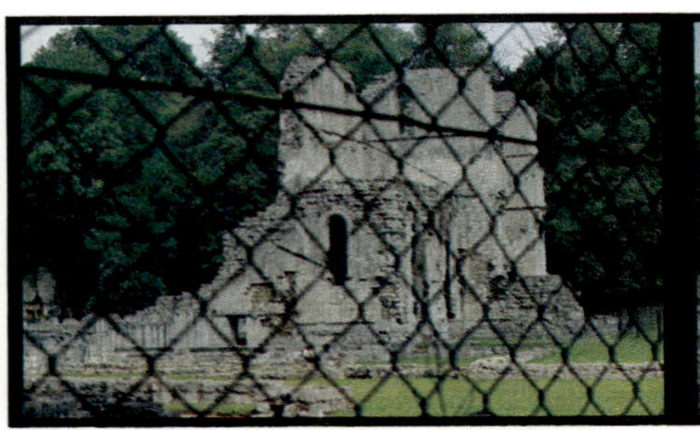

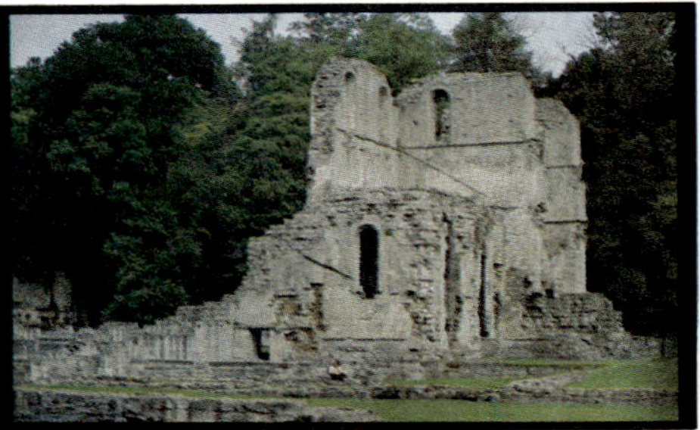

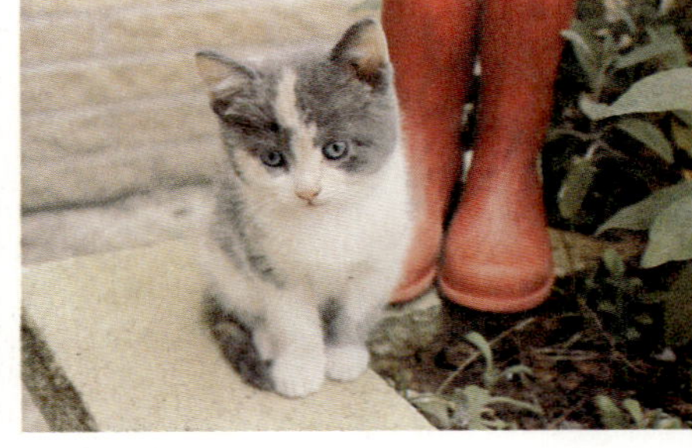

ELIMINATING FOREGROUND

Sometimes, you won't be able to get past a foreground obstruction to photograph a distant subject. This happens at zoos, sports fields and other places that have fences, windows and gratings. Make the obstruction as unobtrusive as possible by focusing selectively.

The picture above left was made without considering selective focus. The photographer used an aperture of *f*-16 for good depth of field. He didn't preview depth of field before exposure to see what the effect would be. The fence is out of focus but clearly visible.

For the second picture, the photographer moved as close as possible to the fence and used maximum lens aperture to limit depth of field as much as possible. The fence was so close and blurred that it's invisible in the picture.

OBTRUSIVE BACKGROUND

Sometimes, a background doesn't help composition. Background may be detailed or colorful and distract the viewer's attention. If a different subject position or camera viewpoint are impractical, use selective focusing to subdue the background. Make it as blurred as possible by using a large lens aperture. Keep the main subject sharp.

In the photo, above right, the sharp background of red boots and green leaves distracts your attention from the gray kitten. The zone of sharp focus is too deep for best composition.

The solution here was to use maximum lens aperture and focus on the kitten's head. This blurred background and part of the cat. The background, though still bright, is less emphatic than before.

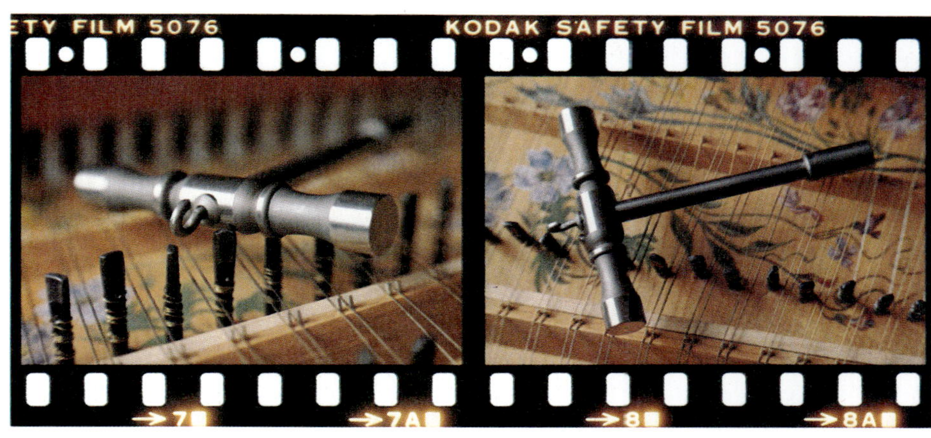

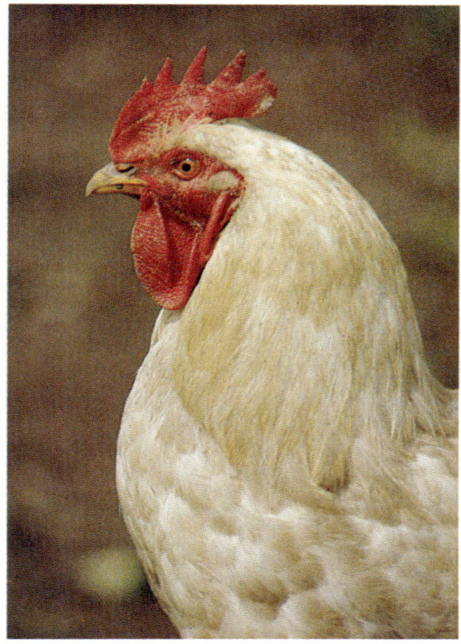

CONTROLLING THE SUBJECT

Sometimes, you have to go beyond camera controls to get the picture you want. Two photos above show this. For the composition at left, image magnification and exposure conditions limited aperture selection—the photographer couldn't stop down enough to sharply reproduce the whole tool within the narrow depth of field.

To get a better picture, he decreased image magnification by increasing subject distance. Then he shot from overhead, making sure that the subject was within the depth of field established by the unchanged lens aperture and slightly lower magnification.

Prefocusing—Instead of trying to focus on a moving subject, why not let the subject move to your focused distance? Do this by prefocusing on a certain spot. When the subject moves to that spot, take the picture.

Use this technique when shooting subjects with predictable motion. If the subject is unpredictable, you may have to use some bait, as was done for the rooster. Some corn was just out of the picture. The photographer focused on the corn, moved the camera and exposed the picture when the rooster approached the grain.

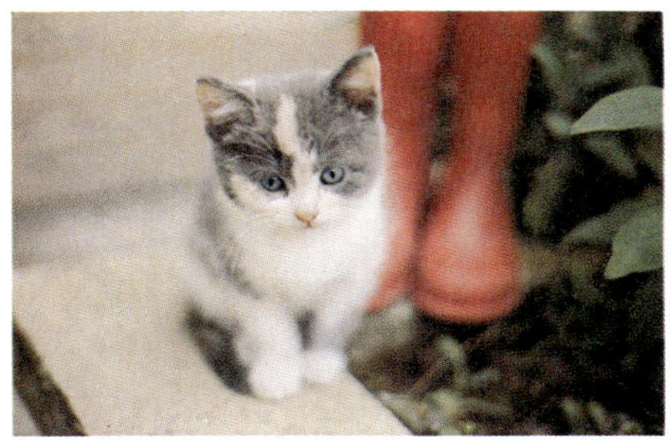

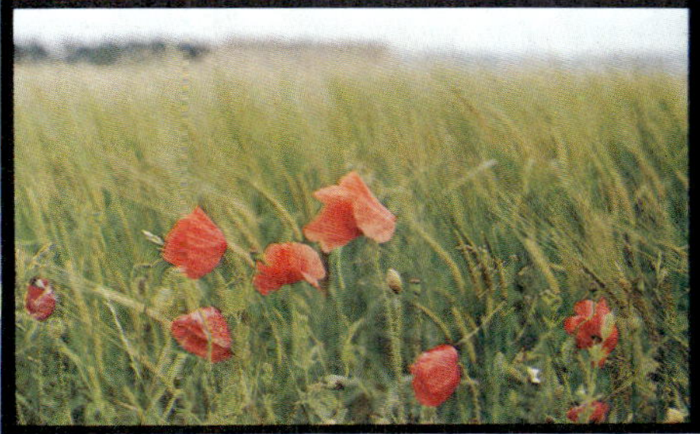

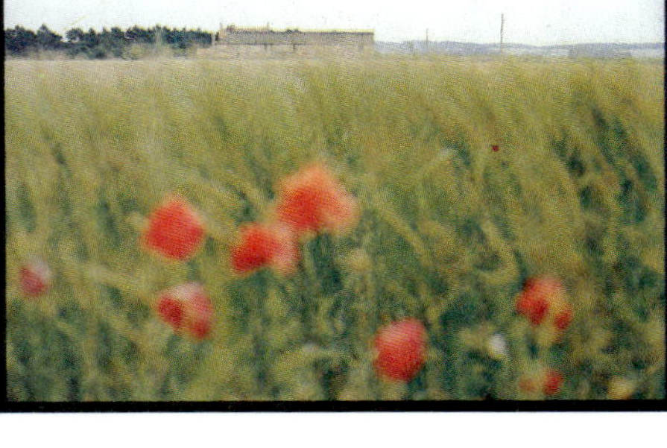

SELECTIVE EMPHASIS

By now you've probably realized that selective focus can also be called *selective emphasis*—you emphasize something by making it sharp. For some scenes, deciding what to emphasize is easy. With other scenes, it's not.

For example, in the field scene pictured above, there are three basic ways to record the view. Sharp focus can include just the poppies, just the building and horizon, or everything. The first two cases are shown.

If everything were in focus, the viewer may be confused about the purpose of the photo. It may not have a main subject. This is OK if you want to give everything equal emphasis.

The above photos show how picture information radically changes if only part of the scene is in focus. Neither is necessarily better than the other. If you like to photograph flowers, make the left-hand picture. If you like buildings, make the one at right. If you like buildings and flowers, put everything in focus. Or, try all three possibilities on film. When you "bracket compositionally," you'll have more than one picture for more than one use.

Viewpoint & Perspective

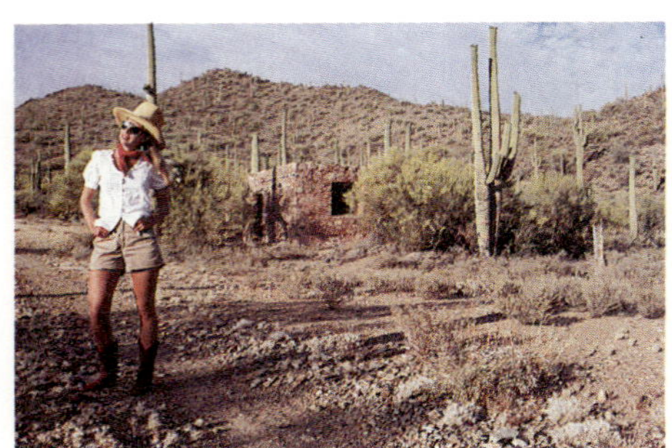

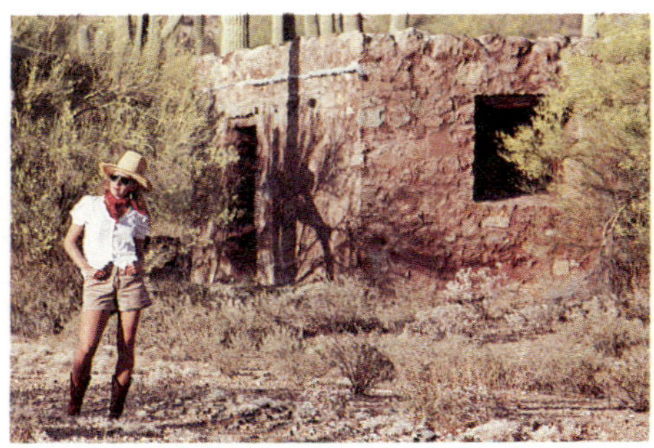

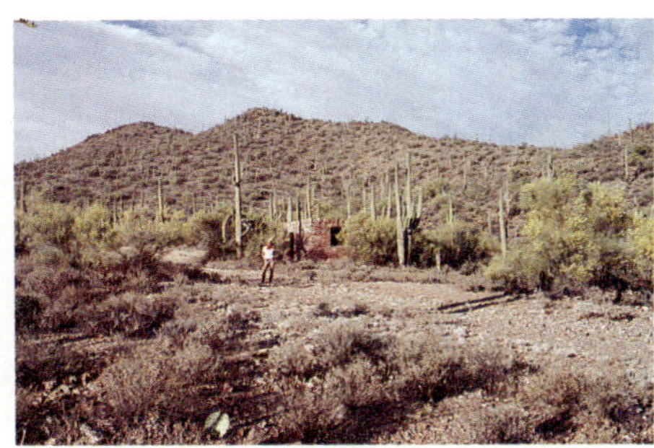

Choice of camera position, or viewpoint, is critical to a good photograph. But viewpoint doesn't only refer to the angle from which you shoot—it also relates to the distance between you and your subject. Notice how, as you change distance, the relationship between near and distant objects changes. This relationship is known as *perspective*.

By moving close, you can make a person look tall and prominent in front of a distant house. As you move away from the person, you'll notice that the house becomes relatively larger and more prominent.

Changing Perspective—To control perspective in your photography, you need two things. First, you need an awareness of what you are seeing in the viewfinder, so that you can deliberately choose the best position from which to shoot. Second, you need a selection of lenses of different focal lengths, so that you can fill the image area on the film, no matter how far away you are.

In the left and center photos, the model is about the same size. When the photographer took the left picture, he was relatively close to the model. She is dominant in front of the distant scene. A 35mm lens was used.

For the second photo, the photographer moved much farther away. Note how the distant building seems to have grown in size, and now dominates the scene. To fill the film area at this distance, a telephoto lens was needed—a 200mm lens was actually used. Compare this with the right picture, which was made from the same distance as the center photo, but with the 35mm lens.

You can see from this example that a careful choice of viewpoint and lens gives you a lot of creative control.

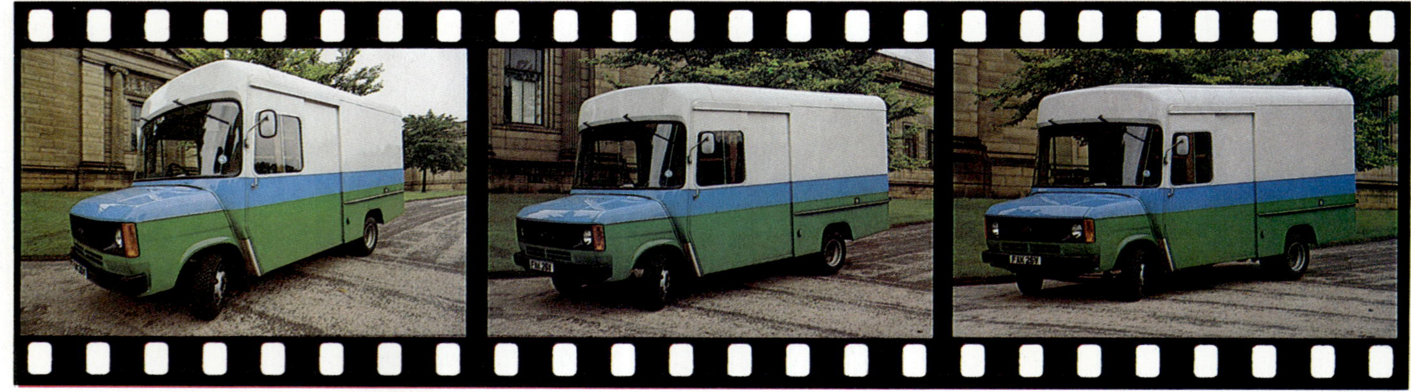

CHANGING LENS AND VIEWPOINT

For these three photos, the photographer made the truck about the same size on film. Each photo was made with a different lens and viewpoint. These changes created noticeably different images.

24mm Lens—The photographer was close to the front of the truck. This viewpoint exaggerated and distorted the truck's size because the foreground was much closer to the camera lens than the back of the truck. The top and bottom of the truck are converging.

Make this kind of photo for special effect or when you are in a small space and must use a wide-angle lens up close.

50mm Lens—This photo was made with a 50mm lens at a farther subject distance. The relative distances between the photographer and front and rear of the truck are smaller, so there is less convergence of lines and less distortion.

100mm Lens—The photographer used a 100mm lens and backed up even more to make this picture. When you compare it with the middle photo, you can see that the truck top and bottom are now nearly parallel. This is because of the increased subject distance.

Notice too that the background seems to be closer to the truck. In fact, the tree seems to be growing bigger in each picture! The last photo is best if the image is to picture the truck as accurately as possible.

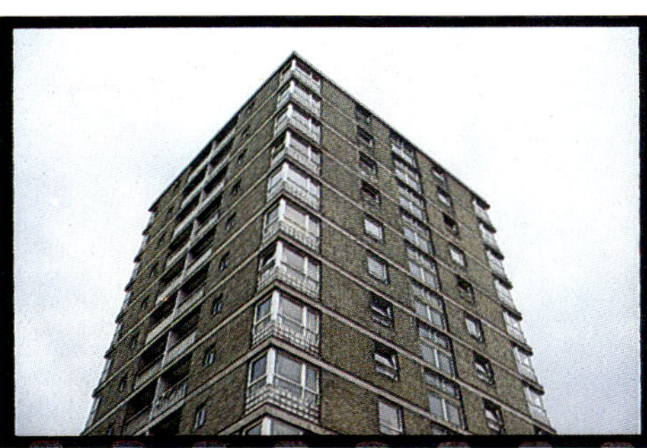
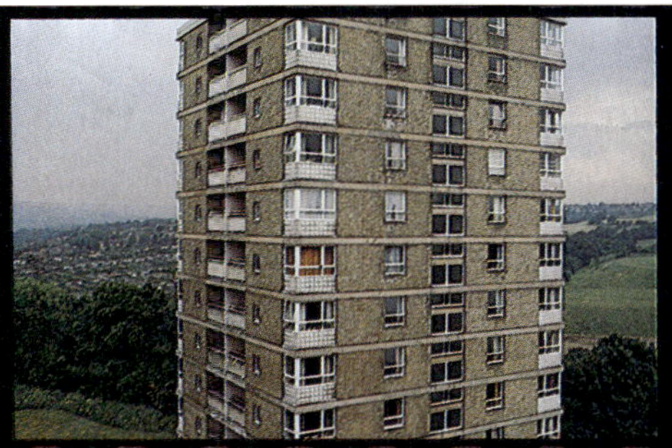
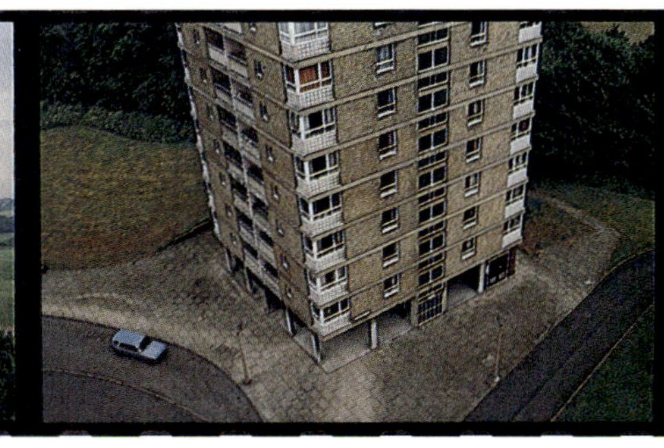

CONVERGING VERTICALS

This happens when the camera film plane is not parallel to the main subject plane. It results from a tilting viewpoint, such as when you photograph a tall nearby building by pointing the camera up. The top floor of the building is farther away than the first floor, so its image is smaller and at a different angle. This makes receding vertical lines seem to converge and the building seem to lean backward. The photo at far right shows that converging verticals will also happen if you tilt the camera down.

Some photographers like this effect to exaggerate a building's height. However, architects usually don't like the effect because they design buildings not to lean!

Correcting Verticals—If you agree with architects that the effect is unattractive, you have to change viewpoint. Get farther away or higher so the lens can see more of the whole building without your tilting the camera. Converging verticals disappear when the film plane and building sides are parallel.

The middle photo was made with the same lens as the photo at left. The photographer shot from a middle floor of an adjacent building. Notice that the building sides are parallel to the vertical sides of the film frame.

To photograph more of the building he would need to go farther away or use a shorter focal length lens. This would also show more background.

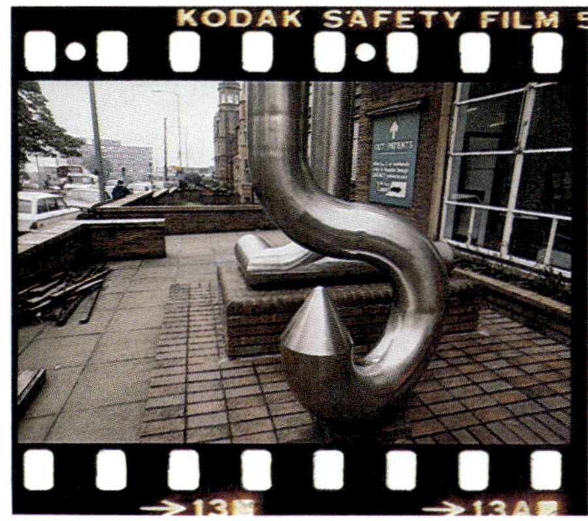

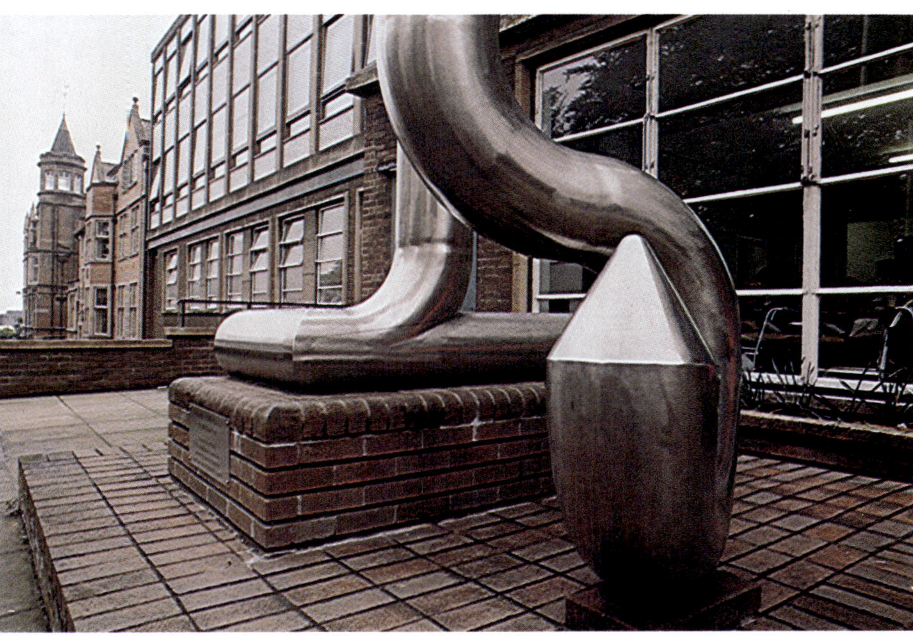

FINDING A BETTER VIEWPOINT

As mentioned earlier, the best viewpoint is rarely the first one. Typically, some detail—not an overall view—attracts you to a scene. If you take the picture from where you saw the detail, the lens will probably give you an overall view.

This is what happened with the above scene. The photographer noticed the metal sculpture and took a picture without thinking. He inadvertently imaged cars, pedestrians, the street and a blank sky. The sculpture and its relationship to the building are not very apparent.

The larger photo was made after more careful consideration of what attracted the photographer to the scene—the sculpture's base and placement. He changed viewpoint and photographed from a low level. This shows that you don't always have to change lenses to get a better picture.

People Photography

People are the most interesting and popular photographic subjects. A picture with a person in it is almost always better than a picture of the same scene without human interest. Capturing a person's qualities on film is also challenging. You have to be aware of technical considerations *and* human factors like gestures, expressions and moods. When you can handle both, your people pictures will please you and your subject.

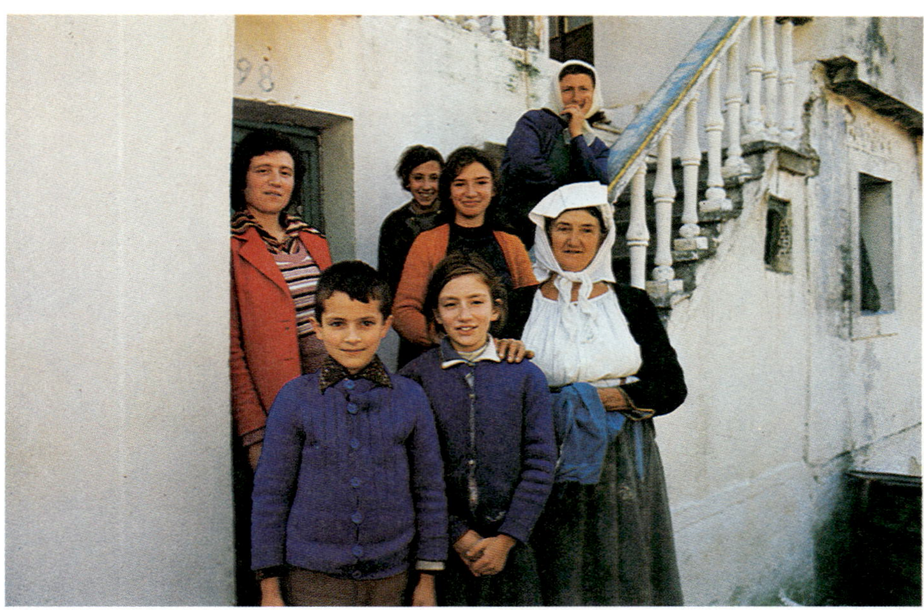

POSSIBLE METHODS

There are as many kinds of people photographers as there are people. Each photographer has his or her own best way of working. Finding yours may take some time. When you try different methods, you'll see that some give good results and others don't. Eventually, you'll give up methods that won't work for you, and develop those that do.

You can photograph someone formally or informally. With formal shooting, *you* are in total control. Lighting, background, pose and other important photographic decisions are your responsibility. Examples of formal people photography are a school portrait or a passport photo.

Informal photography means more casual, less controlled picture taking. You do the best with the situation at hand and try to achieve a natural-looking image, not a photograph of record. A photo that goes into a family album is an example of this.

You may want to specialize with single-person pictures, and further specialize by photographing just children or adults. Or, you may prefer group photography, as shown here. Some group photography can be financially rewarding, as can wedding photography. People are *always* willing to buy *good* photographs of important events.

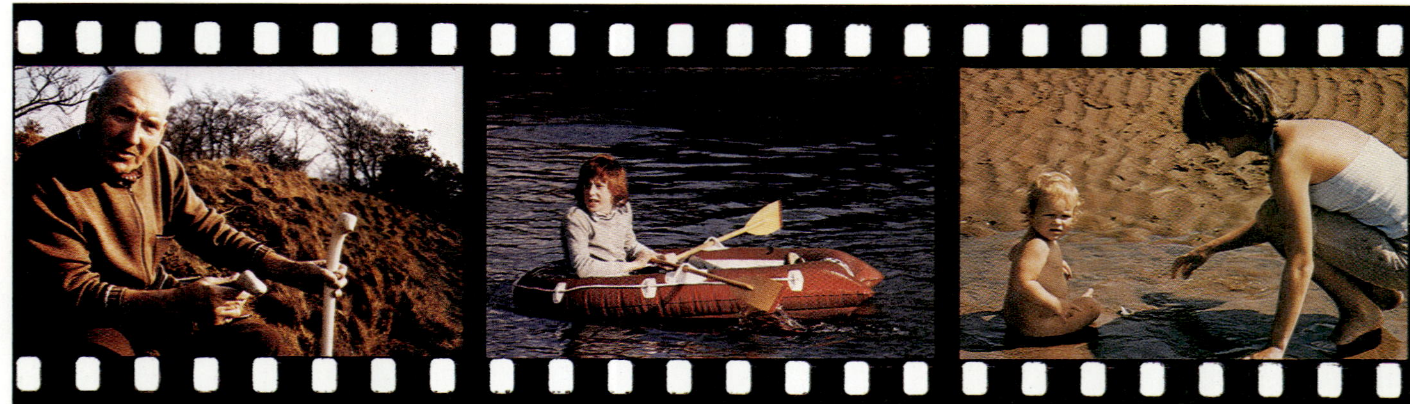

EXPRESSIONS & GESTURES

When you capture a subject's natural expression or gesture on film, the image shows the viewer something more than what the person looked like and was wearing that day.

An informal approach is the best way to capture gestures and expressions. Talking to the subject while you photograph is the best way to elicit an expression. For example, tell a joke if you want someone to give a natural smile or laugh. Don't request specific expressions—it rarely works!

ENVIRONMENTAL PORTRAITURE

This style of shooting shows the subject and his typical, or favorite, surroundings. The background and other elements tell the viewer something about the subject, such as his hobby or interests.

If you want to photograph a chef dressed in white cooking clothes and hat, it's best to picture him in his kitchen, not in the backyard of his home. The food or cooking tools shown in the scene will tell the viewer about the man's occupation.

INTERACTION

When informally photographing small groups, it is generally best to show interaction among group members. This helps avoid the stiff, posed look that is characteristic of too much group photography. When people begin ignoring the camera, they'll act naturally, giving plenty of sincere expressions and gestures for you to record.

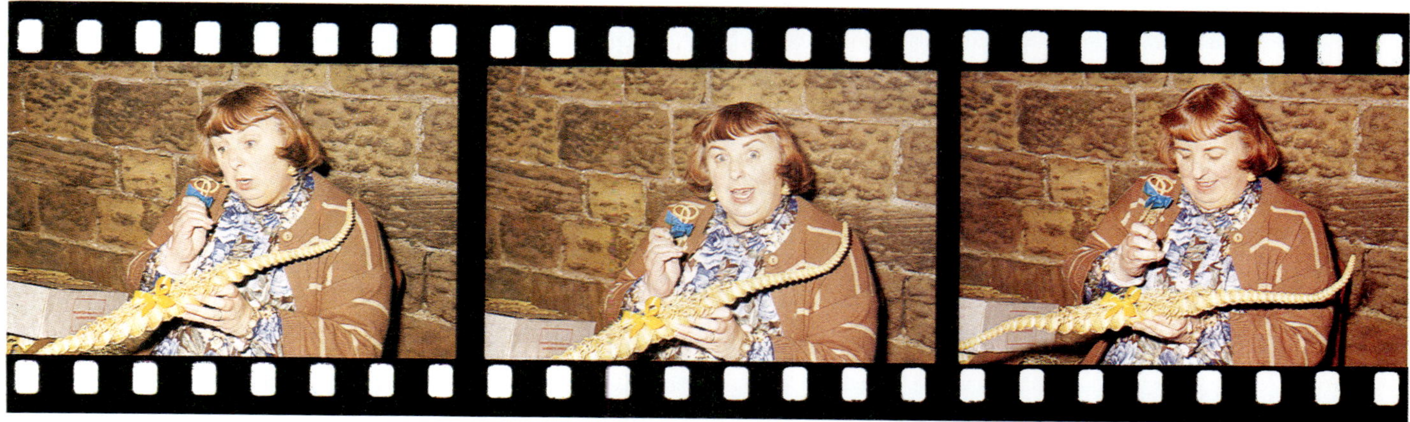

AN HONEST APPROACH

When you want to photograph someone, especially a stranger, it is always good policy to ask permission. Explain why you want the picture and what you want it to look like. People are usually so flattered by your attention that they will cooperate—sometimes long enough for a formal picture.

Others may prefer their privacy and consider your camera intrusive. If so, respect their wishes. Better to not get a picture than to make someone angry.

How To Do It—After getting permission, begin shooting to get the subject used to your presence. Try to determine the person's patience with you. If your subject appears to have little, you'll have to do your best quickly. Maybe you'll have time for just one picture. If the person is very patient, then you can make many exposures. This is ideal because the first photo is rarely best, as illustrated above, left.

Use different viewpoints and compositions if possible and change lenses if necessary. Consider giving general directions to the subject, such as which way to look, where to put hands, and whether to smile or not.

When you've finished, you may want to send your subject a print or two in gratitude, so remember to get a name and address.

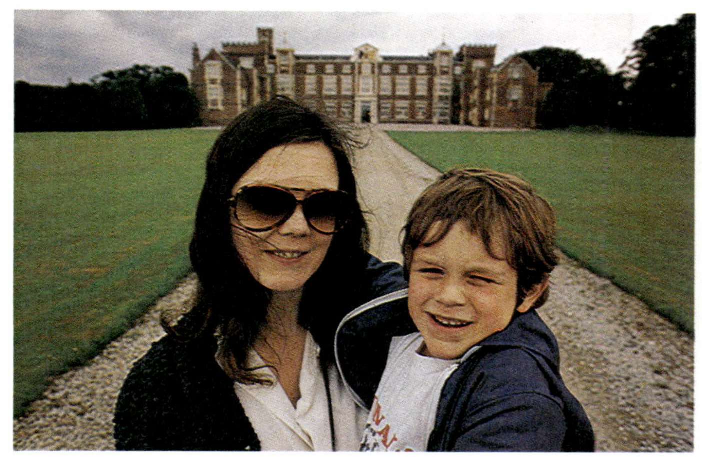

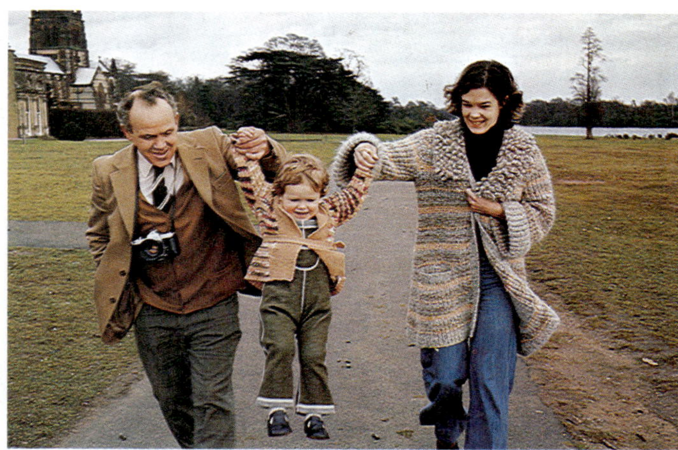

VACATION PICTURES

These are probably the first people pictures we take. In fact, many people use a camera only to record travels with their family. Not all of your vacation pictures will have people in them, but the best ones usually will.

Instead of recording an experience quickly and automatically, take care to expose and compose well. Good vacation pictures can help you relive a wonderful time for many years.

People and Place—If you use a wide-angle lens, you'll be able to include both people and place in the image. The photo above left shows one good way to do it. The subjects are in the foreground, filling empty image space created by the lawn and gravel road. Even though the building is in the background, it is quite prominent. You can also put close subjects at the side of the frame or in the middle-ground area. However, if they are in the background, they'll be very small and unrecognizable.

Posed or Unposed?—If you want to remember a new acquaintance from your trip, then perhaps a posed portrait is best. If you want to record some local activity such as an overall view of people at a marketplace, unposed pictures may be best.

With familiar people, such as family members, unposed photos work well. Generally, the closer the subjects, the more posing they will do automatically.

Making Portraits

A portrait tells the viewer about the subject. In fact, the word *portrait* is derived from *portray,* which is exactly what a successful portrait does.

Formal or Informal?—Deciding which way to make a portrait depends on many factors. How well do you know the person? What does he or she want in the picture? Is it a photo of record or just for fun? Is background necessary for more information? These are just some of the things to consider.

Formal portraits are usually made indoors, under controllable studio conditions. Control of everything is the photographer's responsibility. Basically, the goal is to idealize the subject—make him look as he wants to be remembered. You need to choose a subject pose from a large set of standard poses photographers have used for a long time. Try new ideas, of course, but be aware that traditional poses have lasted because they work.

An informal portrait may require some decisions from the subject. Ask his opinion about what he wants to do or see in the picture. The subject may know a good location or time of day for interesting light. You both want a realistic and casual record of how the subject looks most of the time. The environmental portrait shown above was made with this in mind. Some tips for good results with formal and informal portraiture follow.

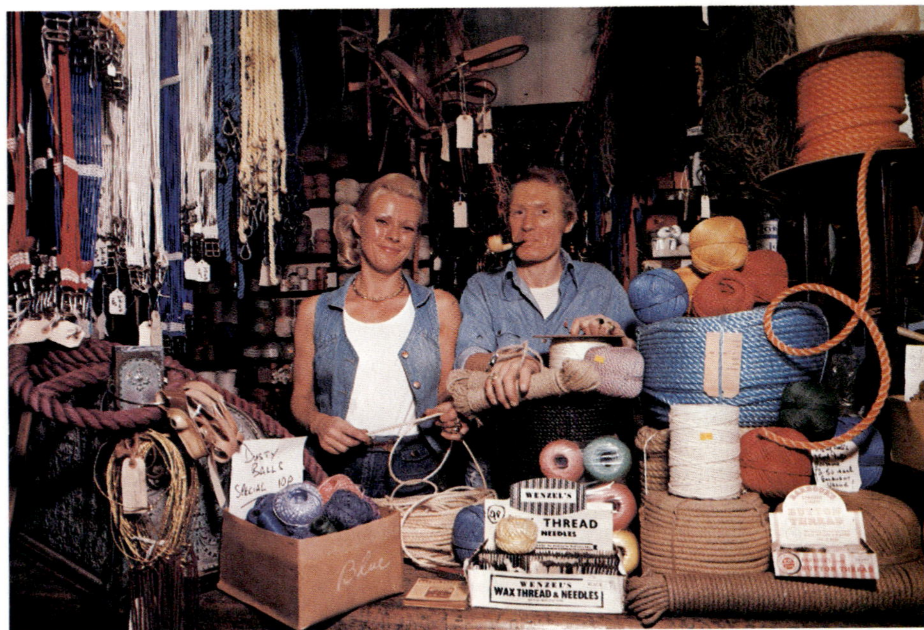

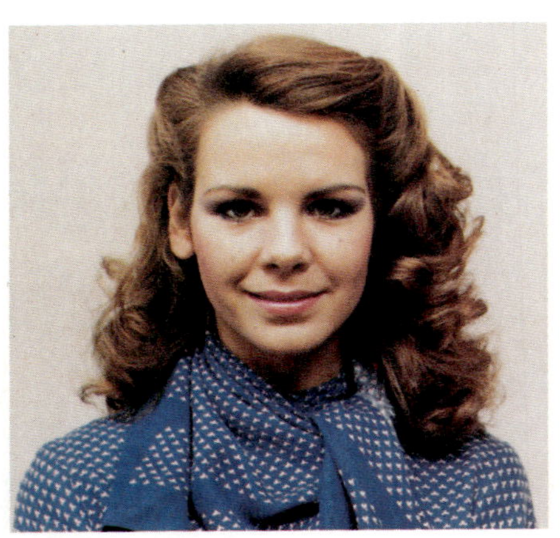

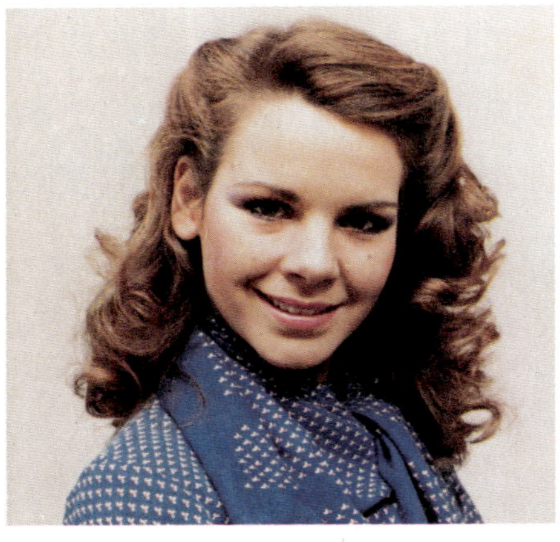

HEAD-AND-SHOULDER POSES

This is one of the most popular poses—useful for both formal and informal pictures. When you use a 50mm lens, you aren't too close or too far away.

The above picture shows a basic head-and-shoulder pose. It is fine for photos of record like a passport or other ID photo. However, it lacks artistic interest. There are many ways to change it for improved composition.

Have the subject turn the body so one shoulder is closer to you than the other, and tilt the head to the side, a bit down, or even away from you. Try different types of eye contact. Have the subject lean forward for best effect. Give directions while looking through the camera viewfinder.

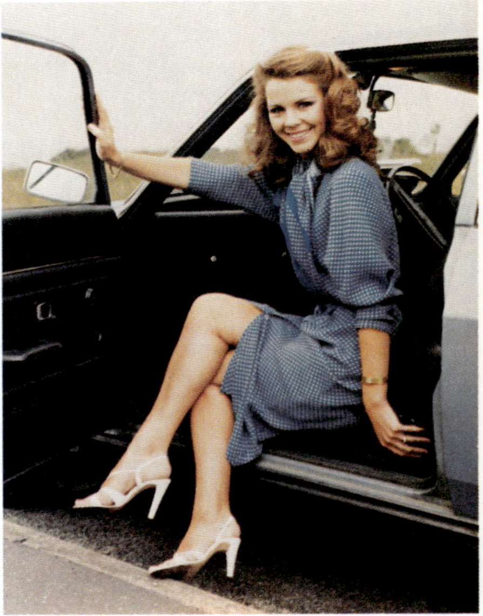

FULL-LENGTH POSING

Try to avoid showing a full-length pose with the person standing straight. This doesn't give a good composition—even if you use the 35mm format vertically. Instead, have the subject try a seated pose.

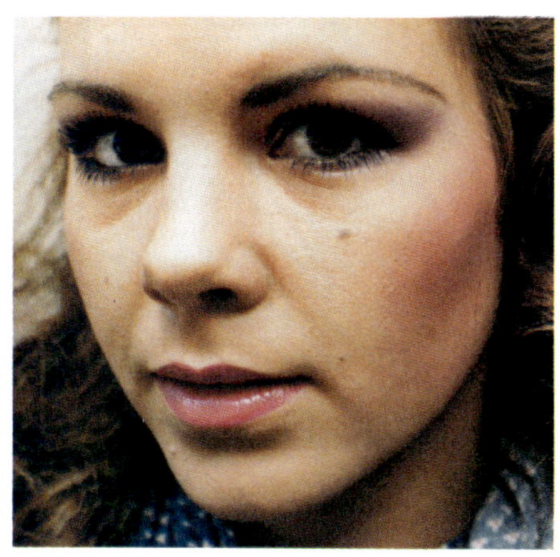

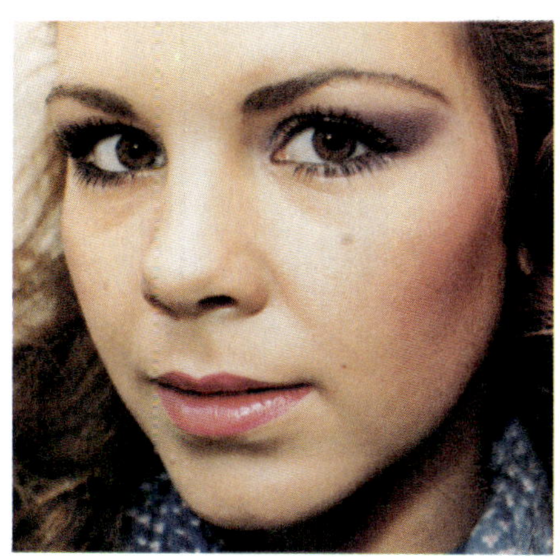

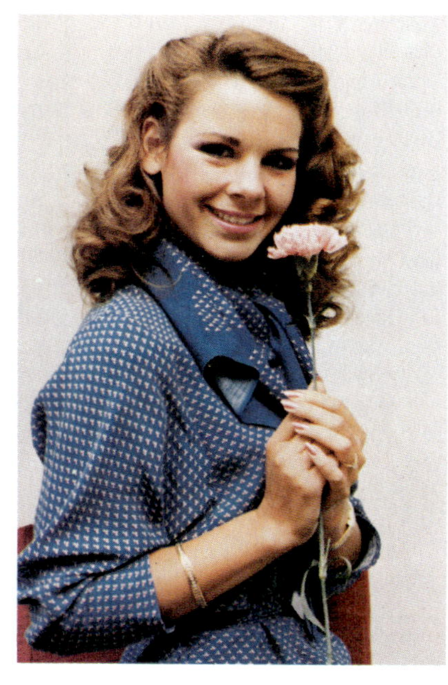

THE EYES HAVE IT

A strong portrait usually has good eye contact between subject and viewer. For this reason, always consider how the eyes will look in the picture. Focus on the eyes or lashes to make them sharp.

Lighting Tips—If light comes from directly overhead, the eyes may be shadowed, as shown above. This can happen on overcast days, at midday when the sun is high, or when you use bounce flash.

You can brighten dark features by bouncing light toward the subject or using fill flash, described earlier. Use a large white or silver card to reflect the main light source. If you use fill flash, attractive small highlights will show in the eyes, as shown above.

HANDS

Pose the hands so they do not detract from the subject's face. Keep them looking relaxed and near the body so they don't look distorted or unnatural.

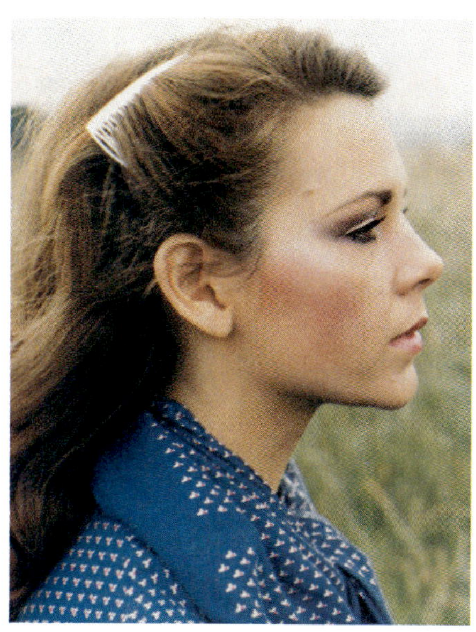

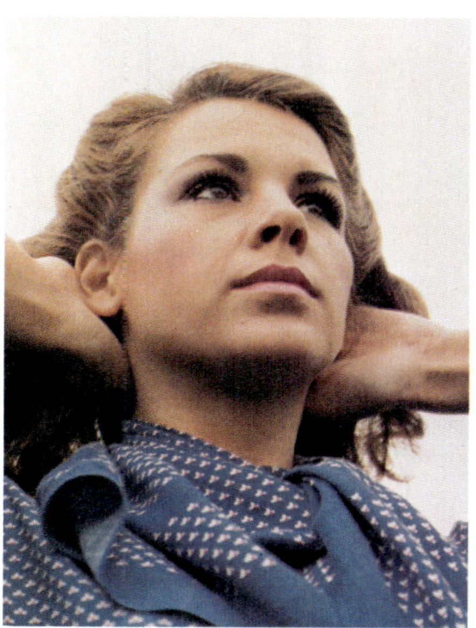

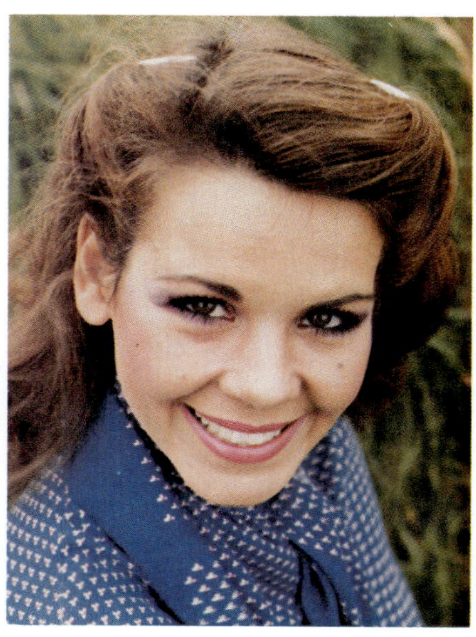

CAMERA ANGLE AND VIEWPOINT

Try a variety of camera angles and viewpoints. Photograph from the side for a strong profile. If you base exposure on a bright background light, the subject will silhouette, which can also be a nice effect.

You don't have to face every subject at eye level. Put the camera below eye level for a low viewpoint. It emphasizes the eyes and nostrils, makes a small chin look bigger, the nose shorter and broader, and the face almost rectangular.

A high viewpoint does the opposite to facial features. It emphasizes the hair and forehead and makes the chin look smaller. The face appears more triangular than usual.

Candid Photography

With this type of people photography you have no control over your subject, the lighting or background. This is part of the challenge. The reward is that you can document people as they really are without making them self-conscious with your camera.

The best candid photographers are quiet and unobtrusive. They seem to blend into their surroundings and remain unnoticed. Using a 35mm camera helps because it is small and quiet. When possible, meter and make exposure-control settings before you start taking pictures. Then when you are ready to shoot, only small changes will be necessary. Or, use an automatic-exposure camera when shooting average scenes.

PERMISSION?

You can take candid photographs of people in public places. It isn't illegal. If you are noticed, wave and look friendly. Most people will smile back and feel flattered. If someone asks you to stop photographing them, it is polite to do so.

There *are* some restrictions on what you can do with candid pictures. For example, if they are to be used for advertising, you must have the subject's permission in writing. If you sell them to a magazine because the photos have newsworthy information, you don't need permission.

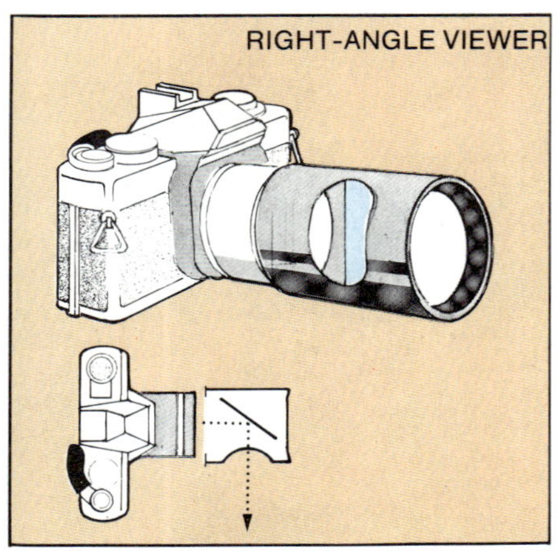

SPECIAL VIEWFINDERS

Pointing a camera at someone can look conspicuous, possibly ruining a candid photo. The two accessories shown here can help you avoid this problem. The right-angle attachment reflects the lens axis 90°. You can point the camera straight ahead and photograph someone at your side. The attachment looks like a lens hood and can be used with lenses from 50mm to 200mm. The image you see is reversed—the subject's right side is at the left of the focusing screen and vice-versa. This makes it difficult to use with a moving subject because a subject moving to the left looks as if it's moving to the right.

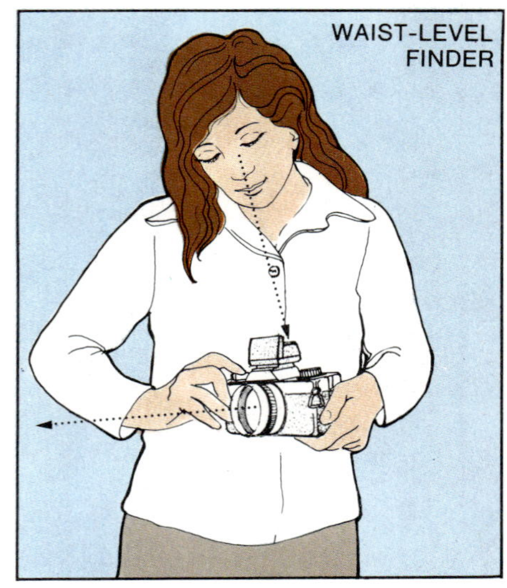

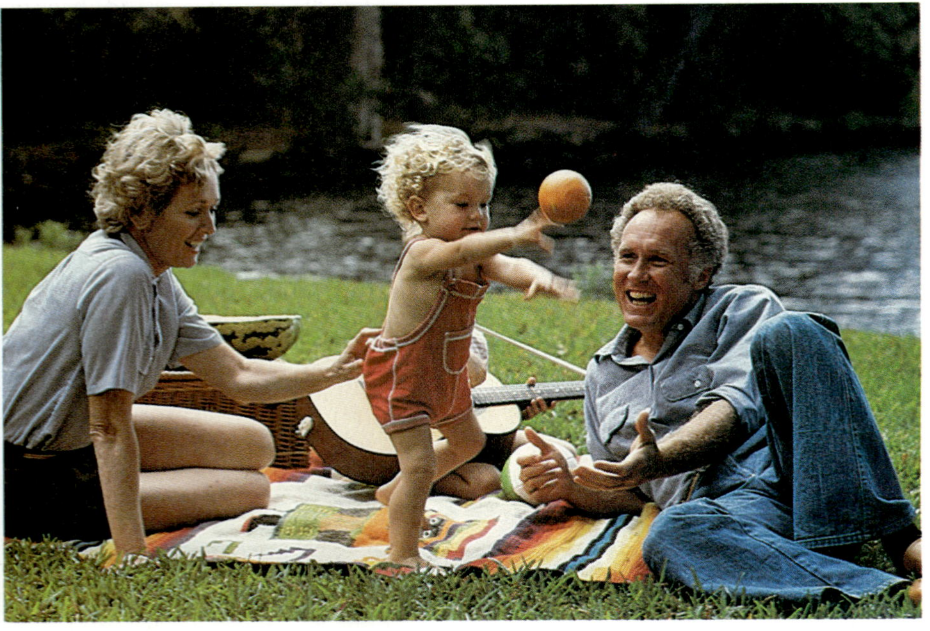

FAMILY CANDIDS

Making candid pictures of your family and friends who know and trust you is usually easier than making candids of strangers. Familiar people will relax and ignore you even when you take pictures. If you make a habit of carrying your camera, people will naturally accept it and your candid photography.

Because you don't have to be unnoticeable, you can try a variety of viewpoints, camera angles and lenses. You may even want to give some small directions if you think a striking image will result. Don't try to control the situation too much, however, or the picture may look posed.

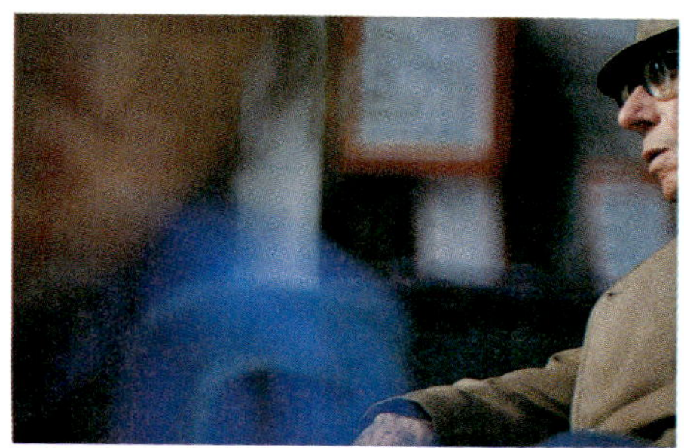

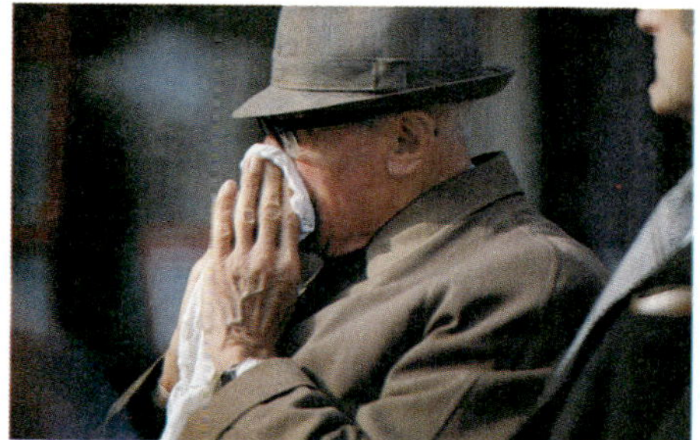

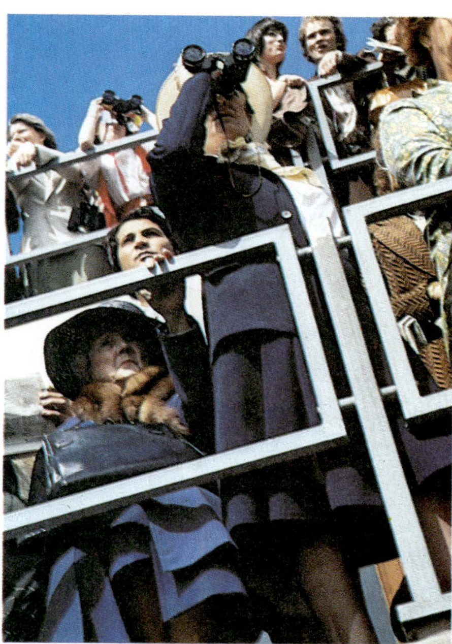

The waist-level finder is an accessory viewfinder. Not all camera systems offer this accessory. With one on your camera, you view the focusing screen image from overhead, not at eye level. This way you don't have to hold the camera to your eye, as people expect. You can make pictures while people think you're doing something else. And, you can face forward while shooting sideways.

VIEWING TECHNIQUES

You can adjust exposure and focus without pointing the camera directly at your subject. This is sometimes necessary to avoid being noticed. Aim a bit to the side of the subject. If he notices you, he'll probably think you're photographing something other than him. Typically, he'll lose interest in what you are doing.

As shown above, when you aim to the side of the subject, include some of him in the composition to make a final focus check and to know exactly when to gently swing the camera and expose film. After making the picture, swing the camera back to the original aim point and stay ready for the next picture.

Using Wide-Angle—With a wide-angle lens on your camera, you can focus extremely close and include a large view. This is a good way to make candid pictures up close. Use fast film, a fast shutter speed, and a small aperture like *f*-16. Set the lens focusing ring so depth of field extends from close to far subjects. You won't have to manually focus on subjects in that range. Hold the camera at waist or chest level for informal compositions.

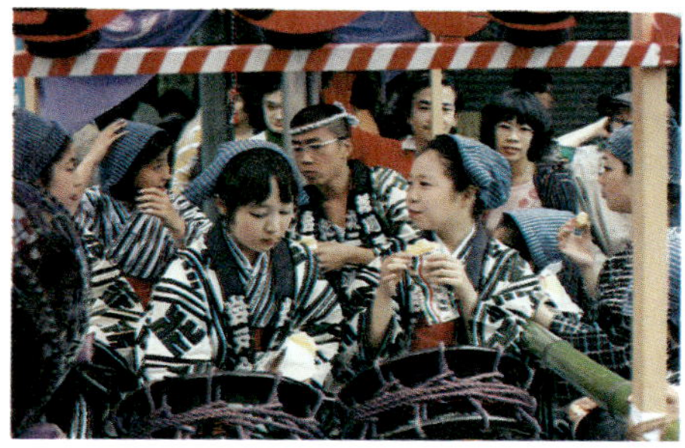

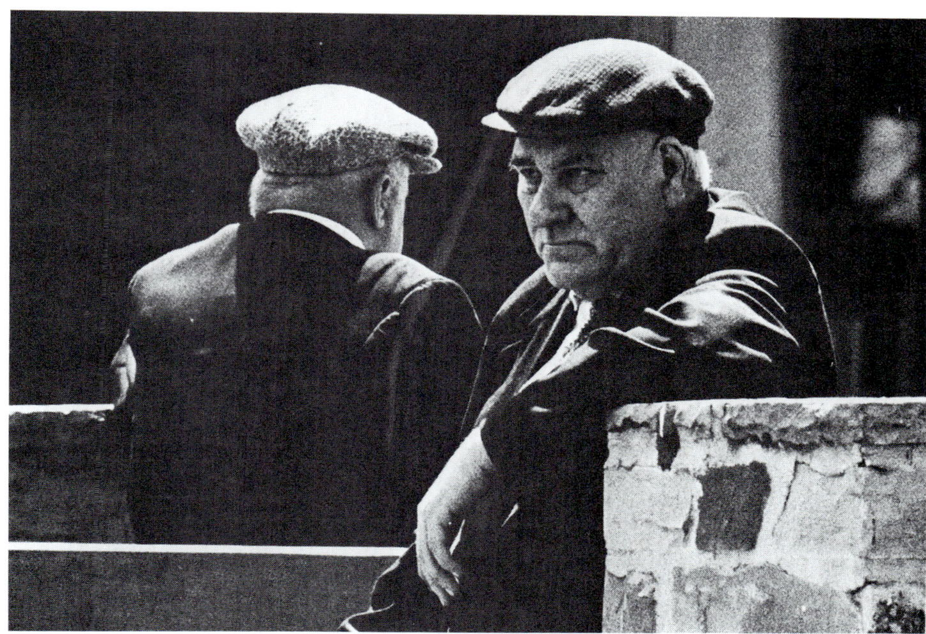

TELEPHOTO LENS

This lens is helpful because you can photograph from farther away than if you use a 50mm lens. The longer subject distance makes you less noticeable. Even if your subject sees you pointing your camera at him, he can't be sure that he is the subject, especially if other people are nearby. This may keep the person's expression and actions natural and relaxed.

Zoom Lens—A telephoto zoom is great for candid photography. You can get far away, and adjust composition in the viewfinder without having to change camera position. By adjusting lens focal length you can zoom in to exclude surrounding elements or zoom out to show more.

B&W PICTURES

Making candid portraits in b&w is a good idea if you do your own processing and printing. Even if composition isn't perfect, you can *crop* the image when printing the negative. You can enlarge just the part you like to make the strongest picture.

Landscapes & Scenic Views

There are lots of good reasons people photograph landscapes and scenic views. Good landscapes are all around you, waiting to be photographed at any time of year. In fact, some people like to photograph the same scene at different times of day and year. Environmental conditions vary to give a wealth of exciting pictures.

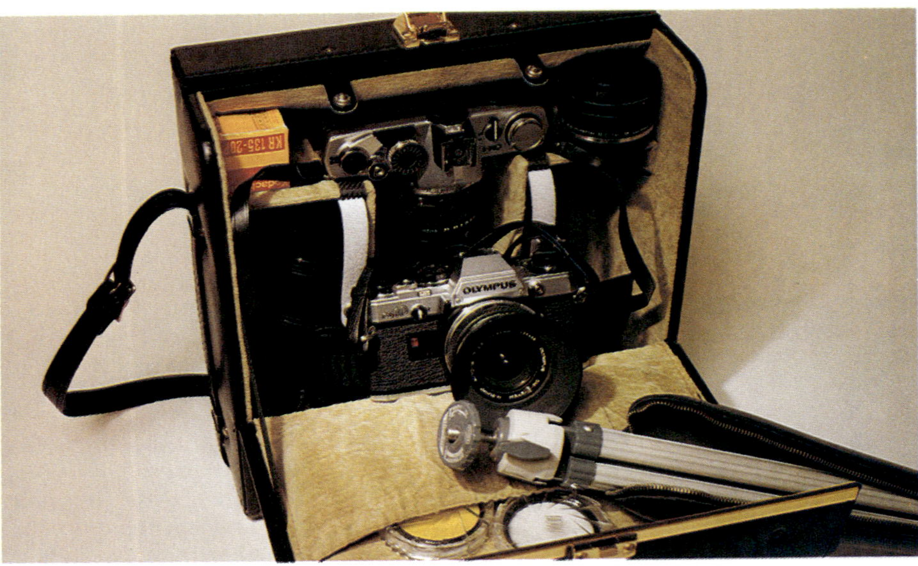

WHAT YOU NEED

In addition to the right equipment, you need patience and perseverance to make good landscape photos. Your first view of the scene is probably not the best camera viewpoint. Landscapes pictures can be unique if you search for exciting places to shoot from. Climb a tree, if you can, or lie on the ground if you need to. You may have to get up early for the right light, or stand in a cold fog to capture a misty mood. Walking around a scene to find the best viewpoint may necessitate a muddy hike.

Equipment—When photographing out in the field, use a tripod, so you can use any shutter speed and not worry about camera shake. Bring plenty of film—about twice as much as you plan to shoot. You don't want to run out of film in case conditions are great or a lot of bracketing is necessary.

An assortment of lenses is useful. A wide-angle lets you get the wide view of a scene. A telephoto enlarges distant details and seemingly compresses background and foreground.

Bring skylight, polarizing, yellow and red filters. The last two are used for b&w shooting.

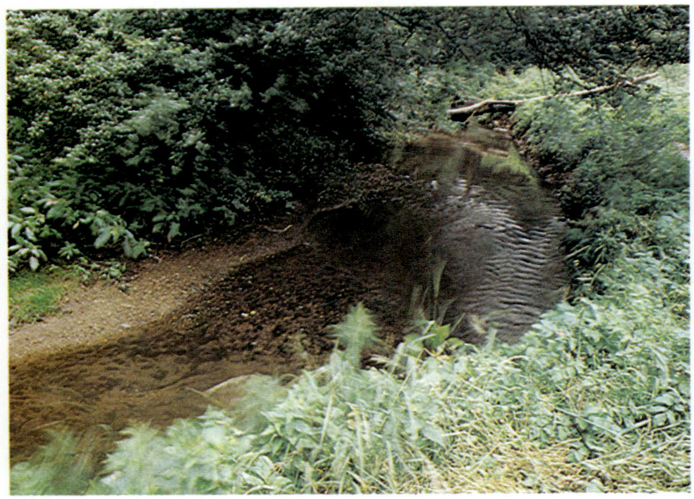

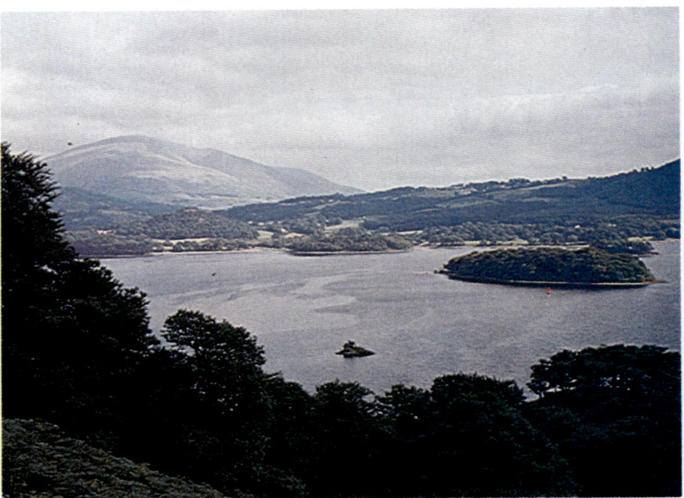

LONG EXPOSURES

Even if you photograph on a sunny day, a slow shutter speed may be necessary. For example, suppose you use ASA 25 slide film for good reproduction of detail. The Sunny Day *f*-16 rule says that exposure-control settings on a clear sunny day are *f*-16 at 1/30 second. If you want to set *f*-22 on your wide-angle lens for maximum depth of field, shutter speed should be 1/15 second. A polarizer on the lens absorbs about two exposure steps, making shutter speed about 1/4 second. If the day wasn't sunny, exposure time would be even longer.

With long exposures, moving objects like grass and foliage in the wind will blur on film, as shown above. The farther away they are, the less noticeable the blur. You can use this effect creatively with moving water. Or, exaggerate it by photographing with slow speeds on windy days.

BLOCKING HAZE

When you photograph distant scenes or at high altitudes, haze and invisible ultraviolet radiation can give color photos a bluish cast, as shown above. B&W pictures have lower contrast and distant detail is not clear. Minimize haze by using a skylight filter with color and b&w film. It also absorbs some blue. With b&w film you can use a yellow, orange or red filter to darken the sky and cut haze.

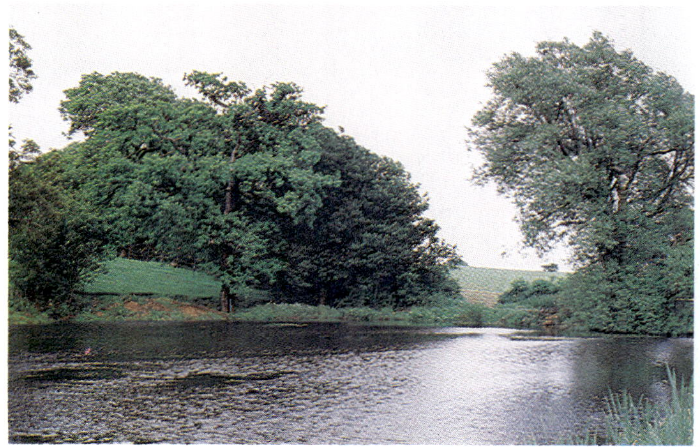

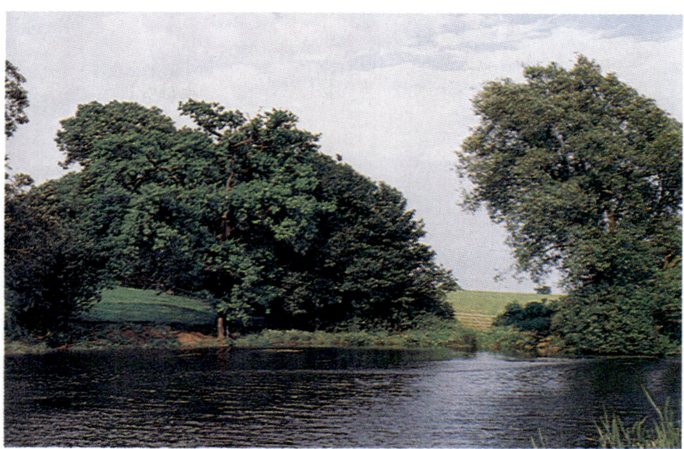

WAIT FOR THE RIGHT LIGHT

Good lighting is essential for good landscapes. What is right light depends on the scene you want to photograph. If you want to capture a feeling of depth, the scene should have shadows. This will show texture and contribute to a three-dimensional effect in the image. Strong shadows result from bright sunlight at a low angle. This typically occurs on a clear day during the first two or three hours after sunrise and the last two or three hours before sunset.

If the landscape doesn't need the effect of depth, light from a cloudy sky is OK. This diffused lighting simplifies a composition full of details by giving even illumination.

The two photos above are examples of both types of lighting. The landscape at left was made under a cloudy sky. A few minutes later the clouds parted to let the sun shine through. The second photo has more shadow and a brighter look to it. The slight color difference happened because the light on overcast days has a slightly bluer color than direct sunlight. This can be corrected with filtration. Which landscape do you prefer?

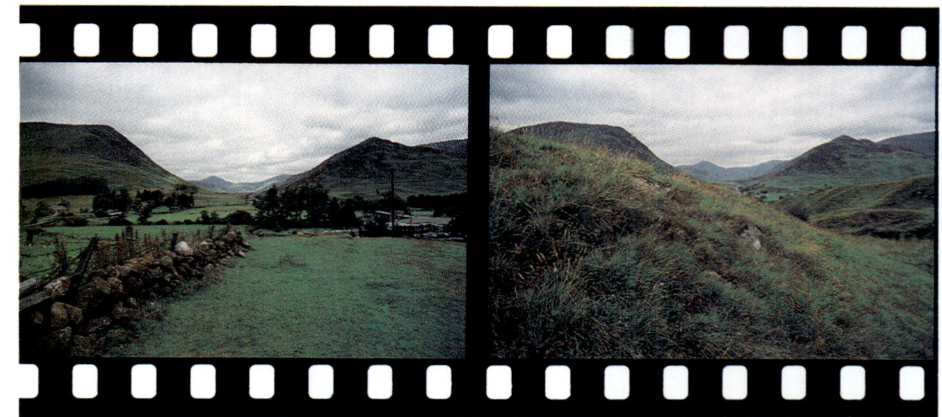

USE THE FOREGROUND

As you walk around a scene, notice how the foreground in view changes. The background seems to change much less because it is farther away. By moving just a few feet you can usually photograph a completely different foreground, yet still retain essentially the same background. Exploring a scene leads to the best pictures.

The above two photos illustrate this. The one at left emphasizes depth. The wall leads your eyes into the background. To make the other picture, the photographer moved a few feet away from the first viewpoint. The background is practically unchanged, but the new foreground gives you the impression of a different place.

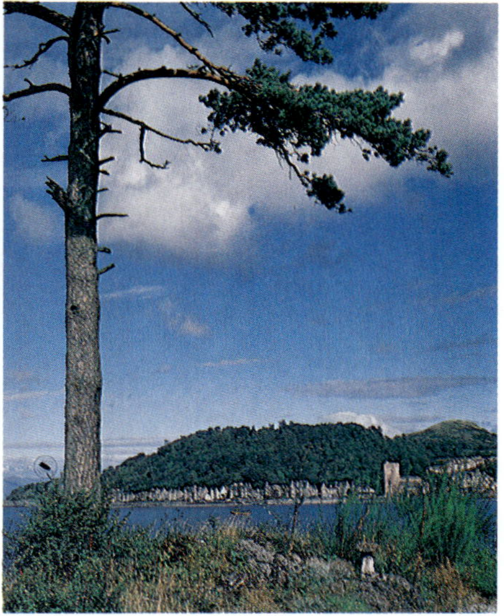

Foreground Frame—When distant elements interest you most, it is easy to forget about the foreground, with the result that you'll have either an empty or a distracting foreground. Include a foreground element to frame the main subject, as shown here. It gives a sense of depth and helps complete the composition.

Good Pictures in Bad Weather

Not only good weather leads to good pictures. *Dramatic* weather does too! The effects of wind, rain, fog or snow can add extra interest to an otherwise ordinary scene. Exciting environmental conditions are fun to photograph, but they can also cause some problems.

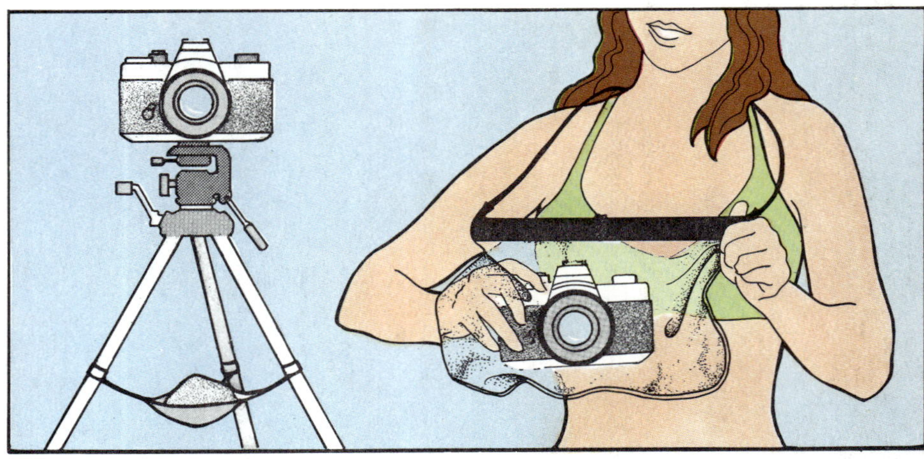

SECURE YOUR TRIPOD

Use a tripod with spiked feet to hold securely in wind or on wet ground. Splay the legs out as wide as possible for extra stability. In high wind, the tripod may still shake a bit. If so, fill a bag with something heavy, like stones, and sling it underneath the camera, as shown. When taking the picture, block wind with your body and exert slight downward pressure on the camera top to help steady the assembly.

WEATHERPROOFING

Protect yourself from the elements by using a windproof parka, raincoat or poncho, warm coat or other appropriate outdoor wear. If the garment is spacious, you can keep the camera inside when not shooting.

Equipment—You can use your camera without protection in a gentle rain or at the beach on a windy day. Be sure to protect it when not taking pictures. If you need to use it a lot and keep it ready, weatherproofing is necessary to avoid getting the camera too wet, dusty or salty.

If you don't use a weatherproof camera like the Nikonos or Fujica HD-S, consider a weatherproof accessory for your camera. Camera stores carry special plastic bags like the one shown. It keeps your camera dry and free of sand and dust.

The camera lens looks through a special viewing port built into the bag. Some photographers make their own bags by using clear plastic food bags. Cut a hole in the bag for the camera lens to look through. Secure the bag with tape or a rubber band.

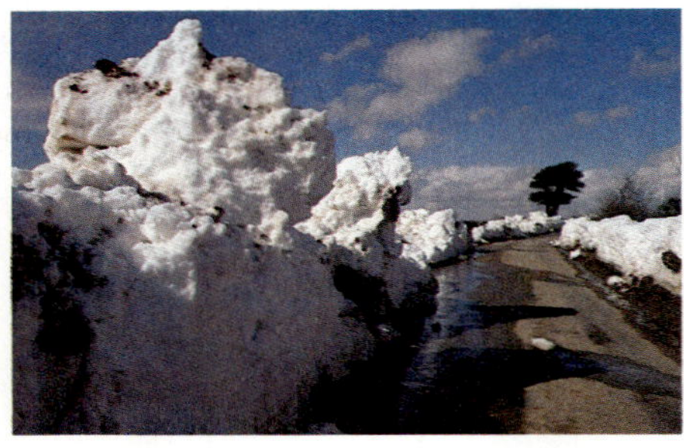

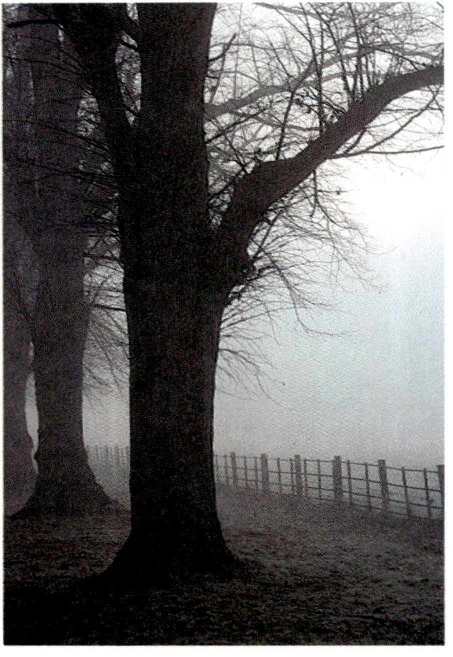

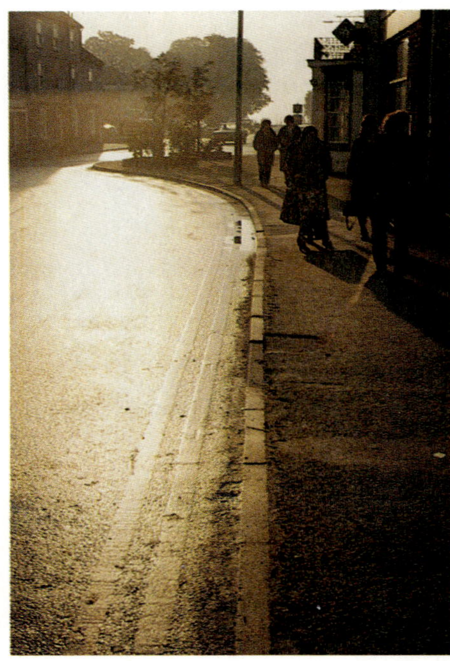

COLD WEATHER

It can be difficult to handle the camera when it is very cold outside. Here are some tips for best results.

Use warm gloves or mittens with finger flaps. Try not to breathe directly on the camera. Your warm breath may condense and ice up the camera or fog the lens. Batteries have less power when cold; in extreme cold an electronic camera may malfunction. Keep the camera warm under your coat when not using it or get an external camera-battery pack that you can keep warm in your coat.

Film can get brittle so rewind it slowly, or do it when the camera is warmed. While the camera is warming up, put it in a plastic bag with a small bag of silica gel. Let it sit in a warm place for a couple hours. Condensation will form on the bag, not on the camera and film.

NON-AVERAGE SCENES

Many of the scenes you'll want to shoot in bad weather are non-average. Some are shown here. As described earlier, getting

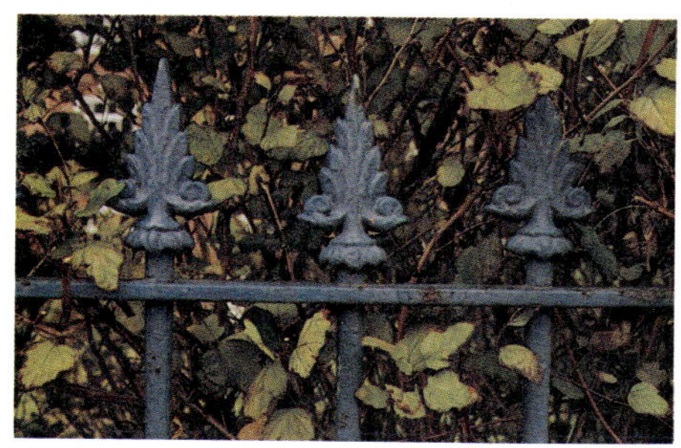

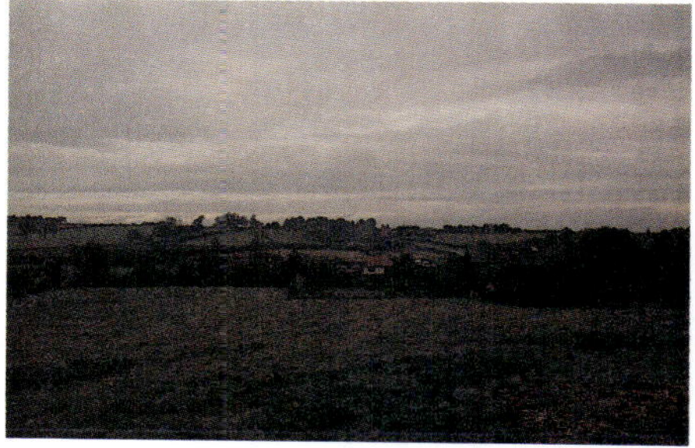

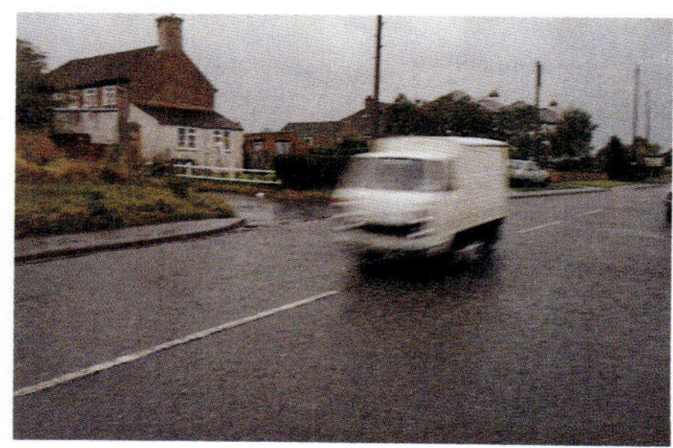

PROBLEM LIGHTING

Often, bad weather means clouds and relative darkness. These conditions affect the way you see and take pictures. When it is overcast, lighting is even because the sky acts as a large light source. This is good for two-dimensional or complex scenes with a lot of detail. It's not good for scenes that you want to reproduce with a three-dimensional look. See the left and center photos above.

In addition, the light from a cloudy sky is likely to reproduce with a bluish cast on color film. You can filter this out with a skylight filter if you want, although the cast may contribute to the mood of a dreary day. When in doubt, make filtered and unfiltered photos, then choose the one you like.

Exposure—When dark conditions are low-contrast, a colorful scene will appear somber. Bracketing in unusual light or bad weather is recommended.

Dim light also necessitates relatively slower shutter speeds and larger lens apertures. This may limit the depth of field you want or cause a moving subject to blur, as shown in the photo above right. If you don't want to use these effects creatively, use the fastest film available.

Filters—You can improve some scenes by using filters creatively. The effect can be subtle or obvious. It depends on the scene and what you want to show.

For example, use a blue graduated filter to make a white cloudy sky look bluer. Or, use a different color for an unnatural effect. Make a scene look foggier by using a diffusion or fog attachment. Use a pale colored filter to give an overall color cast to the photo.

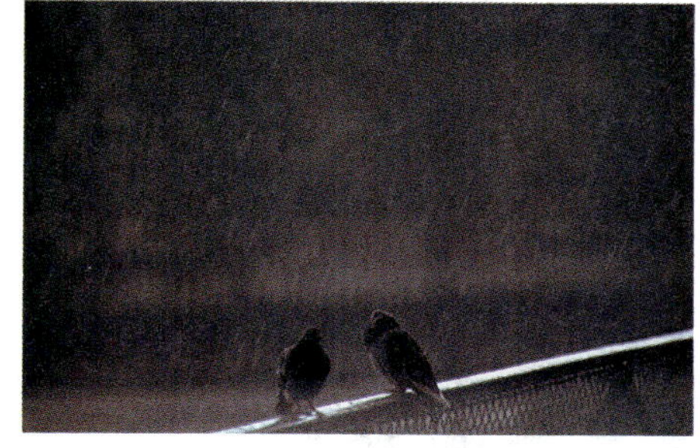

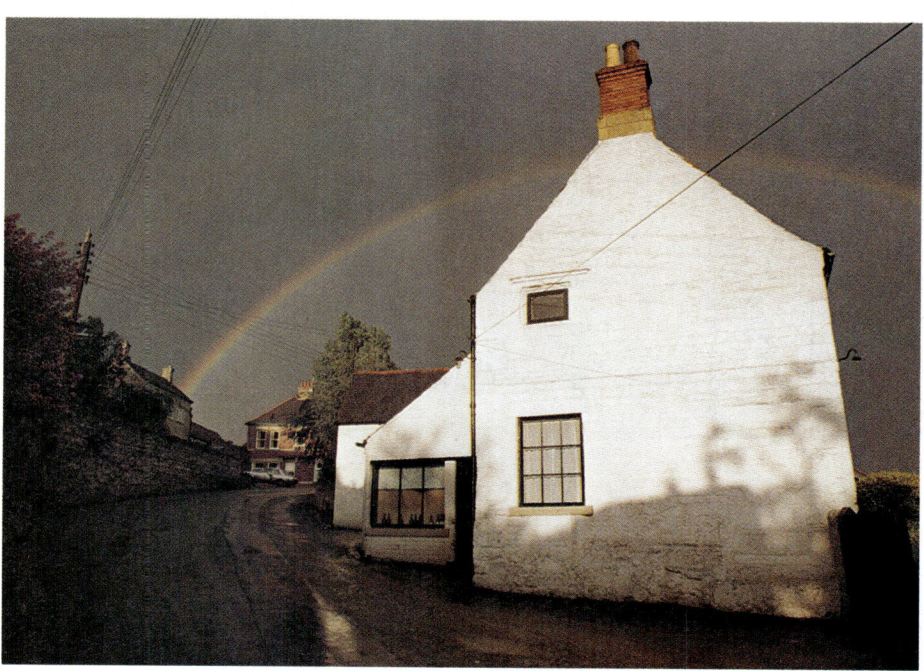

good exposures requires interpreting the camera's exposure recommendations. Or, you can meter a midtone area and base exposure on that reading. Compose and take the picture. If you are shooting an unusual scene, bracket exposures to be sure to get the picture.

Snow—If you photograph snow on a bright day, the camera meter "assumes" that you are photographing an average scene, rather than white snow. The recommended exposure settings will reproduce the snow as gray. Because you want the snow to look white, give the film about two steps more exposure than the meter recommends.

Mist and Fog—Best exposure for this kind of scene depends on your personal preference. For a dark, dreary picture, gray mist or fog is effective. Some pictures look most interesting with white mist. Bracket one step on either side of your best estimate of correct exposure.

Rainbow—Meter on the gray sky and underexpose a half step to get saturated colors in the rainbow.

Cityscapes

You may prefer taking pictures in your city or town to making trips to the country. If you live and work in a city, it's easier too. Instead of making special trips to take pictures, you can carry your camera with you during your daily activities. This way, you'll be ready to take a picture at almost any time.

POTENTIAL SUBJECTS

City life is exciting because of its variety. You'll see different kinds of people, activity, architecture, trees and flowers. Finding enough subject matter is rarely a problem.

Human Interest—People make a city fun to photograph. It's difficult to shoot buildings and streets without including people. So use human interest to improve your photos.

You can use people as foreground or background elements. Take candids, or informal portraits. Usually, the best formal portrait is the environmental kind, such as photographing an architect in front of a building he designed.

Activities—Take your camera with you to the next street fair, political rally or parade held in your town. Some people like to photograph sporting events—others

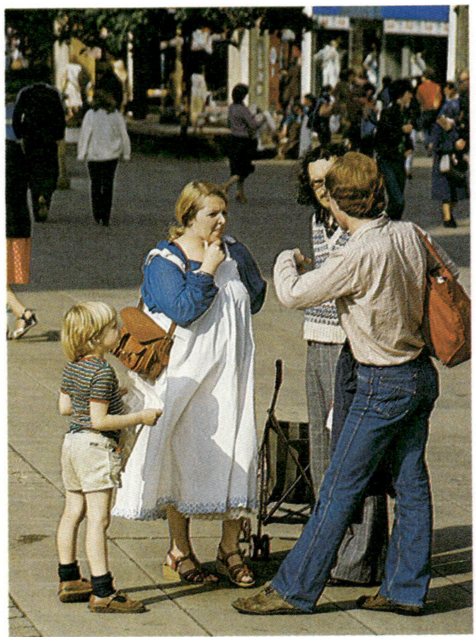

always seem to appear at house fires.

Architecture—Taking good architectural photos is like making an historical document of where you live. Buildings are always being built, remodeled or torn down, giving a changing cityscape to explore.

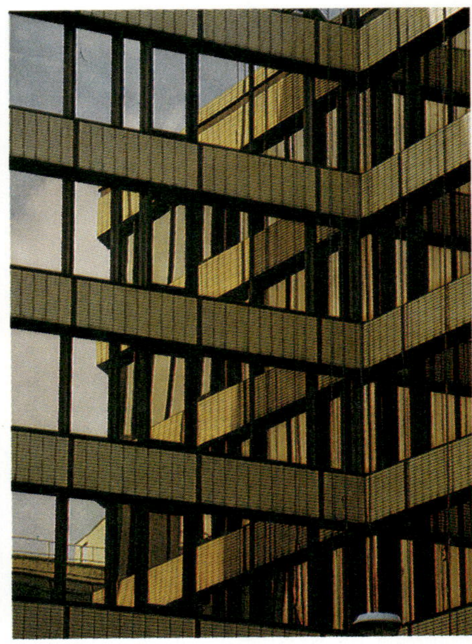

Some modern buildings are also fun to shoot abstractly. Consider reflections, close-ups and distorted wide-angle views.

Foliage—Visit city parks and photograph the people, trees and plants, or all of them. Try contrasting the urban and natural parts of the landscape.

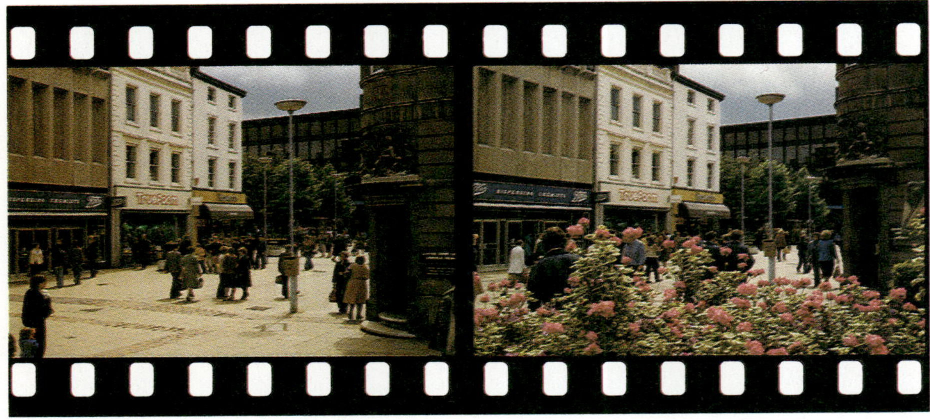

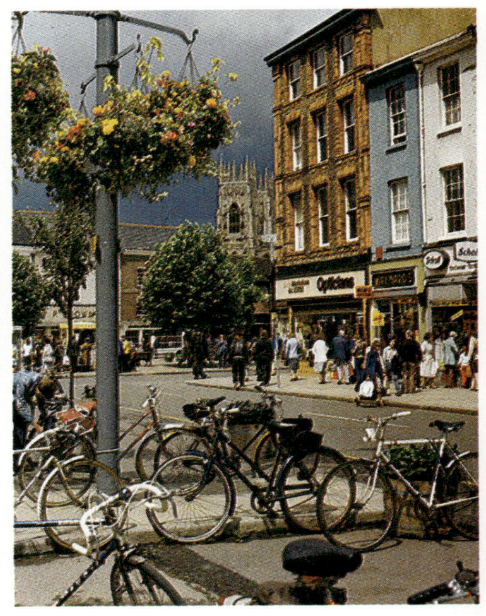

COMPOSITIONAL CONSIDERATIONS

Most of the tips mentioned for making good landscape pictures also apply when making cityscapes. For example, the two pictures above show the importance of finding the best viewpoint when using a wide-angle lens.

To photograph buildings on both sides of the street, the photographer had to back up from his original viewpoint and use a 35mm lens. This not only put the buildings in the field of view, but also included too much of the street. He filled this empty space by moving to his right and including some nearby flowers, with a lower viewpoint.

Put variety in your city pictures by using different lenses, horizontal and vertical formats, close-ups and special filtration. Being creative with everyday scenes will sharpen your photographic skills.

10 a.m.

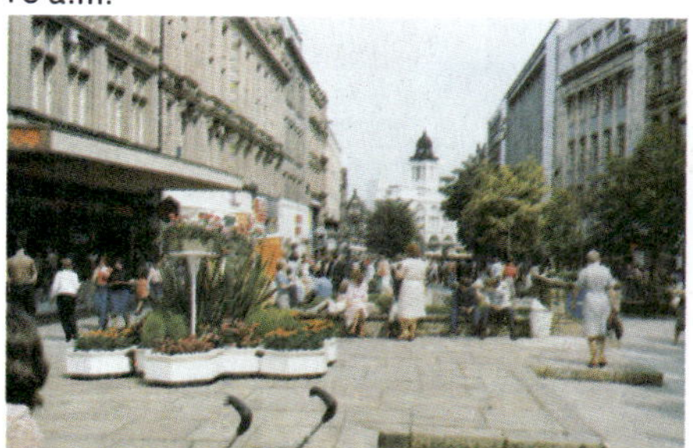

1 p.m.

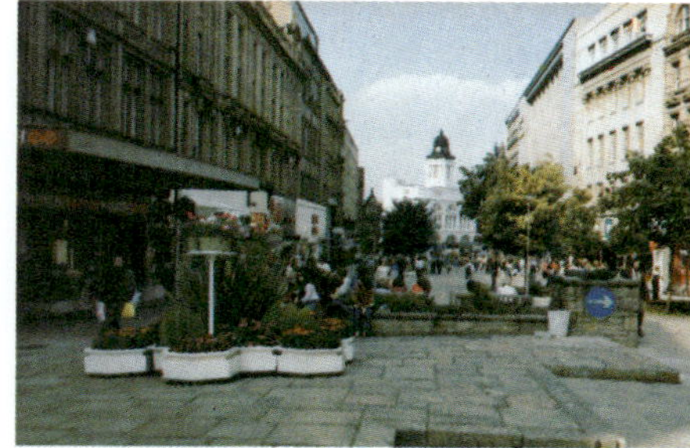

4 p.m.

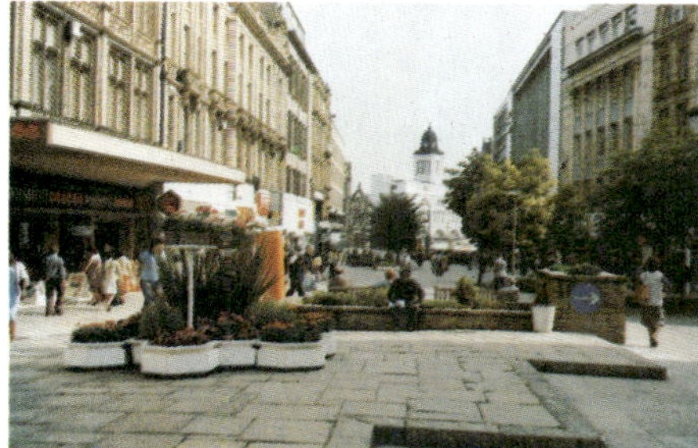

7 p.m.

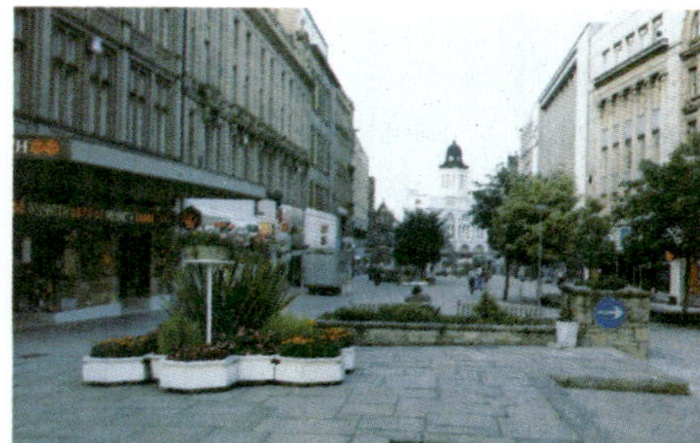

TIME OF DAY

The photos on this page show how lighting conditions can change during the day. Tall buildings block direct sunlight much of the time. Therefore, the brightest cityscapes usually occur at midday. Shadows are small because the light is directly overhead.

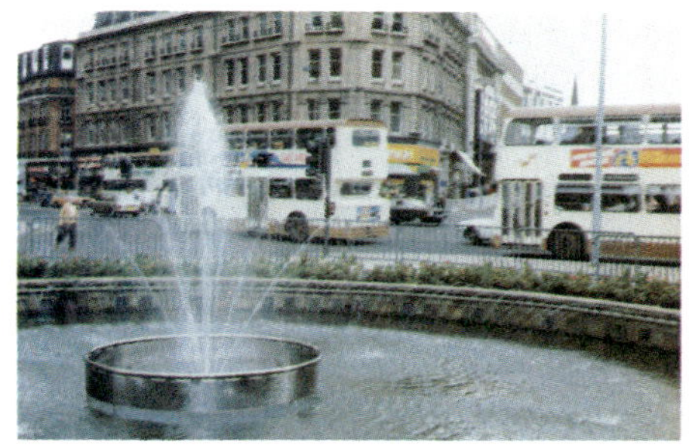

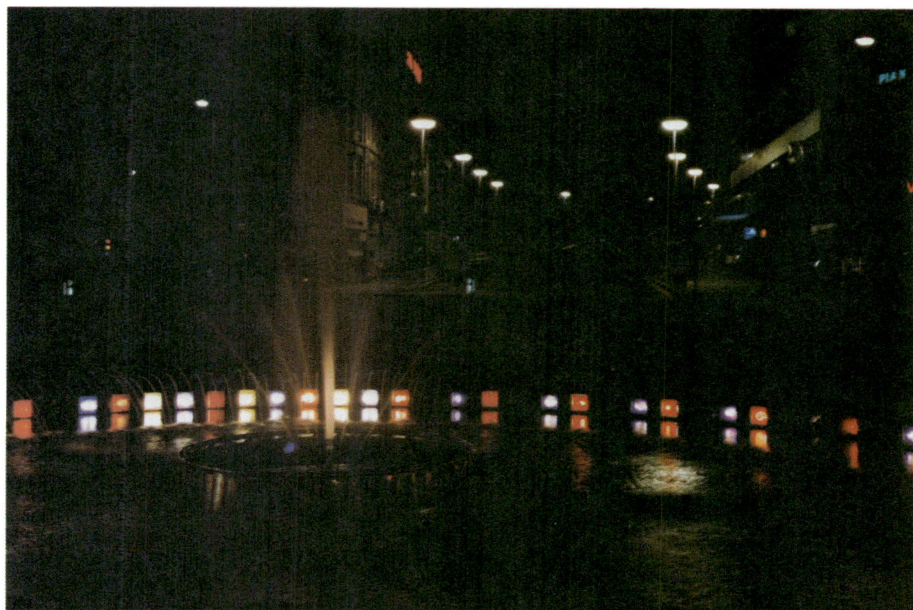

CITIES AT NIGHT

City scenes that may be uninteresting by day can be exciting to photograph at night. Street and car lights can add special lighting effects, while the darkness can hide unattractive details that you don't want to show.

For example, the above picture of the fountain has too many distracting background elements. Colors are drab too. In the photo at right, made at night, distracting background elements aren't visible. If cars had driven by during exposure, trails of light would have passed through part of the black background.

Exposure—In predominantly dark scenes, move close to significant bright areas and meter them. Use the recommended settings and move back to recompose. Try to exclude dark areas from the metering pattern; otherwise, the meter recommends settings that give overexposure.

Use the camera on a tripod because most expcsures will be relatively long. You won't be able to handhold the camera without causing image blur. Bracket extensively on the side of overexposure when shooting scenes at night. This is necessary because general-purpose films look underexposed with shutter speeds of 1/2 second or slower, because of film *reciprocity failure.*

Photographing Interiors

You don't always have to go outside to photograph. You can record interesting scenes in your household and in public buildings such as museums and churches.

Interior photography can be more challenging than photographing outdoors. Usually, the light is not as even or bright, requiring flash or slow shutter speeds. Color film is not balanced for the light from most interior lighting, requiring filtration. To record a large area in a confined space, a wide-angle lens is necessary.

WHAT TO SHOOT?

The variety of potential indoor pictures is enormous. You can record personal possessions for insurance purposes. Make environmental portraits of people in their favorite rooms. Record a day in the life of your household. Photograph a room before, during and after redecorating.

USEFUL ACCESSORIES

Use the camera on a tripod to eliminate camera shake. The camera film plane must be parallel to the walls if you want vertical lines to reproduce vertical. Use a tripod with a bubble level or get an accessory level that fits in your camera hot shoe, as shown above.

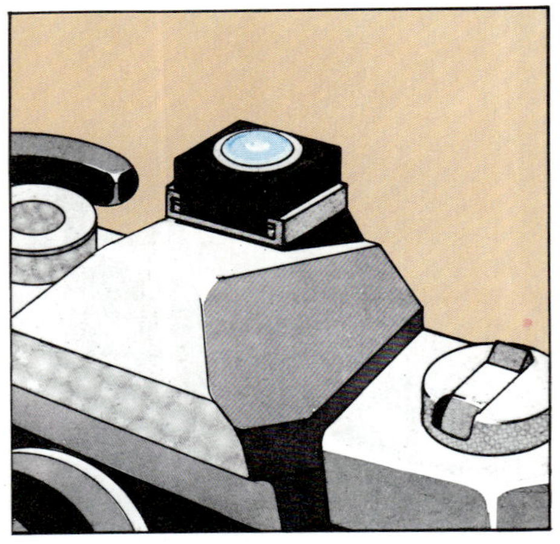

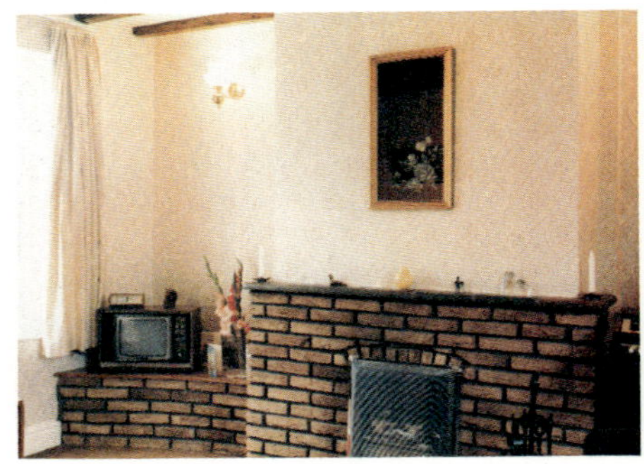

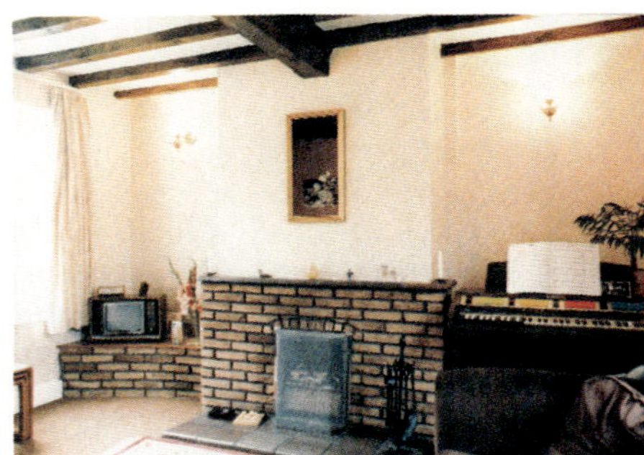

A wide-angle lens is ideal when you want to record a wide view within a confined space. The top photo was made with a 35mm lens, the bottom with a 24mm lens.

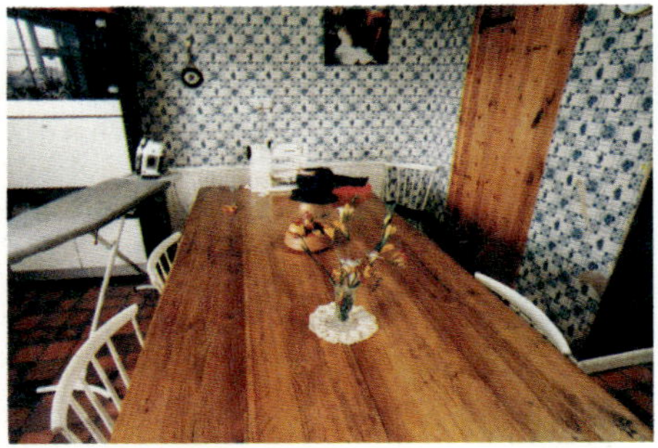

CAMERA VIEWPOINT

When you photograph an interior at eye level, you may record too much ceiling. When you point the camera down to avoid imaging the ceiling, as shown above, the room seems to tilt and looks distorted.

Avoid these problems by carefully considering what you want to show in the picture. If the ceiling is interesting, use a high viewpoint. If furniture or seated people are most interesting, use a lower viewpoint, as shown at right. Notice that the wide-angle lens used for this picture included part of the ceiling. In addition, the camera film plane was vertical, so vertical lines in the picture do not seem to converge. The photo is a realistic record of the scene.

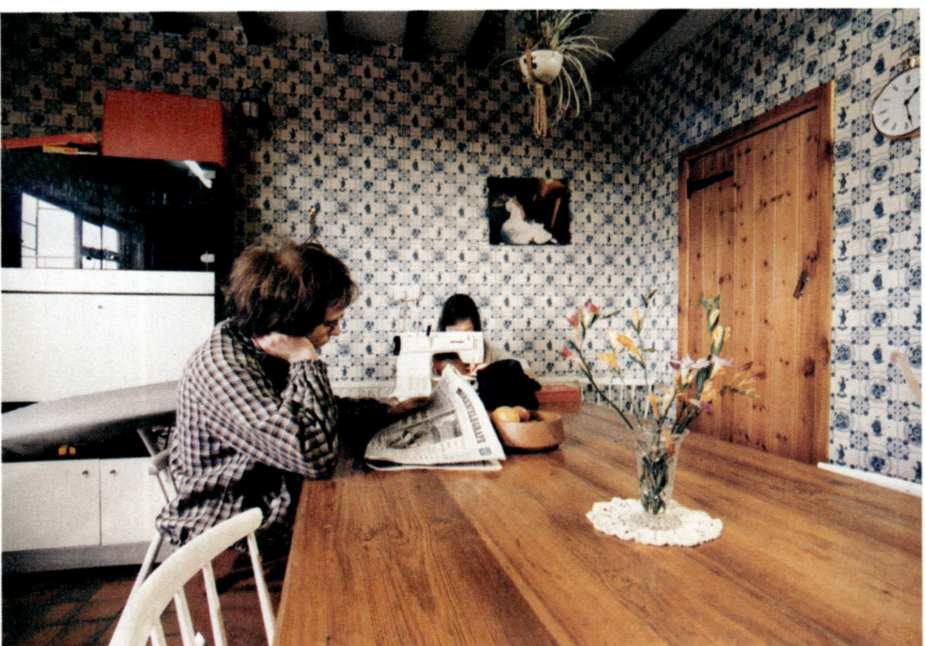

People and Scale—Use people to indicate the size of a room or its contents. Putting people in different places in the scene also adds to the effect of depth in the image.

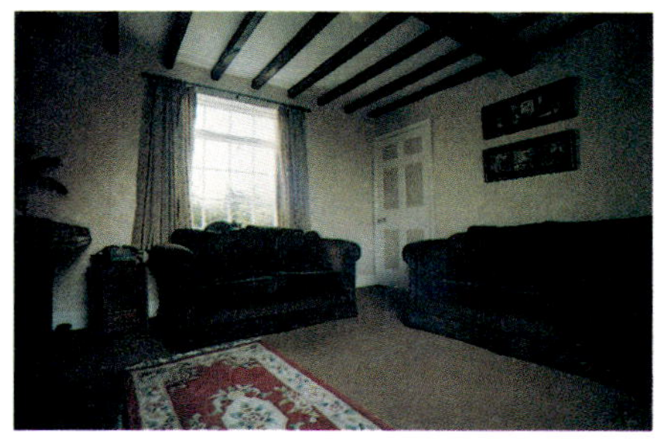

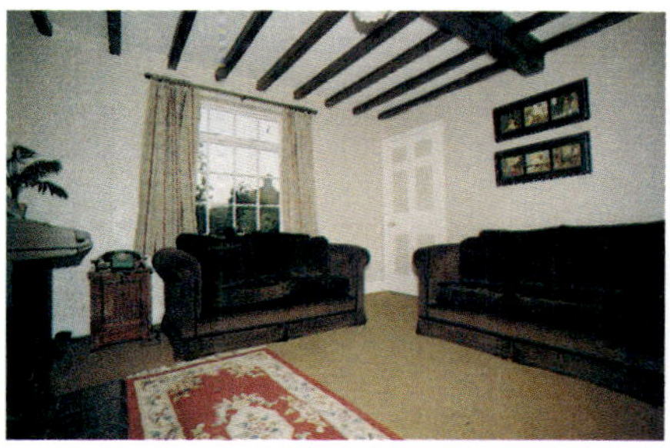

FLASH OR WINDOW LIGHT

If you are photographing a small area or subject near a large window, you'll probably like the effect of soft, even light coming from outdoors through the window. Direct sunlight through the window may also be pleasing.

However, neither of these conditions may be adequate if your subject is large or far from the window. The lighting probably won't be even—far subjects will reproduce darker than those close to the window. In addition, you'll probably base exposure on lit areas and include the window in the field of view. This makes the window reproduce white. If you don't want this to happen, give less exposure so outside detail shows on film. But this may make the room look dark, as shown above left.

Flash—One way to get even lighting is to use flash. The simplest way is to use it mounted on your camera. Be sure that the beam covers the area your lens sees. If you use a focal length shorter than 35mm, you may need an accessory beam spreader over the flash window.

For big rooms, or if you want to minimize shadows, bounce the light from the ceiling. Or, you can manually trip the flash two or three times while an assistant holds the shutter open on B. Bounce light from different parts of the ceiling.

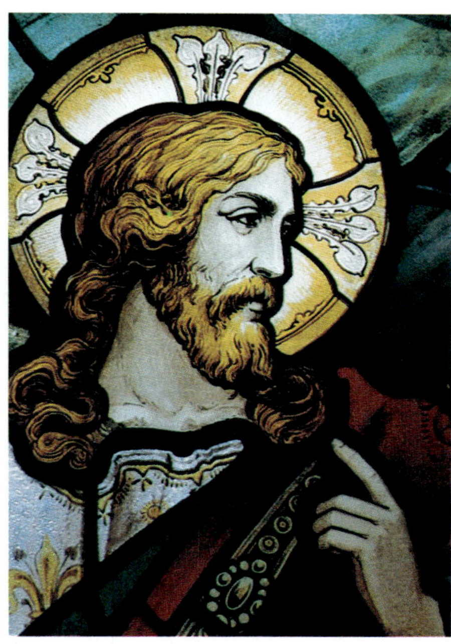

STAINED GLASS

Meter just the stained glass. Use the recommended setting and recompose if necessary. Use a bubble level to make sure the film plane is parallel to the stained glass.

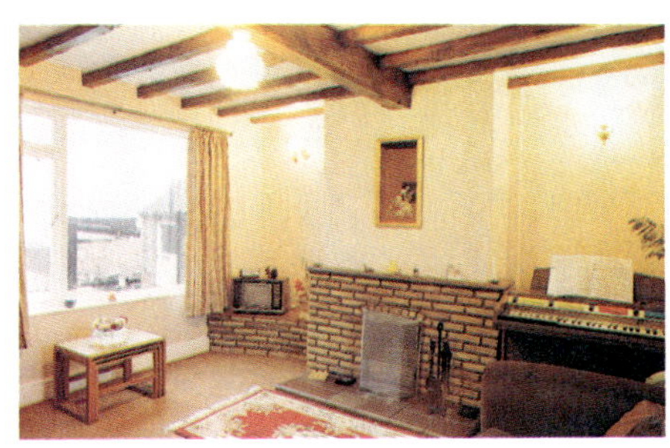

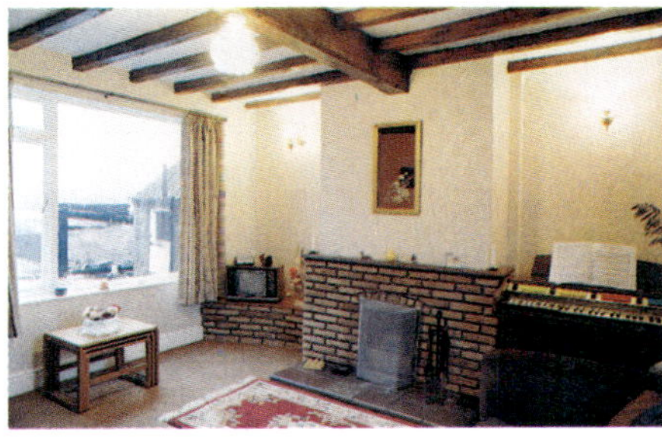

COLOR BALANCE

Shooting interiors in color can be difficult when the lighting is mixed. As shown above, you may want to use window light and household lamps for even lighting. If you use daylight film, household lamps reproduce too orange, above left. If you use tungsten film, above right, the exterior view reproduces too blue.

One way to solve the problem is to use one light source exclusively and use the film balanced for that source. If you use daylight film, try bounce flash to brighten dark areas not lit by window light. If you use tungsten film, close the drapes.

If you can't exclude one offending light source, try to minimize it compositionally. Use the film that most closely balances with the predominant source.

Using Filters—Sometimes, you won't have the color film you need to photograph an interior. In these cases, use a light-balancing filter so the light matches the color sensitivity of the film.

Suppose you have daylight film in the camera and want to photograph a room lit by household tungsten lamps. A standard blue 80A filter will absorb much, but not all, of the excess orange light. The leftover will give the image a slightly warm cast. Most people will like this effect in a color slide. The cast can be corrected in a print made from a color negative.

Or, suppose you have tungsten-balanced film in your camera. Photographing by just window light will create an unappealing blue cast in the picture. Avoid this by using an orange 85-series filter over the lens. The right one to use depends on the tungsten-balanced film in your camera. With film balanced for 3200K light, use the 85A filter. The 85B filter absorbs excess blue to balance with 3400K tungsten film.

Many modern interiors are lit by fluorescent lamps. This light reproduces on daylight film with a bluish-green cast. The easiest way to avoid this color cast is with an amber-colored light-balancing filter. It's called different things by different manufacturers, such as FLD, FL-D or FL-DAY.

Better Action Pictures

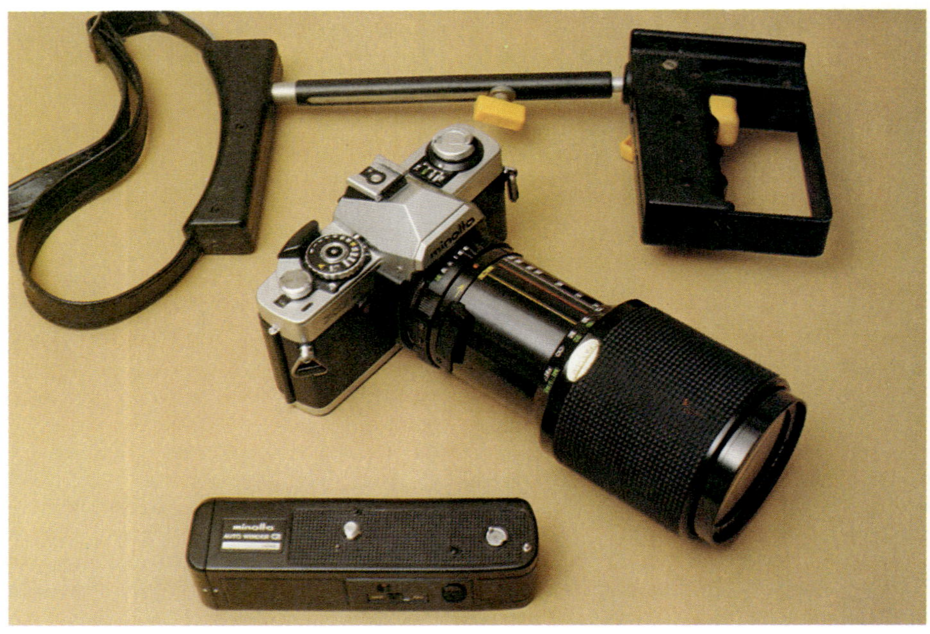

One of photography's most fascinating characteristics is the ability to record a moment for the viewer to ponder leisurely. When that slice of time is extremely short, such as with 1/1000-second or flash exposures, we are able to appreciate action and movements that we may otherwise miss. This is why good action pictures have visual impact.

WHAT YOU NEED

In today's busy world, fast-moving subjects seem to be everywhere. You may want to photograph moving vehicles, animals in motion, or athletic performers. Doing it well demands three things: familiarity with your subject's activity, knowledge of your equipment, and fast reflexes.

Equipment—A camera with a top shutter speed of 1/1000 second or faster is essential. As mentioned earlier, these speeds will freeze most moving subjects. Use fast film so you can use these fast shutter speeds together with a relatively small lens aperture.

If your subject is far away, as happens at many sporting events, a telephoto zoom lens is very useful. Your subject will be on the move, but you are probably restricted to where you can go. For quick and easy camera operation, use the camera and zoom on a shoulder grip, shown at top.

An autowinder or motor drive lets you make sequential exposures quickly, without having to manually advance film. After each exposure, the accessory advances film for you. This lets you concentrate on the scene you see in the camera viewfinder.

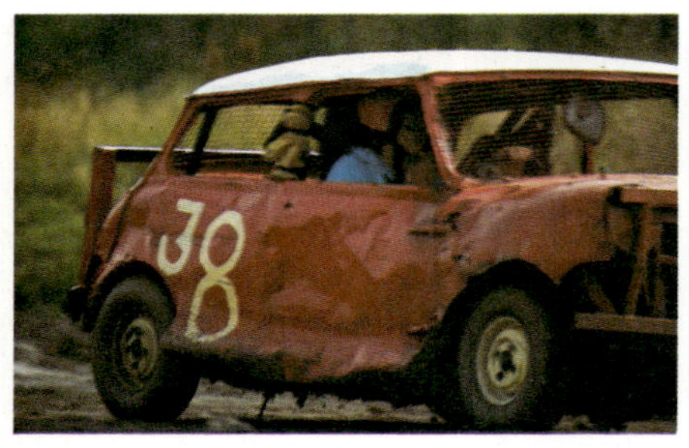

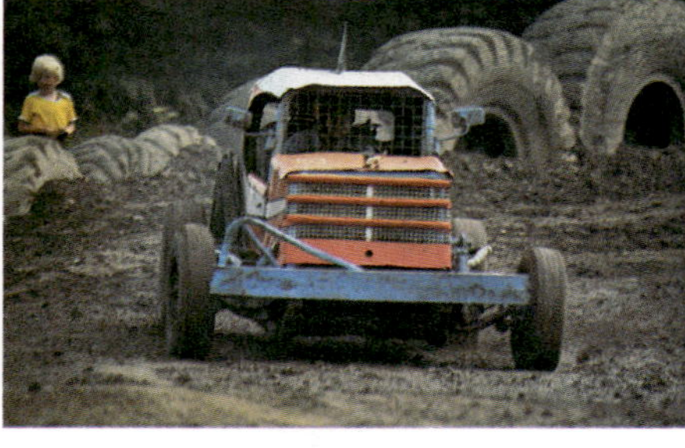

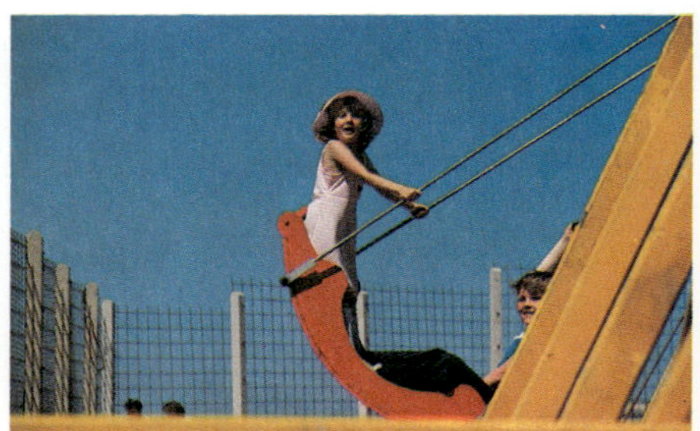

ANTICIPATE ACTION

You'll get better action pictures when you know about your subject's activity, so you can anticipate what will happen next. You're better able to be in the right place at the right time and have a suitable lens on the camera.

In addition, you must compensate for the slight time delay between wanting to take the picture and actually exposing film. This varies from photographer to photographer. Only practice will decrease your time delay. Press the shutter button just *before* the anticipated action occurs. If you see the action in the viewfinder, it's already too late to make the photo.

The above photo is a good example of this. The photographer waited until the front of the car was at the right of the frame. The car kept moving during the time delay between seeing the motion and actually exposing film.

ANGLE AND SHUTTER SPEED

Angle, shutter speed and subject speed determine the amount of image blur on film. Generally, when the subject moves toward you, a slower speed is possible without image blur. As the subject moves more perpendicular to you, a faster shutter speed is necessary to freeze action.

Image blur is not necessarily bad. Because your subject is moving, a blurred effect may give the image most impact. For specific recommendations, see pages 14 to 17 for useful tips on controlling image blur.

PEAK ACTION

Many regular and predictable motions have peak times. These are transition times between motion in one direction and the switch to the opposite direction. For example, a jumping basketball player can jump only so high. When he reaches his peak, he is temporarily almost still before coming down again. The still time is *peak action.* In the image it can imply action and drama. Even though it looks stationary, it helps define the action by showing the limits. Observe this by looking at the picture of the girl in the swing. Other subjects that have exciting peak actions are pole vaulters, gymnasts, divers and tennis players.

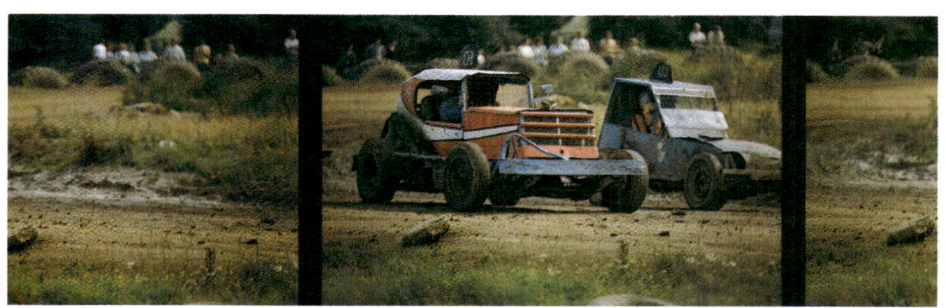

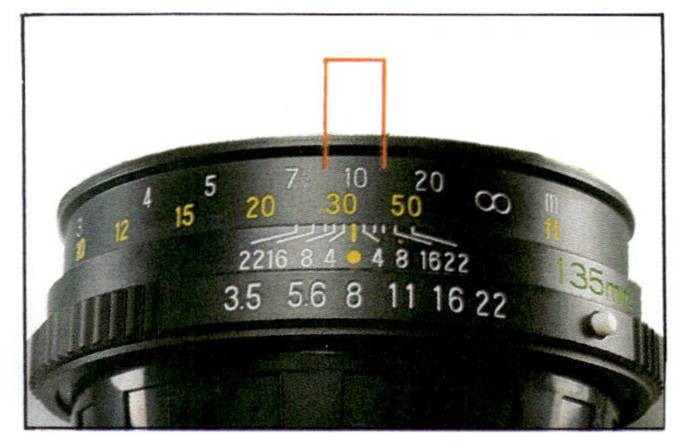

TIPS FOR GOOD FOCUS

Following a moving subject by looking through the viewfinder of an SLR is easy. The image you see is right side up and laterally correct. What isn't always easy is maintaining good focus as you move the camera to follow the moving subject. If you use a zoom lens on the camera, your task can be even more difficult.

You should know how the focusing ring on your lens works. When you know which direction to turn the ring to focus, you can find best focus quickly, without moving the ring back and forth, possibly missing the shot.

Preset Focus—If your moving subject has a predictable motion, then the best way to get good focus is to preset it on an element that is about as far away as your subject will predictably be. This is illustrated in the above series of photos.

The rock you see at the extreme left is on the road traveled by the race cars. The photographer focused on this rock, envisioning a composition of two cars on the road near the rock. Then he sighted the two cars approaching. He followed their progress by keeping them centered in the viewfinder. When they were in the area of the envisioned composition, he depressed the shutter button to take the picture you see in the middle.

Depth of Field—The photographer was also sure to keep the rock and road in the zone of sharp focus, as indicated by the depth-of-field scale on the lens. Remember that about one-third of the depth of field is in front of the focused distance and two-thirds behind it.

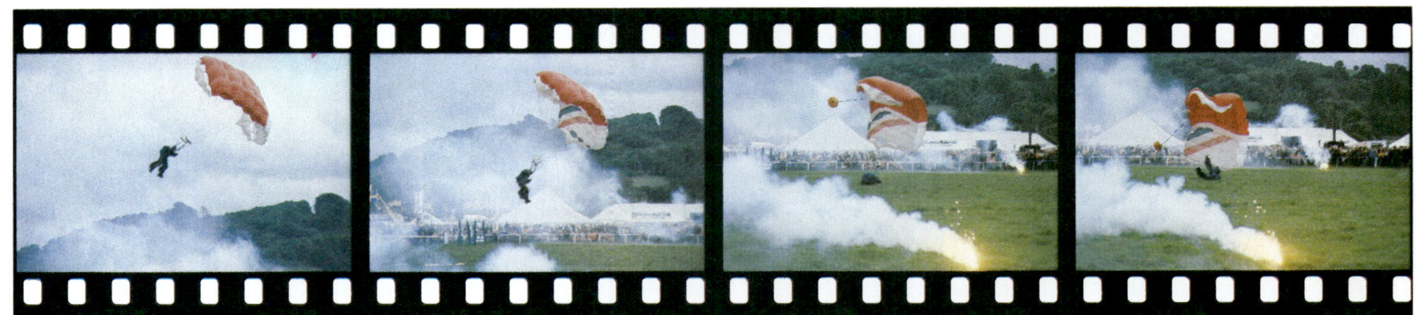

An understanding of your subject and the action helps you expose film at times of peak action. For example, sports photographers must know the rules and actions of the game if they want exciting pictures. You have to anticipate the action and push the shutter button just *before* the peak.

AUTOWINDERS AND MOTOR DRIVES

These accessories minimize the time delay caused by manually winding film. Also, it is one less step to worry about, so you can keep your attention on the subject you see in the viewfinder and be constantly ready to press the shutter button.

With an autowinder, you can expose about two frames per second at the fastest camera shutter speeds. A motor drive gives faster sequential shooting—about five frames per second, maximum.

Shooting many frames quickly may help you get the picture you want when the action is rapidly changing, as illustrated above. Instead of making just one or two pictures, you can expose a lot of film quickly. Later, you can choose the best of the bunch, as was done here, right.

Don't use an autowinder or motor drive as a substitute for anticipating action. It's possible to miss a good photo even though you've exposed 36 frames in less than 18 seconds!

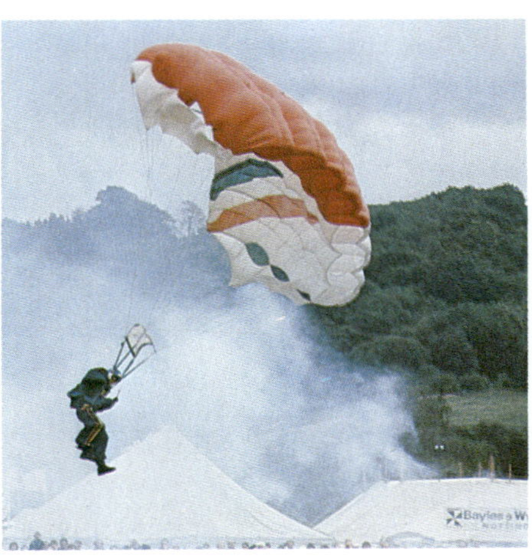

Making Multiple Exposures

Accidentally making more than one exposure on a frame of film can be frustrating. You've ruined two potentially good pictures to make an unusable third one! This is why most modern cameras have a built-in, double-exposure prevention mechanism.

However, intentionally making multiple exposures on a single film frame can also lead to unique and exciting images. Doing it purposefully can be a way to get spectacular pictures.

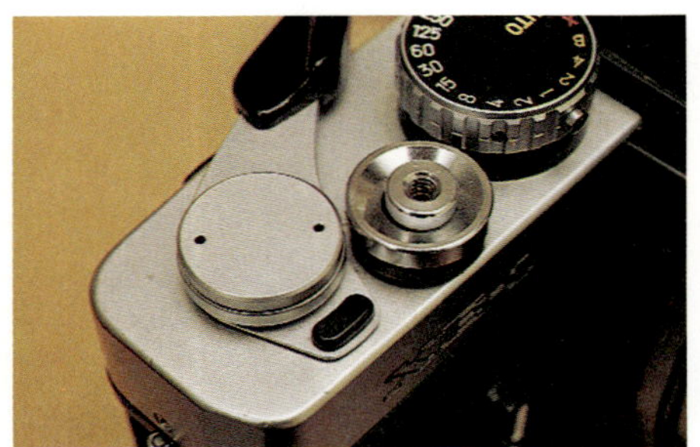

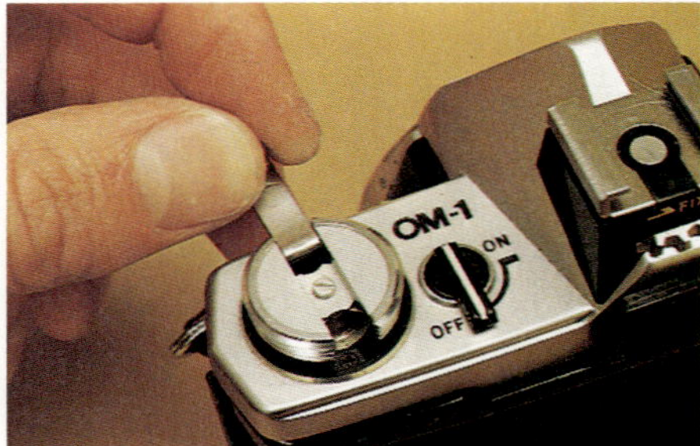

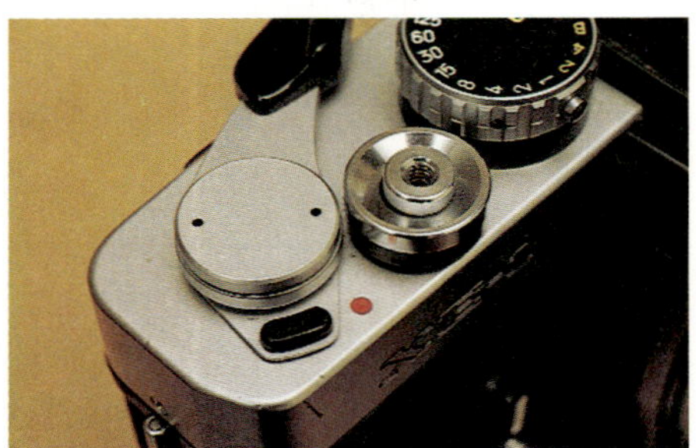

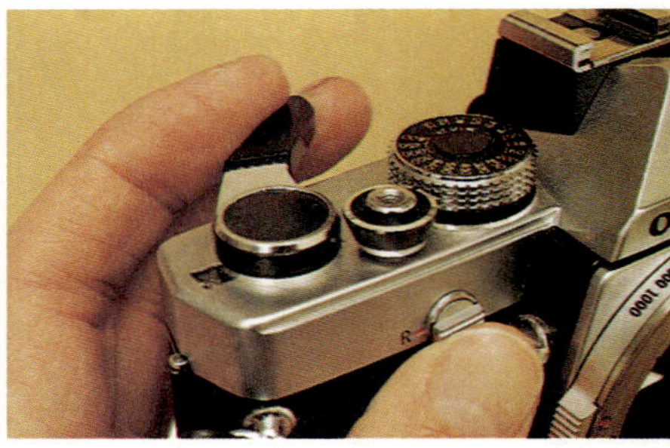

CAMERA OPERATION

Many cameras have a multiple-exposure control that releases the film-advance mechanism from the camera's film-wind lever. After making the first exposure on the frame, engage the multiple-exposure control, as shown in the left set of pictures. Typically a red dot is uncovered. Then turn the film-wind lever to cock the shutter; it won't wind film. Make the next exposure and repeat the process for subsequent exposures on the same frame.

If your camera doesn't have a multiple-exposure control, you have to trick it. Turn the film-rewind lever, as shown above right, to take up film slack. Make the first exposure on the frame. Then engage the film-rewind button while holding down the film-rewind crank. Turn the film-wind lever. This cocks the shutter but doesn't advance film. Make the next exposure. Repeat the process for subsequent exposures on the same frame.

The first method gives good registration of the superimposed images. The second method, however, is non-standard so the film may slip a bit every time you turn the film-wind lever. Good registration is not guaranteed. For this reason, shoot an extra unexposed frame for safety before and after the multiple-exposure frame.

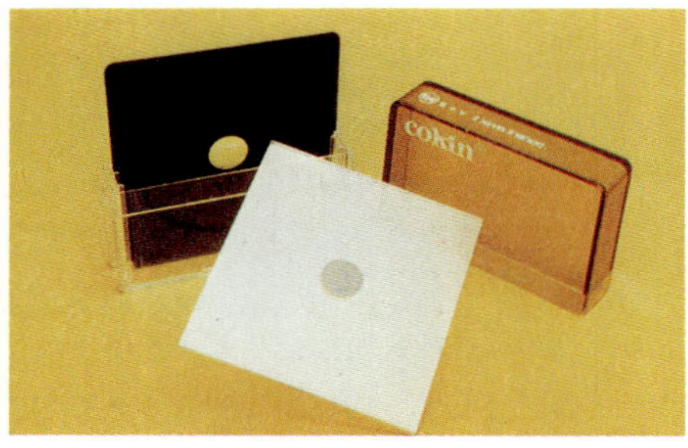

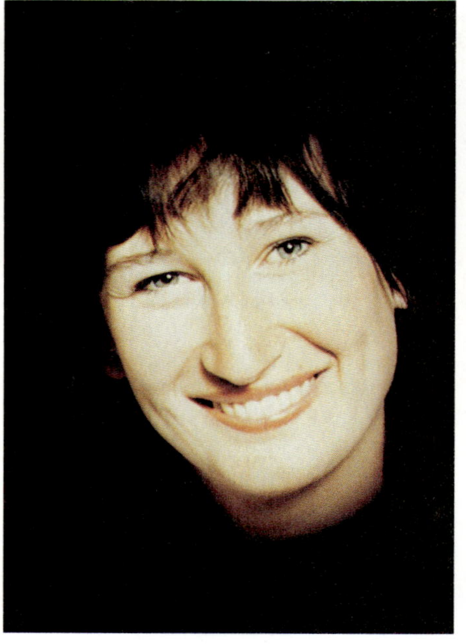

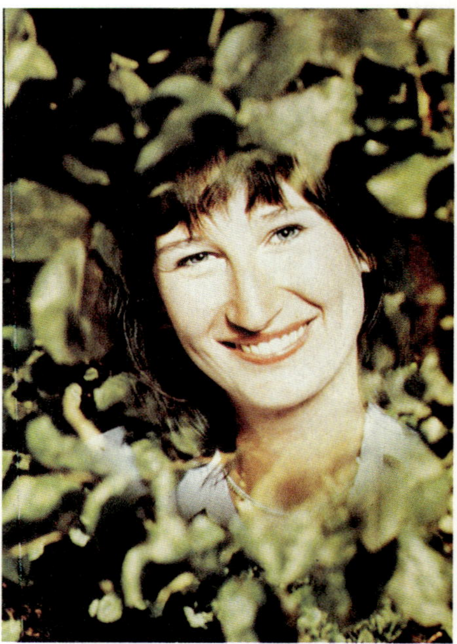

MULTIPLE-EXPOSURE MASKS

With multiple-exposure masks, you can combine two scenes without having image overlap. No exposure correction is necessary. These accessories are available as part of filter systems mentioned earlier. A Cokin model is shown here.

Two masks are part of each kit. One mask at a time is held in front of the lens in a holder that attaches to the lens. One mask is mostly black with a clear area. The paired mask is a *negative* version of the first one. It is clear where the first is black, and vice-versa. The example shown above was made with a center-spot mask kit. Others are available to give left/right combinations and more complex superimpositions.

Meter both scenes without the mask in place. If using an automatic camera, meter and then set shutter speed and aperture manually. Install the mask and take the picture. The first exposure in this example was with the mask that had the hole in it. It prevented light from surrounding the subject's face on film. The second mask had a black spot in a clear field. It blocked exposure to the central, already-exposed area and let the foliage expose the film in the previously-masked areas.

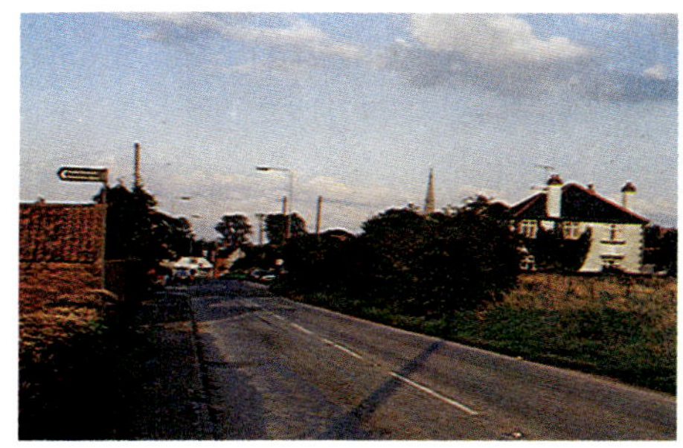

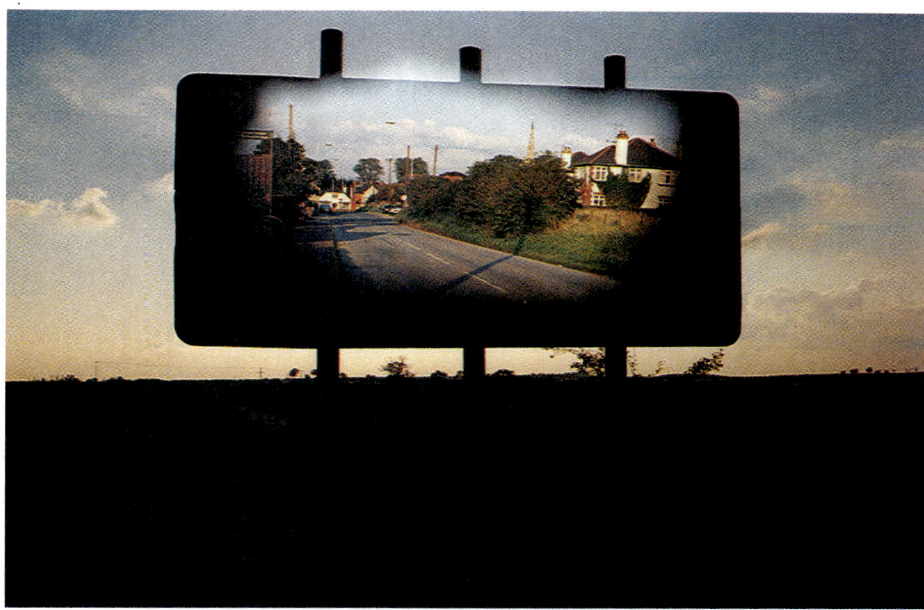

COMBINING IMAGES

Superimposing normal exposures makes the image progressively lighter. Bright areas add up exposure and will eventually reproduce as white. Overlapping dark areas also reproduce lighter than you'd expect. A little later, you'll see how to compensate for this effect by making each exposure a fraction of normal.

Exposure correction is unnecessary if you are careful to superimpose bright areas onto very dark areas. The dark area contributes little, if any, light to the multiple exposure.

For example, the first exposure for the photo above right was a silhouette of the billboard. The photographer based exposure on the background sky to reproduce the foreground as black. This is normal for a silhouette. Later, the photographer exposed the same frame to the scene you see at left. He used an opaque card with a hole cut into it to block exposure from areas other than the billboard. Normal exposure was used for the second image.

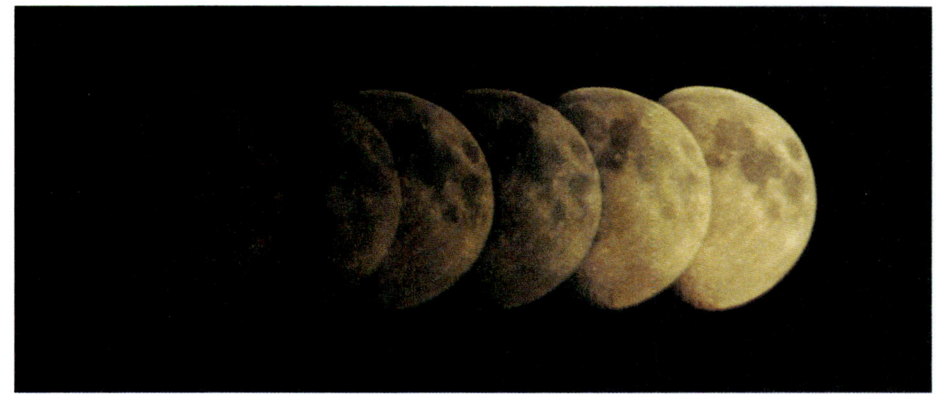

EXPOSURE CONSIDERATIONS

The above photo is a good example of how you can use exposure creatively when making multiple exposures. In this case the photographer used progressively more exposure for each moon image. The fifth image received full exposure. This kind of creative control is practical when there is a large dark background. If there is minimal overlap, you can make each exposure normally or a fraction of normal.

Making Fractional Exposures—As mentioned earlier, image overlap creates a lighter picture—one that is possibly too light and overexposed. Avoid this problem by making *each* exposure a fractional part of the total.

For example, if a normal exposure for two scenes of a double exposure is *f*-8 at 1/125 second, expose each at *f*-11 at 1/125 second. Each image is underexposed by one step, half normal. Added together, however, they give a normal exposure. For a triple exposure, give each image one-third the normal exposure.

This guideline works well if each scene has approximately equal amounts of light and dark areas, and there will be overlap of bright areas. Don't use this technique with multiple masks or when one or more of the scenes is predominantly dark, as in the illustration at the top of this page.

Using the Film-Speed Dial—You can use the camera film-speed dial as a multiple-exposure-control device. Multiply the normal film speed by the number of exposures you want to make. Set this number, or the closest standard film-speed number, on the film-speed dial. Meter each scene normally and use the recommended settings for each exposure. Be sure to reset the film-speed dial when the multple exposure is finished.

For example, if you want to make four exposures on a frame of ASA 100 film, set the film-speed dial to 400. The camera then "underexposes" each image by two steps—each gets one-quarter of normal exposure. Because it happens four times, total exposure is about correct.

Copying Your Pictures

Making high-quality duplicates of your prints and slides is a useful skill. For example, you may want an enlargement of an old family photograph but can't find the negative. All you have to do is re-photograph the print with slow-speed b&w film and make an enlargement of the processed negative.

Copying photos can be as simple as using your camera on a tripod and taping a print to a wall. If you do it this way, use a small level to be sure that the film plane is parallel to the copy subject.

Or, suppose you want to enter a photo contest but don't want to send your original slide. Make a copy slide that looks just like the original and send it instead. Your original won't be lost or damaged in shipping and handling.

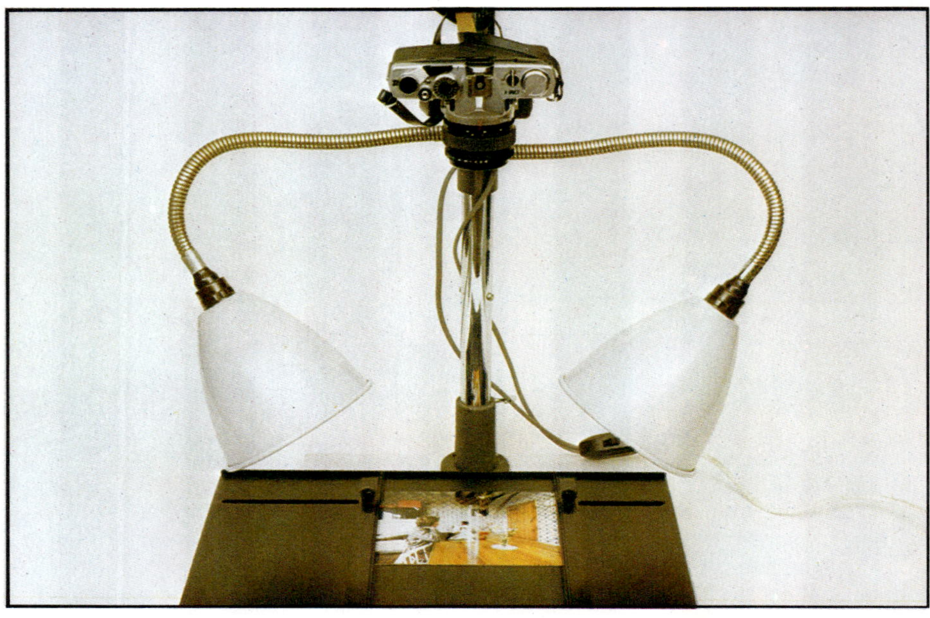

COPY STAND

A copy stand, shown at right, is a useful aid to get good results. With a copy stand, you can photograph flat objects like prints onto negative or slide film. The camera mount holds your camera with the lens axis perpendicular to the plane of the copy subject. This puts the film parallel to the print, so the image is not distorted.

You adjust the subject distance by sliding the camera mount up or down the vertical column. Subject distance depends on required image magnification and lens focal length. For copy work you can use the close-up equipment mentioned earlier. A macro lens is most convenient.

Accessory Viewfinder—If you do a lot of copy work, you'll get tired of looking down through the camera's standard eyepiece every time you want to compose or focus. A handy accessory called a *right-angle viewer* clips over the standard eyepiece. It lets you view the focusing

COPYING SLIDES

There are a lot of good reasons to copy your best slides. If you project slides often and long enough, they can fade. Therefore, some people store original slides carefully and project high-quality duplicates. As mentioned earlier, you can also use duplicate slides in competitions or for other photographic uses and not worry about losing or damaging an original.

The easiest way to make a duplicate slide is when you expose the original. If you are sure about the exposure, and subject and lighting won't change, expose more than one frame of film. Use the same exposure-control settings for each frame. This is not bracketing. It's a convenient way to make identical pictures.

Accessory Slide Copier—Many camera and independent manufacturers make an accessory for copying or improving existing slides. Some of these copiers attach to a lens at the front of a bellows or extension tube. With this setup you can magnify part of the slide, selectively cropping the image. In addition, you can use filters to alter the color balance of the duplicate for improvement or special effect.

Less-expensive slide duplicators attach to the camera body and use built-in lenses.

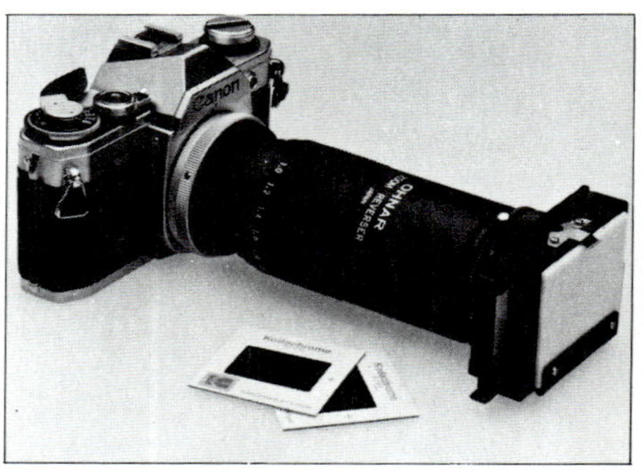

Two types are available. One gives just same-size slide duplicates. This is OK if you don't want to crop an original image. If you do, then get a variable-magnification copier. Typically, this device has a magnification range from 1.0 to 2.0.

Film and Lighting—Use slow color slide film when duplicating your slides. This gives the duplicate image good color and fine grain. You don't have to worry about slow exposure times if they are faster than one second. The camera doesn't have to be rigidly supported because the copier is attached to it.

Typically, a copy image made with conventional color slide film has more contrast than the original. This may be OK.

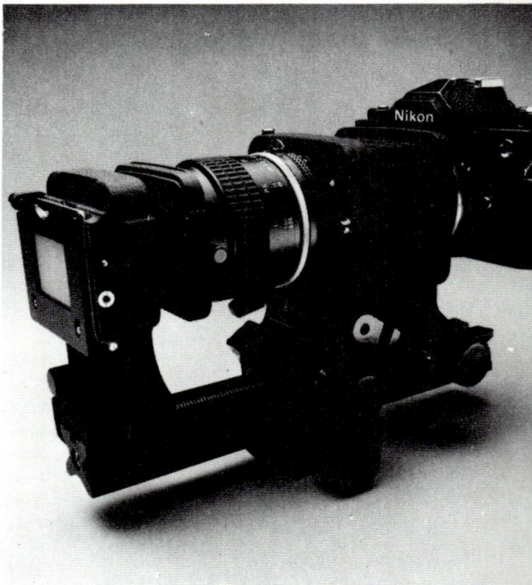

If you don't want this contrast rise, use one of two Ektachrome slide duplicating films. SE Duplicating Film SO-366 is balanced for use with electronic flash. The other, labeled 5071, is balanced for 3200K light and an exposure time of about one second. Be sure to balance film with the light to avoid an objectionable color cast.

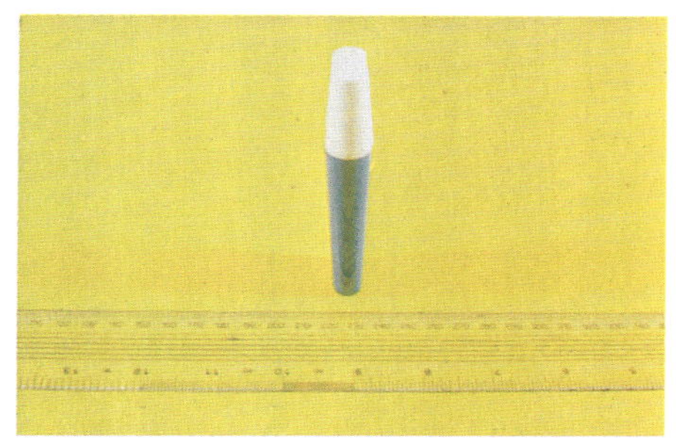

screen at a 90° angle to the lens axis when you move your eye to the viewer's eyepiece. You can view the same way without this accessory if you use a waist-level viewfinder or an SLR that has a removable pentaprism.

LIGHTING

Even lighting is important for print copying. If the lighting is uneven, the copy image will have light and dark areas that the original didn't have.

Most photographers use two identical lights for even lighting. The lights can be tungsten bulbs or flash. Generally, tungsten bulbs are easier to use because metering is easy and you can see whether the illumination is even or not.

Test this by standing a pencil or pen in the middle of the copy subject. If the cast shadows are the same length and darkness, the lights are OK. If shadows aren't identical, adjust one light until shadows look the same.

USING FILTERS IN COPY WORK

Old b&w prints can fade with age and turn brownish. Making an improved duplicate b&w image is usually easy. Use a pale yellow filter on the lens and expose slow-speed b&w film. Underexpose about one-half step and develop the film for about 50% longer than normal. This will give a negative image with good contrast so you can make a clear print with a continuous range of tones.

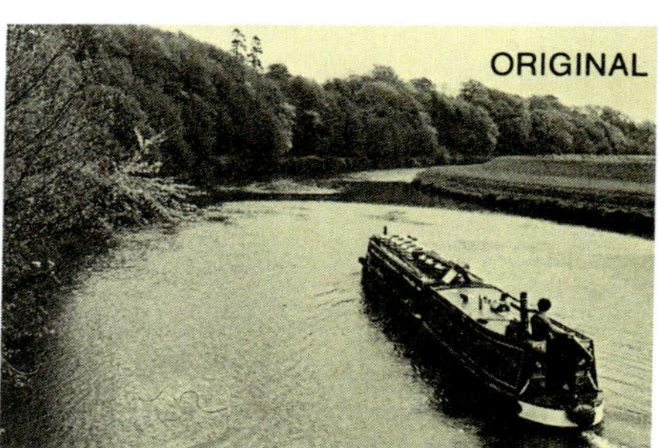

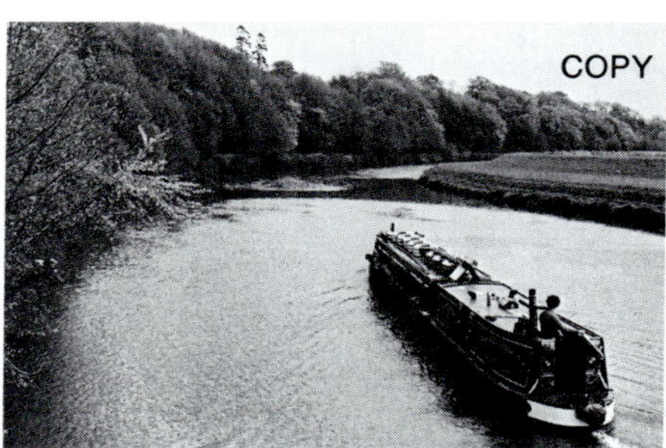

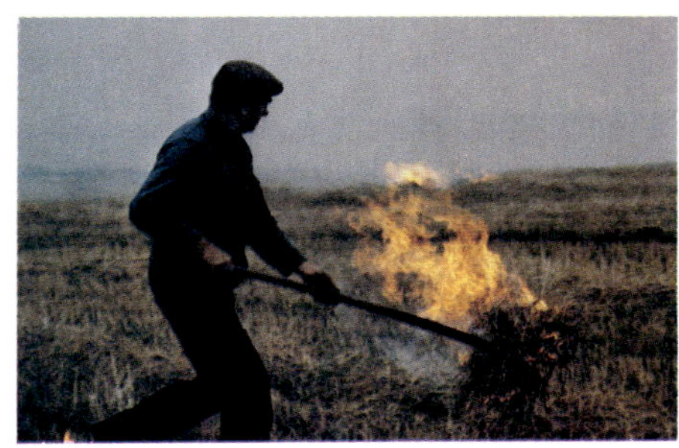

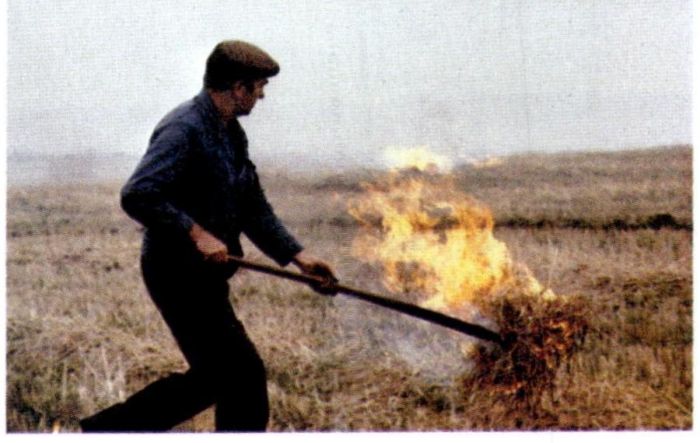

Exposure—A frosted piece of acetate behind the original slide diffuses the back light used to illuminate the slide. Getting good exposure can be as simple as pointing the camera at the appropriate tungsten lamp or midday daylight reflecting from a white piece of paper. Your camera's built-in meter will recommend good exposure for an original slide having relatively equal amounts of bright and dark areas. If the slide is non-average, make an exposure correction as described earlier.

If you use electronic flash, make an exposure test for a life-size setup. Set up the flash a certain known distance from the diffuser. Then use guide-number calculation to get an initial lens aperture. With life-size magnification, open aperture two more *f*-stops from the initial aperture.

Use the flash manually and bracket exposures two steps in each direction in half-step increments. Record each exposure and check the resultant slides with your notes. For subsequent life-size duplicates, use the aperture that gave the best duplicate. For example, the above left dupe is underexposed. The other looks good, so the aperture used for that slide is standard for the setup used.

For subsequent shooting, be sure to set up the flash exactly as in the test. For larger magnifications, make the aperture adjustments in the table, above, for increasing exposure.

APERTURE ADJUSTMENT DUE TO MAGNIFICATION

M	Open Aperture (steps)
1.0	2
1.1	2
1.2	2-1/3
1.3	2-1/3
1.4	2-1/2
1.5	2-2/3

Image Manipulation

You can continue to be creative with an image even after making the slide or print. With some of the methods described here, you can salvage a bad photo or make a good one even better. When learning these techniques, it's best to practice with old prints and slides that you'd normally throw away. Then you won't have to worry about ruining a good image because your experiment failed.

Materials for Prints—Pictured here are some of the materials you need for working with b&w and color prints. Art-supply stores have these, and more, for creative print manipulation.

You can color b&w prints with transparent liquid dyes, opaque inks or special colored pencils, not shown. Some of the coloring aids come with built-in applicators. Dyes are concentrated and must be diluted with water before use. Apply them with a fine-tipped brush, such as #0 or #00.

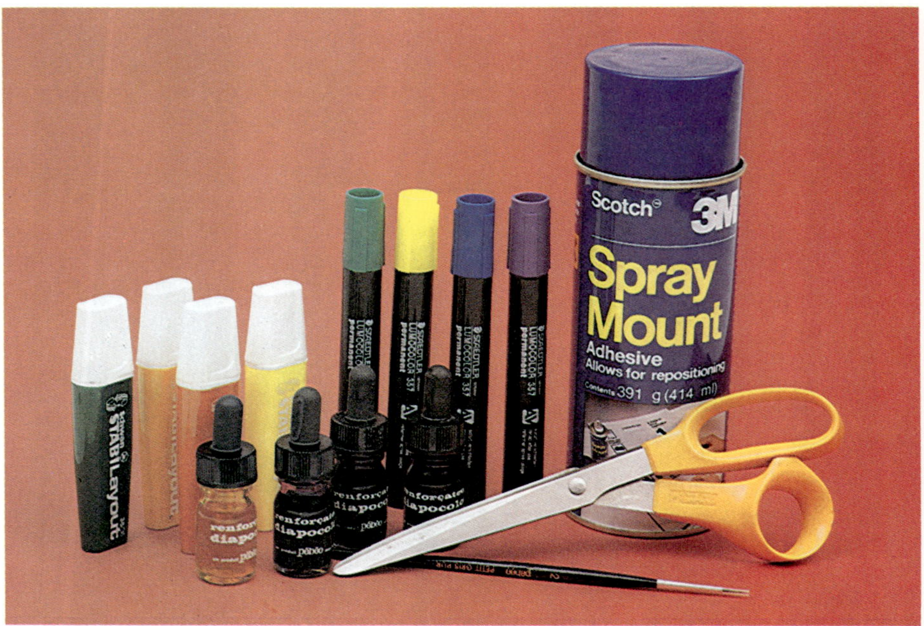

Art glue and scissors or a razor knife are useful when you want to create a *collage* from color or b&w prints. A collage is a picture made from pieces of other pictures.

Materials for Slides—The simple slide-manipulating technique described here doesn't require any materials other than glass slide mounts, available from your photo dealer.

More complicated slide and print techniques for special effect include bleaching, toning, multiple exposures and more. A more complete discussion is in *How To Create Photographic Special Effects*, by Allan Horvath, also published by HPBooks.

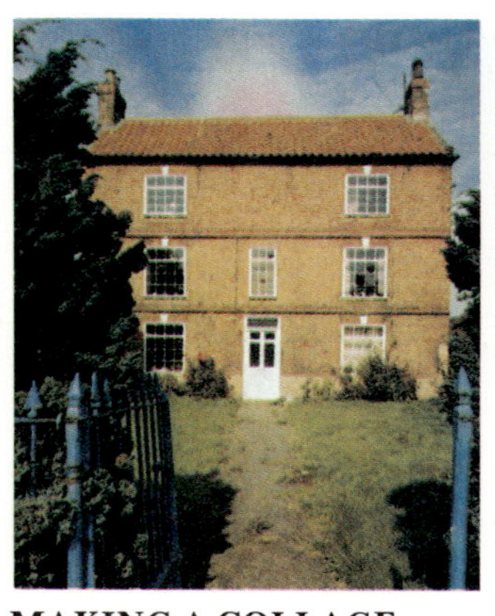

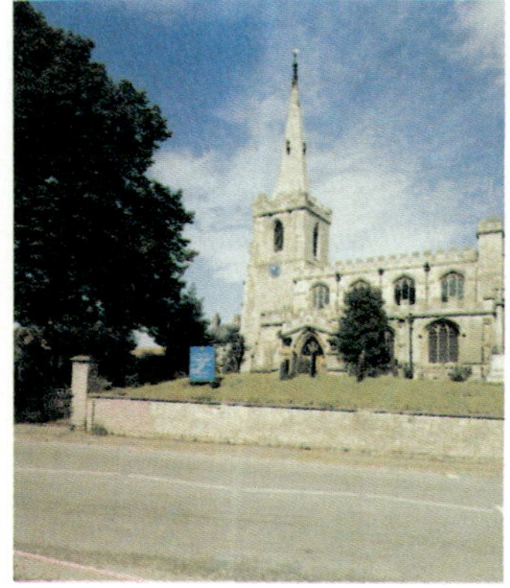

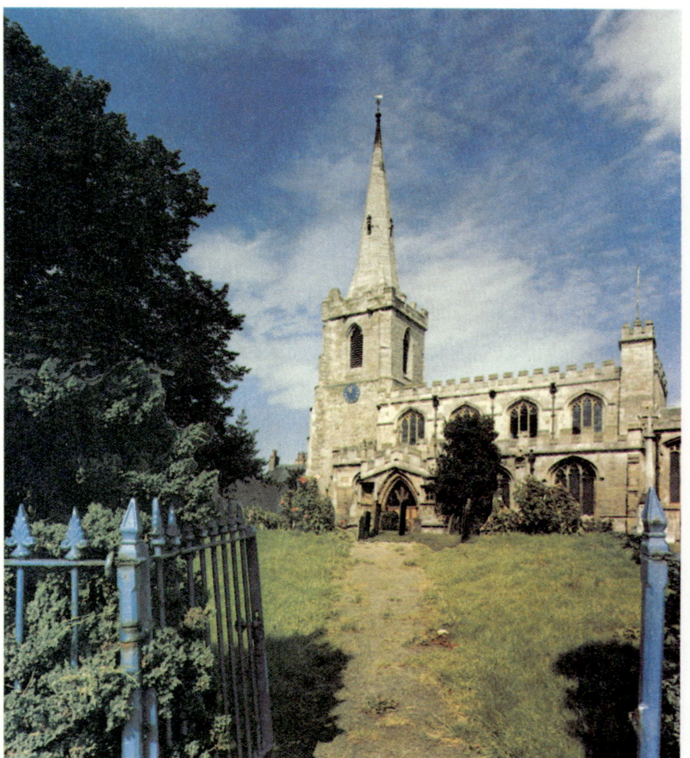

MAKING A COLLAGE

Shown at right is a realistic-looking collage. It was made by carefully cutting out the foreground of the print at left and gluing it onto the center print. The two original images were made on the same day with the same camera and lens. The lighting for each was similar. Areas that didn't match well were handcolored with special dyes made for color prints, available from your photo dealer.

It's easiest to make unrealistic-looking collages. Cut out pieces of a print and darken the edges with ink from black pen. Apply rubber cement or spray glue to the back of the pieces and glue them onto a large background print. You can combine color and b&w photos and use magazine illustrations too. If you don't want to make the collage permanent, hold down the pieces with a sheet of glass and photograph the assembly with b&w or color film.

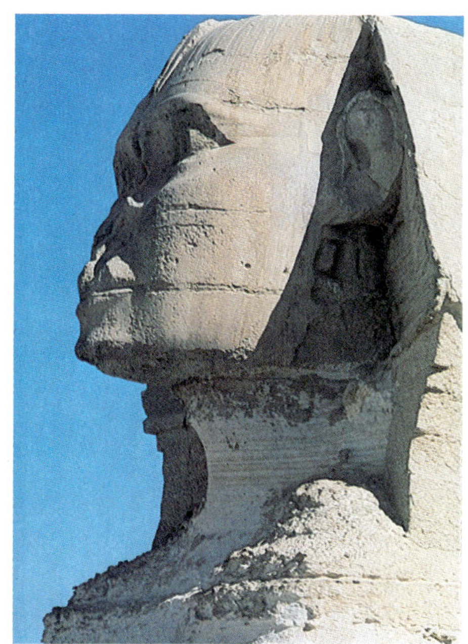

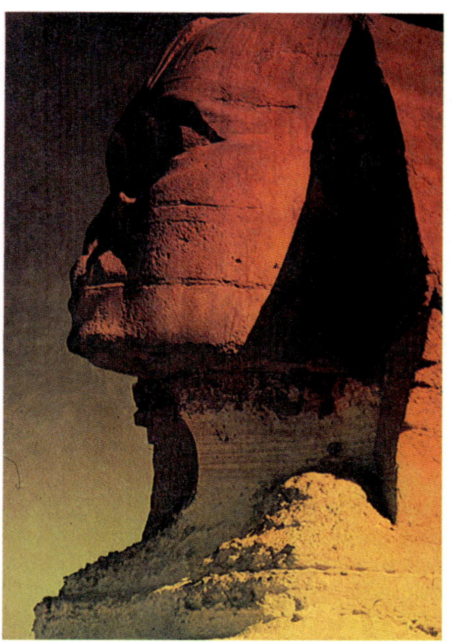

SLIDE SANDWICH

When you put two or more slides together in a glass slide mount, you've made a *sandwich*. With this technique, illustrated above, you can make images that would be difficult or impossible to make with the camera. It's fun and easy, too. Your sandwiches don't have to be permanent. You can photograph or print the sandwich and reuse the slides for another sandwich.

Combine slides that are lighter than usual—two slides with normal density will look too dark. Save your slightly overexposed slides. One slide should have strong colors. Important subject details shouldn't overlap. The detail of one slide should overlap the empty area of the other.

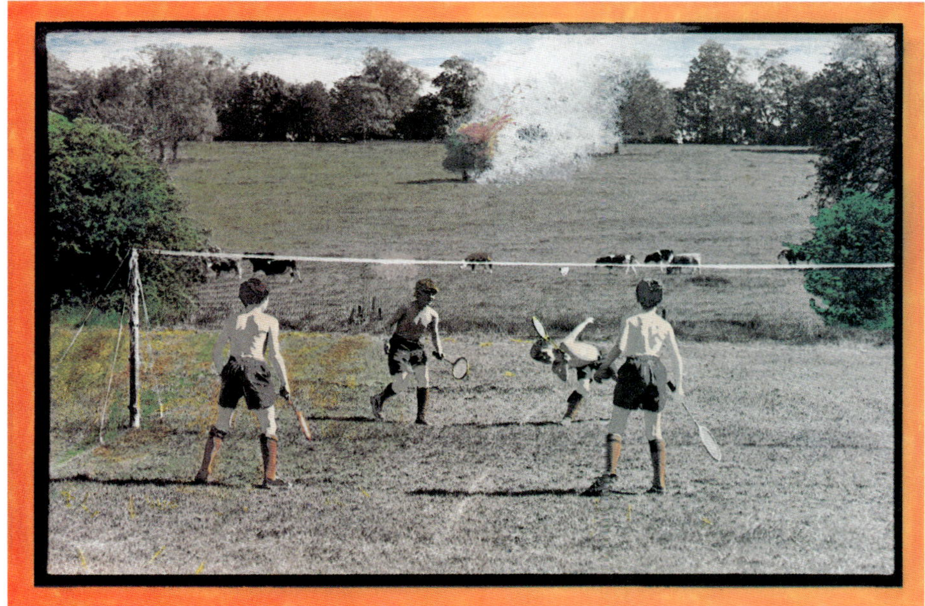

COLORING PRINTS

The number of different ways to hand color a b&w print are enormous. You can do it realistically or not. Color all of the print or just part of it. Use strong, bold colors or subtle tints. Use opaque or transparent colors separately or combined. You can remove parts of the image you don't want and add details you do want. Create graphic lines and shapes. Much of the above was done in the example print you see here.

The print was made on a *matte-surface* b&w printing paper. It "grips" the coloring material better than a *glossy-surface* paper. After coloring the image, the photographer sprayed a "fixative" over the print to protect the print fom smearing and abrasion.

Coloring Methods Used—The bushes at left and right and some of the grass were colored with dilute solutions of watercolor dyes, such as Dr. Ph. Martin dyes. The color shows best in light areas and lets print detail show through. It tints detail, but doesn't cover it.

Light areas of the boys' bodies were painted with opaque inks. This covered the detail, but added a contrasty "graphic" look to the image. The top of the badminton net was accentuated with white opaque ink. A cow intersected by the line of the net was "removed" with gray ink speckled on the print to simulate the texture of background grass. The background burning bush was made with transparent colors over opaque white.

Realistic-looking clouds were added with a fine felt-point blue pen. Orange and black felt-tip pens were used to make the decorative border around the image area.

Storing Slides & Negatives

As your interest in photography increases, you'll be creating a large collection of photographs. Being able to organize and store your images will aid your appreciation of them. When you want to show a print, enlarge a negative, or create a slide show, you don't want to waste time trying to find the right picture.

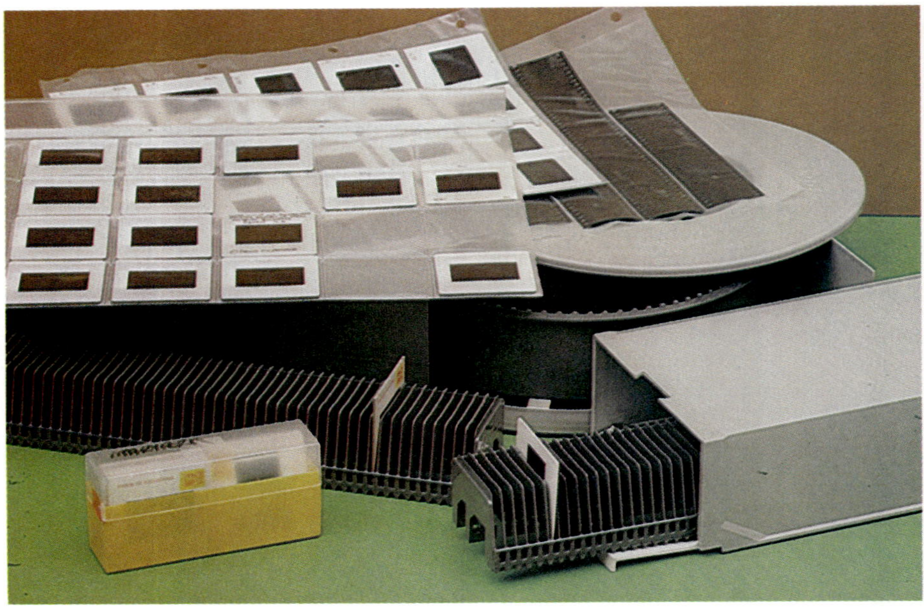

STORING SLIDES

Before filing slides, you should edit them. Divide them into three categories: those you'll keep and show, those to be discarded, and those that aren't bad enough to throw away but aren't good enough to show.

The photo at right shows four ways to store slides. The one that is best for you depends on how you use the slides. If you process your own slides and use them just to print from, store them as you would negatives. Cut them into strips, unmounted, and store them in flexible plastic pages you can put in a ring binder.

A more popular method is a sturdy slide page that holds about 20 mounted slides. It's easy to view all the slides on the page at once. You can also see data written on the cardboard slide mount. The page fits into standard ring binders.

If you project your edited slides a lot, keep them in projector trays. Make a list of the slides in the tray so you can pull one out if necessary for another slide show.

These methods are good for "keeper" slides. An economical way to store less good slides, is to put them in the box they came in. Put similar slides together—landscapes in one box, portraits in another. Subdivide categories as necessary and label each box.

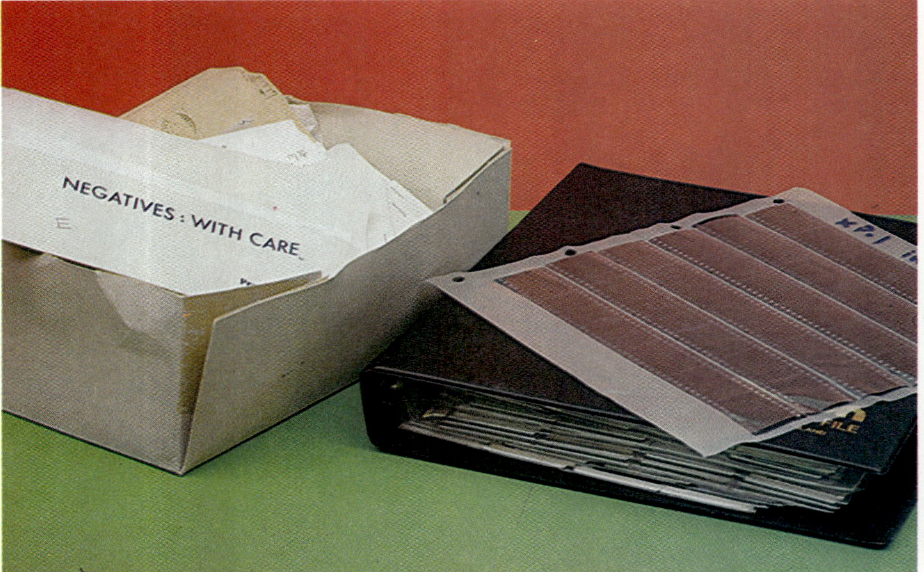

NEGATIVE STORAGE

The photo at right shows good and bad ways to store negatives. At left is an old box containing envelopes with negatives inside. Finding a certain negative in this disorganization takes a lot of time.

At right is a binder that holds individual transparent sheets. Each sheet conveniently holds strips of negatives. Your photo dealer has sheets that hold 36 frames of film. This lets you store a roll of exposures together. It's easy to view and evaluate the negatives by holding the sheet up to a light. The binder-and-sheet system keeps stored negatives flat and clean. In addition, they are easy to label and locate.

Labeling Negatives—This goes a long way toward making organization and printing easier. Make a contact print of each negative sheet and put the contact sheet in the binder with the negative sheet. Label both the contact sheet *and* negative sheet with identical useful information.

One way is to date the pictures with a code, such as 4/83, to represent April 1983. Add to this code a letter to represent how many rolls you've shot that month. For example, 4/83/C stands for the third roll you shot in April 1983. If you shoot more than 26 rolls in a month, use AA and so on after using Z. Include on the back of the contact print the film and processing you used for that roll.

When you make a print from the fifth frame on that roll, label the back of the print with exposure information and the code 4/83/C-5. This makes it easy to find that negative frame again if you want to reprint it.

If you don't want the expense of negative sheets, use negative sleeves that hold film strips together. Tape the sleeve to the back of the contact print and store both in a binder.

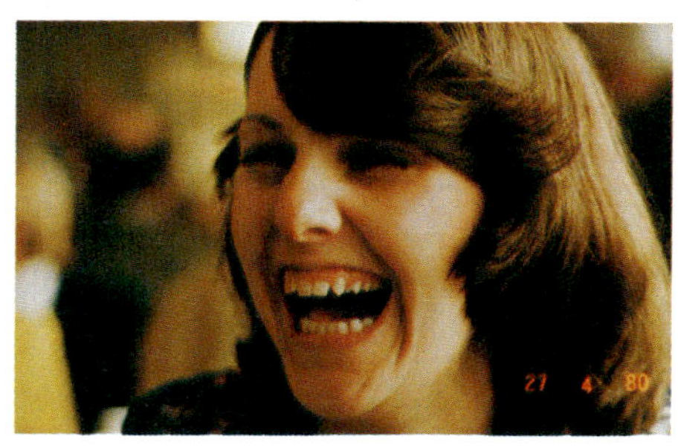

SLIDE DATA

It's sometimes useful to know when you took a picture. For this reason, the processing month and year is usually printed on cardboard slides. If this isn't enough information, then write more on the cardboard slide mount. Consider including the following: the day you *took* the picture, the subject shown, and exposure-control settings. Relying on your memory for all of this can be difficult. Write it down after making the picture and transfer the information later to the processed slide.

Data Back—Many SLR cameras offer an accessory data back that photographically imprints the time of day or date on your images, as shown above. You can turn off this feature when you don't want to print any information in the image.

CLEANING FILM

Handle negatives and slides carefully. Hold them by film edges or mounts. To avoid touching them with your fingers and leaving unsightly fingerprints (right), wear lintless white cotton gloves. These are available from your camera dealer. Remove dust with a small blower or with a gentle burst of air from an aerosol can designed for this purpose.

If you do get fingerprints on the image, clean it with a film-cleaning liquid, also available from your local camera store. Apply the liquid to a soft lintless cloth and gently rub the image.

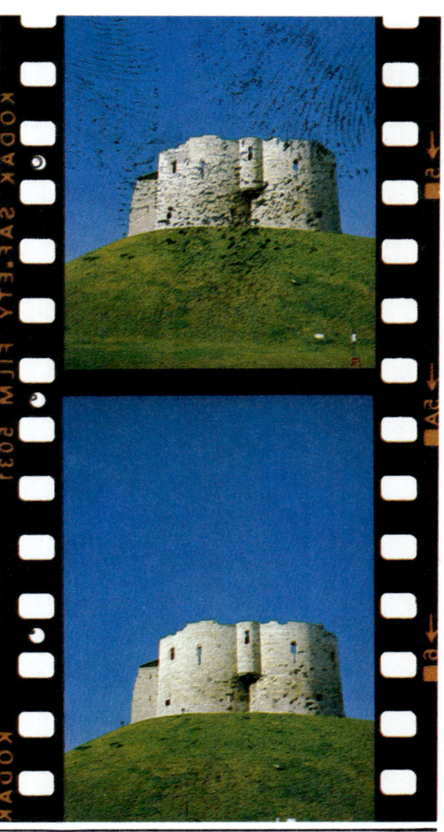

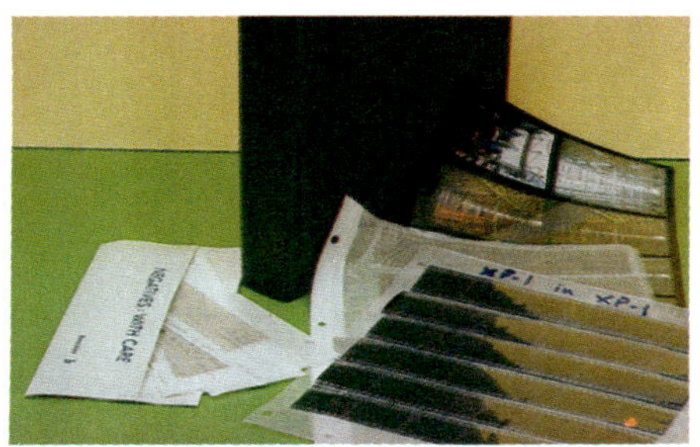

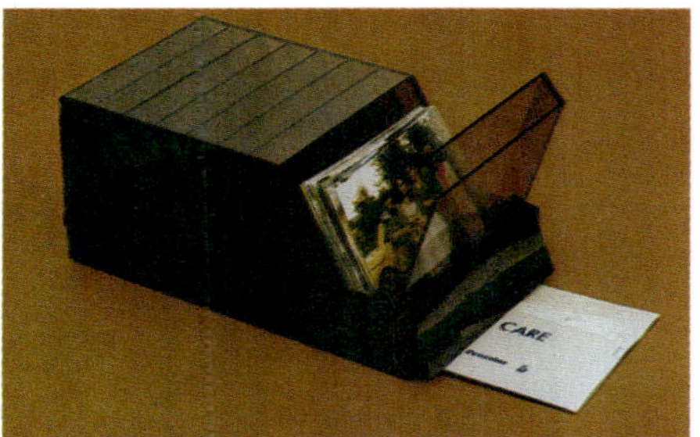

STORING PRINTS

If you have small 3x5 inch prints made from your favorite negatives, then your favorite storage system may be a photo album. If you don't like photo albums, or want to view prints individually, then the Gepe print box shown may be better. It holds over 60 prints and protects them from dust and light. In addition, a drawer underneath conveniently holds negative envelopes.

Another useful device for small prints is the Roto-Photo, also shown. Clear plastic sleeves hold photos that rotate around a spindle. It's easy to quickly find the picture you want to see.

Bigger Prints—If you have enlargements made or do your own printing, you'll get prints bigger than 3x5 inch. More likely they'll be 5x7, 8x10 or 11x14 inch. These are ideal for framing—it's a way to store and appreciate your prints at the same time.

When the print isn't on display, store it in a box that photographic paper came in. If you don't have any, check with your local photo dealer for some empty ones. Keep prints in a cool dry place.

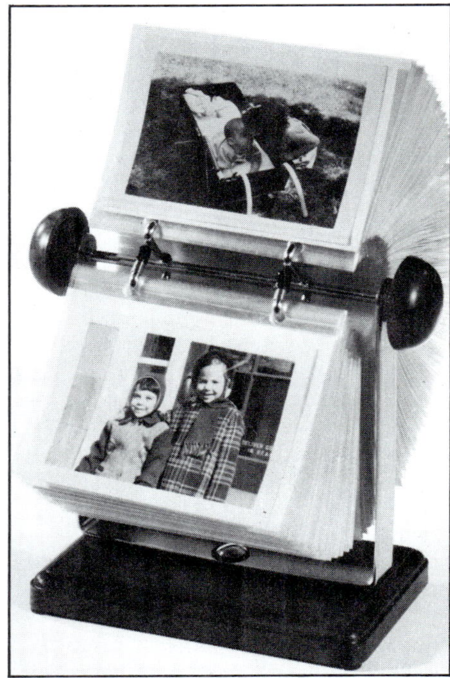

Index